GREAT CLOCHE

COLLINS INLET

FRENCH RIVER

MANITOWANING BY

MANITOWANING

BYNG INLET

GEORGIAN BAY

PARRY SOUND

COVE ISLAND

CABOT HEAD

SAUGEEN PENINSULA

125 DEEPEST SOUNDING

CAPE CROKER

GRIFFITHS ISLAND

CHRISTIAN ISLAND

PENETANGUISHINE

FISHING ISLS.

OWEN SOUND

MIDLAND

Huronia

SAUBLE

NOTTAWASAGA BAY

SAUGEEN R.

Petun Country

THORNBURY

Nottawasaga River

COLLINGWOO

KINCARDINE

CANADA

GODERICH

BAYFIELD

FRENCH SETTLEMENT

GRAND BEND

ETTLE OINT

ONTARIO

D1535164

UNITED COLLEGE LIBRARY
FACULTY OF ARTS

977
La25-9

DISCARDED

UNIVERSITY OF WINNIPEG
PORTAGE & BALMORAL
WINNIPEG 2, MAN.   CANADA

216 760 9

CHANGED

A2167609N

UNITED COLLEGE LIBRARY

FACULTY OF ARTS

LAKE HURON

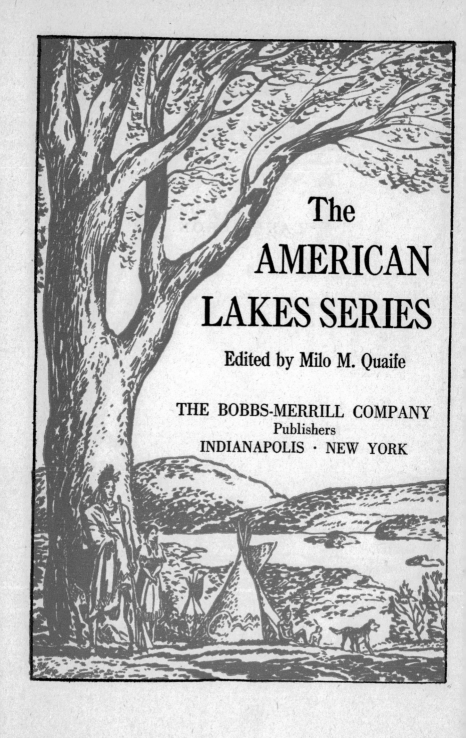

The
AMERICAN
LAKES SERIES

Edited by Milo M. Quaife

THE BOBBS-MERRILL COMPANY
Publishers
INDIANAPOLIS · NEW YORK

F
55
.L3

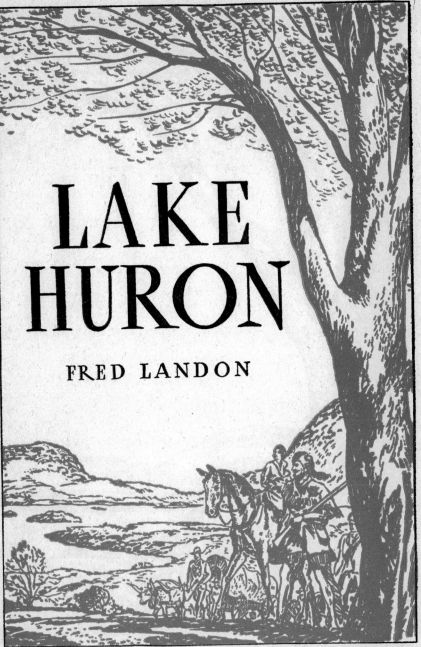

LAKE HURON

FRED LANDON

COPYRIGHT, 1944, BY THE BOBBS-MERRILL COMPANY

PRINTED IN THE UNITED STATES

TO MY DAUGHTER

Mary

UNITED COLLEGE LIBRARY
Faculty of Arts
ACCESSION No. 12441

EDITORIAL INTRODUCTION

Save for Lake Victoria in Africa, Superior, Huron, and Michigan are the largest lakes in the world. Along with Erie and Ontario they constitute a chain of fresh-water seas without parallel elsewhere on the globe. Moreover, unlike Lake Victoria, their shores are occupied by two of the world's most progressive nations, whose people are surpassed by none in intelligence and industry. It follows as a matter of course that the Great Lakes exert a well-nigh incalculable influence upon the continent to which they belong.

First of the chain to be discovered by white men was Lake Huron. Since its French discoverers knew nothing as yet of the other lakes, they called it *La Mer Douce*—the sweet or fresh-water sea. Beside it was founded, before the middle of the seventeenth century, the first center of French civilization west of the lower St. Lawrence Valley, and this became a training ground for the further advance over the remaining lakes and the Mississippi Valley. Until the close of the seventeenth century Lake Huron was a part of the principal highway between Lower Canada and the Upper Country, and a great international highway it remains at the present day. Oddly enough, however, its scenic and other resources have been but little advertised. Probably few Americans have ever learned that both the largest and longest fresh-water island in the world lies in Lake Huron, nor can even the brightest radio expert give the precise number of its remaining islands.

In the planning of *The American Lakes Series* it has been constantly kept in mind that while the volumes are written by scholars they are intended for the use and enjoyment of laymen. All of the authors are competent historians, familiar with methods of historical investigation and specialists in their own particular fields of study. All have been chosen, too, for their ability to write and for their sympathetic understanding of the language and interests of common men and women. All have striven to combine the qualities of scholarly accuracy and popular interest, believing that the sober truth of American history requires no fictitious adornment and that, properly presented, it suffers from no lack of drama or of glamour.

It is the good fortune alike of publisher and reader that Professor Landon has written the story of Lake Huron. He was in earlier years a lake sailor and has traversed its waters scores of times. He knows their every mood, as he also knows the men and the ships that sail them. He is an accomplished historian, whose scholarship is attested by many titles and honors—President of the Ontario and the Canadian Historical Societies, President of the Ontario Library Association, Fellow of the Royal Society of Canada, member of the editorial boards of *Agricultural History* (Washington) and the *Northwest Ohio Quarterly* (Toledo), and Librarian and associate professor in the Department of History of the University of Western Ontario. A veteran journalist, he is incapable of producing a dry-as-dust recital. Instead, his narrative recreates the drama and the feel of life which is the essence of all good historical writing. It sets a high standard for the volumes which are to follow in *The American Lakes Series*. No comparable description of Lake Huron has ever before been written; its like will not soon be seen again.

M. M. QUAIFE,
Detroit Public Library

FOREWORD

A LAKE, says the dictionary, is a large body of water contained in a depression of the earth's surface and supplied from the drainage of a more or less extended area.

But a lake has no history, apart from that which the geologist may provide, until men come into some relation to it. Then it acquires a personality; it may be feared or it may be loved, may thwart men or may make their life happier.

The geologists tell us that the Great Lakes originated very recently in the physical evolution that has taken place on our planet. They tell us also that these waters have always been fresh. But, as men measure time, that is all far in the past and not a matter of human record. We know the Great Lakes only from the beginning of the seventeenth century when Europeans first reached their borders and brought back word of these vast inland waters. Moreover it was the better part of a man's lifetime from the initial discovery until the last of the five had been visited.

Though Longfellow chose the shore of Lake Superior, "the shining Big-Sea-Water," as the setting for his Hiawatha legends, he might quite as properly have placed the story on the north shore of Lake Huron, for this whole region upward to Lake Superior is alike in its character and coloring, and everywhere the early home of the Indian. The traveler who sails up Lake Huron, leaving behind the broad open waters and sandy beaches of the lower region, is suddenly confronted with a new landscape, broken and bold, for he is viewing the southern rim of the great Laurentian Shield which lies in a half circle around Hudson Bay. The transition is so sudden as to be startling.

Lake Huron, unlike its sister lakes, has no great cities and few industries located on its shores. During eight months of the year the steamboats are always in sight from the shore line of Michigan, but few enter its harbors. So closely do they follow a definite course between Detour and the St. Clair River that it might be likened to a river channel set down in the lake.

They pass by, bearing the products of northern mines and northern lands to the mills and markets below. But the cheap transportation provided by this lakes system has been a factor of highest importance in promoting the prosperity of the continent. It has brought about the supremacy which the United States has attained as an iron and steel-making country, and it has enabled Canada to send her wheat to world markets.

This book is a history of Lake Huron and of the St. Clair River into which it empties. It is an attempt to tell of some of the happenings around and upon these waters in the years since Champlain first saw a portion of Georgian Bay. These happenings relate to men and to ships, for ships have personality too, and much will be said of them in these pages.

History has a way of disinterring the record of very humble folk who never dreamed that some day their names might appear in print. Some of these will figure in the story of Lake Huron, side by side with people more famous, because something that they did or something that they said makes the record of their times more clear to us. History does not relate to the great alone but to all men, and the humble folk are always the more numerous.

So, now to the story.

TABLE OF CONTENTS

Part I

EARLY DAYS ON LAKE HURON

CHAPTER   PAGE

1. CHAMPLAIN'S FRESHWATER SEA 17
2. THE PATHFINDERS 28
3. OLD HURONIA: CRADLE OF MARTYRS 39
4. WHEN FUR WAS KING 61
5. WAR COMES TO LAKE HURON 71

Part II

ISLANDS, SHORES AND RIVERS

6. ALONG THE MICHIGAN STRAND 97
7. UP THE CANADIAN SHORE 115
8. AROUND THE SHORES OF GEORGIAN BAY 137
9. ALONG THE ST. CLAIR RIVER 148
10. AMONG LAKE HURON'S MYRIAD ISLANDS 175
11. THE MAGIC ISLAND IN THE STRAITS 200

Part III

FOUR LAKE HURON STORIES

12. A VICTORIAN LADY VISITS LAKE HURON 233
13. WILLIAM BEAUMONT: "BACKWOODS PHYSIOLOGIST" . . 247
14. "PIRATICAL DOINGS ON THE RIVER ST. CLAIR" 257
15. THE *Pewabic* AND THE *Asia* 272

TABLE OF CONTENTS—*Continued*

Part IV

THE SHIPS AND THE MEN WHO SAIL THEM

CHAPTER   PAGE

16. THE SURVEYORS AND THEIR CHARTS 285

17. GEORGIAN BAY SHIPS AND SAILORS 304

18. THE GREAT STORM OF 1913 325

19. "THE STATELY SHIPS GO ON" 335

20. LAKE VESSELS PAST AND PRESENT 345

    EPILOGUE 366

    ACKNOWLEDGMENTS AND BIBLIOGRAPHICAL NOTE . . . 375

    INDEX 383

LIST OF ILLUSTRATIONS

FACING
PAGE

An Early Map of Lake Huron 36
Old Sainte Marie I Today 37
Presque Isle Lighthouse 80
A Lake Huron Fisherman 81
Loading Limestone at Alpena 102
One of the Self-Unloaders 102
An Old-Time Lumber Hooker 103
The *United Empire* 103
In Schooner Days 134
An Indian Rendezvous on Drummond Island 135
An Indian Encampment on Lake Huron 135
Looking out upon the Straits 230
A Corner of Old Fort Mackinac 230
Within Old Fort Mackinac 231
Old Fort Mackinac 231
Dr. William Beaumont 262
General George Gordon Meade 263
The Lost *Asia* 294
Happy Days on Georgian Bay 294
Waiting the Word to Go 295
Lake Carriers of Today 326-327
The *Colonel James M. Schoonmaker* 326-327
The Largest on the Lakes 326-327
A Great Lakes Oil Tanker 326-327
The *Governor Miller* 326-327
The *Colonel James Pickands* 326-327
The *South American* 326-327
The *City of Cheboygan* 326-327
The Entrance to Lake Huron 358

Part I

EARLY DAYS ON LAKE HURON

Chapter 1

Champlain's Freshwater Sea

*Yet thoughts even now
throb at my heart, bidding me venture
the deep waters, the tumult of waves.
Now and always desire is urging
my heart to wander and seek out the land
of strange peoples far away hence.*

—THE SEAFARER (Old English Elegy)

LAKE HURON, lying central in the chain of inland seas, was the first of the Great Lakes to be seen by a white man, and history has accorded the honor of its discovery to Samuel de Champlain, founder of Quebec and "Father of New France." On a day in late July of 1615 his canoe emerged from the mouth of the French River and to the south and west he saw a body of water beautifully blue, extending to the horizon. Today we call it Georgian Bay. "Because of its great size," he wrote, "I named it the Freshwater Sea."

Champlain was quite unaware that what lay before him was but an arm of a great lake situated to the westward and that beyond were other seas of this "sweet" water which, with their connecting rivers, would one day carry a commerce greater than any other similar waters on the face of the earth. Nor, if we may judge by his last map, had he learned much more of these lakes, save by rumor, until a few months before his death in 1635 when Jean Nicolet returned to Quebec with wonderful stories of the places he had been and the things he had seen in his journeys westward.

Champlain records his discovery of Lake Huron in such laconic fashion that we might wonder whether he appreciated the im-

17

portance of the event. Only a few lines in his journal—and then he hurries on to tell of other things. We can understand this if we remember that the journey had been undertaken not primarily to discover new lands and waters but for ends connected with Indian trade and the building up of French influence. It was gratifying to find that the Indian stories were based upon fact, and the open waters of the bay were a welcome change from the hard labor of crossing portages and running through dangerous rapids. But the job in hand was to reach the country of the Huron Indians. No time, therefore, was wasted on exploration; that could be attended to later.

Champlain had come to Georgian Bay by the Ottawa River route, the only feasible and known way at that time. He was not unacquainted with the lower section of this route since two years before he had gone far up the Ottawa, deluded by a lying guide into the belief that the Northwest Passage, will-o'-the-wisp for so many explorers, was to be found in that direction.[1] But the expedition of 1615 had less visionary and more practical aims. The Huron tribes were to be brought into a pact of friendship with the French and the way paved for the barter of French goods for the valuable furs which the Indians would collect. To provide for intercourse with the tribes he would meet, Champlain had brought with him young Etienne Brulé, whom he had sent into the wilderness years before and who now, by his knowledge of Indian life and Indian languages, could act as interpreter.

The Ottawa River route lay through what was then a wilderness and large portions of which are still wilderness. There were seemingly endless portages to be traversed in order to pass from one water to another or to avoid swift and dangerous rapids in the rivers. Canoes and baggage had to be carried over rocks and

[1] It is believed that during this journey of 1613 Champlain lost the astrolabe by which he determined his latitude and that it was this instrument, bearing the date 1603, which was found on a farm in Renfrew County, Ontario, in 1867, near the course which Champlain must have been following. Though he makes no mention of the loss in his journal it is significant that after June 6, when he was in this region, the explorer ceases to record the latitude. The instrument, after being in private hands for many years, is now in the possession of the New York State Historical Society.

through swamps, amid a tangle of fallen trees rotting where storms or age had left them. Hardships and dangers were always present for the travelers in their frail canoes.

At Lake Nipissing they had halted for two days. The Indians on its shores were dreaded by other tribes as sorcerers, but to Champlain they proved hospitable and the stay in their village made a welcome break in the toilsome journey. The French River brought the party out to the great open water, the Indian "Lake of the Attigouautan," Champlain's "Freshwater Sea." To the south lay the country of the Huron and toward this destination the canoes threaded their way, moving through the maze of islands which fringe the eastern shore. Decades were to pass before there was more than a vague idea of the contours of the bay and of the lake itself farther to the west, and it was more than fifty years after Champlain's discovery before the relation of the several lakes one to another became at all clear. If we may judge by their maps, the outline of Lake Huron seems to have been extremely puzzling to the early explorers and geographers.

Champlain was not the first white man to look out upon one of the Great Lakes but he was the first to record the fact. Father Le Caron, one of the four Récollet missionaries whom he brought to Quebec in 1615, anticipated him by a few days, and Etienne Brulé, who had been roaming the country since 1610, living with the Indians and almost one of them in his manner of life, may have seen these waters years before Champlain came that way. But Le Caron was more interested in pointing the way to heaven than in charting earthly shores, while Brulé, illiterate and irresponsible, had no idea of the importance of the information which he from time to time passed on to Champlain and others.

If merely seeing portions of the Great Lakes had constituted discovery, Etienne Brulé would deserve the honor in abundant measure. He was the first white man to bring back knowledge of the region beyond Lake Huron and there is more than a possibility that in his wanderings he may have seen all of the Great Lakes save Lake Michigan. He had gone up the Ottawa River five years before the journey made with Champlain and in the intervening period may easily have looked out upon Georgian Bay. When Champlain sent him in 1615 on a mission to the Andastes at the headwaters of the Susquehanna River he must have encountered Lake Ontario. There is some evidence that he visited Lake Superior in 1622, perhaps in search of copper mines, and he was in the country of the Neutral Indians, in what is now Southwestern Ontario, in 1624, probably visiting the north shore of Lake Erie at that time. Nor were his travels confined to the lakes region. When he was sent to the Susquehanna River it is believed that he traced this stream to its mouth and he may also have followed Chesapeake Bay to the ocean. But of all this and much more he wrote not a word.

Brulé is a somewhat pathetic figure as he has come down to us in the narratives of Champlain. He was scarcely more than a boy when he first went to the Algonquin country in 1610. When he returned to Quebec a year later he was dressed as an Indian and could speak the Indian language. But as years went by and he continued his wanderings he became in some ways more degraded than the Indians themselves. When the English challenged the French hold on the St. Lawrence in 1629 Brulé sold his services to the enemy. Champlain, taken a prisoner at the surrender of Quebec, met him at Tadousac while being conveyed to England and in his journals records the severe reprimand which he administered.

"To think of you," said Champlain, "brought up from early boyhood in these parts, turning round now and selling those who put bread into your mouth. You are losing your honor; you will be pointed at with scorn on all sides, wherever you may be. Better would it be for you to die than to live in the world under such conditions; for whatever happens you will always have a worm gnawing at your conscience. Remember that God will punish you if you do not mend your ways."

The warning was almost prophetic. Brulé went back to the Huron country after Champlain's departure and continued his debauchery. There, in 1632, he was killed in a drunken brawl and eaten by his Indian associates. When Champlain returned to Canada he declined to exact any retribution from the Indians, giving as a reason that Brulé by his treason had ceased to be a Frenchman.

It was Champlain's concern for the souls of the Indians that brought Father Joseph Le Caron to Canada in 1615. Moved by the degradation of the native races, living, as he wrote, "like brute beasts, without faith, without law, without religion, without God," he sought missionary assistance and turned for help to the Récollet convent near his own home town, Brouage. Three friars and a lay brother were set aside for work in New France and, embarking with Champlain at Honfleur, they arrived in Quebec at the end of May 1615.

Of these pioneer Récollet missionaries, Joseph Le Caron is best remembered. He was impatient to begin his labors among the Huron Indians, the field to which he had been assigned after counsel with his brethren. By the first of July he had set out from the site of Montreal, accompanied by twelve armed Frenchmen, a week ahead of Champlain, who had the same destination in view. Clad in his coarse gray robe, with heavy wooden sandals on his feet and with the knotted cord of his order about his waist, he must have been a strange figure in the midst of the painted Indian canoemen. From a surviving fragment of one of his letters we obtain a glimpse of his experiences:

"It would be hard to tell you," he writes, "how tired I am with paddling all day, with all my strength, among the Indians; wading the rivers a hundred times and more, through the mud and over the sharp rocks that cut my feet; carrying the canoe and luggage through the woods to avoid the rapids and frightful cataracts; and half starved all the while." But amid these hardships he found consolation: "When one sees so many infidels needing nothing but a drop of water to make them children of God, one feels an inexpressible ardor to labor for their conversion, and sacrifice to it one's repose and life."

Le Caron left no record of his first view of the Freshwater Sea,

For him it had no interest other than as a way by which he might arrive at his mission field. Champlain, following close behind, overtook him at the palisaded Huron village known as Carha-gouha. There, on August 12, they joined in what must have been for both of them an event long remembered, the first celebration of the Mass among these savage Indians, the first Mass ever celebrated in what is now the province of Ontario. As Le Caron raised aloft the Host, there knelt before him the twelve Frenchmen who had accompanied him on the long and painful journey. There also was Champlain, who had made it possible for him to undertake his task, and near by also the young man Brulé, the first of the *coureurs de bois*. And all about were the Indians for whose salvation Le Caron had come, gazing in wonder and curiosity at the strange rites of the white man.

Le Caron remained in New France until the surrender of Quebec to the English in 1629. When peace came three years later the Récollets were eager to resume their labors but obstacles appeared, and Le Caron never again saw the tribes to whom he had dedicated his life. He died at Ste. Marguerite in France on the very day that the treaty was signed which restored Canada.

So great is the part played in the early history of New France by the black-robed followers of Ignatius Loyola that the services of their predecessors, the Récollets, usually pass with little mention or are forgotten entirely. But to these gray-cloaked priests, most austere of the disciples of St. Francis of Assisi, belongs the honor of first bringing the offices of religion to New France. Their order had no large resources to meet the expenses of missionary work in this distant colony and at Quebec they encountered hostility from the merchants, most of whom were fanatically opposed to their efforts. The interpreters, who might have made the way easier by instructing them in the Indian tongue, refused assistance. Despite such handicaps and the constant physical difficulties which attended their work, the Récollets were instrumental in planting the Cross from Tadousac to the far-off shores of Lake Huron.

In the history of French enterprise overseas no chapter has greater romance or interest than that which records colonial development in America. It was France, not England, which in the seventeenth century was thinking imperially, and we may properly admire the grandeur of the French design which from its inception grasped at a continent and not a seaboard. French claims extended from Quebec to New Orleans while Britain's colonies were still huddled to the east of the Alleghenies. It was a thin line, traced by the waterways, and its weakness caused constant concern, but it represented a great idea. It was Frenchmen who first traversed the wide areas of the West and the names which they attached to lands and waters remain with us as memorials of their enterprise.

Champlain stands pre-eminent among the empire builders of his time. His achievements are the common possession of the United States and Canada. For over thirty years he labored to build for France a colony that would strengthen her position among other nations. The doggedness with which he stuck to his task through difficulties and dangers of every kind excites our admiration. His narratives tell in the most direct and simple fashion of adventures which might easily have been extended into thrilling tales. When he did give greater freedom to his pen it was chiefly in his description of the Indians and their customs which he realized would be of interest to his European readers. There are times when we learn of his own adventures only through some notice of Indian practices. When he tells us, for example, that the Huron carried those men wounded in battle in rude, woven baskets we find that he learned this through personal and painful experience. But in telling it there is no trace of self-pity—that is not Champlain's way.

In common with his contemporaries he was thrilled by the thought of discovering a short route to China, and the possibility of finding the "Western Sea" occurs and recurs in his writings. The need of Indian friends along the waterways leading westward toward this goal drew him into alliance with the Huron rather than the Iroquois and had fateful consequences for the colony on the St. Lawrence and fateful consequences for the later history of France in America. But the way to the Orient, always seemingly just over the horizon, constantly eluded him, as it did so many others.

Champlain's concern for religion and for the conversion of the Indians was not less than his zeal for the welfare of the colony and his ardor for exploration. He brought to New France the first missionaries, Le Caron and his associates. He was absent in France when the Jesuits first arrived at Quebec in 1625 but upon his return he gave to them the same constant support that he had given to the Récollets. The Jesuit Paul Le Jeune, who preached his funeral sermon in 1635, said of him:

"Truly he led a life of great justice, equity and perfect loyalty to his King and towards the Gentlemen of the Company. Those whom he left behind have reason to be well satisfied with him; for though he died out of France, his name will not therefor be any less glorious to posterity."

Paul Le Jeune was right. Champlain's fame has steadily grown with the passing of more than three centuries. At Crown Point on Lake Champlain, which he discovered in 1609, there stands an impressive memorial lighthouse, erected in 1912. Affixed to it is a bronze plaque which was brought to America by a distinguished delegation from the government of France. At Quebec, overlooking the broad St. Lawrence; at Ottawa, the capital of Canada, the site of which Champlain visited in 1613; and at Orillia, near the location of the village where Champlain spent the winter of 1615-1616, are other impressive monuments. The states of New York and Vermont and the province of Quebec all have municipalities bearing the name of the "Father of New France," while the geologists have gone even further and have applied the name Champlain Sea to the extension of the Gulf of St. Lawrence which in the postglacial ages covered the present St. Lawrence Valley and the lower part of Eastern Ontario.

Champlain was a native of Brouage, about eight miles south of Rochefort on the Bay of Biscay and in the Department of Charente-Inférieure. On a monument erected there in 1878 one may read that he was born "toward 1570," though 1567 is the date more commonly accepted. Today his natal town, formerly a place of importance, is little more than a modest, almost deserted village, situated in the center of a marshy territory from which the sea long ago retired. On the ancient ramparts, now almost hidden by vegetation, may be seen the arms of Cardinal Mazarin, who conducted the government of France during the boyhood of Louis XIV and was "Captain of Brouage." Large iron rings attached to the masonry of the crumbling harbor walls recall the days when ships came to this port and when the boy Champlain received the first impulses to voyage to far-off lands.

There is another town in France, also a seaport, which has interesting associations with Champlain. This is Dieppe, where in the early morning hours of August 19, 1942, Canadians, some of them descendants of pioneer colonists in New France, attempted the first invasion of the German-held continent since British troops withdrew from Dunkirk. Dieppe in prewar days was the port of entry for thousands of English-speaking folk on their way to Switzerland, Italy or Paris, as well as being a popular holiday resort in itself. Its gleaming cliffs, white sandy beach and its clean-looking streets took on a different aspect that August morning, when fighting was hand to hand and when its casino, formerly a place of relaxation and enjoyment, became a place of carnage and death. Dieppe was once the chief seaport of France, and Champlain must have known it well. He was a soldier before he became a sailor and when Henry IV entered the town and received the allegiance of Aymar de Chastes, governor of Dieppe, it is quite possible that Champlain was with his royal master. And it was also under the auspices of old Aymar de Chastes, who had resolved to undertake the colonization of Canada, that he made his first voyage to America.

"Going from time to time to see the Sieur de Chastes," writes

Champlain, "judging that I might serve him in his design, he did me the honor to communicate something of it to me, and asked me if it would be agreeable to me to make the voyage, to examine the country, and to see what those engaged in the undertaking should do. I told him that I was very much his servant, but that I could not give myself license to undertake the voyage without the commands of the king . . . but that, if it should please him to speak to the king about it, and give me his commands, that it should be very agreeable to me, which he promised and did, and received the king's orders for me to make the voyage and make a faithful report thereof."

Thus it is probable that the plans for the first voyage to Canada were discussed under the roof of the grim old castle which overlooks Dieppe town and harbor. In peacetime days a visitor might wander through grass-grown courts to its rooms of state, bare of furniture and with whitewashed walls, where kings and princes were once entertained or held court. Below the castle and opposite to the casino stands the old stone gateway to the town, its turrets crowned by cone-shaped roofs. In imagination we can picture Champlain passing through that gateway in 1624 with his young wife, returning to France after four years at Quebec. She was but twelve when she was betrothed and only during the brief period spent in Canada was she ever with him. He makes no mention of her in his writings but St. Helen's Isle, opposite the city of Montreal, was named after her.

Through that same old gateway Champlain passed again in 1633, to embark upon his last voyage. He was then more than sixty years of age and had spent almost thirty years in New France, but his purpose was still high and his ardor undaunted. When the shores of France receded from view his active life was nearing its close. He died in Quebec on Christmas night of 1635. The records tell us that over his grave a little chapel was reared but nothing is said of its location. Documents of the time indicate that it still stood in 1661, but after that date no mention is found. Possibly it perished in one of the little town's numerous fires. Thus the burial place of the "Father of New France" and the discoverer of Lake Huron remains unknown. Nor is there an authentic portrait; the one which is so often reproduced is the work of a nineteenth-century artist and was given to the public only in 1854.

But while we know nothing of his face or figure, Champlain lives on as the outstanding personage in the early history of New France—soldier, sailor, explorer and empire builder. He led French enterprise into the Great Lakes region. He discovered Lake Huron and we may well believe that he would have found keen pleasure in seeking out more distant regions and waters, but there was the King's business to be looked after at Quebec and elsewhere, so it was left to others to carry on the work which he had begun.

Measured by years, it was a long time before there was even rudimentary knowledge of Lake Huron and of its sister lakes. But when we remember that the population of all New France even beyond the middle of the seventeenth century was no more than that of a small town, and remember also the variety of activities which occupied the people's attention, we may well marvel at the speed with which geographical knowledge accumulated. Bit by bit, a fact here and a fact there, interior America gradually came to have understandable form, and the map makers of Europe in their turn delineated it for the use of those interested in the opening up of the New World.

Chapter 2

The Pathfinders

And they looked to the West and
searched it with their eyes,
And there was the endless forest
and the sharp star.
—STEPHEN VINCENT BENÉT

IT IS one of the anomalies of American history that exploration of
the Great Lakes began at a point almost central in the chain,
proceeded then in directions leading farther from the French
settlements on the St. Lawrence and only later came to the waters
that were nearest. Lake Erie, most southerly of all, was the last to
be explored, and Champlain had been in his grave more than a
generation before any white man descended Lake Huron, though
long before this the upper regions of the lake had become known
to missionaries and traders and above all to the nimble *coureurs
de bois.*

There were reasons, of course, for a situation which led men off
into Lake Michigan and Lake Superior before any voyager paddled
along the heavily timbered shores of lower Lake Huron. Missionaries and traders came year after year by the Ottawa River route
and pushed out beyond the confines of Georgian Bay. The St.
Mary's River was traced to the steep descent by which the waters
of Lake Superior flow toward Lake Huron and a daring Frenchman pushed his canoe through the Straits of Mackinac and out
upon the waters of Lake Michigan. Champlain's original "Fresh-
water Sea" was increased to three, and yet however far men
traveled there seemed always to be lands and waters beckoning
farther westward.

Surely, it was reasoned, in that direction would be found the way to China and the East. A London merchant in the days of Queen Elizabeth, Apsley by name, wrote that he expected in his lifetime to see a letter carried in three months to China by a route that would be discovered across the American continent somewhere between the forty-third and forty-sixth parallels. The familiar story of Nicolet, clad in brilliant Oriental silk with pattern of birds and flowers, meeting the Winnebago Indians in what is now Wisconsin, was not unique in its time, for when Captain George Waymouth sailed the *Discovery* into Hudson Straits in 1602 his "preacher," Master John Cartwright, who had been to Persia, wore a brand-new clerical gown with which to impress the natives on his arrival in China. And we may recall also that when Thomas James left England in 1631 "to discover the north-west passage into the south sea" he carried with him a letter from James the First, the reigning monarch, addressed to the Emperor of Japan. Visions of a short passage to the riches of the East were much in the public mind in that first half of the seventeenth century.

Trade was also an influence affecting the direction of exploration—the fur trade and the copper mines of Lake Superior and the dreams of stores of precious metals to be found at some point beyond the horizon. These lured men on year after year. Champlain had trade in mind when he crossed the wilderness area between the St. Lawrence and the country of the Huron. And so it was with those who came after him. Save for such restless spirits as Brulé, exploration was a means to an end, not an end in itself.

Yet another reason existed for the curious order in which the lakes became known and understood. To the south of Lake Ontario and westward to the Niagara River (in itself a barrier by its mighty falls) were the tribes comprising the Iroquois Confederacy, blocking the penetration of the western country by way of the upper St. Lawrence and the lower lakes. Not until de Tracy's slashing attack upon the Mohawk villages in 1666 was it possible to follow this natural highway westward, but once the Indian threat had been removed, exploration of the lower lakes system quickly followed.

To Etienne Brulé belongs the undisputed honor of being the first white man to penetrate the regions beyond Georgian Bay and beyond Lake Huron. Brulé returned to Huronia in 1618 after his mission to the Andastes, and before proceeding to the St. Lawrence he paddled for ten days along the north shore of Lake Huron. According to Champlain he would have gone still farther had it not been for a rumor of preparations for war by unfriendly tribes. Five years later, on this occasion accompanied by Grenolle, he followed the same course and probably ascended the St. Mary's River to the Sault. From the records that have been left to us, it is impossible to say whether these men actually saw the broad expanse of Lake Superior above or merely heard of it from the Indians, and it is equally impossible to say whether the ingot of copper which they brought back as a sample of Lake Superior's riches was taken, as they claimed, from a working mine or was secured in trade at the Sault. But one important fact they did record, namely that the waters which came tumbling down from the north were fresh and sweet.

Jean Nicolet's journey westward in 1634 comes next in the chronological record of exploration. This man's career is of striking interest. He was twenty years old when he landed at Quebec in 1618 and like Brulé he was sent off to become acquainted with Indian life and languages. Sixteen years of wilderness life eminently fitted him for the mission upon which he was sent in 1634 by Champlain, that he should go to the far West and bring back information of peoples and places and of the opportunities for trade. Curiously, this important journey was practically forgotten until less than a century ago. Nicolet's experiences, related by him to the Jesuits, were duly chronicled in their journals, where they lay unnoticed until the historian John Gilmary Shea came upon them. It was then revealed that Nicolet was the first white man to visit Lake Michigan and Green Bay and present-day Wisconsin.

The shores of Green Bay furnished the stage for Nicolet's dramatic meeting with the Winnebago Indians. In his robe of Chinese damask, with all its embroidered decoration, and with a huge horse pistol in each hand, which he fired at intervals, he made his first acquaintance with the inhabitants of the region. But neither here, nor elsewhere in all his journeys, did he find any people whose costume resembled that of the Orient. The damask robe, with all its birds and flowers, was obviously out of place among peoples who wore little beyond a breechclout, and we may judge that it was soon discarded and placed with other less necessary baggage.

The stage accessories were not wasted, however. Impressed by the Oriental robe, and probably even more by the man-made thunder, thousands assembled to see the *manitou-iriniou,* the "Great Spirit man." Chiefs rivaled one another in setting out feasts, and it is related that at one gargantuan repast the choice parts of one hundred and twenty beavers were devoured. Nicolet found no difficulty whatever in concluding a treaty of peace between these people and the middlemen Huron whereby the volume of furs destined for the French storehouses on the St. Lawrence would be much augmented.

These early explorers, as they neared the mouth of the St. Mary's River or the Straits of Mackinac, must often have looked southward toward the vast open expanse of Lake Huron and wondered how all this volume of fresh water finally found its way to the sea. Were there other great lakes and rivers as yet unknown? The Indians talked vaguely of waters to the south just as they talked of great waters to the west, but it was difficult to understand or interpret their stories. In the end it was the missionaries who provided the first clue to this geographical mystery by establishing the existence of Lake Erie.

La Roche Dallion, a Récollet who was in the Huron country with Father Le Caron, was the first to cross the peninsula from the Georgian Bay region to the country lying north of Lake Erie. Here was the home of the Neutral Indians, tribes who sought to live at peace with both Huron and Iroquois though hesitating not at all to engage in war with other nations. When Dallion made his visit they were fairly numerous, living in villages scattered at intervals from near the Detroit to the Niagara River. Remains of several of their villages have been discovered and excavated, one such, known as the Southwold Earthwork, being unique in having had a double row of palisades as defense. But these people all disappeared at the middle of the seventeenth century—victims, like the Huron, of Iroquois fury—and we know comparatively little about them.

Dallion's journey, made in the autumn of 1626, lay through a heavily forested country, penetrated only by obscure trails. He had taken with him as interpreters and traders two Frenchmen, Grenolle and La Vallée, and with their assistance friendly relations were established with the Neutrals, who even consented to his remaining among them as a teacher of religion and adopted him as a member of the tribe. But in the end he became the victim of Huron malice. Jealous of their privileged position as middlemen in the fur trade and fearful that the Neutrals might enter into direct trade with the French, the Huron sent messages to the Neutrals stating that the French were a people who fed on snakes and venom and that they had tails. They even anticipated the Dionnes by declaring that French women bore six children at a birth. Dallion, ignorant of these slanderous stories, was maltreated, and in the end almost lost his life. His visit, however, confirmed the idea that there were other waterways connecting Lake Huron with Quebec and that probably these were shorter than the route by way of Lake Nipissing and the Ottawa River.

Fourteen years later two Jesuits, Fathers Brébeuf and Chaumonot, repeated Dallion's exploit, tramping through the forests for five days before arriving at the first Neutral village. It was November, cold, wet and stormy, and the reception they received was even more hostile than that accorded to Dallion. The Huron once again had poisoned the minds of the Neutrals and had even sent agents to bribe the young warriors to kill the priests.

Father Charles Lalemant, in the *Relation* of 1641, gives an account of this mission and Chaumonot has told of it also. The missionaries, half-starved and half-frozen, were driven from the doors of the cabins and subjected to endless indignities, especially at the hands of the pretended maniacs who were to be found in every village and who were regarded with superstitious awe by their fellows. The Neutrals were in terror of the priests, believing, as the Huron had told them, that they were sorcerers. The priestly garb, the sign of the cross, the breviary, inkstand and writing materials, all lent color to the Huron slanders, and the Jesuits barely escaped with their lives. One potential religious gain came unexpectedly. Journeying along a snowbound trail one day, the fathers were admitted to the cabin of a native woman and were allowed to remain for more than three weeks. Chaumonot seized the opportunity to compile a dictionary and grammar of the Neutral tongue, an achievement which Lalemant thought would have been worth several years' sojourn in the country. But dictionary and people alike subsequently disappeared.

Map makers of Europe were soon utilizing the additional information secured by the Jesuits. Lalemant's effort to explain the connection between Lake Huron and Lake Ontario, based upon what he was told by the two missionaries, is confusing, but it is interesting to note that both Lake Ontario and Lake Erie had received their present names by that date. He mentions the Niagara River but not the Falls, the first mention of the latter being by Father Ragueneau in the *Relation* of 1648.

The northern portion of Lake Huron was no mystery by 1640. Brulé had led the way westward from Georgian Bay more than twenty years before, Nicolet had gone even farther in that direction, and there were probably others in this early period who followed the north shore but of whom no record remains. Father Isaac Jogues and Father Charles Raymbault of the Jesuit mission in Huronia went to the Sault in the fall of 1641, and their narrative shows that the earlier confusion between Lake Superior and Lake Michigan was beginning to clear.

But dark days were ahead. Beginning in 1643 and continuing for years the Iroquois carried on relentless and almost uninterrupted warfare against the French and their Indian allies. Determined to drive their competitors in the fur trade entirely from the field, they raided, burned and massacred Huron, Petuns, Neutrals and Algonquin alike. The Dutch at Albany supplied the weapons and profited in return by the trade that was diverted to their hands. There were years during which not a single canoe came down the Ottawa River, and it was an event in 1653 when three canoes followed the old sixteenth-century route from the upper reaches of the Ottawa to the sources of the St. Maurice and finally came in safety to Three Rivers. Montreal had not bought a beaver skin for a year.

This is the period in which the Iroquois fell upon the Jesuit missions in the Huron country. The story of this spiritual enterprise, told elsewhere in this volume, is one of the most dramatic episodes of its time and short-lived though it was, it has remained a great chapter of Canadian history. It may be observed, however, that the massacre of such men as Brébeuf and Lalemant was purely incidental to the main objective, the extermination of the Huron. The beaver lands of the area between the Ottawa River and the Great Lakes were the prize which the Iroquois won by their persistent attacks and when the Huron and other tribes had been dispossessed they themselves occupied the country in large numbers every winter.

French enterprise in America had been brought to a standstill by 1650 and gained ground only slowly after that date through the sheer daring of such men as the intrepid Radisson and Groseilliers who penetrated far into the West and brought back rich prizes. On an August day of 1660 they led a fleet of fifty canoes loaded with furs, a veritable argosy, to the docks at Quebec. It is little wonder that they were received as conquering heroes. France now came to the rescue of her colony overseas, provided military aid, took complete control of the government and soon dealt withering blows to Iroquois prestige.

The time had arrived when the lower lakes would become known. Heretofore Lake Ontario, nearest of all to French settlements on the St. Lawrence, had been closed entirely by the Iroquois menace. There is no record of a white man having descended the St. Lawrence from Lake Ontario until 1653 when Father Poncet made such a journey, nor is there record of an ascent of the river to the lake until 1657 when Father Simon Le Moyne went to the Iroquois country by that route. Missionary enterprise was responsible for both these daring journeys and missionary enterprise was to extend further the geographical knowledge of the Great Lakes system. Jesuits had heretofore been the only ecclesiastics to be found among the Indian tribes; now they had rivals in the Gentlemen of St. Sulpice, seigneurs of the Island of Montreal. With the approval and backing of Jean Talon, the great intendant of New France after 1665, the Sulpicians established themselves among the Iroquois villages on the north shore of Lake Ontario and within four years the whole north shore of the lake was known. Their stations soon extended even beyond the head of Burlington Bay at the west end of the lake.

The year 1669 cleared up all the mystery of the lower lakes. More than fifty years had passed since Champlain had discovered Lake Huron but no one had yet descended to the St. Clair River. This was now the achievement of Louis Jolliet, who was later to be associated with Father Marquette in the discovery and exploration of the Mississippi River. Jolliet, one of the earliest native-born Canadians to win fame, had received a good education, first at the Seminary of Quebec and later in Europe, where he had continued his scientific studies. Talon, eager to develop the wealth of the colony, was prompt to make use of such a man and in 1669 sent him to the Sault with supplies for Jean Peré, an experienced *coureur de bois,* who had gone there the year before to investigate anew the Lake Superior copper mines.

Jolliet failed to find Peré and he was unable to pursue any independent investigation because of a threatened Indian war on Lake Superior. But these very circumstances led him on to a far more important achievement. While at the Sault he rescued from the stake an Iroquois prisoner whom he determined to take back with him to Quebec. The prisoner suggested that they follow a route directly south from the St. Mary's River. And so for the first time a white man descended Lake Huron to the St. Clair River, and passing through Lake St. Clair and the Detroit River came out upon Lake Erie. Had good luck attended, Jolliet might have traversed the whole water system from the Sault to the Niagara River but as he moved along the north shore of Lake Erie he found increasing danger from bands of Andastes and, when about half the length of the lake, he landed, hid his canoe and proceeded eastward by an overland route.

Now came a most unexpected incident. Between the Grand River and Burlington Bay, Jolliet met a party of more than twenty Frenchmen bearing their canoes through the forest and headed southwest. Robert Cavelier de la Salle was the leader of the expedition but with him were two Sulpician priests, Dollier de Casson and René de Bréhant de Galinée. The date was September 24, 1669, and except for the fact that the two parties were following Indian trails, the meeting was quite accidental. The encounter was to have highly important results, for after a winter spent on the north shore of Lake Erie, not far from the present town of Port Dover, the two priests made their way westward to Lake Huron. Jolliet had come down the Michigan side of the lake; they went up on the Canadian side and so within a year both shores became known. The two Sulpicians arrived at the Sault on Pentecost Day, the twenty-fifth of May, 1670. "We were received," Galinée wrote, "with all charity [and] received the communion with so much the more joy, inasmuch as for nearly a month and a half we had not been able to enjoy the blessing."

On the wall of the old Seminary of St. Sulpice at Montreal the visitor may still see a tablet reading: "Francois Dollier de Casson, first historian of Montreal, captain under Marshal de Turenne, then priest of St. Sulpice during thirty-five years. He died in 1701, curé of the parish."

We learn further that he was a native of Brittany, that he came from a noble family, and that after serving for some time as a cap-

AN EARLY MAP OF LAKE HURON

Sanson d'Abbeville, geographer-in-ordinary to King Louis XIV of France, made this map in Paris in 1656, basing it upon information received from the French authorities at Quebec. Early geographers found difficulty in getting Lake Huron's two large bays in proper relation to the lake itself.

Photos by Royal Ontario Museum of Archaeology

OLD SAINTE MARIE I TODAY

The Jesuit Order hopes when the war is over to reconstruct Sainte Marie as
it was in 1649. Excavations conducted during 1941-1943 have revealed the
general plan and some of the foundations of buildings. The upper photo
shows the site on the little River Wye before excavations began. The lower
photo shows two bastions and a connecting wall. These are the oldest ruins
in Canada apart from some at Quebec.

tain of cavalry he abandoned the sword for the church. Of Galinée
we know less, since he was in Canada only three years, though it is
to him that we are indebted for the extensive narrative of the joint
expedition and also for the map of their journeys which he placed
in Talon's hands. "It was," says Dr. James H. Coyne, who has
edited the journal[1], "the first map of the upper lakes at first hand,
and marks a notable advance in cartographical knowledge. From
actual observation Galinée . . . traced the River Detroit, Lake St.
Clair and the St. Clair River into Lake Huron, the east and north
shores of Lake Huron to the Mackinac Islands, and the St. Mary's
River with its islands."

With these discoveries and others that were to follow immediately in the far West, France was laying the foundations for what
promised to be a great empire in the heart of the continent. Settlement was increasing on the St. Lawrence and men were pushing
ever farther into the West. When Jolliet returned to Quebec in
1674 with news of the discovery of the Mississippi River the future
of France in America seemed assured. By control of the waterways
in a great arc that would extend from the Gulf of St. Lawrence to
the Gulf of Mexico, the rival English colonies were to be penned
in along the Atlantic Coast with no back country in which to
expand.

This great conception was ruined by the ambition of Louis XIV
to dominate Europe. In 1672, the very year in which the successful
search for the Mississippi began, he embarked upon the first of
that series of Continental European wars which in the end wrecked
both homeland and colonies. Henceforth there was meager aid
for New France and the dreams of men like La Salle and Frontenac
faded away. Eighty years were to pass before the final struggle
for the control of the continent, but the weaknesses that were to
determine the outcome may be seen in that initial period of European conflict.

Today, as we look back upon French enterprise in America, we

---

[1] The journal of Galinée, translated and edited by Dr. James H. Coyne, is printed
in Ontario Historical Society *Papers and Records*, IV (Toronto, 1903).

can see that while much was eventually lost, certain nonmaterial things remained as a permanent legacy of the times. French names scattered all over the western country indicate to us the deep penetration of the wilderness by explorers and missionaries and traders. The foundations of religion were laid in this era by men who were seldom far behind the front rank of western advance. The Christianizing of the Indian was always a definite part of French policy, and the mission stations which were established here and there about the lakes were not of lesser importance in the minds of most administrators than forts or trading posts. They were frequently the first outpost of civilization in their localities.

The record of French missionary effort in America, going hand in hand with exploration, is one of the most fascinating aspects of the period. Whether it was the solitary priest resident among an Indian band on some remote part of Lake Superior or such a planned campaign as found its highest expression in the Jesuit activities on Georgian Bay, no sacrifice, not even that of life itself, was too great for the representatives of the Cross. The story of these missions continues to be a source of inspiration for thousands of people. It is a story well worth the telling.

THE
UNIVERSITY OF WINNIPEG
PORTAGE & BALMORAL
WINNIPEG 2, MAN. CANADA

DISCARDED

FACULTY OF ARTS

Chapter 3

Old Huronia: Cradle of Martyrs

*Three hundred years have gone, but the
    voices that led
The martyrs through life unto death
    are heard again
In the pines and elms by the great
    Fresh Water Sea.*

          —E. J. PRATT

ON BLEURY Street, in the heart of Montreal and adjoining the massive Church of the Gesu, stand the buildings of St. Mary's College, provincial center of the Jesuits in Quebec. The gray stone walls abut the sidewalk and narrow little windows are so close to the passer-by that the curious might be tempted to peer through. Behind those windows and separated from the noisy street only by the thickness of the walls is a long, narrow room in which are preserved the Canadian archives of the order for more than three hundred years. Here are letters and reports that came down from the Huron country in the days when Brébeuf and Lalemant and their heroic comrades were seeking the salvation of the savage tribes. Here are manuscript Indian dictionaries, laboriously compiled, often amid the smoke and stench of Indian cabins, each word a matter of patient search as to its exact meaning and in its spelling an attempt to reproduce the pronunciation. Here is the journal of Marquette with its declaration that what it contains is a true account of the places he has been and the things he has seen. Thousands of documents fill the shelves from floor to ceiling.

The story of the missions among the Huron on Georgian Bay has often been told, but however often told and however well related it still bears repetition as new light is thrown upon its incidents. It is a unique story in that highly educated Europeans were permitted over a period of years to be spectators of the clash between two uncivilized powers and to witness the virtual annihilation of a savage nation at the hands of its assailants. When the Jesuits first saw the Huron they were a proud people, confident of their ability to withstand attack and even to carry war to their enemies. Twenty-five years later the missionary priests were shepherding a pitiable remnant on an inhospitable island in Georgian Bay and making plans for their removal to a yet more distant refuge. All phases of this tragedy were chronicled by these competent observers.

Interest in the story centers chiefly today about the figures of the men who gave their lives in devotion to their savage charges. On June 29, 1930, with impressive ceremonial in St. Peter's in Rome, Pope Pius XI presided over the rites of canonization of the eight Jesuits who suffered death between 1640 and 1650 within the present bounds of the United States and Canada. Five of these men perished in the Huron country—Fathers Jean de Brébeuf, Antoine Daniel, Gabriel Lalemant, Charles Garnier and Noël Chabanel.[1] None save Brébeuf was past middle life; all were of good birth and highly educated. They were products of the Catholic revival which gave to the church a renewed zeal and to its orders a devotion to the ascetic life almost without parallel. Dominicans and Franciscans, Sulpicians and Trappists, Ursulines and Sisters of Charity, all rose in this period to new heights of service. Yet in aggressiveness and daring and sheer devotion to the salvation of souls, none could compare with the disciples of Ignatius Loyola. They were the spearhead of the church militant. Molded by the spiritual exercises prescribed by their founder, they had a common aim, a common mentality and, some have suggested, even a common type of countenance. Their motto was *Ad majorem Dei gloriam* (To the greater glory of God), and they constantly exemplified it in their utter disregard of hardship and suffering and their contempt for

---

[1] The others were Fathers St. John de la Lande, Isaac Jogues and René Goupil, who suffered martyrdom in the Iroquois country, Goupil in 1642, the others in 1646.

worldly affairs, except as these contributed to the saving of souls. Nowhere have they a nobler record than in their missions to the Huron Indians.

The Huron country was roughly the territory at the southern end of Georgian Bay, lying between Lake Simcoe and the Severn River on the east and Nottawasaga Bay on the west. It formed the upper two-thirds of the present county of Simcoe and the traveler who goes north from Toronto to Midland passes directly through the former habitat of the Huron tribes. For a century and more farmers have been coming upon old burial pits, ash heaps and other indications of the once numerous Indian villages. Great numbers of tomahawks and arrowheads have been found at the scenes of ancient battles. Historians with their documents and archaeologists with their spades have been studying the country for a long period, yet much remains to be learned and some of the most interesting discoveries have come only within the last decade.

Samuel de Champlain, the "Father of New France," was also the father of the missions to the Huron Indians. His deeply religious nature was stirred by the thought that this heathen people might be Christianized and to this end he brought members of the Récollet order to Quebec in 1615. When their resources proved inadequate to the undertaking he gave his support to the Jesuits who succeeded them. The task was challenging. The tribes living to the south of Georgian Bay were as yet almost untouched by white influence and while almost constantly at war were settled in villages and had a primitive agriculture. The Jesuit mind quickly pictured an Indian nation Christianized, set apart from white men and governed by the Church. The dream was never realized but the effort toward its accomplishment forms one of the most dramatic stories of American history.

Jean de Brébeuf was the first Jesuit to enter the Huron country and he was still there and died for his faith when the enterprise came to disaster. Today he is invariably the central figure in any pictorial representation of the North American martyrs and this pre-eminence seems to have been conceded to him from a time soon after his death. He was born in 1593 in Normandy, that province of northern France which contributed so much to the racial stock of French Canada. Father Charles Lalemant described him as "a pious and prudent man, and of robust constitution," and all that we know of him indicates that he possessed in large measure a practical common sense derived from his Norman ancestry. He entered the Jesuit novitiate at Rouen in 1617, but five years later his health had become impaired. Perhaps because of this, his courses of study were shortened and it is said that he never studied dogmatic theology at all. "Still," says one of his biographers,[2] "he knew enough to solve the difficulties of the sorcerers and the sachems who sat around him at the council fires near Lake Huron."

Brébeuf's nature, "like a furnace white hot," would have welcomed martyrdom at any time. When persecution was at its height in 1637 and death seemed imminent, he wrote in farewell to his superior, Le Jeune: "We are perhaps about to give our blood and our lives in the cause of our Master, Jesus Christ. . . . Blessed be His Name forever, that He has chosen us, among so many better than we, to aid Him to bear His cross in this land!"

He frequently claimed to have seen visions of angels and devils and of the glories of the other world. One such vision, which came to him in the winter of 1640, was of a great cross approaching from the direction of the Iroquois country.

"How large was it?" his companions asked.

"Large enough to crucify us all," was the grim response.

There are many references to Brébeuf's bodily strength and he himself on occasion made play with his name, saying that he was an ox, fit only to bear burdens. The record of his journeys and of the privations which he endured are proof of his great vigor yet, strangely, when the final testing came he succumbed to the torture of the Iroquois in less than four hours while the frail and weak Lalemant lasted for nearly seventeen. Possibly it was the titanic

---

[2] T. J. Campbell, *Pioneer Priests of America.* 3 vols. (New York, 1910), II, 70.

power of will with which he resisted his tormentors' efforts to break him down which finally snapped the life cord.

Brébeuf first went to the Huron country in 1625, accompanied by a fellow Jesuit, Anne de Noüe, and the Récollet priest, La Roche Dallion. But these companions soon withdrew and until 1629, when the English seized Quebec and expelled the French, he toiled alone. No record remains of his experiences during those four years but the knowledge which he acquired of the language and customs of the Huron must have been of inestimable value when, following the restoration of Quebec to France in 1634, he resumed his labors.

This second attack upon the stronghold of heathen superstition was to be on a larger scale, Brébeuf being accompanied by Fathers Ambrose Davost and Antoine Daniel. The journey to the Huron country was accomplished in the face of difficulties which few men would have surmounted. It was reckoned to be nine hundred miles from Quebec to Huronia and even Brébeuf, with his giant strength and his past experience of such journeying, nearly despaired of arriving at the destination. Davost was robbed of his baggage and his precious writing materials and abandoned by his Huron companions among the Algonquin of Allumette Island. Daniel was likewise deserted and left to shift for himself. Yet both men, making their way through a wilderness of which they were almost entirely ignorant, managed to arrive safely at their goal.

Brébeuf has left us an unforgettable picture of the hardships of such a journey. The missionaries were not mere passengers in the canoes but were themselves required to toil hour after hour, day after day, with the paddle, work for which they were unfitted and in which they had little experience. Thirty-five times in this journey the canoe and its contents had to be lifted from the water and carried over rough portages. Even more often missionary and Indians alike had to wade waist-deep in the rushing current of rivers, hauling their craft where it was impossible to paddle. When the long day of toil closed, their bed was a bare rock and their food the thin porridge prepared from some crushed Indian corn. And always there was the stench of tired-out savages and the stings of an infinite number of mosquitoes and gnats. To men of culture and refinement the strain of such surroundings was severe, but Brébeuf adds yet one more item: "the long and wearisome silence to which one is reduced, I mean in the case of newcomers, who have, for the time, no person in their company who speaks their own tongue and who do not understand that of the Savages."

In contrast to the streamlined Indian, with his breechclout, moccasins and some daubs of paint, no costume would seem less suited to wilderness travel than the long black robe of the Jesuit. With this handicap the missionaries had to make their way through mud and water and tangled forest trails, at the same time carrying their share of the common burdens. It is characteristic of the thoroughness with which the Jesuit order regulated its affairs that not long after this journey of 1634 Brébeuf was commissioned to prepare instructions for those who might be called upon to journey with the Indians.

"You must be prompt in embarking and disembarking," was one of Brébeuf's very practical admonitions. "Tuck up your gowns so that they will not get wet, and so that you will not carry either water or sand into the canoe. To be properly dressed you must have your feet and legs bare; while crossing the rapids you can wear your shoes, and, in the long portages, even your leggings. Be careful not to annoy anyone in the canoe with your hat; it would be better to take your nightcap."

And there was also the important warning that the savages had no sense of propriety. Brébeuf's Jesuit brethren would be forced to witness, as he also had been forced to witness, gross obscenities and indecencies. "Leaving a highly civilized community," Brébeuf wrote to his associates, "you fall into the hands of barbarous people who care but little for your Philosophy or your Theology. All the fine qualities which might make you loved and respected in France are like pearls trampled under the feet of swine."

But he was able to offer a compensation for such trials of their faith. "Jesus Christ is our true greatness," he wrote, "and having found Jesus Christ in his cross, you have found the roses in the thorns, sweetness in bitterness, all in nothing."

There was need of consolation and inspiration for the men who were to live among the Huron. On the walls of their mission chapels were pictures showing in vivid colors the torments of Hell, pictures which fascinated their savage charges, yet on more than one occasion the only comparison they could make for the scenes about them was that it was Hell itself on earth. Iroquoian cruelty to captives is everywhere recorded with horror and detestation but the Huron also were no amateurs in this barbaric practice. No amusement was more enjoyed than the torture of an enemy, Iroquois preferred. The Jesuits at first questioned the propriety of being present at such horrible festivities but decided that as they could not prevent the practices they might possibly ameliorate the captive's sufferings and even find opportunity to baptize him. Thus we have authentic accounts in their narratives of the ghastly types of torture which were later inflicted upon some of the missionaries themselves.

The frequent necessity of living with the Indians in their rude dwellings, whether through lack of other shelter or during missionary journeys, produced a severe mental strain. "Now that we have Christians in every village," wrote Brébeuf in 1636, "you shall have to tramp for miles along unbeaten trails to reach them, carrying on your back whatever luggage you wish to bring along. There you shall have to stay two or three weeks and share an Indian family's cabin with its inconceivable wretchedness and inconvenience."

The smoke and overpowering stench, the indecencies and lack of all privacy in the rude dwellings must have been cruelly revolting to sensitive minds. The vessels in which the wretched food was prepared were never cleaned. Sick and diseased savages were in close and constant contact with those that were well and with the white men. Though the Huron were more advanced than the Montagnais tribe, to whom the Jesuits also went, and had much more inventiveness, they never achieved adequate provision for their comfort in the wintertime. The Jesuits refer frequently to the torture which they suffered from the smoke in Indian dwellings. The fumes when stirred up by a winter wind would become so dense and biting that throats, nostrils and eyes were in a continual state of inflammation.

"One would prefer the blow of a tomahawk," wrote one of the fathers, "to living during whole years the life one must lead here every day while working for the conversion of these barbarians. If you go to visit them in their cabins you will find there a miniature picture of Hell, seeing nothing ordinarily but fire and smoke, and on every side naked bodies, black and half roasted, mingling pellmell with the dogs which are held as dear as the children of the house, and share the beds, plates and food of their masters. Everything is in a cloud of dust and, if you must go in, you will not reach the end of the cabin before you are completely befouled with soot, filth and dirt."

But life in Huronia was not all grim and horrible. However intent these men might be on the task before them, they were not unmindful of the human comedy being enacted about them and in their writings we find many pleasant little pictures of Indian life. Nor was it a forbidding land in which they dwelt. It was for most of the year a smiling country, fertile lands intersected by pleasant little rivers. The winters were severe but there was also the smiling spring, the warm months of summer and the mild autumn days of harvest with all their splendor of color.

There must have been many evenings when, at the close of a day of toil, the fathers sat together, watching the setting sun, talking perhaps of days gone by and of friends far away, days in Paris or Rouen or other ancient French cities. What a contrast between Paris or Rouen and the life of an Indian village near the shore of Georgian Bay!

When the Jesuits first came to the Huron country they estimated the population at thirty thousand, scattered in a score or more of villages. From time to time these villages were moved to new locations as the fields about them became exhausted or when the accumulation of filth was beyond what even an Indian could stand. Brébeuf, upon his return to Huronia in 1634, chose a small settlement known as Ihonatiria as the place of residence for himself and his two associates. Three years later two villages known as Ossossané and Teanaustayae became the missionary centers. A further change was made after 1638 when Father Jerome Lalemant succeeded Brébeuf in the office of superior. One of his first acts was to provide for a census of the Huron nation. The population was found to be about twenty thousand in all, divided among thirty-two villages and hamlets, adults numbering about twelve thousand. After careful study Lalemant decided that instead of scattering his forces throughout the several villages it would be well to have a central residence from which the fathers could go out to their charges and to which they would at intervals return for rest and refreshment. "It was of our thoughts," he wrote, "that while building a house remote from the neighborhood of the villages, it would serve among other things as a retreat and a place of recollection for our Gospel laborers who, after their combats, would find in this solitude a place of delight."

The site chosen was on the bank of the River Wye, a little stream emptying into one of the indentations of Georgian Bay. Though it was less than a mile to the bay and several of the Huron villages were at no great distance, the place was somewhat isolated. The first structure erected was but an ordinary Indian long house, covered with bark and no more pretentious than those in use elsewhere. One end was partitioned off to provide a chapel. In the next few years more permanent buildings were added, of wooden construction but placed upon stone foundations—a residence, a chapel and storehouses for grain and roots. At a date not earlier than 1646 and probably not before 1648 protecting walls and bastions were added. The place was known as Sainte Marie.

More than a score of Jesuits are recorded as having lived within this center and even a greater number of soldiers, artisans and lay helpers were to be found there. Six men who resided at Sainte Marie were among the eight martyrs who were canonized in 1930. Five who lost their lives in Huronia have already been mentioned— the sixth was Isaac Jogues whose death took place in the Iroquois country to which he had been sent on a special mission in 1646.

One of those in residence during the last days was Joseph Bressani, Italian by birth, who had come to Canada in 1642. He fell into the hands of the Iroquois two years later and was cruelly tortured over a period of more than two months. During one week he was brought out nightly to provide a spectacle for young and old. At times details of Indian torture were so horrible that the Jesuits, candid as they were in such matters, did no more than allude to them. This, it would appear, was true of Bressani. His captors, in the end, seem to have reached their capacity for cruelty and let him pass into the hands of Dutch traders who sent him off to France. Writing at this time to the General of the Jesuits at Rome, he said of his condition:

"I do not know if your Paternity will recognize the handwriting of one whom you once knew very well. The letter is soiled and ill-written; because the writer has only one finger of his right hand left entire, and cannot prevent the blood from his wounds, which are still open, from staining the paper. His ink is gunpowder mixed with water, and his table is the earth."

Bressani arrived in France in the autumn of 1644, but in the following spring he was again at Quebec, horribly disfigured yet eager to resume his duties. He was sent at once to the Huron country, arriving there in the autumn of 1645. Fate did not bring to him the martyr's crown but in heroism and self-sacrifice he falls not a whit below those so distinguished.

The Jesuit writings tell us much concerning the activities of the period during which Sainte Marie was headquarters of the mission work. Long years of patient sacrifice seemed at last to be bringing fruit. There had been a time when the fathers thought themselves fortunate if by some subterfuge they might secretly place a drop of water on the head of a dying infant and so rescue it from perdition. But now there were some real converts, drawn by Christian teaching from their heathen practices. In half a dozen Indian villages, bearing new and Christian names, St. Ignace and St. Joseph, St. Louis and St. Michel, were rude little chapels in which the converts assembled at the sound of the bell to receive instruction from one of the fathers.

The cause was gaining but it was far from triumphing. Indifference, if not actual hostility, was still shown by the greater number of the braves. Converts were loath to abandon the feasts, the dances and the games which formed so important a part of the social life. The medicine men, with their incantations and charms, were the sworn enemies of the priests and embraced every opportunity to vilify and slander them. When misfortune fell upon the villages, pestilence, famine, fire or war, it was at once attributed to the "black robes." "It is the priest that kills us," was the oft-repeated cry. "Before he came we were happy and prosperous. He has bewitched the country."

Indeed, it did seem that an evil influence had fallen upon the Huron nation. Pestilence and battle had decreased their numbers and their spirits were low. From a time before white men ever entered the country there had been conflict with the Iroquois and the menace was now becoming greater each year. In 1645 the Huron sought an alliance with the Andastes who dwelt on the banks of the Susquehanna, but without success. Two years later there was no communication between Huronia and Quebec—the way was barred by lurking Iroquois. Broken in spirit, dejected and fearful, the nation seemed incapable of taking even the most obvious measures for its defense.

In 1648 a Huron party succeeded in making its way as far as Three Rivers on the St. Lawrence, and when attacked at that place routed its assailants, the warriors proudly bearing the scalps back to their own country. It was a hollow triumph, however, for in their absence another Iroquois war party had entered Huronia and on the fourth day of July made a sudden attack on the mission

village of St. Joseph, the Teanaustayae of former days, once Brébeuf's headquarters.

As always, there was no warning. Father Daniel was on the
point of dismissing his converts at the close of Mass when the
savage war whoop was heard. In a moment the invaders were
within the walls, killing young and old alike. Daniel fell pierced
by a score of arrows and bullets. His body, hacked and torn, was
cast into the flames of his burning church. He was the first of the
Huronia martyrs and had served his order for twenty-eight years.
He was a native of Dieppe.

The final blow came in March of 1649. Through the preceding
winter an Iroquois party, numbering at least a thousand warriors,
had moved stealthily through the forests, arriving in the very
heart of the Huron country without discovery. On March 16, before daylight, the palisaded mission station of St. Ignace was attacked and within a few minutes was in complete possession of the
invaders. Fugitives carried warning to the near-by village of St.
Louis, most of whose inhabitants at once fled, but the warriors,
numbering less than one hundred, decided to fight it out. The two
Jesuit missionaries who were present, Brébeuf and Gabriel Lalemant, elected to remain with them.

The defense of St. Louis was almost the last gesture of defiance
of the Huron. Three times the enemy was beaten back from the
wooden palisades which surrounded the town and when breaches
were made in the walls a hand-to-hand struggle continued. But in
the end the fighting rear guard was struck down and those who
survived were made prisoners, the two Jesuits with them. The
town was in flames as the victorious Iroquois returned to St. Ignace.
There at the end of tortures so devilish as almost to bar description and too revolting to be dwelt upon, died the second and third
of the martyrs of Huronia. Lalemant had been in the country less
than eight months, Brébeauf more than eighteen years.

News of the Iroquois attack came quickly to Sainte Marie. At nine o'clock thick smoke and the reflection of flames were seen in the direction of St. Louis. A few minutes later two Huron, breathless and shaking with fear, brought word of its capture. The day that followed was filled with suspense for Father Ragueneau and for his fellow Jesuits. Fugitives came in, many of them wounded or burned, seeking refuge and help. While attention was being given to these suffering people thoughts constantly turned to the brethren elsewhere. Where was Brébeuf? Where was Lalemant? The day passed with the question unanswered, nor was it fully answered until four days had passed. But in the meantime there was much to do. At any moment Sainte Marie itself might hear the dreaded war whoop. Prayers were said without ceasing. Vows were made to Saint Joseph, patron saint of the colony. Iroquois scouts appeared on the edge of the clearing but none approached the fort. Elsewhere, however, there was ferocious fighting and even a seeming change of fortune. But by this time the Iroquois raiders had satisfied their blood lust and had turned homeward, dragging numerous prisoners with them, many of whom they tomahawked as they journeyed. But before they left they bound numbers of helpless captives to stakes within the bark houses of St. Ignace and then set the place afire.

On the morning of March 20 an armed party set out from Sainte Marie to search for the bodies of the missing brethren. The snow of mid-March still lay deep in the forests and along the trails, here and there dyed deep red where some unfortunate prisoner had been tomahawked. No doubt existed as to the fate that had befallen the two missing priests. Huron who as prisoners had witnessed their torture and had later escaped had told of the horror attending those last hours. All that they told was confirmed by the condition of the bodies found in the ashes of St. Ignace. Fire and the knife, red-hot stones and boiling water had all been used to satisfy Iroquois vengeance.

"We saw no part of his [Brébeuf's] body," wrote Ragueneau, "from head to foot, which was not burned, even to his eyes, in the sockets of which these wretches had placed live coals."

"I saw and touched all the wounds," wrote Christophe Regnaut, a lay brother who was present with the party. "We buried these precious Relics on Sunday, the 21st of March, 1649, with much Consolation." The place of burial was within the walls of Sainte Marie on the little River Wye.

When the mission buildings were abandoned in the next few weeks the bodies were exhumed, the flesh removed from the bones and reburied. But the bones themselves were regarded as precious relics and Regnaut has recorded for us the reverence which was given to them.

"All the bones were well scraped," he writes, "and the care of drying them was given to me. I put them every day into a little oven which we had, made of clay, after having heated it slightly, and when in a state to be packed, they were separately enveloped in silk stuff. Then they were put into two small chests, and we brought them to Quebec, where they are held in great veneration."

In later years Brébeuf's family in France sent to Quebec a silver bust, the base of which was made to contain his skull. It was for a long time in the custody of the Jesuits at Quebec but in the late eighteenth century was given into the care of the Hospital Sisters of the Hôtel-Dieu, in whose venerable institution it may still be seen.

Gabriel Lalemant, who perished with Brébeuf at St. Ignace, came of a good Parisian family belonging to the curious hereditary *gens de robe* (practitioners of the law). The emphasis which has always been placed upon the vigor and strength of Brébeuf has its contrast in the frequent references to the weakness of Lalemant. Both Ragueneau and Bressani mention it, and Marie de l'Incarnation expressed her astonishment at finding one so delicate in such surroundings as New France afforded. There were, in all, three Lalemants sent from France to the Indian missions. Charles Lalemant, who arrived in 1625, was an uncle of the martyred Gabriel. Jerome, a younger brother of Charles, went to Huronia as superior in 1638 but was superior at Quebec in 1648 when the Iroquois holocaust began. He died at Quebec in 1673 and his brother Charles survived him but one year.

Two more names were yet to be added to the roll of Huronia's martyrs. In the Petun country, lying along the south shore of Nottawasaga Bay, were two missionaries who remained at their post even after the tragedy of March 1649, though they were distant but two days' journey and knew that at any time the Iroquois might search them out. The blow came some months later. The mission station of St. Jean was attacked in December and there Father Charles Garnier fell before the bullets of the invaders. Wounded and dying, he dragged himself from one to another of his Indian converts, giving them absolution, until a blow from a tomahawk ended his own life.

His co-worker at St. Jean, Noël Chabanel, who had left two days before in company with some Indians, was deserted by all save one when the Iroquois war cries were heard. His companion, an apostate Huron, in the end turned upon the missionary, killed him and threw his body into the Nottawasaga River. The roster of Huronia's martyrs was completed.

The Iroquois raids of 1649 ended the Huron as a nation. Fifteen villages had been burned and their inhabitants massacred or scattered. Terrified groups sought refuge with the Petuns or with other tribes to the north and west. Some fled to the Neutrals or to the Erie. As for the Jesuits, it seemed that all for which they had labored during more than twenty years had been destroyed almost in a day. To save even some remnant of the Huron was the immediate task. Ragueneau, superior of the mission, at first thought of Manitoulin Island as a place of refuge. On further consideration, however, Christian Island, then known as Isle St. Joseph, was chosen. It lay to the north of Huronia and so close to the mainland that the movement of people and possessions could be carried out with little danger. Some large rafts, hastily constructed of logs, and one small boat served as transport.

On May 15 the Sainte Marie mission was burned. In a letter written to the superior at Quebec, describing the last day on the mainland, Ragueneau penned what may well be described as the epitaph of the Jesuit enterprise. "On each of us," he wrote, "lay the necessity of bidding farewell to that old home of Sainte Marie—to its structures, which though plain, seemed to the eyes of our poor savages master-works of art, and to its cultivated lands, which were promising us an abundant harvest. That spot must be forsaken which I may call our second Fatherland, our home of innocent delights, since it had been the cradle of the Christian Church; since it was the temple of God and the home of the servants of Jesus Christ. Moreover, for fear that our enemies, only too wicked, should profane the sacred place, and derive from it an advantage, we ourselves set fire to it, and beheld burn before our eyes, in less than one hour, our work of nine or ten years."

On the shore of Christian Island a new Sainte Marie soon arose, this time a veritable fortress of stone and cement, with walls and bastions and surrounded by a deep moat. No Iroquois attack, however strongly supported, could have broken its defense. To this stronghold the remnants of the Huron gathered during the summer and autumn of 1649, coming fearfully from the forests and the wilds where they had fled for shelter. Some were wounded or suffering from burns, many were sick, all were hungry and dejected. The Jesuits ministered as best they could to the immediate needs but their resources were few and the demands were heavy. Over all hung the shadow of the winter that would come. Through summer and autumn efforts were made to store up food against the oncoming cold. Any kind of food that would support life was sought, acorns even, but Christian Island had little to offer.

The days began to shorten and colder winds came in from the waters of the bay. The first snows fell and the depressed savages crouched about their fires. A people who had gone through the experiences that marked the spring of 1649 were in no condition to resist disease. When spring of 1650 came, half of those who had crossed to the island were dead. We do not know the number of those who perished; it may have been in the thousands.

Little more remains to be written of the Huron. It was evident that to remain on the island would mean death to many. To return to the mainland would tempt the Iroquois to further attacks. In the end two Huron chiefs waited on Father Ragueneau and suggested that those who had survived should be removed to the vicinity of Quebec where, under the shelter of its fort and garrison, they would have protection. Ragueneau must have suffered deeply in making his decision. Removal to Quebec meant the complete abandonment of the missionary enterprise upon which so much effort had been expended. But there was no alternative, and on June 10 a flotilla of canoes began the long retreat eastward. We can picture Ragueneau with sad eyes looking back at the vanishing shores of the Huron country. "It was not without tears," he wrote, "that we left the country which possessed our hearts and engaged our hopes; and which, even now reddened with the glorious blood of our brethren promised us a like happiness. But yet, self must be forgotten and God left for God's sake."

So they came down to the settlement at Quebec and there first found a home on the Island of Orleans. Later they removed to Ste. Foy and then to Lorette where today a few of their descendants may still be found. Others who had been scattered by the Iroquois attacks removed to Manitoulin Island, to the shores of Lake Superior and some even yet farther west to the Mississippi country. The Huron as a nation were no more.

All this happened long ago. What of Huronia today, what of Sainte Marie, what of St. Ignace, what of Christian Island? Does this modern age concern itself at all with the story of a religious enterprise that came to an end nearly three centuries ago? The answer is that at no time in the past has there been such public interest in the story of the Jesuit missions as is manifest today. Nor is this interest confined to antiquarians and devotees of religion. The Huron missions have long been a theme for historians. Today they have become a theme for novelist and poet. Artists and musicians gain inspiration from the story. Newspapers record the discoveries made during excavation of the sites. Huronia has become news.

One circumstance alone might account for much of the popular interest. When Pope Pius XI in 1930 officiated at the canonization of the eight Jesuit martyrs he gave to the United States and to Canada their first saints. The event was of interest to the whole Christian world but of particular interest to North America. It had long been expected that such distinction would be accorded to the men who gave all for the cause to which they had dedicated their lives. Four years after the death of Brébeuf and Lalemant, the Archbishop of Rouen, whose jurisdiction extended to New France, had ordered an official investigation into the circumstances surrounding their deaths. More than two and a half centuries later a wider inquiry, relating to all of the martyrs, was instituted at Quebec. But in such matters the Church moves slowly and another quarter century passed before the seal was finally placed upon the virtues of these men.

Sainte Marie, because of its close association with the closing years of the Huron mission, has in recent years become the subject of close study and investigation. The Jesuit records tell us that it was abandoned and burned in 1649. During the next two hundred years its site was almost forgotten, for when the Huron mission came to an end Jesuit activity was turned to other directions. Moreover, the order itself fell upon evil days, being suppressed by Pope Clement XIV in 1773. The English government decreed that the members of the order then in Quebec might hold their lands while any remained alive, after which the properties would pass into the possession of the Crown. A grim sort of comedy ensued as officialdom sat by watching the gradual decrease in numbers. The Jesuits were mostly old men and by 1785 but four were living. Seven years then passed without a death, but after 1794 one lone member of the order remained, Father Jean-Joseph Cadot. His death took place on March 16, 1800, one hundred and fifty-one years to the day after the martyrdom of Brébeuf and Lalemant.

Forty years went by after the death of Father Cadot before the black robe of the Jesuit was again seen in Canada. Then, at the instance of Bishop Ignace Bourget, who had himself begged from the papal authorities the privilege of joining the order, a small group, six in number, came to Montreal from Kentucky. These men were deeply interested in the work of their predecessors and in 1844 Father Pierre Chazelle made a journey to the site of Sainte Marie. Probably no one other than wandering Indians or hunters had visited the place since 1650. Eleven years later another member of the order, Father Felix Martin, also visited the site and has recorded that at that time remains of the old walls and foundations were standing to a height of about three feet.

After this time considerable destruction of the ruins took place. The early settlers in the district saw the rude foundations on the bank of the River Wye but knowing nothing of their history treated them with little respect. Stone from the walls was hauled away as material for barn foundations and for the abutments of a near-by bridge. Except for one brief period the site was in private hands and vandalism and desecration was for many years almost unchecked.

Today, however, all is changed. Sainte Marie has once again become the property of the Jesuits. On the high hill beneath whose shadow it nestles there stands a great church, the Martyrs' Shrine, to which each year tens of thousands of pious Roman Catholics make pilgrimage. Moreover, having acquired the historic site, the Jesuits have determined that Sainte Marie shall be restored, and as a preliminary to this a systematic excavation of the site has been made, the work being entrusted to the staff of the Royal Ontario Museum of Archaeology.

The writings of the seventeenth-century Jesuits tell surprisingly little about Sainte Marie and no contemporary plan or drawing is known to exist. Excavation, however, has provided abundant information. In plain view today stand the remains of the defending walls and foundations of the buildings which stood within them. They are the oldest masonry structures in Canada except some at Quebec. The place is shown to have formed a rough parallelogram about 180 feet in length and about 93 feet in breadth. At each corner there were stone bastions, while additional protection was afforded by a moat along two sides.

Within the walls there have been unearthed the foundations of several structures, probably the residence and chapel, and also storehouses. Various objects of interest have also come to light. The ruins of an old forge tell of ironworking to meet the needs of this remote post. Seeds of various grains and vegetables confirm the Jesuits' own records of farming experiments designed to better the living conditions of the Huron. A mason's trowel and axes also reveal some of the general activities during the 1640's. One ax that was uncovered still retained a portion of its handle.

A medal which came to light bears the images of St. Ignatius Loyola and of St. Francis Xavier. Since the inscriptions include the word *"beatus"* rather than *"sanctus"* it is clear that it was made before their canonization in 1622. Another find of human interest was a small silver sewing set, scissors, bodkin and a tiny needlecase still containing two needles. Fragments of fine Venetian glass form yet another relic of the days of occupation. Sewing case and glass may well have come from some friend in France to the missionary so far away, little objects of refinement in the midst of so much savagery.

After Sainte Marie no other site in the Huron country has as great religious interest as St. Ignace, where Brébeuf and Lalemant met death. We learn from the Jesuit writings that it was a palisaded village, built in 1648 and therefore occupied less than a year before its destruction in March 1649. So short a period would produce no extensive ash heaps as evidences of human occupation and its wooden construction would leave no such remains as are found at Sainte Marie.

Father Chazelle looked for it without success in the forties, as did also Father Felix Martin in the fifties. Late in the nineteenth century Father Edward Jones, archivist of the Jesuits, undertook the task of exploring Huronia and in 1898 he fixed upon a site which seemed to satisfy all requirements. Ten years later he admitted that he had erred and that what he had actually found was St. Louis, where the two Jesuit martyrs were taken prisoner. Other theories were advanced by scholars from time to time but none stood the test. In the end it remained for a completely unlettered man to present evidence leading to the most promising site that has yet been suggested for St. Ignace, a site so far accepted by the Jesuits themselves that the order has purchased the property to ensure its preservation.

Alphonse Arpin, a citizen of Midland on Georgian Bay, had from his youth a deep religious interest in the story of the Jesuit missions. As a boy he tramped the country where the missionaries had worked, and since he himself could not read he had others read to him the printed records until finally he had memorized whole passages of the Jesuit writings. Brébeuf and Lalemant were to him living personages and in his mind grew a pious wish that he might discover the place of their martyrdom. For years he searched and at last found a site which seemed to conform in all particulars to the descriptions in the writings of the early Jesuits. His discovery, however, might have died with him had he not by a strange coincidence encountered one who was following the same quest.

On a day in 1932 he was at the railway station at Medonte, Ontario, and there met a stranger who explained that he had come to test his own theories as to the location of St. Ignace. This was Thomas G. Connon, of Goderich, a Protestant by faith. Arpin told Connon of his own search and of the site which he had found. In company they visited the place not once but many times and checked its distance from other known sites by pushing a bicycle wheel to which a cyclometer was attached. Their findings as to distance were strikingly in accord with the Jesuit records.

Both men died in 1936, convinced in their own minds that they had found St. Ignace. But more definite evidence was required, such evidence as might be brought to light by a trained archaeologist. The investigation was continued by President W. Sherwood Fox, of the University of Western Ontario, who secured the services of W. J. Wintemberg, an official of the National Museum of

Canada. Wintemberg began his excavations in the late summer of
1937. For several days the men under his charge carried on their
work with no results whatever. Then, following a hint in Connon's
records, operations were shifted to a neighboring field and almost
at once there was discovered a line of post molds indicating the site
of an ancient village. Further excavations during 1938 indicated
that the village had an area of ten acres and that it had been completely encircled by palisade defenses. In one of his reports
Wintemberg declared: "I know of no other site in the neighborhood that fulfills all the requirements of Father Ragueneau's description given in the Jesuit Relations of 1649," and this view is
held by all who have been associated with the investigation.

Christian Island, where Huron fled for refuge after the Iroquois massacres of 1649, and from which a remnant went to Quebec in 1650, is today again a mission station of the Jesuit order.
Father Labelle's little stone church is the center of religious life of
those Indians on the island who profess the Roman Catholic faith.
Sisters of Service teach the children the rudiments of learning and
the essentials of religion. The bell in the cross-crowned tower
calls them to worship just as the bell called the unfortunate Huron
during that starving, freezing winter nearly three hundred years
ago. But all is peaceful today. Occasional visitors come to the
island to see the place so closely related to the events of long ago.
In 1942 the quiet was broken as men salvaged hundreds of tons
of steel from the wreck of the steamer *Mapledawn* which went on
the rocks of the island as long ago as 1924. But they, too, have
gone and quiet has returned. Christian Island is left with its
memories.

Chapter 4

When Fur Was King

There was in the forest trade that freedom which many civilized men feel when they come into touch with savage life, and even the element of gambling which made the profits of the trade so largely a matter of chance seems only to have added to its attractiveness.
—WILLIAM BENNETT MUNRO

DURING the period in which Jesuit missionaries were seeking the salvation of the Huron tribes on Georgian Bay, daring explorers and adventurous traders were extending the bounds of French influence. Popular interest tends to center upon the happenings in old Huronia because of their tragic character and spiritual significance, but these were not the only important phases of Lake Huron's history in this time. Even before 1650, when the Jesuit effort in Huronia came to an end, interest was shifting to regions farther west, to the St. Mary's River and Lake Superior, to the Straits of Mackinac and Lake Michigan.

The French River and Ottawa Valley route to and from Montreal was to continue even beyond the eighteenth century as a highway between the St. Lawrence Valley and the West, but an alternative route was opened when Jolliet in 1669 descended Lake Huron, following the present Michigan shore, and when a year later Sulpician missionaries ascended these same waters. These voyages revealed what was eventually to become an all-water route from the head of the lakes to the ocean. Jolliet was soon followed by others, the beginnings of the marine traffic which today moves continuously during the season of navigation between the entrance to the St. Clair River and the passages leading to Lake Superior and Lake Michigan.

Father Louis Hennepin, that strange disciple of St. Francis who once admitted that his great ambition was an "Inclination to travel," has given us an account of the first voyage ever made by a ship on Lake Huron, that of La Salle's *Griffin* in the summer of 1679. This historic ship, the first to ply the waters of Lake Erie and Lake Huron, had been built on one of the creeks flowing into the Niagara River. The ship entered the waters of Lake Erie on the seventh of August to the accompaniment of a *Te Deum* and the boom of a little cannon. Four days later the *Griffin* reached the entrance to the Detroit River and sailed through its pleasant waters to the shallow little lake above which La Salle named Sainte Claire. Equally pleasant were the days spent on the St. Clair River. It was the twenty-third of August, Father Hennepin tells us, when with the help of twelve men hauling at ropes the little ship was finally brought through the rapids of the St. Clair River and out upon Lake Huron. "We sang Te Deum a second time," he wrote, "to return our Thanks to the Almighty for our happy Navigation." Many a vessel after the *Griffin* was to be detained by these same rapids and those aboard were to give equal thanks for passage out on the broad sparkling waters of the lake.

On leaving the river the *Griffin* was set to a course north-north-east but as this brought the vessel near land it was changed to north-northwest and soon they were crossing Saginaw Bay. Lake Huron was not kindly toward these pioneer voyagers, for they experienced both calm and gales, ran into shallow water and could find no anchorage. A tempest came down, so severe that all seemed lost, and they fell to their knees in prayer. All except one. Hennepin tells us that the pilot could not be made to pray and did nothing but curse La Salle for bringing him into such a "nasty lake" after he had had long and happy years of navigation on the ocean. Doubtless it was because the pilot stayed on his job instead of falling to his knees that vessel and crew survived the storm. Better weather came at last, and on the fourth day after entering the lake the *Griffin* came to St. Ignace of Michilimackinac on the north shore of the Straits and anchored in six fathoms of water.

Seven years after the *Griffin* had passed through the rapids of the St. Clair a fort was established there by Daniel Greysolon, Sieur du Lhut. This aristocratic *coureur de bois,* with his brother Charles, had been active in the Lake Superior region in the effort to encircle the English on Hudson Bay and hold the western fur trade for France. The post at the mouth of Lake Huron was named St. Joseph and to it came in 1687 the young Louis Armand de Lom d'Arce, Baron de Lahontan, sent by Governor Denonville with a detachment of soldiers and Indians to take over the command from du Lhut.

This young Frenchman served in Canada between 1683 and 1693, at times holding commissions of considerable responsibility. His letters from New France and his various memoirs, written in racy style, are important sources for our knowledge of the colony during the time he was present, but they have suffered a strange fate. Because of certain indiscretions in some of his writings, much else has been subjected to criticism and grave doubt. His reference to the character of the women who were brought out in groups from France as wives for the settlers and his attitude toward the accepted doctrines of Christianity were bound to stir up resentment. At the same time his account of a journey to the Mississippi region where he claimed to have found populous nations, Eokoros, Esanapes, Gnacsitare and others with equally fantastic names has, from his own day to the present, been received with incredulity. But apart from these he left in his writings an extensive body of knowledge of the most varied character with regard to both the colony of New France and the Indians of the wilderness.

Lahontan and his party left Niagara in early August, made the laborious passage around the cataract, were threatened on the way by a band of Iroquois and emerged upon the waters of Lake Erie, where the crude heavy craft of their enemies were no match for their own light birchbark canoes. Lake Erie was calm and the diet of the travelers was enriched on the way by wild turkeys which ran in flocks of fifty or more along the shore.

It was September 6 when they entered the Detroit River, more than a month since their departure from Niagara. Eight days later they were at the little picketed post established by du Lhut the year before. "You cannot imagine the pleasant prospect of this Streight," wrote Lahontan, "and of the little Lake[1]; for their banks are covered with all sorts of wild Fruit-trees. 'Tis true, the want of Agriculture sinks the agreeableness of the Fruit; but their plenty is very surprising." Deer were abundant and when the party came to the little islands in the Detroit and St. Clair Rivers the animals were chased into the water and killed by the Indians.

Lahontan, passionately fond of hunting, found the life at St. Joseph pleasant during the autumn months, but the winter that followed, with its scanty and monotonous diet, was less to his liking. On the first day of April he set out with most of the garrison for Michilimackinac. His pretext was the necessity of securing a supply of provisions, but we may suspect that what he really wanted was a more active and exciting existence than was afforded by the lonely little post at the entrance to the St. Clair, with dense forests behind and the great lonely lake in front. Since his journal makes no mention of encountering ice we may conclude that the spring season had come early. A gentle gale brought the canoes to Saginaw Bay, which they were six hours in crossing. Apparently the course followed led them well into the bay, for he speaks of two islands which afforded welcome shelter from the wind.

"Before you have crossed this Bay," he wrote, "the Coast is all along full of Rocks and Shelves, one of which that I saw was six Leagues broad: But above it the Coast is clean and low, especially towards the Sand-River, which lies half way between that Bay and a place called l'Anse du Tonnere. This last place is reckoned thirty Leagues off the Bay."

It is of interest to note how early Thunder Bay had acquired that name. No point on the west shore of Lake Huron was more often mentioned by early travelers and while Lahontan says nothing of thunder being heard when he passed the place the majority of other

---

[1] The "little Lake" to which Lahontan refers is Lake St. Clair and the "Streight" refers to the whole passage from Lake Erie to Lake Huron.

voyagers assert the frequency of the phenomenon. But this was not the only Thunder Bay on the lakes. On the northern shore of Lake Superior and at the south end of Georgian Bay the name is also found, and probably it was first applied for the same reason.

Jonathan Carver, the first traveler in the western country during the British regime and the first to publish an account of travels in the region now known as Wisconsin, voyaged up the west shore in 1766 accompanied by William Bruce, a British trader. He makes particular mention of Thunder Bay: "Nearly half way between Saganaum Bay and the north-west corner of the lake," he wrote, "lies another which is termed Thunder Bay. The Indians, who have frequented these parts from time immemorial, and every European traveler that has passed through it, have unanimously agreed to call it by this name, on account of the continual thunder they have always observed here. The bay is about nine miles broad and about the same in length; and whilst I was passing over it, which took me up near twenty-four hours, it thundered and lightened during the greatest part of the time to an excessive degree."[2]

Carver, speculating on the cause of the unusual amount of thunder, could see no reason for it, since the country in general was not subject to any such disturbance. He wondered if the shores of the bay or the adjacent high lands were either "impregnated with an uncommon quantity of sulphurous matter, or contain some metal or mineral apt to attract in a great degree the electrical particles that are hourly borne over them by passing clouds." In the end he decided that the solution of this and other philosophical questions confronting him might well be left to the discussion of abler heads than his own.

For two centuries the fur trade dominated the economic life of the Lake Huron region and after 1701, when Cadillac founded Detroit, the Michigan shore and the waters below had an important

---

[2] Jonathan Carver, *Three Years Travels Through the Interior Parts of North-America, for More Than Five Thousand Miles* (Edinburgh, 1807).

place in the business. Michigan was itself one of the great fur-bearing areas of the Old Northwest, and Detroit and Mackinac became the two most important centers for the carrying on of the enterprise.

The fur trade, whether under French, English or American auspices, was opposed to settlement. The hostility shown to Cadillac's plans for a colony at Detroit was the reflection of the attitude taken both by traders and by government officials who might profit indirectly by the trade. It was manifested also in the Royal Proclamation of 1763, issued from London after the cession of Canada by France, closing the whole western country to settlement. "Let the savages enjoy their deserts in quiet," said the English Lord Commissioners on one occasion. "Were they driven from their forests the peltry trade would decrease."

Michigan's delay in advancing to statehood when other areas farther west had reached such status may be attributed in part to the opposition of fur-trading interests and the deliberate misrepresentation of the nature of the country. Steamboats carrying the immigrants to the West passed by Michigan in favor of Illinois and Wisconsin. It is true that vessel owners preferred to carry such people to their most distant port, increasing their revenues thereby, but they were aided in this by the generally prevalent idea that Michigan lands were unsuitable for settlement. The Hudson's Bay Company later pursued the same policy with regard to the Canadian Northwest, its officials testifying before British parliamentary committees that there was no extensive agriculture possible in what is now one of the great wheat-growing countries of the world. They, like the fur companies in American territory, realized that settlement meant the doom of their trade in furs.

When Antoine de la Mothe Cadillac founded the little post of Detroit in 1701 the rivalry of England and France for control of the fur trade was at its height. It was a rivalry which contributed not a little to the series of border intercolonial wars in the last of which the whole destiny of the continent was changed.

Sault Ste. Marie had been the first important center of the trade but was later supplanted by Michilimackinac which so grew in importance that the post at the Sault had dwindled before the end of the seventeenth century to little more than a station on the route to the West. The rival English trader was early on the scene, even at the distant post of Mackinac, paying higher prices for the furs which the Indian collected, offering his own goods at a price below that which the French asked, and, what was often most influential of all, prepared to exchange the exciting firewater for peltries. To meet such a challenge France had the advantage of holding many key positions and having men of remarkable skill and daring to administer her affairs in the far interior.

Cadillac saw in the strait connecting Lake Erie with Lake St. Clair a position strategic both for defense and for trade. A post set here would be an effective barrier to the English effort to reach the western tribes. Around it might be gathered a stout little colony, and it could be made a center for the Indians of a large area who would bring their peltries here rather than to other posts. Had Cadillac been given a free hand from the beginning much more might have been accomplished. But he was no sooner installed at Detroit, ready and eager to carry out his plans, than he found the post handed over to the jurisdiction of the Company of the Colony of Canada. Trade did not flourish under its management, with the numerous restrictions then hedging it about.

In 1705 Cadillac returned to Detroit. Unfortunately most of the restrictions remained to handicap his efforts but he was successful in drawing many Indians within his influence, so much so that Michilimackinac was reduced for a time to unimportance. Cadillac left in 1710 to become governor of Louisiana, and from then until France ceased to rule in America the fortunes of Detroit varied with the character or ability of the official in control. By the 1740's the generally disturbed conditions resulting from border warfare were adversely affecting trade, the English becoming more aggressive than at any time in the past. The threat of the impending struggle for the continent was plainly felt.

British policy after the conquest of Canada contemplated the free licensing of traders, presents for the Indians to insure their friendship, and concentration of the trade, if possible, at a few large posts rather than at numerous smaller stations. The new policy of free licenses contrasted sharply with French monopolistic ideas but the freedom of trade which it encouraged led to such bitter competition and scheming practices that in the end it proved disastrous. More farseeing traders, realizing that only ruin could come from such a situation, eventually formed companies which in the end themselves became a partial monopoly even though there was no actual prohibition of the individual trader.

In the thirty-five years of British rule at Mackinac the Loyalists, settled on and around the Niagara River area, and the French and others on the Detroit River found a market for their produce among the fur traders in the northern country who seldom attempted anything larger than a vegetable garden. These supplies were carried up Lake Huron in small government sailing vessels. In 1793 about 4,000 bushels of Indian corn and nearly 200,000 pounds of flour went from Detroit to Mackinac and Sault Ste. Marie, and three years later John Askin at Detroit had a contract with the North West Company to supply it with 1,200 bushels of hulled corn and 12,000 pounds of flour in each of the succeeding years. Some of this corn was procured from Delaware Indians who had been brought to Upper Canada by Moravian missionaries and settled on the Thames River.

Despite the fact that British sovereignty was extinguished in the Northwest in 1783 and the illegal possession of such posts as Detroit and Mackinac terminated in 1796, the influence of the British fur-trading companies continued strong until after the War of 1812, when they were finally excluded by Congress from operations within the United States. It was then that the American Fur Company, chartered in 1810 with John Jacob Astor as the head, entered upon its heyday and sought to drive out all other competition. More ruthless business methods have rarely been known than those that were practiced against the independent traders. As for the source of the trade, the peltries themselves, the policy appeared to be to exploit to the limit regardless of the future.

The fur trade at Detroit during the American regime was not, as at Mackinac, dominated by one company or individual but was divided among a number of traders, each having his own employees whom he sent into the Indian country. These agents took their merchandise with them and returned to Detroit in the spring with the furs which they had been able to secure. In the early 1820's as many as eight or ten firms were engaged in the trade and a rough estimate of the furs collected and sent from this post in 1822 placed the value at $300,000. It was the chief business of the town, but a writer in the Detroit *Gazette* laid his finger on its weakness when he wrote: "How much more consoling it would be could we feel that even a small portion of our fur could return to our territory in cash to be expended in erecting mills. . . . Instead all furs which are collected by our merchants go towards payment of debts contracted for foreign fabrics or in exchange for them, not only the fur but the money received for them."[3]

One of the fur-bearing areas tributary to Detroit in this period was the Saginaw Valley. The American Fur Company had established a post near the present site of the city of Saginaw in 1824 and had also several outposts elsewhere along the river. One of the independent traders, Louis Campau, acting for a group of Detroit merchants, had come to the neighborhood of this American Fur Company post in 1816 and set up his headquarters near by. Bitter feeling developed on the part of the company's agent and the feud, being taken up by the Indians, threatened to drive the company from its location. For a time it was unable to do any trading. Only when more diplomatic managers were sent to the spot was peace restored and business resumed.

The middle thirties saw the trade distinctly on the decline. Astor sold out his interests in the American Fur Company in 1834 and retired from the trade. The old name was retained by his successors but the end was nearing for the business that had occupied men

---

3 Ida A. Johnson, *The Michigan Fur Trade* (Lansing, 1919), 144.

around the Great Lakes since the early years of the seventeenth century. Cutthroat competition had exacted its price; fur-bearing animals were becoming scarce, and some were nearing extinction.

The decline of the fur trade did not mean the immediate end of the companies. Like the Hudson's Bay Company, which today probably has greater revenues from its large stores in Winnipeg and elsewhere and from the sale of its lands than is received from any fur trade, so the American Fur Company adjusted itself for a time to changing conditions. When William Cullen Bryant was at Mackinac in August 1846 he visited the company's old warehouse looking for some Indian embroidery. "Here on the shelves," he recorded, "were piles of blankets, white and blue, red scarfs and white boots; snow shoes were hanging on the walls, and wolf-traps, rifles and hatchets were slung to the ceiling—an assortment of goods destined for the Indians and half-breeds of the north." The warehouse had become a general store.[4]

---

[4] William Cullen Bryant, *Letters of a Traveller; or, Notes of Things in Europe and America.* (New York, 1850), 297-298.

Chapter 5

War Comes to Lake Huron

---

*The conquest of Canada is in your power. I trust I shall not
be deemed presumptuous when I state that I verily believe
that the militia of Kentucky are alone competent to place
Montreal and Upper Canada at your feet.*

—HENRY CLAY (1810)

*A country defended by Free Men, enthusiastically devoted
to the cause of their King and Constitution, can never be
conquered.*

—GENERAL ISAAC BROCK (1812)

LAKE HURON saw no naval engagement during the War of 1812
comparable in any way to Perry's victory over the British
fleet at Put in Bay, nor was it the scene of such extensive
naval construction as took place on both Lake Ontario and Lake
Erie during the course of the struggle. It was, nevertheless, the
scene of several exploits which for sheer daring are scarcely rivaled
elsewhere during the war, and the effect of these operations upon
the northwestern area was of high importance to the contending
forces, and might conceivably have profoundly influenced the final
peace settlement.

When hostilities came in the early summer of 1812 there were
but two centers in the Lake Huron region where settlements existed and where business activity was to be found. These were
Mackinac and Sault Ste. Marie. Mackinac since the summer of
1796 had been occupied by an American garrison, final recognition of American sovereignty over this frontier post having been
assured by the Jay Treaty of 1794. At Sault Ste. Marie the opposed
nationals could look at each other across a narrow stretch of river.
But at both places Canadian fur-trading interests were highly influ-

ential, the North West Company, founded in the very year of English recognition of American independence, extending its trading activities far to the north and west.

We recognize today that it was the pressure of western opinion and the drive of western men which largely influenced the United States to declare war. There were national grievances which furnished diplomatic argument for initiating hostilities—the restrictions on American commerce and the outrageous way in which the claim to right of search was at times conducted. But it is doubtful if, in the face of New England's opposition, these would have been sufficient to turn the scale had not the representatives of the agrarian West, with an almost completely united front, threatened and blustered at Washington until Madison finally yielded.

From the year 1795 when, by the Treaty of Greenville, vast areas of land had been ceded in central Ohio, the Indians had been steadily falling back before the advance of white settlement. Prior to the War of 1812 they had agreed to no less than nine separate cessions of territory and their more farseeing leaders recognized that before many years their whole life would be changed. Agriculture must supplant hunting and the trade in furs. The two modes of life could not exist together. In this period, so critical for the Indians, leadership of a high order arose in the Shawnee chieftain Tecumseh who sought to bring the tribes into a great Indian confederacy. When the war finally came he promptly joined with the British and until his death in 1813 gave highly effective aid.

Canadians have always regarded the War of 1812 as primarily aimed at the conquest and acquisition of the province of Upper Canada and there is much in the political oratory of the American West in the prewar period which might lead to such a view. The young patriots who were elected to the House of Representatives in 1810 and who were branded "War Hawks" by old John Randolph, made no secret of their territorial ambitions. "I am not for stopping at Quebec," said Henry Clay from Kentucky, "but I would take the whole continent." John C. Calhoun, with equal fervor, could assure Congress: "I believe that in four weeks from the time a declaration of war is heard on our frontier, the whole of Upper Canada and a part of Lower Canada will be in our power." With leaders so confident there was little hesitancy on the part of the rank and file in the West in supporting what was expected to be an easy conquest.

But the British provinces had their "War Hawks" also, though this is not usually given much prominence in Canadian schoolbooks. The merchant class, with its headquarters in Montreal but with financial interests ramifying over half the continent, saw in the situation which Clay and his friends were creating the possibility of regaining the fur-trading empire which had been their preserve before the surrenders made by British diplomats in 1783, at the close of the War for Independence, and in 1794 by John Jay's famous treaty. For them this was no war of defense; they would gladly turn it into a war for the reconquest of that which had been lost to them.

"Posterity will hardly believe," they declared, "although history must attest the melancholy and mortifying truth, that in acceding to the Independence of the Thirteen Colonies as States, their Territory was not merely allowed to them, but an extent of Country, then a portion of the province of Quebec, nearly of equal magnitude to the said Thirteen Colonies or States, was ceded, notwithstanding not a foot of the Country so ceded was at the time occupied by an American in Arms, nor could have been, had the war continued."[1] John Graves Simcoe, first lieutenant governor of Upper Canada, had dreamed that by peaceful means he might woo the American colonies back to the British fold, but these aggressive Canadians would waste no time on persuasion or blandishments. They would fight for what they wanted. They did not even wait for the declaration of war to make known their ambitions and to offer assistance. As early as January 1812 the Deputy Quartermaster General at Montreal, Captain Gray, was able to assure Sir George Prevost, the Governor General and Commander of the Forces, of the support and help of the fur traders.

---

[1] *Public Archives of Canada,* Series Q, CXXX-CXXXI, 117-118.

"The heads of the companies," he wrote, "are exceedingly grateful to Your Excellency for taking an interest in the protection of their Trade. . . . They will enter with zeal into any measure of Defence, or even offence, that may be proposed to them. . . . They express every wish to be useful in the common cause. . . . They have tendered all their vessels for the service of the Govt. if the Exigencies of the War should make it necessary to call for them. In short they are full of Loyalty and Zeal, and manifest a degree of public spirit highly honorable to them. By means of these Companies, we might let loose the Indians upon them throughout the whole Extent of their Western frontier, as they have a most Commanding influence over them."[2]

The merchants even came forward with plans for the opening of a campaign on Lake Huron, suggesting an attack upon Mackinac and the removal of the British garrison from St. Joseph Island to Sault Ste. Marie. They themselves would take the offensive on Lake Superior, "acting in concert with the forces at the Straits of St. Mary's." The effect of such operations would, they believed, be "to dislodge the enemy from any position he may take upon the Lake and in short exclude him entirely from any participation in the navigation or Commerce of Lakes Superior, Huron and Michigan."[3]

When war came this was almost exactly the plan of operations decided upon for this region and the British cause had no more zealous advocates or assistants during the whole period of the struggle than these men who saw an opportunity that might never come again of redeeming *Canada Irredenta* for themselves and their Indian allies.

The sharp, swift stroke by which the British force captured Fort Mackinac at the very opening of hostilities was not only dramatic but had immediate effect upon operations elsewhere. By this one

---

[2] Gray to Prevost, Montreal, January 13, 1812. *Michigan Historical Collections,* XV (1909), 70-72.

[3] *Ibid.,* 71.

operation, conducted without loss of life, indeed without the firing of a single shot, the most important post in the Northwest, the key to the whole region, was made a British center of operations and continued so during the remainder of the struggle. The loyalty and assistance of thousands of Indians, many of whom might perhaps as easily have been drawn to the American side, was insured, and the loss of Mackinac was one of the factors in determining Hull to surrender Detroit exactly one month later.

Fort Mackinac in June 1812 had a small garrison, less than sixty men, under command of an artillery officer, Lieutenant Porter Hanks. It was sixteen years since the fort had been taken over from the British, who had then retired to St. Joseph Island, and in the interval little had been done to strengthen the defenses. The works erected so carefully by Captain Patrick Sinclair after 1781 commanded the approach to the island which every visitor of today sees, but nothing had been done to insure against attack and invasion from some other portion of the shore line. Mackinac was a long distance from the lower lakes region where American forces were then gathering, but St. Joseph Island was an even greater distance from Montreal. Yet the garrison at St. Joseph received word as early as July 8 of the declaration of war and received two other messages regarding operations before their attack of the seventeenth, while in that period Lieutenant Hanks appears to have been entirely ignorant of the outbreak of hostilities. He had, it is true, observed certain ominous signs—Indians leaving the island in considerable number and British traders conspicuous by their absence. These happenings, in the end, induced him to make inquiry on his own account.

The British post on St. Joseph Island was under the command of Captain Charles Roberts,[4] an officer of experience, who had a garrison no larger than that at Mackinac, chiefly a detachment of the Tenth Royal Veteran Battalion, old men. But for offensive purposes in this operation he had a much greater force, as we shall pres-

---

4 Captain Charles Roberts was an uncle of Lord Roberts ("Bobs"), famous British commander in India and in the Boer War.

ently see, and he had the advantage of being in a position to take the initiative.

From what we know of Roberts and of his superior in Upper Canada, General Isaac Brock, the fall of Mackinac might just as easily have come a week earlier. It was the halting indecision of Sir George Prevost, the commander in chief at Quebec, which on this occasion, as on other occasions during the war, held back younger and more active officers. Prevost had received word on June 25 of the declaration of war upon England, but he still believed that something might intervene to delay an actual outbreak of hostilities. Consequently his first message to Roberts counseled only vigilance to protect the post and, significantly, to protect the interests of the "Gentlemen of the North West Company."

General Brock, at York (now Toronto), learned just a day later than Prevost that war had been declared, information coming to him through a private source. Where Prevost had counseled caution Brock suggested action and gave Roberts authority to move at once if he thought wise. But Prevost was hesitant and Brock was forced to send a second express practically canceling his earlier instructions. Roberts was ready for an immediate movement against Mackinac when this second message arrived, and he even knew that the American garrison had received no reinforcements.

Then came Brock's third message, ordering action. It arrived on the fifteenth and within twenty-four hours the expedition was under way. It is worth while to look at the composition of this force, for it was varied in character. First of all, there was the regular garrison of forty men and four officers, disciplined and capable of obeying orders. Next there were 180 Canadian *voyageurs,* and finally 300 or more Indians. The total force was over 500, but Roberts must have had some doubts in his mind as to what the Indians would do should there be any real resistance at the island.

Those days of waiting during June and early July of 1812 must have been extremely trying for Lieutenant Hanks and his garrison. He was aware that relations between his own country and England were approaching the breaking point and that war might come at any time. Day after day he must have scanned the horizon to the east, watching anxiously for the arrival of some vessel off Lake Huron which would give him definite information on the state of affairs. But none came. In his difficulty he took counsel with the American traders on the island, particularly with Michael Dousman, who was a captain of militia. Dousman had suspicions that all was not well, since two of his agents who had been on Lake Superior and had, as he knew, returned to the Sault, had failed to make an appearance at Mackinac. Finally it was decided that Dousman, who owned property on St. Joseph Island, should go there and learn what he could of the situation. He embarked on July 15 but never reached his destination. Instead he ran straight into the British force headed for Mackinac and was brought back as a prisoner.

The expedition under Captain Roberts left St. Joseph at ten o'clock on the morning of July 16, traveling in the North West Company's brig *Caledonia* and in a fleet of bateaux and canoes. It was fortunate that the *Caledonia* was available since it gave a vessel of some strength in case of resistance, capable also of bearing a considerable amount of supplies. Roberts was none too sure of the Indians and so, before landing his force, he sent one of the British traders present, accompanied by the prisoner Dousman, to warn the civilian population and to conduct them to another part of the island where a guard would be placed over them.

At daylight on July 17 the situation was this: At a point on the back of the island, ever since known as British Landing, the invading force was ashore and moving rapidly and unopposed toward the heights. In the village Dousman and others were going from door to door awakening the people and hastening them to the place of safety. It was the unusual quiet in the village which first alarmed Lieutenant Hanks, but before he could ascertain the reason the garrison heard the whoops of the Indians in the woods encircling the fort. Hanks was no coward and was prepared to defend his post but when he perceived that the enemy was in force on the heights above him, that their gun commanded his position and that their numbers were evidently much superior, he recognized that resistance would be fatal.

He had not long to wait. The British force had completed its preparations for attack by nine o'clock and soon after a message came to him, demanding surrender. The summons was brought by Dousman and other members of the trading community who knew enough of the British strength to advise that resistance would be useless and that surrender was the only alternative to bloodshed, perhaps massacre.

The Articles of Capitulation were brief. The fort was to be given up and the garrison sent to the United States, not to serve until regularly exchanged, for which the officers were to pledge their word of honor. The vessels in the harbor, with their cargoes, were to remain in possession of their owners, and there was to be no interference with private property. Citizens of the United States were required to take the British oath of allegiance within a month or leave the island.

Roberts and a portion of his force descended from the heights to the old fort and the American garrison was paraded. There were sixty in line and one man in hospital. Three deserters from British regiments in Canada were found among the sixty: Hugh Kelly from the Forty-ninth, Alexander Parks from the Royal Artillery and Redman Magrath from the Fifth. It must have been a trying moment for these three gentlemen, knowing as they did just what sort of punishment was inflicted upon deserters under the hard British discipline of those days. Visions of the lash laid on their bare backs several hundred times must have made their knees shake as the officers spotted them.

But two of them were in rare good fortune. Parks and Magrath were "an excellent drum and fife" and Roberts decided to keep them with him until further orders. Perhaps he thought that they might instill some of the Spirit of 1776 into his old veterans, of whom he had none too high an opinion. "The men I have here," he wrote, "tho' always ready to obey my orders are so debilitated and worn down by unconquerable drunkenness that neither the fear of punishment, the love of fame or the honor of their Country can animate them to extraordinary exertions, it is painful to me to be obliged to draw such a picture, but truth and justice demands it."

The paroled garrison and such American citizens as chose to leave were soon sent to Detroit aboard two small schooners. Roberts took every precaution for their safety while passing through the St. Clair River region where an attack was a possibility, sending along an interpreter and three Indians well acquainted with the tribes residing in that area. Poor Lieutenant Hanks who had been forced to surrender Mackinac was killed a few days after his arrival at Detroit by a cannon ball from across the river which crashed into the room where he happened to be.

In his report to General Brock, written within a few hours after the capitulation, Roberts gives as one reason for his swift move that he was fearful of abandonment by the Indians if they were not soon employed. On the other hand, the fact that he did move with decision gave him a prestige with the red men well illustrated by their actions while on the island. Instead of pillaging and other outrages there was order and decency.

"It is a circumstance I believe without precedent," he wrote, "and demands the greatest praise for all those who conducted the Indians, that although these people's minds were much heated, Yet as soon as they heard the Capitulation was signed they all returned to their Canoes, and not one drop either of Man's or Animal's Blood was Spilt, till I gave an Order for a certain number of Bullocks to be purchased for them."[5]

The *voyageurs,* "Canadian Engagées" as Roberts terms them, had an important role in the expedition. Half of them were unarmed, but their contribution was to man the boats and, on arrival, to haul one of the six-pounder guns to the summit of the island. A few days after the surrender the *voyageur* force was increased by

---

[5] Roberts to Brock, Michilimackinac, July 17, 1812. *Select British Documents of the War of 1812,* edited by William Wood, 3 vols. (Toronto, 1920-1928), I, 434.

the coming of reinforcements from Fort William. When word came to St. Joseph that war had been declared an express was immediately sent to the fur-trading post five hundred miles away and nine days later the northern contingent arrived.

Captain Roberts was in possession of Mackinac but his troubles were by no means at an end. In a letter written on July 29 he lays bare some of his difficulties, one of the chief being his uncertainty as to the loyalty of the Ottawa. This tribe had been expected to form a part of the expedition against Mackinac but they failed to arrive until several days after the surrender. "It is now evident," wrote Roberts, "that they were encamped all this time at no great distance, waiting to hear the result of our attack."

His other native allies, chiefly Chippewa, were more reliable and he thought of bringing over all the members of this tribe in the neighborhood of St. Joseph and settling them on Mackinac, thereby making himself independent of the doubtful Ottawa. His own force was so few in number that he had to use the Indians and he could only hope that reinforcements would reach him before an attempt was made to recapture the place. He would have been in better spirits had he known more of events elsewhere. On August 16, the very day on which Detroit surrendered to Brock, Roberts wrote, detailing the trickery of the Ottawa, the "dreadfull consumption of Provisions" by the Indians who were flocking in from all quarters with their wives and children, the weakening of his force by the departure of the *voyageurs* for the winter hunting grounds and the conduct of some of his own men—"one of them is now in Irons for striking an Officer in the execution of his duty."

"The Spark which gave Life to every proceeding at the commencement of our operations seems to have nearly expired," was his lament. But he was cheered by a letter from Major General Sheaffe which pointed out to him that the capture of Detroit and of General Hull and his army had removed the grounds of some of his difficulties, and that all he had done had received official approval. A word of confidence and of praise was worth much to him at that moment.

Detroit News Photo

PRESQUE ISLE LIGHTHOUSE

One of the older lighthouses on the Michigan shore of Lake Huron. By day it stands out dazzlingly white and by night flashes its warning to vessels passing by.

Photo by A. G. Atkinson

A LAKE HURON FISHERMAN

L. H. ("Louie") MacLeod, of Bayfield, Ontario, one of the best-known fishermen on the Canadian shore of Lake Huron.

Roberts must have been sorry to see his Canadian *voyageurs* leave. They may have been difficult to control but they were stout, resolute fellows who could be counted upon when there was hard work ahead, much more so than the poor old drunken veterans of his own command. With his blue *capot,* his gaudy sash, his deerskin leggings and his gay beaded pouch, the *voyageur* was a figure long to be remembered. Joseph McGillivray has left us a lively picture of the Corps of Canadian Voyageurs which came into existence in the fall of 1812, just such fellows as were under Roberts for a short time.

"It was quite impossible to make them amenable to military law," he wrote. "They generally came on parade with a pipe in their mouths and their rations of pork and bread stuck on their bayonet. On seeing an officer, whether general, colonel, or subaltern, they took off their hats and made a low bow, with the common salutation of 'Bon jour, Monsieur le Général' or 'le Colonel,' as the case might be, and, if they happened to know that the officer was married they never failed to inquire after the health of 'Madame et les enfants.' On parade they talked incessantly, called each other 'pork eaters,' quarreled about their rations, wished they were back in the Indian country again, &c., and when called to order by their officers and told to hold their tongues one or more would reply, 'Ah, dear captain, let us off as quick as you can; some of us have not yet breakfasted, and it's upwards of an hour since I had a smoke.' . . . In vain the subaltern winked, in vain the captain threatened, in vain the colonel frowned; neither winks, threats, or frowns, could restrain the vivacious laugh, silence the noisy tongue, or compose the ever changing features into any thing like military seriousness."[6]

Captain Perry's victory over Captain Barclay's fleet on September 10, 1813, changed the whole picture west of Niagara. Procter's British force which had been holding Fort Malden on the

---

[6] Grace Lee Nute, *The Voyageur* (New York, 1931), 164-165.

Detroit River, and thereby the entrance to the upper lakes, was forced to retreat, and being overtaken on the Thames River was badly defeated at Moraviantown. From that time until the end of the war most of the British province of Upper Canada, from Burlington Bay on Lake Ontario westward, was in American hands or helpless against American raiders. As for Mackinac, the way was at once wide open for an attempt at its recapture. The lateness of the season, however, and the repairs needed by the ships which had taken part in the battle on Lake Erie, made it necessary to postpone any movement against the island until the next year.

Captain Richard Bullock of the Forty-first Regiment was in command at Mackinac when word was received of the American victory on Lake Erie. Bullock had led the detachment which marched into Detroit on August 16 "with Drum and Fife to the tune of the British Grenadiers." He had fought at Queenston Heights and had been at the action on the Maumee in May 1813. The retreat of Procter left him isolated at Mackinac unless supplies could be sent overland from Lake Ontario to Matchedash Bay and thence by boats to the island. Autumn gales prevented the arrival of any such assistance but Bullock managed to lay in enough food for most of the winter by buying everything that could be obtained in the near-by settlements.

During that winter of 1813-1814 plans were made by the American command for an assault in force upon Mackinac in the spring and, realizing the danger to which the post was exposed, the British command laid its plans to strengthen and defend the island, so vital to the interests of the great fur-trading companies. Captain Bullock had suggested the building of some small gunboats at Matchedash Bay in order to keep communications open and had also asked for additional men and guns. The gunboats were not built but effective aid was brought to the island garrison before the real danger arose.

About the end of February, Lieutenant Colonel Robert McDouall, of the Glengarry Light Infantry, led a party overland to the head waters of the Nottawasaga River. This stream empties into Georgian Bay not far from the present town of Collingwood. With him were shipwrights, twenty-one seamen, eleven artillerymen with four guns, and two companies of the Royal Newfoundland Regiment. A cairn and tablet erected in 1938 by the government of Canada marks the place where during the winter of 1813-1814 McDouall's men cut down the trees, sawed out the timbers and constructed thirty bateaux of large size. These were loaded with provisions and military supplies and on April 19 began the descent of the river. Six days were occupied in bringing the heavily loaded boats through the twistings and shoals, and then began the hazardous journey, amid great fields of floating ice, across Georgian Bay and upper Lake Huron. Nineteen days after leaving the river the flotilla was at Mackinac, having lost but one boat, the crew and cargo of which was saved. The successful navigation of the lake in such an unfavorable season was due in no small measure to Lieutenant Robert Livingston, an officer of the Indian Department, who had served in his youth as a midshipman in the Royal Navy and who acted as pilot.

McDouall, on his arrival at Mackinac, took charge of the post and continued in command there until the end of the war. He had scarcely become acquainted with the place before he faced a situation calling for prompt decision and stout action. Word came to him on June 21 that the important trading post of Prairie du Chien had been occupied by a force sent by General William Clark, Governor of the Missouri Territory. It was imperative that an effort be made to regain the place and McDouall did not hesitate. He quickly detached a small force from his garrison, provided them with a field gun and attached to the expedition the 155 Sioux and Winnebago warriors on the island. An artillery sergeant, Keating by name, led the party which at Green Bay was joined by other volunteers, raising the number of white men in the force to 120. The Indians were also augmented to 450. The journey of more than 600 miles was made in nineteen days. The post was at once invested and the American force of three officers and seventy-one men surrendered forty-eight hours later.

While these events were taking place the American ships which were to take part in the expedition against Mackinac were being assembled and put in readiness for the work ahead of them. Because of the importance of the operations a separate command had been authorized for the upper lakes and to this post Captain Arthur Sinclair was appointed. He was a capable officer and an experienced seaman and set himself with vigor to the task of getting his little fleet in readiness. There were unexpected delays and not until June 25 was the squadron ready to sail.

Sinclair had five ships under his command. First of all were the brigs *Niagara* and *Lawrence,* both of which had taken part in the battle on Lake Erie. Then there was the brig *Caledonia* which had once belonged to the North West Company and which had carried Captain Roberts and his men to Mackinac in July 1812, but had been captured at Fort Erie in the following October. To these three ships were added the schooners *Tigress* and *Scorpion,* which had also shared in Perry's victory.

At Detroit troops to the number of 600 were taken aboard, with Colonel George Croghan in command and Major Andrew Hunter Holmes as his second. Five hundred Ohio volunteers joined the force at Fort Gratiot. Difficulty was experienced in moving the larger and heavily laden vessels over the shallows of the St. Clair Flats, resulting in a delay of more than a week, and it was not until the twelfth of July that the white sails were at last spread to the strong breezes of Lake Huron.

The plan of campaign was not to proceed directly to Mackinac but first of all to destroy the little British post which had been set up on Matchedash Bay, thus eliminating any possibility of assistance coming from that quarter. But Sinclair quickly found that he had undertaken a hazardous enterprise in venturing into the uncharted waters of Georgian Bay.

"Being unable to procure a pilot for that unfrequented part of the lake," he wrote to the Secretary of the Navy, "and finding it filled with islands and sunken rocks which must inevitably prove the destruction of the fleet as it was impossible to avoid them on account of the impenetrable fog with which this lake is almost continually covered, and finding the army were growing short of provisions from the time already elapsed, it was agreed between Colonel Croghan and myself to push for this place [St. Joseph Island] where we should procure such information as would govern our future operations."

It was discouraging to have failed in the first portion of the projected enterprise. As the fleet groped about in dense fog, in constant danger of smashing up on some unseen rock, those days of search for the Matchedash post must have dampened the spirits of all aboard. Nor was there anything in the occupation of St. Joseph Island that could uplift them. The post had been abandoned by the British and the garrison withdrawn to Mackinac, nothing of value being left behind. The only consolation afforded at St. Joseph was the capture of the little schooner *Mink*, belonging to the North West Company, which was intercepted on its way to the Sault. Captain Sinclair learned thereby that Prairie du Chien had been recaptured by the detachment sent from Mackinac, but that in doing so the island's garrison had been weakened. A side expedition to Sault Ste. Marie was not entirely barren of results, but was less successful than anticipated as the fur traders had been warned of an impending attack and had removed their property.

The movement against Mackinac itself began on July 26, but it was not until August 4 that a landing was actually made on the island. McDouall, in command of the place, had been well informed as to the dispositions of the American fleet from the time of its arrival at St. Joseph and wrote to his superiors that the garrison was in highest spirits and ready for any attack. And so it proved when Croghan finally landed his men on the west side of the island and began to move them against the defenses on the heights. The commander explained later that his plan was not to attempt to storm the heights but to establish himself in some favorable position from whence he might "by gradual and slow approaches" achieve his goal.

The difficulty lay in the fact that to reach the desired favorable position the force must pass through many dense woods where Indians might lurk in ambush. Croghan and his men had not advanced far before they found themselves under fire of the British guns and on endeavoring to change their position and, if possible, outflank the defending force they again came under fire, this time from Indians concealed in the forest. Major Holmes fell almost at once and Captain Desha, next in command, was severely wounded. Confusion followed and, though there was stiff fighting for a few minutes, Colonel Croghan saw that it was impossible to advance farther and ordered the forces withdrawn. In addition to the two senior officers mentioned, there were nearly sixty other casualties. McDouall's force numbered 140 men of the Royal Newfoundland Regiment and Michigan Fencibles,[7] and about 150 Indians, but he had the advantages of concealed position and familiarity with the ground. He had fought a purely defensive action and had won without the loss of a single man. The next day, under a flag of truce, a party came from the *Lawrence* and took away the body of Major Holmes. Forty years later one of the members of the Campau family of Detroit related that the body of Holmes was placed in a crude coffin carved out of a log and brought to Detroit for burial, trailing all the way in the water behind the ship to which it was tied by a rope. It was in memory of this officer that Fort George, constructed by the British on the summit of the island, was renamed Fort Holmes by Colonel Anthony Butler, the commander of the American force which took over Mackinac when it was returned to the United States by the terms of the Treaty of Ghent.

With the failure of the attack on August 4, operations on Lake Huron took on another character. It seemed possible that Mackinac might be brought to surrender by cutting off all communication between the garrison and its base of supplies on Georgian Bay. As

---

[7] The Michigan Fencibles was "a corps enrolled from the voyageurs and hangers-on at Mackinac, whom the war and its disarrangement of the fur trade had left stranded." Louise Phelps Kellogg, *The British Régime in Wisconsin and the Northwest* (Madison, 1935), 308.

the whole squadron would not be required for such an effort, two of the larger ships now sailed away to the lower end of the lake, leaving the *Niagara* and the schooners *Tigress* and *Scorpion* to handle the situation.

One particular objective was the capture or destruction of the schooner *Nancy* which, so far as the American commander knew, was the only vessel left to carry supplies to Mackinac. The *Nancy* was owned by the North West Company when the war began. She was promptly put at the service of the British military authorities and during 1812 carried troops and stores between Detroit and Fort Erie. She narrowly escaped capture in the St. Clair River after the battle on Lake Erie and came to Mackinac in October 1813 with her sails and ropes so badly damaged that she had to be sent to the Sault for repairs. When McDouall took over at Mackinac in the spring of 1814 it was proposed that the *Nancy* be made over into a gunboat but in the end she continued on transport work and had made two successful trips before the appearance of the American fleet in upper Lake Huron. Fear that she might fall into Sinclair's hands caused word to be sent to the post on the Nottawasaga River to move the little schooner as far upstream as possible and to have her remain there until more favorable times.

The Nottawasaga River follows a peculiar course before it empties into the bay. For miles it runs parallel to the shore, only a short distance inland, thus forming a sort of long narrow peninsula of sand hills covered with thin timber. From offshore there was no indication that such a place of shelter existed. About the middle of July the *Nancy* had approached the river mouth, returning from Mackinac, and there found a young lieutenant of the Royal Navy, Miller Worsley, and a detachment of seamen. The schooner was immediately loaded for another run to the island but before she set sail Colonel McDouall's message was received and the *Nancy* was at once towed about two miles upstream to a point where she would be completely concealed by the sand hills. As further protection a small blockhouse was erected and three guns placed in position.

The American ships, arriving offshore on August 13, had no idea that the vessel so eagerly sought was within easy gun range. Colonel Croghan received a most pleasant surprise, therefore, when a landing party moving inland suddenly saw the masts of the schooner and, investigating further, found that she was lying on the farther side of the river under the shadow of a blockhouse and guns.

Next morning Sinclair ran his ships in close and opened fire, without much effect at first as the target was not visible. But by landing howitzers and firing over the intervening trees and sand hills he made Worsley's position so untenable that it was decided to abandon both schooner and blockhouse and blow them up. The guns had been spiked and a train of powder laid to the little vessel when a shell burst inside the blockhouse, starting a fire. This quickly communicated itself to the schooner which, with its cargo, was almost completely destroyed. The blazing hull sank in the river, its trading and fighting days at an end. In time the sunken timbers formed a shoal which gradually became an island, a sort of earthy coffin for the little vessel. In 1924 Dr. F. J. Conboy, at that time an official of the Ontario government, visited the spot and found a cannon ball of twenty-four pounds' weight, presumably one of those fired by the American vessels on the day in August 1814 when the *Nancy* met her end. This aroused curiosity as to the actual resting place of the vessel and led to the discovery of the charred hull. The timbers were in such good condition that there was no difficulty in raising them. Today the hull rests on the island which it created long ago, a spot which has been transformed into a pleasant little park.

There are several contemporary references to the *Nancy* which indicate that her builders had taken special pride in their work. John Richardson, a Montreal fur merchant, one of the original owners, wrote on September 23, 1789: "The schooner will be a perfect masterpiece of workmanship and beauty. The expense to us will be great, but there will be the satisfaction of her being strong and very durable. Her floor timbers, keel, keelson, stem and lower futtock are oak. The transom, sternpost, upper futtocks, top-timbers, beams and knees are all red cedar. She will carry 350 barrels."

The *Nancy* was launched in September 1789, "a very beautiful and substantial vessel," with a figurehead, made by the carver Skelling of New York, of "a lady dressed in the current fashion with a hat and feather." Richardson wrote with pride from Niaggara when she came there: "She is spoken of in such a high strain of encomium as to beauty, stowage, and sailing, that she almost exceeds my expectation." And when the hull came from its long resting place all that had been said as to beauty of line and excellence of materials and workmanship was well proved. The timbers and planks were sound and hard. Red cedar and oak of the vintage of 1789 had withstood storms and buffetings in her sailing days and had fought off decay during the years since her burning timbers went with a great hiss and a cloud of steam beneath the waters of Nottawasaga.

The attack upon Mackinac on August 4 was the first chapter in these naval operations of 1814, and the destruction of the *Nancy* the second. But there was a third chapter as well which lacked none of the dramatic qualities of those which preceded. With the *Nancy* out of commission, Captain Sinclair felt that further operations could be left to the two schooners and he therefore sailed away in the *Niagara*. His instructions to Lieutenant Daniel Turner were explicit. He was to maintain a blockade of the Nottawasaga River until fall storms made his position untenable, "suffering not a boat or canoe to pass in or out of this river." But at the same time he was authorized to cruise at intervals in the vicinity of St. Joseph Island to cut off any fur canoes headed for French River.

Turner would have been wise had he examined the Nottawasaga River more carefully. Its entrance had been effectually blocked, so Sinclair believed, by cutting trees which fell into the channel, but Turner made no search upstream beyond the captured blockhouse. Had he done so he would have found, at no great distance, a hundred barrels and more of provisions, together with two bateaux and a large canoe. Had he been vigilant he might even have captured young Worsley and the naval detachment which had escaped into the bush after their blockhouse was blown up.

Worsley, keeping an eye on the American vessels, eventually found them absent and determined to run for Mackinac with his men and some of the provisions. The river entrance was easily cleared and on the night of August 18 the party entered the bay. Six days of hard rowing brought them to the vicinity of St. Joseph Island where they suddenly found themselves at no great distance from the American blockaders. As it was impossible for the heavy bateaux to pass without being seen, Worsley concealed them in a quiet bay and then, loading his men, twenty-five in all, into the big canoe, set out for Mackinac.

McDouall must have been a surprised man when Worsley and his seamen landed on the island. He knew little of what had recently transpired on Georgian Bay and had been anticipating a possible return of Sinclair's squadron and another attempt to take the island. But Worsley had plans in mind which he quickly communicated. Why not attempt the capture of the *Tigress* and *Scorpion* before they returned to their duties off the Nottawasaga?

No time was lost. Next day four boats loaded with troops and guns, and accompanied by two hundred Indians in canoes, left for the Detour passage. One of the two American vessels was soon discovered and it was decided that a night attack would be most likely to succeed. On the evening of September 3, the weather calm and the night dark, the convoy headed silently for the ship lying at anchor. So well was the operation conducted that Worsley's own boat was but ten yards away when the first alarm was given. The attacking force quickly gained the decks of what proved to be the *Tigress* and a few minutes sufficed to overpower the officers and crew.

The prisoners were immediately sent away in boats and a canoe party was detailed to watch for the *Scorpion* which was supposed to be near by. On the night of September 5 information was received that the sister ship was beating down toward the captured *Tigress,* apparently ignorant of the events of two days before. Later in the night, when the wind fell, she anchored within two miles' distance, giving no signals of any kind.

Lieutenant Worsley kept the American colors flying on the *Tigress* and at daybreak of the sixth, with but a jib and foresail, ran down toward the *Scorpion.* A few sailors were kept in plain view but the soldiers lay on the deck covered with their greatcoats. The ruse was entirely successful. The *Scorpion* proved an easier prize than the *Tigress.* When within a few yards Worsley opened fire, the two vessels came swiftly alongside each other and the boarding parties were over the sides and on the other deck before the *Scorpion's* crew realized what had happened. Two men belonging to the captured vessel were killed and two wounded; Worsley had one seaman wounded. The American ships were taken to Mackinac, the *Tigress* being later renamed *Surprise,* perhaps in joking reference to the manner of her capture, and the *Scorpion* becoming H. M. S. *Confiance.* With the menace of these two vessels removed, the Mackinac garrison could at once open communication with Georgian Bay and with the lower end of the lake. The captured vessels were sent to Nottawasaga Bay and returned with ample provisions and supplies. For the remainder of the struggle Mackinac and the St. Mary's River were free from threat.

Colonel McDouall in his official report on these operations gave glowing praise to Worsley, recommending him to the naval authorities for promotion. The War of 1812 produced its share of intrepid officers on both sides, and Worsley for sheer daring and cool courage stands high among them. Lieutenant A. H. Bulger of the Royal Newfoundland Regiment, which participated in the cutting out of the *Tigress,* paid his tribute also to its officers and crew. "The defence of this vessel," said his report, "did credit to her officers who were all severely wounded, she had 3 men wounded & 3 missing supposed to have been killed and thrown overboard immediately." Sailing master Stephen Champlin, who was in command of the *Tigress,* was one of the most severely wounded.

A grapeshot, after passing through the flesh of his right leg, shattered the bone in the left. He was operated upon at Mackinac and was shortly after paroled to Erie. After the war he assisted the American commissioners in determining the international boundary along the upper lakes.

It was the fifteenth day of May 1815 when a messenger brought to McDouall at Mackinac Island the first news of the treaty of peace and its terms. The letter had been on its way two months. In the reply which McDouall penned four days later all his pent-up chagrin and bitter disappointment are exposed. "My perplexity is as great as ever," "I see with great pain," "I cannot disguise my fears" are phrases which indicate his frame of mind. He knew that a few weeks hence he would have to meet an incoming American garrison, see his own flag hauled down and that of his recent enemy raised in its place. What would be the effect upon the Indians, his allies?

"The surrender of this most important Island," he wrote, "the key to the whole Western Country, & which they fully expected would be retained by us, if followed up by that of St. Josephs, and the adjoining Islands, will be to them such conclusive proofs of our disgrace, & absolute submission to the American Government, that it would be most grossly deceiving ours, to hold forth the expectation of being joined by a single Indian, in the event of another war. Their neutrality is then, the utmost, perhaps, that we can hope for, & that is more to be desired than expected."[8]

He also wrote from Mackinac to Captain Bulger at Prairie du Chien: "Our negociators, as usual, have been egregiously duped; as usual, they have shown themselves profoundly ignorant of the concerns of this part of the Empire. I am penetrated with grief by the restoration of this fine Island—'a fortress built by nature for herself.'"[9]

---

[8] McDouall to Forster, Michilimackinac, May 15, 1815. Wood (ed.), *Documents*, III, 532-536.

[9] Louise Phelps Kellogg, *Op. cit.*, 327.

McDouall's feelings could not be compared, however, with those of the Canadian merchants who, from the outbreak of hostilities in June 1812, had looked forward hopefully and expectantly to the recovery of their old trading area in the Northwest. Great Britain had let them down in 1783 when she ceded to the independent states all the territory west to the Mississippi River, and though they had received thirteen years' grace by the continued occupation of the frontier posts, in the Jay Treaty they had again lost out.

Once more they were to meet disappointment. Though the American position at the opening of peace negotiations was poor, the representatives of the republic won a striking victory in the diplomatic game at Ghent. Britain has seldom had more incompetent officials designated to deal with an important matter than the three who met John Quincy Adams, Henry Clay and Albert Gallatin. Lord Gambier, Henry Goulburn and William Adams by comparison were but mediocrities. It is true that one of their original demands was that the greater part of the old Northwest should become an Indian state under British protection, and, further, that there should be a revision of the international boundary westward from Lake Superior. But these demands were promptly rejected by the American commissioners who even threatened to break off negotiations and sail for home. The bluff, for bluff it was, proved effective, and the British government, worried by affairs in Europe more than by the situation in America, abandoned its position. The Northwest and all other territory was to remain in the exact status which had existed before the war came.

News of the abandonment of all claims to the western territory was received by the merchants with surprise and consternation. All the hopes built up by the capture and retention of Mackinac, the prompt recapture of Prairie du Chien after it had fallen into American hands, the seizure of the *Tigress* and *Scorpion,* enterprises in which fur-company men, ships and employees had participated to the full—these had all gone for nought. The fact that scarcely any Canadian territory was in American hands at the close of the war, while the Atlantic coast was under blockade by the

British fleet—these circumstances, too, apparently had had no influence upon the final settlement. Ruin of the trade centering around Mackinac was almost complete. In April 1816 Congress ruled that only American citizens might receive licenses to carry on their business within the territorial limits of the republic. "The retreat of the fur trade to the northwest, which had begun as far back as the American Revolution, had become a rout and had ended in complete withdrawal."[10]

It was more than thirty years since a group of aggressive young Scots, centering on Montreal, had pooled their brains and their resources in the formation of the North West Company. North America has had few business groups more shrewd and daring. In three decades they achieved remarkable results, their organization extending practically from ocean to ocean. But there had always been competition from the Hudson's Bay Company and now that competition was to be keener than ever. The Canadian West was changing, beaver was becoming scarcer and it was not easy to reduce the expenses of such a widespread concern. It is probably true that the North West Company was saved from bankruptcy by its union with the Hudson's Bay Company in 1821, just six years after the war had been brought to a close.

The British regime in the Northwest, as an eminent historian has suggested, was but an interlude in the Americanization of a French settlement. "The British traders came and went, took their toll of . . . furs and enriched themselves at the Indians' expense. They built numbers of trading posts on the lakes and rivers but these were transitory. They developed no institutions, assumed no governmental functions, built up no new settlements. The British régime was a wilderness régime, perpetuated solely in the interests of the fur trade."[11]

The War of 1812 had been "the final episode in the long struggle between settlement and the fur trade in the region of the Great Lakes."[12]

---

[10] D. C. Creighton, *The Commercial Empire of the St. Lawrence 1760-1850* (New Haven, 1937), 183.

[11] Louise Phelps Kellogg, *Op. cit.*, 329.

[12] D. C. Creighton, *Op. cit.*, 175.

Part II

ISLANDS, SHORES AND RIVERS

Chapter 6

Along the Michigan Strand

Majestic woods of ev'ry vigorous green,
Stage above stage, high waving o'er the hills,
Or to the far horizon wide diffused,
A boundless deep immensity of shade.
                                        —THOMSON
In a moment the ashes are made, but a forest
is a long time growing.
                                        —SENECA

THE Michigan coast line of Lake Huron extends two hundred miles northward from the St. Clair River to the region of Mackinac and the Detour passage. One-third of the distance northward, Saginaw Bay breaks in as a long arm to the west and, seen from the deck of a vessel crossing its mouth, the coast line becomes indistinct or may for a time entirely disappear. When it reappears it is as part of a great irregular arc that stretches northward from Au Sable Point to Thunder Bay Island and then northwesterly from Presque Isle to Cheboygan and Bois Blanc Island. Four rivers cut through to the lake—the Saginaw, Au Sable, Thunder Bay and Cheboygan—rivers that once brought the logs down from the great inland forests but today are pleasant streams having little commercial importance for the areas they traverse.

Upbound shipping, seeking the shortest course to the Straits of Mackinac or to Detour, passes within a few miles of large portions of this coast, leaving trails of black smoke always in view during the months of navigation. Farther out in the lake and less distinctly seen are the downbound boats following their designated lane of traffic toward the St. Clair River. By night the vessel lights gleam out over the waters. In the pilothouses men watch for the flashes from the lights along the shore and check their course thereby. Many a ship has come to grief on this coast, and even today there is need of constant watchfulness despite all the aids that have been provided.

In earlier days old Fort Gratiot at present-day Port Huron was the first sight to greet the mariner coming off Lake Huron. Samuel A. Storrow, of Massachusetts, who was Judge Advocate in the army during the War of 1812, visited the place in 1817. He wondered that no effort had been made during the recent war to insure command of the entrance to the St. Clair River until the struggle was nearly over. Situated on a slight eminence within a few hundred yards of Lake Huron, the guns of a well-constructed work would have commanded both the narrow entrance and the Canadian bank opposite which was but a few feet above the water.

"Within the range of the guns of the fort," said his report, "there is a fishery, which for years, perhaps ages, has given sustenance to the tribes inhabiting the lower parts of Lake Huron. From this and other causes they have ascribed to it a moral value even beyond its due, and rarely pass without making it, as much from superstition as convenience, a resting place on their way below."[1]

Old Fort Gratiot, from which during its entire life of sixty-five years not a hostile shot was ever fired, was named after its builder, Captain Charles Gratiot. He was with General Harrison in the spring of 1813 when it was decided that an effort should be made to recapture Detroit surrendered the year before by Hull. Perry's victory over Captain Barclay on Lake Erie solved this problem but still left the St. Clair River frontier unguarded and open to a flank attack from Upper Canada. To this was added a hostile attitude on the part of the Indians in Eastern Michigan. These considerations led to the building of a stockaded embankment at a site about 1,000 feet below the lake and on ground that was twenty feet above the river. Quarters were provided for a small garrison. The place was occupied until 1821, then abandoned and was soon

---

[1] "The North-West in 1817: a Contemporary Letter," *Wisconsin Historical Collections*, VI (1872), 156.

in bad repair. A few years later, at a time of unrest among the western Indians, some new log buildings were erected and subsequently covered with boards. Final abandonment of the post came in 1879.

Despite its rather prosaic history, as far as military activities are concerned, Fort Gratiot did have an occasional place in larger events. It must have been an exciting day around the fort when on July 12, 1814, Colonel Croghan's force arrived from Detroit on its way to attempt the recapture of Fort Mackinac. Captain Gratiot accompanied the expedition when it headed up Lake Huron and took part in the attack upon the island stronghold. Later he was with the detachment which raided the Nottawasaga River and destroyed the schooner *Nancy*. His name has been perpetuated in Michigan by Gratiot County, by two townships, by avenues in Detroit and Port Huron and by the Gratiot Turnpike.

There were exciting and tragic days, too, when the troopships bearing men westward to the Black Hawk War became pestilence-ridden with cholera. Then the fort was turned into a hospital. But since that time little has happened to break the dull monotony of the place. Major John Richardson, a Canadian officer, wrote rather cynically in 1848 that he found Fort Gratiot "looking as unmilitary as most American forts do in its daubing of white paint." On the other hand he thought that the village on the American side had better-looking houses than were to be found at Sarnia.

Captain Daniel Lysons (afterward Sir Daniel Lysons) of the First Royal Regiment, then in garrison at London, Upper Canada, had occasion to visit Fort Gratiot in 1842 in connection with an investigation which he was making into the political sentiments of the American population along the border. Upper Canada had not yet quite recovered from the effects of its rebellion five years before, and there had been some extremely unpleasant border incidents after 1837. Captain Lysons carried letters of introduction to officers of the United States Army along the international boundary and found them most ready to co-operate in heading off any unfriendly moves against Canada. But his experiences at Fort Gratiot village were not of the most pleasant, as he recorded them many years after in his reminiscenses:

"According to my instructions," he wrote, "I went to Detroit, and then on to Fort Graciot at the foot of Lake Huron. At the latter place I put up at 'The Hotel', a dirty pot-house full of wild-looking roughs. After I had gone to bed an old Irishman, who had waited on me and given me a good deal of information, came up to my room and told me that I had better 'clear out sharp.' I had obtained all the information I required so I made my escape in a waggon which my friend procured for me. I heard afterwards that I had got into a regular hornet's nest of sympathizers."[2]

Though Port Huron's history goes back to 1686 when old Fort St. Joseph was built, it was not until after the War of 1812 that a community grew up. Originally there were several little hamlets on the St. Clair and the Black River flowing into it, the best known being Desmond. These were united in the later thirties to form the village of Port Huron. Like many other Michigan ports it had its lumbering era, which reached its peak in the 1870's and then gradually declined. With lumber abundant, shipbuilding naturally developed and elsewhere in this volume will be found some account of this particular activity. Today, where there was but a village a century ago, is a city which stretches for miles along the river and even along the shore of Lake Huron, where pleasant homes are set in the shade of the old forest bordering the sandy beaches. Just above the entrance to the St. Clair River is Fort Gratiot light, one of the oldest on the lakes, erected in 1829, always a welcome beacon to ships descending Lake Huron.

Thomas Alva Edison spent his boyhood and early manhood in Port Huron. The Edison family had been forced to leave the neighboring province of Upper Canada at the time of the uprising of 1837 and had settled in Milan, Ohio, where the future scientist and inventor was born. The removal to Port Huron came in 1854 when he was seven years old. Edison wrote in afteryears of the place as he first knew it: "The town in its pristine youth was a

---

[2] *Sir* Daniel Lysons, *Early Reminiscences* (London, 1896), 156-157.

great lumber center and hummed to the industry of numerous saw-mills. An incredible amount of lumber was made there yearly until the forests near-by vanished and industry with them."[3]

The Edison home in Port Huron was a spacious colonial dwell-ing set amid pines in the old military reservation on the bank of the river. The house had originally been built by Chancellor Wal-worth of New York State for his daughter, whose husband was the purveyor of Fort Gratiot. Young Thomas Edison had his first laboratory in the basement of this house. Arranged on shelves were scores of bottles containing various chemicals, all of which were labeled "Poison" so that no one would disturb them. When he became interested in telegraphy the basement laboratory be-came a network of wires. An interesting story is told of his in-genuity in this latter field. One day in the sixties an ice jam in the St. Clair broke the cable connecting Port Huron and Sarnia and communication was cut off. Edison, who was at the time employed on one of the railroads, boarded a locomotive and by whistle blasts corresponding to the Morse code began to call the town across the river.

"Hello, Sarnia, do you get me?" was sounded shrilly over the water.

At first there was no response, but after four or five attempts an operator in the Canadian town recognized the message and soon there were answering toots.[4]

From the beach at the Fort Gratiot light, a marine prospect, always interesting, opens up. To the east the wide beaches of the Canadian shore fade into the distance, the greenery of the forest fringing the blue of the waters. The whole expanse of Lake Huron lies to the north and northeast. A few miles up the lake the Huron lightship rocks ceaselessly at its anchor, a guide for the vessels entering or leaving the St. Clair River. Far to the north on the horizon is the smoke of up-and-down-bound boats, and nearer are the boats themselves. At times there are a dozen or more in view,

[3] *Michigan History Magazine* (Lansing, 1920), IV, 177.
[4] *Ibid.*, 189.

swinging around the lightship as they near it, and then, with increasing speed as they are urged on by the swift current, passing
under the International Bridge. More than 20,000 vessels go beneath this steel arch each year.

The spirit of this pleasant little Michigan city, so beautifully situated on river and on lake, is rich with memories of its long past.
Memories of Frenchmen—explorers, soldiers, priests, traders and
voyageurs who passed this way when the fleur-de-lis was the symbol
of empire in the interior of the continent. Memories of the Indians,
and of the canoes bearing cargoes of furs to Detroit. Memories of
bugle notes sounding from old Fort Gratiot and the voices of
officers on its parade ground. Memories of the schooners and the
old lumber hookers coming from Saginaw Bay and the grinding,
crunching noise of rafts of logs being guided through the rapids.
Each of these marked an era in the city's past. Nor, save for the
fact that it is so familiar to us, is the present less rich in romance.

Michigan in its early days was one great forest. The southern
area was a part of the hardwoods region of the Ohio Valley, having
little or no pine or spruce and varying in species according to the
nature of the soil and the amount of drainage. Northward from
the latitude of Saginaw Bay to the Straits of Mackinac and beyond
was the home of the evergreens but there were also northern hardwoods, largely maple and beech. The pine was Michigan's greatest tree and from it chiefly was drawn the wealth of the lumbering
era. On the sandy lands where pine predominated there were older
stands so clear from undergrowth or brush that a team of horses
might easily be driven for miles where no road existed.

These northern forests, abounding in game, formed the haunts
of the Chippewa. The streams running through them teemed with
fish, and waterfowl of many kinds were abundant during a considerable part of the year. Passenger pigeons came in such flocks
that they darkened the sky, and wild turkeys were numerous and
easily caught. Here and there on the jack-pine lands were tracts
which the Indians kept clear by fires, providing summer camping

Michigan Department of Conservation Photo

LOADING LIMESTONE AT ALPENA

The limestone trade has grown to large proportions in connection with the iron industry and also for chemical and construction purposes. The vessel shown above is the *Charles C. West,* operated by the Rockport Steamship Company.

Photo by James McCannell

ONE OF THE SELF-UNLOADERS

The steamer *Dow Chemical* was built in 1912. These vessels are used particularly in the limestone-coal trade. More than thirty of them are now in service on the Great Lakes.

AN OLD-TIME LUMBER HOOKER

Scores of wooden vessels similar to the *I. Watson Stephenson* were employed in the lumber trade out of Saginaw Bay and other ports in the eighties. This old vessel ended her days in 1935.

THE "UNITED EMPIRE"

Built at Sarnia in 1883, this wooden passenger boat was in service until 1915. The photo was taken as she left for Lake Superior on the first trip in 1901. Strengthening arches were still a feature when she was built. The *United Empire* was familiarly known as "Old Betsy."

grounds free from mosquitoes and producing an ample supply of huckleberries.

Bela Hubbard, who accompanied Dr. Douglas Houghton on the first expedition sent out by the newly constituted State Geological Survey, gives an account of the Saginaw country as he saw it in 1837. As yet the lumberman's ax had not been applied to the great northern primeval forest. Going overland from Detroit to the Shiawassee River, the party descended by this stream to the Saginaw River, passing through extensive Chippewa reservations where native clearings sometimes extended for miles along the riverbank, many acres being covered with crops of corn, the chief food. But the Indians were still nomadic and the so-called villages were only resorted to at such times as cultivation and harvesting of their food supply required. Their chief occupation was trapping and hunting, and the presence of trading houses met with here and there in the wilderness gave evidence of the barter that was carried on.

The Saginaw River marked the last of the occasional clearings that had been encountered on the journey from Detroit. The forests through which the party had been passing were of mingled growth: "Oaks not gnarled and spreading as in more open lands, but at once massive and tall, and centuries old; the elm, that most graceful and majestic of trees of any land; the tulip or whitewood, magnificent in size and height above even the Titans of the forest; the broad and green-leaved linden; the clean-bodied beech; the saccharine maples, so superb in their autumnal dresses; the giant sycamore, ghost-like, with its white naked limbs; these with other kinds, each possessing its own peculiar grace, and a use and a beauty almost unknown in other lands."[5]

Saginaw at the time of Bela Hubbard's visit comprised about fifty frame houses with several stores, warehouses and a church. There were two small sawmills in operation and a large frame hotel was under construction. The fur trade of the Saginaw coun-

---

[5] Bela Hubbard, *Memorials of a Half-Century in Michigan and the Lake Region* (New York, 1888), 73.

try had been exploited at least from the time of the Revolution onward. One of the earliest traders to enter the region was James V. Riley who came to Detroit (apparently from Albany or vicinity) in 1781 and went to Saginaw Bay a year later. On a visit to Mackinac he made the acquaintance of one George Shead who had a squaw wife at Au Sable River and a child, Nancy, born in 1783. About this time Shead was drowned, and Riley was sent by his Detroit employers to winter at the Au Sable, where he took over Shead's squaw, whose name appears in the Saginaw Treaty of 1819 as Menaweumegoqua. This treaty, negotiated with the Chippewa, brought to the government all of eastern Michigan north of the Hull cession of 1807 and as far north as Alpena.[6]

A fort was constructed on the west side of the Saginaw River in 1822 to serve as a safeguard upon the Chippewa, who were troublesome and anti-American. An epidemic of fever prostrated almost the entire garrison in 1823, and as a consequence the place was abandoned. A few settlers came into the region but were not welcomed by the fur-trading interests, who industriously spread reports of the unfriendly attitude of the Indians.

The lumbering industry in the Saginaw region was in its infancy when Hubbard visited the district. The two little sawmills which he found in operation increased in number during the next two decades, so that in the later fifties there were more than a dozen operating on the Saginaw River and its tributaries. Prospectors, or timber "lookers" as they were termed, ranged through the forests selecting tracts that promised high returns and purchasing these for about $1.50 an acre. The thirty years after 1850 were a period of wasteful exploitation scarcely rivaled in American history. The pine forests were cut to the last acre but over many areas only

---

[6] The upper boundary of the cession of 1819 ran from about present-day Kalamazoo northeasterly to the source of Thunder Bay River, thence down it to the lake at Alpena. Nearly all the country remaining north of this line was ceded by the Treaty of 1836. In these and other treaties pieces of land were reserved for the Indian tribes and some grants also made to individuals of Indian descent. But as settlement pressed in, these reservations were in turn ceded, and the tribal Indians were removed to western reservations about 1840. See George N. Fuller, *Economic and Social Beginnings of Michigan* (Lansing, 1916), 58-59.

the best timber was taken. Fires which raged in the wake of the lumberman's operations left the country a burned-over wasteland, and much of it continues to be so to this day.

Saginaw River and Bay was the chief outlet for Michigan lumbering operations during the 1850's but the demand was so great that soon other areas were being exploited in similar fashion. It was estimated in 1872 that the sawed pine lumber of the state had amounted to two and a half billion feet. Seven years later Governor Jerome in his inaugural message placed a value of sixty million dollars upon the output of that year. In 1883 the cut was estimated by lumber journals at four billion feet and it was computed that the production from Michigan up to that time had had a value of more than one billion dollars.

"The great period of Michigan's lumbering days," wrote W. L. Clements later, "may have been from 1862 to 1880. During these years was begun and carried to consummation, without regard to conservation or the rights of future generations, the destruction of Michigan's white pine forests. Saginaw Valley was the focal center of Eastern Michigan in this destruction; Saginaw River the confluent stream through which logs passed to the mills. Along the river mills were then in course of erection, commerce and population were increasing, which a little later were to make Saginaw and Bay City the busiest communities in the state, and to put an accelerated activity into twenty years which with today's advanced ideas of conservation should have been spread over a century."[7]

Before the 1880's were more than half advanced, it was seen that production in the Saginaw Valley and even elsewhere was beginning to fall off. Originally the rivers and streams had carried the logs to their outlets where the mills were situated. Then it had become necessary to haul the logs longer and longer distances to the carrying streams and eventually railroads were built to bring them out. This was the last stage. As the supplies dwindled, the mills closed down and the machinery was taken elsewhere. Gaunt skeletons of these old mills may still be seen in areas where the cut-

[7] *Michigan History Magazine*, I (Lansing, 1917), 8-9.

over cleaned off all commercially valuable timber, and enormous piles of sawdust indicate sites where not even the skeleton of a mill remains.

Saginaw led the way in the marketing of the timber, but the business gradually moved up the whole Lake Huron shore wherever there was a stream that could float logs and a shelter sufficient to receive a schooner. Tawas, Alpena, Cheboygan all had their day. At Cheboygan one may still see a veritable mountain of sawdust, a thousand feet long, which marks the place where saws hummed for more than half a century. Those were gay, gaudy days for the towns which shared in the industry. The pictures which have come down to us of Mackinac in the spring season when the *voyageurs* were there had its parallel in the throngs of lumberjacks, many of them French-Canadians, who came out of the woods in April as if released from prison and proceeded forthwith to celebrate. Every saloon in town did a roaring business, and gambling joints and resorts of all kinds took away no small part of the winter's earnings in an incredibly short time.

The sawed lumber began to move out from the river ports in the spring as soon as navigation opened. Scores of schooners were engaged in the business and later dozens of steam vessels, each of which could hook on from three to five of these sailing ships and tow them to Detroit or the Lake Erie ports. At times great rafts of uncut logs were taken to Detroit or to Buffalo. The largest recorded was that which passed through lower Lake Huron and the St. Clair River in 1875, towed by two tugs, the *John Owen* and the *Merrick*. This raft, made up of two million feet of oak and a million feet of cork pine to support it, was one thousand feet long. It took eighteen hours to get it through the St. Clair River and sixteen days to move it from Bay City to Buffalo. In a late stage of the business, rafts of logs were assembled at ports on Georgian Bay and brought to the mills on Lake Huron in order to keep them going. Rafts towed on the open lake were a serious menace to vessels, and as late as 1897 the steamer *Cambria,* a passenger boat, was wrecked on Lake Huron when she plowed into a raft of telephone poles.

In loading the barges and lumber schooners a particular technique was required. The lumber was piled in the hold until it was as close to the deck beams as possible, wedges being then driven in to support the deckload, which might be another twelve feet high. The sail had a "lumber reef" taken in it, the boom jaws being shifted up the mast. Thus the vessel was reefed up instead of down as would have been the case were there no deckload carried. Square timber in long lengths required special provision. Some schooners had timber ports built in the transom. These were opened and the end of a big timber inserted. To it was attached a cable drawn by a horse, forward on the ship. When a number of these big timbers had been drawn into the hold in this way, placed on top of ordinary lumber, the usual process of wedging was carried out. If the timbers were not too long they were carried on deck.

One of the tragic aspects of Michigan's lumbering era was the waste caused by forest fires. Hundreds of thousands of acres which once supported heavy stands of timber and gave protection to wild life were thereby made nonproductive. The rush to grasp the wealth of the forests and the carelessness in taking off the growth ruined not only the forests themselves but even the soil cover by which new growth might have come.

Everyone has heard of the great Chicago fire which broke out on the night of October 8, 1871, and during the two following days and nights destroyed large sections of that city. But perhaps few know that on the same night and on the following day and night a fire swept across the state of Michigan, wiping out one small city, almost wiping out another and cutting a swath east from Lake Michigan that was not halted until it came to the shores of Lake Huron. Holland and Manistee, the two places hardest hit, were lumber towns, the buildings all of wood, with the product of their sawmills in great piles to add to the conflagration. The estimated loss in this fire was more than one million dollars of which a considerable proportion was mill properties and manufactured lumber.

Huron and Sanilac Counties on Lake Huron had not passed out of the lumbering stage at the time of this fire, but there were many well-cultivated farms. Over an area forty miles square in these counties, few buildings were left after the flames had died out. Along the lake shore a succession of villages was destroyed, the people who had lived in them being left utterly destitute. Thousands of people were rendered temporarily homeless by this fire.

One incident may be related. William Mann, residing near Sand Beach, was called out of bed by a neighbor in the early hours of October 9. Fire was approaching the place and men were engaged in burying some of their few possessions in the hope of saving them. The Mann farm extended down to the lake and the four children were told to go to the shore and remain there. If the flames threatened them, the eldest, Rachel, a girl of seven, was to take the baby and the others and wade into the water.

There were others on the beach when the children came there. A neighbor, Jim Huxtable, who had a large open boat, took the Mann children aboard with his own family and pushed out a little into the lake where it was easier to breathe. Though he was only a short distance away, the shore was soon lost to sight. During the night the wind increased and he decided to pull in closer but found to his dismay that he was lost. He shouted for help but none came and when daylight broke the boat was far out on the lake, out of sight of land and heavily burdened with four adults and nine children. There was no food and all aboard were drenched with the waves which broke over the sides.

For nearly three days and nights the party was on the open lake. Then, early on the morning of October 12, they saw a hazy gray line in the distance which proved to be the Canadian shore. The boat and its occupants had drifted completely across Lake Huron. One of the children had died during the last night of the journey. These refugees from the Michigan fire were given every care by the Canadian folk and efforts were at once made to communicate with the parents of the Mann children. But telegraph lines were all down in the stricken area and no contact could be made. It was even thought that the parents might have perished. After three weeks, however, William Mann and his wife were found and the children were taken to Port Huron where they remained till the mother arrived. The little child who had died in the boat was buried at Goderich.[8]

Similar but even greater tragedy struck again ten years later. It had been a hot summer and as August of 1881 neared its close, streams and swamps were dried up and vegetation was so parched that it was like tinder. Some small forest fires were already going when on September 5 a southwest gale fanned many little fires until they became merged in one great flame. For three days the conflagration raged with a violence unparalleled in the history of the state. One hundred and twenty-five lives were lost, more than 3,400 buildings destroyed and the property loss was estimated to exceed two millions. Huron and Sanilac Counties were the chief sufferers. Some villages were wiped out; others so badly damaged that there were not sufficient houses left to provide shelter for the homeless.

Eyewitnesses told of great sheets of flame jumping through the air from forest to forest, sometimes skipping completely over a dwelling or a barn. Elsewhere over hundreds of acres only the blackened roots and fallen trunks remained when the flames had passed. The smoke was so dense that the darkness of night seemed to have come down, and out on the lake, vessels were held up by the almost impenetrable black fog. The southwest gale carried the smoke even beyond the lake, and at Collingwood, at the foot of Georgian Bay, the pall of smoke was so heavy that it is still remembered by older people in that district as the dark day of 1881.

Nearly eighteen hundred square miles of the two Michigan counties referred to was burned over, amounting to a million acres. Forty-eight townships in all were affected. Fires also raged in the adjoining counties of St. Clair, Lapeer and Tuscola, but in these there was no loss of life and a limited loss of property. Relief

[8] Information supplied by Mrs. Rachel Mann Stewart to Mr. Victor Lauriston. See London (Ontario) *Free Press.* June 27, 1942.

measures were promptly set on foot for the thousands of homeless people who were found living in every form of improvised shelter, even in dugouts. Some of the dead had remained unburied, and many of the living were suffering from serious burns when help came. Citizens of other states vied in providing help. Money, food, clothing and medical supplies poured in from every side.

The origin of the fire has been attributed, and no doubt correctly, to the practice of burning the brush and log heaps in the process of clearing land. Scores of such fires were alight when the gale came up which carried sparks to adjoining forests where the dry summer weather had prepared the way for disaster.

Little was known of the Michigan peninsula above Thunder Bay River before 1836, when most of the area was ceded by the Indians. Henry R. Schoolcraft has written an account of the negotiations which he conducted with representatives of the tribes at Washington in March of that year. For Michigan it was one of the most important treaties ever made with the red men. On his arrival at Washington, Schoolcraft found a self-constituted delegation of Ottawa chiefs awaiting him, but he found other important Indian interests quite unrepresented and it was necessary to send for them. The cession was made on the general principle of providing limited reservations for the chief villages but allowing the mass of the Indian population to occupy any portion of the ceded lands until they were actually required for settlement. The compensation amounted to about two million dollars or about twelve and a half cents an acre.

Thomas Nye, who went to Mackinac in the following year, mentions only one place on the long coast line above Saginaw Bay. Like many another traveler on Lake Huron, he found the crossing of the bay unpleasant. "A very strong sea and head wind," he wrote in his diary, "boat tossed very much all night." Saginaw Bay probably merited in his opinion the description which the poet Byron gave to a stormy water in another part of the world:

"There's not a sea the passenger e'er pukes in,
Turns up more dangerous breakers than the Euxine."

At Presque Isle, where no landing was possible, the steamboat
on which he traveled, the *Constellation,* was halted for seven hours
while wood scows brought out a supply of fuel. For this, three dollars a cord was paid. Nye says that at this place there were but four
residents, the wood cutters. At Mackinac he was struck by the
transparent water. Crew and passengers bought fine trout of
twenty-five to thirty pounds' weight for fifty cents and whitefish
for a dollar a dozen. But at Mackinac there was no wood to be
had for the steamboat and they had to go on to the Manitou Islands
for a supply.[9]

We have another picture of the Upper Michigan shore in the
narrative of Frederick J. Starin, a native of Montgomery County,
New York, who went to Wisconsin in the spring of 1840. He also
traveled on the *Constellation.* He was on Lake Huron on May 16
and wrote: "On the east the water bounds the horizon, and the
dense forests and habitless beach of Michigan with here and there
a whitened rock to catch the traveller's eye is all that is seen west-
wardly. We passed White Rock which consists of a sawmill and a
log cabin. About one and a half miles above are two or three small
cabins. White Rock itself is under water.... We were soon at the
entrance to Saginaw Bay and from 1 to 3 o'clock P.M. no land
could be seen. About 7 o'clock the boat stopped off Thunder Bay
Island, but no signal being discovered on shore she again proceeded on her journey. There is a lighthouse and comfortable
dwelling on the southern extremity of this island where there are
a few acres cleared. The rest of it is one dense forest, and really a
bleak, lonely, desolate place. About in the middle I discovered a
few miserable huts, probably the abodes of fishermen, saw several
other small islands between it and the main land, all thickly
wooded."[10]

---

[9] *Journal of Thomas Nye Written During a Journey Between Montreal and Chicago in 1837* (Champlain, 1932). Entries of November 12, 13, 14.
[10] *Wisconsin Magazine of History,* VI (Madison, 1922-1923), 79.

White Rock, to which Starin makes reference, was on the Lake Huron shore fifty miles above Port Huron. It was one of the "cities to be" which promoters sold off in town lots in the boom times before the financial panic of 1837. In Detroit's hotel barrooms and in any other place where they might attract attention were to be seen maps and pictures of this place, depicting a magnificent harbor into which steamboats were entering, sawmills busily handling the forest products and a public square about which were grouped a courthouse, churches, schools and, of course, a substantial-looking bank. White Rock was a coming metropolis if one were to believe the statements and the advertising of its promoters, and lots were sold widely and at extravagant prices.

Bela Hubbard had a look at White Rock when he and the exploring party of which he was a member were returning in the fall of 1837 from Saginaw Bay. A large white boulder marked the entrance from the lake but the little river was so shallow that even a canoe could scarcely make its way. "Churches, houses, mills, people—all were a myth. A thick wilderness covered the whole site."

There was but one settler at the place, a Mr. Allen who had come three months before and was then erecting a little sawmill on the stream which gay lithographs pictured as a harbor. Allen and his wife had been waiting all summer for the arrival of the hundreds of families who, it had been announced, were to be the first citizens of White Rock, but none had come. Except for the Allens and their helpers there was not another inhabitant within thirty or forty miles.

"Where the Public Square had been depicted," said Hubbard, "stood several large beech trees. On one of these we carved the names of our party, who were thus registered, for the benefit of future visitors, as the first guests of the 'White Rock Hotel.'"

Before the lumbermen came to strip the forests along these more northerly shores, fishermen had discovered the wealth which was to be had from the waters of Lake Huron. The first steamer to enter Thunder Bay River (in 1852) was the *Julius D. Morton* carrying supplies from Detroit. These were for fisheries which had been established at that point by Captain Harvey Harwood and Captain Walter Scott, who themselves piloted the steamer over the bar. But fishing had been going on in these waters at least since 1835. Gill nets were used in the lake fisheries from an early date. These nets, made by hand, were set on the bottom where they stood upright like a tennis net, the principle being that the fish would not see them and would run headlong into the meshes and be caught behind the head or gill covers.

Pound nets, which instead of meshing the fish led them through a passage or tunnel into a "pot," were introduced on Lake Huron in 1854 in the waters off Alcona County, south of Thunder Bay, and within a few years were found in all the fishing stations as far north as the Straits of Mackinac. Trap nets, a modification of the pound net, first came to this lake around the turn of the century, in Saginaw Bay and off Alpena and Iosco Counties.

As early as 1883 it was claimed for Michigan that it stood first among the states of the Union in the value of its fresh-water fisheries. This position it still holds. No other state has a similar advantageous position for the business. Four of the five Great Lakes touch its borders and with its shore line of 3,121 miles it has jurisdiction over an estimated water surface area of almost 40,000 square miles. Yet, with all the improvements that have been made in boats, nets and other appliances, the total catch is no larger today than it was fifty or more years ago. Like the forests of Michigan, which too were thought to be inexhaustible, the fisheries have been much depleted and in some localities almost exterminated.[11]

Michigan's forests have largely vanished, leaving a sad legacy of nonproductive land. Its fisheries have suffered from exploitation. But in recent years a new resource has come to the front in its limestone, of which abundant supplies exist and which can be easily

---

[11] See John Van Osten, "Michigan's Commercial Fisheries on the Great Lakes," *Michigan History Magazine*, XXII (Lansing, 1938), 107-145.

marketed. Today more than thirty freighters are occupied in bringing down this commodity.

The limestone trade first began to reach noticeable figures during the last two years of the First World War when it was used as a fluxing material in the manufacture of iron. Within a decade the demand for limestone in construction and chemical industries greatly increased, and has gone on increasing, so that today it stands third among the bulk commodities carried by the Great Lakes freighters. The three and a half million tons loaded in 1915 increased to more than seventeen and a half million tons in 1941. The chief loading points are Calcite and Alpena on Lake Huron. At these places special facilities are provided for rapid handling, and as the distance from these points to the Detroit River and Lake Erie ports is much less than from Lake Superior, more trips can be made in a season. Originally, when the limestone was chiefly used in ironmaking, the demand expanded or shrank in relation to the shipments of ore. But now, with other uses added, it is a trade that stands on its own feet.

Chapter 7

Up the Canadian Shore

Miles and miles of lake and forest,
Miles and miles of sky and mist.
　　　—WILFRED CAMPBELL

APTAIN GOTHER MANN's description of the Canadian shore of
Lake Huron as "a great solitude" was true for almost half a
century after he passed along its borders in 1788, sent by
Lord Dorchester, Governor General of Canada, to search out harbors and places capable of defense. Not until the thirties were there
even small settlements at the mouths of the little rivers emptying
into Lake Huron, and it was two decades later before there was any
extensive movement of people into the more northerly part of the
region.

Fathers Brébeuf and Chaumonot may have seen something of
the eastern shore of Lake Huron or of the territory adjacent to it
when they journeyed in the fall of 1640 to the country of the Neutral Indians along the north shore of Lake Erie. But they were too
intent on reaching their goal and fulfilling their missionary purpose
to be much concerned with the wilderness through which they
laboriously made their way, and no precise statement as to the
route which they followed is possible. Tradition of certain Indian
villages which they may have visited, the locations of which have
been confirmed by the excavations of archaeologists, gives us only
faint clues to the way by which the priests reached their destination.
Old stone ruins, found in a few places, have been ascribed to Jesuit
activities but are more likely the remains of some fur trader's or
fisherman's post, the abundance of stone making it a simple matter
to strengthen or even fortify a log dwelling.

The more northerly section of the Canadian shore and the country behind it were within the range of the Mackinac fur traders until the decline of the enterprises centered on that island. Pierre Piché, a French-Canadian, came to the Saugeen River district before 1820 and established a trading post. He was really acting for Dr. David Mitchell, a former army surgeon with the British garrison at Mackinac. Dr. Mitchell supplied him with goods, and Piché managed to obtain and keep control of the best part of the trade in his territory. To obtain the furs it was necessary to travel widely through what was at that time a wild and inhospitable region. In addition to the furs, quantities of maple sugar were also secured from the Indians, and much of this eventually found its way to Detroit.

While many other portions of the present province of Ontario were well settled and advanced, this northern area was scarcely explored before 1845, and it was not until 1848 that a geological examination was made of the lake shore. Fifteen years later a more careful geological survey was carried out which revealed a structure important in relation to the occurrence of petroleum in southwestern Ontario. Vast deposits of salt were also discovered later.

The fur-trading economy of the northern area was short-lived and gave way to lumbering and agriculture. The numerous streams emptying into the lake facilitated lumbering operations and produced also for a time some shipbuilding. But these fell away in the latter part of the century. Today the area from the St. Clair River to the base of the Saugeen Peninsula is all settled farm land, while the lake shore for a hundred and fifty miles is a succession of summer resorts. One reason for its popularity lies in the gorgeous sunsets to be seen over the lake waters. Doubtless the sunrises viewed from the Michigan shore are equally fine, but holidaying folk are more likely to be interested in sunsets than in sunrises.

Sarnia may be regarded as the southern boundary of the Canadian shore of Lake Huron, for even though the city lies for the most part on the St. Clair River, its residential section already touches the lake and moves steadily in that direction. There was early controversy over a name for the little settlement near the outlet of Lake Huron often referred to as The Rapids, some of its Scottish inhabitants desiring it to be known as New Glasgow. The name Sarnia was adopted in January 1836, probably at the suggestion of Sir John Colborne, Lieutenant Governor of Upper Canada, who thereby perpetuated the old Roman name for the island of Guernsey, of which he had formerly been governor.

At that time there was a considerable population of Ojibwa Indians in the neighborhood of the settlement, to whom in 1834 there came as missionary a young Englishman, James Evans by name. A great boulder bearing a tablet has been placed to mark the site of his old mission house. This man, a keen student of Indian languages, later became superintendent of Methodist Indian missions in the Canadian West and, what is of even greater interest, was the inventor of the syllabic characters, a sort of shorthand, by which the Cree Indians were first provided with a form of writing. Today all government proclamations and other notices to the Indians in the West are printed in the syllabics which Evans devised. At Norway House on the far north shore of Lake Winnipeg, where for some years Evans made his headquarters, he printed hymn books, catechisms and portions of the Bible for his Indian charges, making his type from the lead lining of tea chests, his ink from lampblack and oil, and using an old fur press for the actual printing. Through the early 1840's he traveled far and wide in the great Northland, and his diaries and letters form a part of the chronicle of western exploration. At the site of his mission station on Lake Winnipeg the government of Canada has erected a cairn and a bronze tablet commemorating his contribution to the life of its Indian charges.

Sarnia is probably not much interested in Evans today. It is vastly more interested, and quite naturally so, in its great oil refineries, the most extensive in Canada, and in the equally extensive plants established under war conditions for the manufacture of the chemical products used in the making of synthetic rubber.

Twelve miles from Sarnia, near the shores of Lake Huron, is the scene of one of the few communistic experiments which Canada has ever known. Henry Jones, of Exeter, England, a retired purser of the British navy, came under the influence of Robert Owen when the latter was touring England and setting forth his social theories. Jones determined to found a settlement along the lines of Owen's teaching and to this end came to Canada about 1826. His choice of a location fell upon an area at the mouth of a stream known as River aux Perches, the outlet of a shallow lake covering about three thousand acres. Family influence stood him in good stead, for his brother was married to a sister-in-law of Sir John Colborne, later Lieutenant Governor of the province, and he was able to secure a grant of 10,000 acres.

In 1828 Jones brought his followers, chiefly Scottish people of small means, to America, and in due time they arrived at the site on Lake Huron. A large community house, one story high and of logs, was erected. Within this each family had its own apartment, but there was a common kitchen and common dining room. The women attended to the household duties and the care of the children while the men worked in company at clearing the land. Military equipment discarded after the Napoleonic Wars had been brought along, and thin Indian ponies, weighed down by heavy artillery harness, tugged at chains attached to huge clumsy carts which had also come out from England. Never having seen a rail fence, the settlers proceeded to erect such a fence as might have surrounded a field on a long cultivated English farm. They hewed out posts and with auger and chisel made neat holes into which were fitted bars cut with equal precision. At the rate at which they proceeded the big farm would scarcely have been fenced in years. There is a reference in the diary of the Reverend Peter Jones, an Indian Methodist missionary, which indicates that as early as 1829, less than two years after its founding, the settlement was proving a failure. Under date of August 1, Jones wrote:

"In the afternoon we passed a new settlement of white people east of the mouth of the lake. This settlement was formed by a Mr.

Jones, who tried to carry out what is called the Owen system of having all things in common; but I was informed the thing did not work well here, as the colonists one after another left their leader."

The community house soon burned to the ground, and before long most of the original settlers had taken up individual tracts of land. In the end Jones was left alone with his "Toon o' Maxwell," named after Maxwell, Robert Owen's residence at New Lanark in Scotland. The drying up of the colony brought objections to the continued holding of the large original grant and Jones eventually returned to the government all but the thousand acres to which he would be entitled as a retired officer of the navy. So ended one of the most curious of many curious colonization schemes in the province of Upper Canada.[1]

Goderich is the most important town on the eastern shore of Lake Huron and has the only safe harbor, artificially created at the mouth of the Maitland River. Its early history is linked with the operations of the Canada Company, organized in London, England, in 1824, to deal in wild lands and to promote settlement. The objectives of this corporation, as set out in its charter, were more altruistic than its performance, if one may judge by the complaints of those who were supposed to be the beneficiaries of its operations. In addition to vast areas of land held elsewhere in the province the company purchased more than a million acres extending eastward from Lake Huron and known as the Huron Tract. Goderich was the Canadian headquarters from 1827 until 1852, after which the offices were moved to Toronto.

The name of John Galt, a Scottish novelist, is inseparably connected with the earlier operations of the company. In 1820 he had been the London agent for those seeking compensation from the British government for losses suffered during the War of 1812. Perhaps it was this connection which first interested him in the possibility of settling some of Great Britain's surplus population in

---

[1] John Morrison, " 'The Toon o' Maxwell'—an Owen settlement in Lambton County, Ontario," Ontario Historical Society, *Papers and Records,* XII (1914), 5-12.

the new land. He became secretary of the Canada Company and one of its commissioners. He was a man of amazing energy and versatility, "brimming over with ideas and opinions," but his weakness lay in his very versatility, for he constantly had too many irons in the fire.

Guelph and Goderich, at opposite ends of the great Huron Tract, were both laid out in 1827, plans for the streets and public places being prepared under Galt's direction. The visitor to Goderich of today who finds himself lost can blame this Scottish novelist who decided that around a central park the streets should radiate like the spokes of a wheel. Many an automobile driver makes the circle of the hub twice at least before finding the proper outlet.

The most picturesque figure in the early activities of the Canada Company at Goderich was Dr. William Dunlop, popularly known as "Tiger" Dunlop. He was the so-called "Warden of the Forests" and has become almost a legendary figure, so many are the stories told of his eccentricities and his practical jokes. He was a graduate of Edinburgh University and in 1813, at the age of twenty-one, became assistant surgeon in the Eighty-ninth Regiment. Coming to Canada in the fall of that year, he was in the thick of the fighting of 1814, at Lundy's Lane, at Chippewa and at Fort Erie. In this latter engagement he is said to have carried wounded men from the fighting line on his back, himself under fire.

After the close of the War of 1812 he went with his regiment to India and there by his exploits in hunting acquired the nickname of "Tiger" which stuck to him for life. On his return to England he engaged in literary pursuits and was a contributor to several of the English journals. In 1826 he accompanied Galt to Canada in the interests of the Canada Company and continued to be associated with it for many years. He became a member of the Parliament of Canada in 1846 and was later made superintendent of the Lachine Canal. He died in 1848.

His will must be one of the most curious ever admitted to probate in a Canadian court. His landed property he left to his two sisters, Ellen and Elizabeth, "the former because she is married to a minister whom (God help him) she henpecks; the latter, because she is married to nobody, nor is she likely to be, for she is an old maid and not market-rife." His elder brother, John, who was a temperance reformer, was mentioned in the will in these terms: "I leave my silver tankard to the oldest son of old John, as the representative of the family; I would have left it to old John himself, but he would melt it down to make temperance medals, and that would be a sacrilege—however, I leave my big horn snuff-box to him, he can only make temperance horn-spoons of that."

In similar fashion each beneficiary was the victim of some of his mordant wit. To his sister Jenny he left his Bible, "and when she knows as much of the spirit of it as she does of the letter, she will be another guise Christian than she is." His brother Alan received the doctor's silver snuff-box, "as I am informed that he is rather a decent Christian, with a swag belly and a jolly face."

One article that was not bequeathed was a large silver stand which always stood in the center of a huge walnut table. It was a container for twelve bottles of liquor, called the "Twelve Apostles" (the favorite drink, so tradition says, being "Judas").

Both Galt and Dunlop have been suggested as the possible author of what Lord Rosebery once termed "the most exquisite and haunting lament ever written about the Scottish exile." The verses, which were first printed anonymously in *Blackwood's Magazine* for September 1829, have from that time been a matter of interest in literary circles, and numerous articles and several books have appeared discussing their origin.[2] The first lines of the poem read:

---

[2] The question of authorship of this poem has been treated in no less than three books appearing in recent years. Thomas Newbigging published in 1912 *The Canadian Boat Song, a Refutation of the Authorship by "Christopher North" as Urged by Mr. G. M. Fraser and Others* (London, 1912). Edward McCurdy followed with his *A Literary Enigma, the Canadian Boat Song: Its Authorship and Associations* (Stirling, Scotland, 1935). The latest discussion is by G. H. Needler, *The Lone Shieling; Origin and Authorship of the Blackwood "Canadian Boat Song"* (Toronto, 1941). Needler believes that the experiences of Scottish settlers in the Huron Tract supplied the background for the origin of the poem but ascribes its authorship to David Macbeth Moir, one of the Edinburgh group of writers in which Galt was prominent.

"From the lone shieling in the misty island
Mountains divide us and the waste of seas;
Yet still the blood is strong, the heart is Highland,
And we in dreams behold the Hebrides.
Fair these broad meads—these hoary woods are grand,
But we are exiles from our fathers' land."

In John Galt's autobiography we have an account of a visit which he made to Goderich in 1827. He had planned to explore the coast between Cabot Head, at the peak of the Saugeen Peninsula, and the Aux Sables River on Lake Huron to discover, if possible, a safe harbor. Leaving York (Toronto) he journeyed overland to Penetanguishine and there found the gunboat *Bee* placed at his disposal. The letter from the Admiralty authorizing his passage was a specimen of the geographical knowledge extant in some official circles at that time, for it directed the master to take him on Lake Huron "in Lower Canada." On the second day, having rounded Cabot Head, which Galt referred to as the "Good Hope" of the lakes, he saw through the telescope a small clearing in the forest and on the brow of a rising ground a cottage delightfully situated. He wondered if it were "Tiger" Dunlop's location.

"Nor were we left long in doubt," wrote Galt, "for on approaching the place, we met a canoe having on board a strange combination of Indians, velveteens and whiskers, and discovered within the roots of the red hair the living features of the Doctor. About an hour after, having crossed the river's bar of eight feet, we came to a beautiful anchorage of fourteen feet water, in an uncommonly pleasant small basin. The place had been selected by the Doctor, and is now the site of the flourishing town of Goderich. Here we landed and cheerfully spent the night in the log cottage which the Doctor had raised. Among other things which tended to make our success in finding a haven agreeable was the production of a bottle of champagne, probably the first wine drunk on that remote spot."[3]

Goderich was not easy to arrive at in the early years. Many emi-

3 John Galt, *The Autobiography of John Galt.* 2 vols. (London, 1833), II, 80-86.

grants made their way overland, traveling by the road which the company had opened up westward from Guelph and upon which Negroes, escaped slaves from the United States, were among the laborers. Other land seekers came by water, and this method was advised by the company in its advertising, which stated that an agent at Prescott on the St. Lawrence "will forward them to Port Dalhousie, and thence to Fort Erie. From there they are forwarded to Detroit, whence they will proceed in a smaller steamboat up the St. Clair, at the head of which a vessel belonging to the company will transport them [about 60 miles] to Goderich."[4]

Goderich, in its early days, was dependent upon the American settlements to the south for many necessities. A letter written by Dr. Dunlop from Fort Gratiot (now Port Huron) on June 2, 1827, tells of a journey to secure provisions. He had gone from Goderich in a canoe with five Indians, but the lake was so rough that he soon left his companions and proceeded on foot through the woods, doing a good fifty miles in two days, subsisting on ducks and partridge which he shot and broiled by his fire at night.

"I find I shall get abundance here," he wrote, "if only I had a fair wind to bring them up; and as it is at present blowing right in our teeth, I'm not in the sweetest frame of mind. However, there are fellow sufferers. I have wasted only two hours, and there is a party bound for Michilimackinac who have been here for a week, lounging along the beach and wishing the devil had them."

Patrick Shirreff, a shrewd Scot who visited Upper Canada in 1833, looking into the general prospects for emigrating farmers, was critical of the Canada Company and of its settlement at Goderich. The settlers he described as being of the poorest class and seemingly without industry or energy of any kind. The terms on which land was sold proved, he thought, too great temptation to buy more than could be profitably used, and Shirreff found many of the settlers had already left their farms and were working on the company's road-building projects. As for Goderich, he

---

[4] Advertisement in the *Canadian Emigrant* (Sandwich, Upper Canada), December 1, 1831.

described it as having about forty mean wooden houses, scattered irregularly over a considerable space. He was particularly scornful with regard to an item which he had noticed in a Montreal newspaper announcing the formation of a yacht club at Goderich, of which "Captain" Dunlop was president.

"At the time of my visit to Goderich," he wrote, "the population was chiefly subsisting on flour and salt pork, imported from Detroit. The harbor contained three craft of the smallest size, and I did not see a boat or yacht of any description. A steamboat had appeared off the village in 1833, and could not gain admittance to the harbor for want of water. I did not learn the object of her call, but I am sure all the disposable agricultural produce of the settlement, up to the present time, would not freight a nut-shell. The youth of Britain, who anticipated displaying at Goderich the uniform of a yacht club, and having the fair sex greet his triumphant entry into the harbor by the waving of handkerchiefs may delay his departure for half a century."

When the Rebellion of 1837 came, the population in the Canada Company's area was divided in its allegiance. As early as 1835 the "Huron Union Society" had come into existence as a protest against the policies of the company, and when the actual uprising came it was old Colonel Anthony Von Egmond, a veteran of the Napoleonic Wars and a resident of the Goderich district, who led the armed forces which marched on the capital of the province. On the other hand Dr. William Dunlop was at the head of loyal detachments which marched to Sarnia and remained there on guard for some months, their headquarters being the Methodist mission house formerly occupied by the Reverend James Evans. The Huron men were organized by companies and bore such names as the Huron True Blues, the Huron Braves, the Invincibles and one company which modestly designated itself the Bloody Useless.

Goderich and the Huron Tract survived its pioneer difficulties, survived even the policies of the Canada Company, and in due time came into its own. Today Goderich is one of the important grain ports on the lakes and has long been a sailor town. The blasts of the whistles of the big freighters entering and leaving its harbor are music to those who realize how much the trade means to the community.

John Galt and "Tiger" Dunlop were not the only persons of distinction who came into this region in its early days. In the year 1827, when the Canada Company was but beginning its operations, Baron de Tuyle, an elderly Belgian nobleman, became interested in the lands lying along Lake Huron. He sent Henry Wolsey Bayfield, who had surveyed much of Lake Huron after the War of 1812, to select for him suitable areas. Bayfield recommended purchases both at Goderich and farther south at the mouth of the stream which has since been known as the Bayfield River.

At Goderich the baron built a palatial log house, the main hall having sliding doors on all sides so that when required the rooms could be thrown into one. These were handsomely furnished, while the surrounding grounds were laid out in formal lawns, beds of flowers and avenues of trees. The place must have offered a striking contrast to the slovenly, down-at-the-heel premises of the baron's neighbors. Baron de Tuyle died in 1836, but his enterprises were continued by his son, who gave particular attention to the more southerly site, which comprised 1,500 acres on each side of the stream. A town plot, also named Bayfield, was laid out, and there was the prospect for a time that the government might erect fortifications on the bold headlands at the mouth of the river. High hopes were entertained for the future of the place but these were never realized. Today Bayfield is a popular summer resort, but only a few fishing vessels and an occasional yacht from Detroit disturb the waters of its little harbor.

South of Bayfield and along the lake shore is French Settlement, an island of people whose ancestors came from the province of Quebec but who through one hundred years have preserved their race, language and religion. In the late thirties French-Canadian lumberjacks made their appearance in the district, the same roving adventurous type who in an earlier day would have been *coureurs de bois.* Returning to Quebec, they told their friends of this new region so recently opened to settlement where land was plentiful and cheap, where the climate was pleasant and where a great lake furnished abundance of fish.

There were three men in particular who spread the news— Claude Gelinas, Abraham Bedard and Baptiste Durand—and these men not only told of the promised land but came to it themselves and settled down to share all the experiences of their friends in the pioneer life of the settlement. It was chiefly young people who pulled up stakes to move to Lake Huron, a little westward movement, the impetus for which was a succession of crop failures in their native province and a general drop in prices. On the gravestones in the cemeteries near Grand Bend and around the parish church of St. Pierre du Lac Huron in French Settlement one may read the names of those who came in the middle forties and founded the community which, though today scarcely greater in the number of its people than when first established, has lost none of its distinctive character.

The names that appear on the mailboxes or at the farm gates today are the names that appear also on the gravestones— Denomme, Ducharme, Laporte, Mousseau, Brisson, Bedard and others. The original settlers came chiefly from the Quebec counties of Joliette, Berthier, L'Assomption, St. Thomas, Ste. Elizabeth and Levis. Their names fill the parish registers of those counties, though change of residence has naturally added to the variations in spelling. Some of the family names go back to the first century of French migration to Canada. The Brissons, for example, are descended from one René Brisson, born in France in 1635, whose marriage to Anne Vesinat in 1665 is recorded in the register of the parish of Quebec. The Ducharmes trace their ancestry to Fiacre Ducharme, a carpenter, born in Paris in 1628 and married at Quebec to Marie Pacrau in 1659. Of their nine children the oldest, Louis, was killed by the English in one of the border conflicts, and Claude was a victim of the Iroquois while he was serving under Jean Baptiste Le Moyne, Sieur de Bienville. And so the record runs with regard to other families. We do not usually know the exact dates of the arrival of these people in New France, but a clue is afforded by the register of their marriages at Quebec or by the dates of baptism of their children. No other section of North America can compare with Quebec in the completeness of its family records, for which the Church must be thanked.

The original settlement on Lake Huron was a succession of small farms stretching for three miles along the lake front. This land was secured from the Canada Company at about three dollars an acre and the cautious habitants bought no more than they could be sure of holding. During the century since their arrival, however, they have increased their holdings and have spread over an area ten miles long which extends six miles inland. Here, as in old Quebec, the center of religious life and of social life also is the parish church, whose tall steeple is a landmark seen for many miles. Its bell sounds out over the countryside calling to prayer just as the bells along the St. Lawrence have spread their message for centuries, and in the shadow of the church is the school for the children of the community, taught by black-veiled nuns of the Ursuline order. Many of the young people are eventually drawn off to Detroit by the attraction of high wages and the pleasures of city life, but there are always those who, like their hardy ancestors, cling to the land, intermarry, raise up broods of children (one well-known family numbers over twenty) and maintain the population level as it was in the time of their fathers and mothers. They are simple, kindly people, and the soft tone of their French tongue recalls the continuity of the cultural tradition so deeply inbedded in their daily lives.

The name of Paul Kane deserves remembrance for his unique contribution to the record of the North American Indian in the paintings which he made after 1845. Traveling by canoe, dog sled and snowshoe, observing the habits and customs of the red men, he patiently sketched them and their homes, clothing, weapons and utensils. No other such collection can rival his for accuracy and outstanding artistry. From his boyhood he had known the Indians and been sympathetic toward them. At Toronto, to which he came as a child, he played with Indian children encamped on its outskirts, or with Indian companions paddled in a birchbark canoe along the water front and in the little rivers emptying into Lake Ontario. In afteryears he could write: "To me the wild woods were not altogether unknown, and the Indians but recalled old friends with whom I had associated in my childhood."

An early period of wandering both in Canada and the United States, supporting himself by painting whatever came to hand, was followed by four years abroad during which he was able to develop his talent by study and by examining the work of others. In some respects the career of Paul Kane resembles that of Francis Parkman. Both went through a strenuous apprenticeship for the task to which they proposed to give the best years of their lives. Parkman had set himself to tell the story of France and England in America and of the part which the Indian played in the rivalries and ambitions of these two nations. Kane returned to Canada with the determination to "devote whatever talents and proficiency I possessed to the painting of a series of pictures illustrative of the North American Indians and scenery." The painter's task was in a way complementary to that of the historian.

In addition to his pictures, Kane recorded his travel experiences in a book to which he gave the title *Wanderings of an Artist.* It was first published in England in 1859 and with its several beautifully colored plates is now a much sought item of Americana. The opening chapters narrate the journey from Toronto overland to the mouth of the Saugeen River on Lake Huron. The most difficult section was that between Owen Sound and the lake where great swamps and dense forest made the way almost impenetrable. On his arrival at Lake Huron he found the Indians, who had recently been Christianized, holding an old-fashioned camp meeting with boisterous singing and fervent praying under the direction and guidance of a number of Methodist missionaries.

"The Indian Village of Saugeen, meaning 'the mouth of the river,' contains about 200 inhabitants (Ojibbeways)," he wrote.

"It is the site of a former battleground between the Ojibbeways, as usually pronounced, or Chippawas, and the Mohawks. Of this, the mounds erected over the slain afford abundant evidence in the protrusion of the bones through the surface of the ground.

"The land hereabouts is excellent, but only a small part is cultivated, as the inhabitants subsist principally on fish, which are taken in great abundance at the entrance of the river. They also kill hundreds of deer by erecting a fence of brushwood many miles in extent, behind which the Indians conceal themselves; and as the deer, in their annual migrations, are seeking an opening through the fence, they fall a prey to the unerring aim of the Red Man.

"I sketched the principal chief, named Maticwaub, or 'The Bow.' . . . I also took a sketch of a chief named Maskuhnoonjee, or the 'Big Pike.' This man was very proud of having his likeness taken, and put on his chief's medal presented by the Government to those they acknowledged as chiefs. I have never known a chief to barter away one of these marks of distinction, which they seldom wear on unimportant occasions. An interesting girl, the daughter of a chief from Lake St. Clair, gave me much trouble in prevailing on her to sit for her likeness, although her father insisted upon it; her repugnance proceeded from a superstitious belief that by so doing she would place herself in the power of the possessor of what is regarded by an Indian as a second self.

"Wah-pus, 'The Rabbit,' also permitted me to take his portrait. He resides at Owen's Sound, and was formerly as much renowned for his unconquerable fierceness and intemperance as he is now for his temperance and wisdom. This change in his character is attributable to the influence of the Methodist missionaries, whose church he has joined. He was the first Indian I had seen whose hair had been pulled out, all except the scalp lock; this custom is common among many tribes of Indians, though not universal amongst any."[5]

Laurence Oliphant, journalist, war correspondent and world

---

[5] Paul Kane, *Wanderings of an Artist Among the Indians of North America, from Canada to Vancouver Island and Oregon, Through the Hudson Bay Company Territory* (London. 1859), 3-5.

traveler, has left us an account of a similar journey which he made in 1854 between the Georgian Bay and the mouth of the Saugeen River. His mission was to negotiate a treaty with the Saugeen Indians for the surrender of the whole of the upper peninsula. At that time what is now the county of Bruce was rapidly filling up with emigrants from overseas, mostly Scottish folk, though as yet all means of transportation was of the most primitive character. The road which he followed and which ran almost perfectly straight was nothing more than a trace through the woods; fallen trees lay rotting in the mud and stumps with their spreading roots impeded every foot of passage. Every now and then the traveler would come upon a wagon, hopelessly imbedded, with oxen straining to release it and sturdy backwoodsmen, with flannel shirts and boots reaching to their thighs, "imploring, imprecating, belaboring and pushing by turns." Sometimes the way led through long swamps over which fallen trees had been placed to keep the traveler from completely disappearing.

At intervals a bit of snake fencing indicated a settler, and a little log cabin might be seen, with stumps all about and a small plot of potatoes, all looking rather drooping and melancholy. Occasionally, however, the scene was more cheerful, a logging bee, perhaps, with men busily engaged in rolling the fallen trees together and burning them. Huge fires made a jovial crackling and all was excitement. Then the forest would close in again on the road and there would be silence save for the horses' feet.

A settler's hut gave accommodation for the night, a one-roomed dwelling, but the hospitality was hearty and sincere. When the entertainers found that Oliphant was from Scotland, their own native land, nothing was too good for him. Buttered toast for the visitor, and milk, and some little dainties brought from a large chest all expressed good will.

The treaty which Oliphant negotiated, involving an immense consumption of tobacco, together with much palaver, brought to the Crown almost 500,000 acres of land, in return for which the Indians were to receive a considerable annuity. Even at that time squatters were entering the Indian lands, trusting that their claims might be recognized when the tract was transferred to the government. To Oliphant it seemed that a great proportion of the population was composed of land hunters, searching for a location or, having made it, then guarding it against others. Sawmills were springing up, making better use of the timber than merely burning it to clear the ground for the plow. It was the same sort of boom period that at one time or another had come to every western community. Optimism was contagious and men were dreaming of cities that were to be in what was as yet little more than a wilderness.[6]

The Saugeen or Bruce Peninsula, which stretches north toward Manitoulin Island like a great rocky finger, remains one of the most unspoiled portions of the Georgian Bay country. Champlain was reminded of Brittany when he visited it while with the Huron in 1615. "This country is fine and pleasant," he wrote, "for the most part solitary, shaped like Brittany and similarly situated, being almost surrounded and enclosed by the Freshwater Sea." Today a highway leads to the little port at its peak, named Tobermoray, after a little town on the Scottish island of Mull, by the Highland fishermen who came this way in early days. From the highway roads branch off to points on the Georgian Bay, Dyer's Bay, Lion's Head and the Cape Croker Indian reserve, or to Stokes Bay on the Lake Huron side of the peninsula.

The perfect safety with which vessels could lie in the harbor at Tobermoray made it a much-frequented place in the days when the schooners were carrying most of the traffic. The passage between the tip of the peninsula and Manitoulin Island was one in which many a vessel came to grief and from an early day it was avoided in rough weather. Offshore is Cove Island on which in 1858 the government of Canada built an imposing lighthouse, one hundred feet high, circular in form and of stone construction. As

---

[6] Laurence Oliphant, *Minnesota and the Far West* (Edinburgh and London, 1855), 68-80.

seen from the deck of a passenger ship traversing the passage between the bay and the lake, it is dazzlingly white in the sunshine and is one of the sights long remembered. Tobermoray itself received a lighthouse later, and another was placed on Flower Pot Island not far distant.

The peninsula has been properly described as lower Ontario's last frontier, for it was the latest to be settled. It was not an easy country from which to secure a living by agriculture, but lumbering and fishing supported many of its inhabitants and from time to time a wrecked schooner would send to the shore an unexpected addition to the larder. Local tradition tells of one fall storm which brought ashore such vast quantities of lard that little communities far and wide had a full winter's supply of this article. Another wreck provided a store of flour in barrels, and though the outer layer was wet there remained in the center of each barrel a considerable amount of the welcome food.

The whole area of the peninsula was at one time a great forest though today the timber remaining is chiefly second growth and scrub. The lumbermen cleaned off much of the forest during the last quarter of the nineteenth century. There were several severe forest fires during this period, and the general system of taking out the timber was of much the same wasteful character as that which had prevailed elsewhere about Lake Huron.

The history of the Saugeen Peninsula is chiefly related to its earlier Indian ownership and the successive surrenders of their holdings by the tribes resident within the area. Back in 1836 Sir Francis Bond Head visited Manitoulin Island and there concluded a treaty with the Indians by which the land comprised in the original county of Bruce was surrendered by Chippewa and Ottawa in return for Manitoulin Island and certain other small islands. At the same time the Saugeen Indians agreed to surrender their particular hunting grounds and to remove to Manitoulin or to an area north of Owen Sound.

After the signing of this treaty Indians of various tribes again settled on the peninsula and in 1847 a "Royal Deed of Declaration" was issued in which it was stated that they and their posterity were to possess and enjoy the country. At later dates the whole area of the peninsula, with the exception of the Indian reserves, was surrendered to the Crown. The first of these surrenders was in 1851, and consisted of a narrow strip needed for construction of a road between Owen Sound and Lake Huron. Three years later came the important cession negotiated by Laurence Oliphant to which reference has already been made. In 1861 the Colpoy's Bay reservation of 6,000 acres was given up, and in October 1885 the Saugeen Fishing Islands, together with the islands adjacent to Cape Hurd, were placed in the hands of the Crown. Surrenders and land sales have resulted in the building up of trust funds for the Indians of Canada, held and administered by the government, which on March 31, 1942, totaled over fourteen and a half million dollars. From this fund the Indians of the Lake Huron region yearly receive a share by which they benefit substantially. The census of 1939 showed that the Chippewa of the Saugeen, so often mentioned in this chapter, still numbered 398, while the Chippewa of Nawash, in the same general area, numbered 471.

In waters so teeming with fish as were Lake Huron's there must have been something beyond the ordinary which would give the name Fishing Islands to the miniature archipelago off the shore of the Saugeen Peninsula. And indeed it was so. As early as 1831, Captain Alexander MacGregor of Goderich discovered that here was a fishing ground rich beyond anything that he had known. He promptly established a station on one of the many islands, but soon his problem was to dispose of the enormous catches that came to his nets. He solved his difficulty, partially at least, by entering into a contract with a Detroit company to supply to them 3,000 barrels annually at one dollar a barrel. They were to clean, cure and pack the fish so delivered.

The fish caught in this vicinity were chiefly whitefish and herrings, and the manner in which they were taken has been recorded. A watchman was stationed in a high tree near the shore from which he had a clear view of the lake. Suddenly there would seem to be a bright silvery cloud moving through the water. The man on watch would quickly notify the fishermen and the boats would set out with their nets which would be dropped so as to encircle the fish. Then began the work of hauling the net to shore. We have this description of what followed:

"When the fish commenced to feel the pressure from the narrowing of the net the scene was one long to be remembered. There in a small area were entrapped thousands and thousands of fish, sufficient possibly to fill five hundred or a thousand barrels. The water in that circumscribed space seemed to be fairly alive as the fish in their efforts to escape rushed madly about, causing its agitated surface to glitter with the sheen of their silvery sides. All their efforts were futile; the seine was drawn closer to shore and soon the fish were thrown out on the beach, this process being accomplished by a man standing bare-legged in the midst of the net-imprisoned fish, scoop in hand, who soon transferred them from their native element to land where they formed a splendent mass, flapping and gasping life away. At times the catch was so large that the landing of the fish was extended over three days, so that none be lost through inability of the curers to handle so many. At other times, when the supply of barrels or salt was running low, the net was opened to let a portion of the catch escape."[7]

Such enormous takes would seem almost beyond belief were there not contemporary references to the volume of the business. Reverend James Evans, when traveling by canoe from Sarnia to the Sault in the summer of 1838, landed on the islands and preached to the fishermen. "This is a fine fishery," he wrote in his diary. "Sometimes four hundred barrels of herring are caught at one drop of the seine." To carry on such extensive operations substantial stone buildings were erected on Main Station Island, and the ruins of these remained for years after the earlier activity had ceased, their origin sometimes mistakenly attributed to the French.

---

[7] Norman Robertson, *History of the County of Bruce and of the Minor Municipalities Therein* (Toronto, 1906), 22.

Photo by Bury Studio, Sarnia

IN SCHOONER DAYS

A fleet of sailing ships in Sarnia Bay on the St. Clair River waiting for favorable weather in order to go up Lake Huron. This photo was taken about 1871.

AN INDIAN RENDEZVOUS ON DRUMMOND ISLAND

Reproduced from the drawing appearing in Dr. John Bigsby's *The Shoe and Canoe; or Pictures of Travel in the Canadas*. Drummond Island, when Dr. Bigsby was there in the early 1820's, was still occupied by a British garrison.

Photo from Art Gallery of Toronto

AN INDIAN ENCAMPMENT ON LAKE HURON

From the original painting by Paul Kane (1810-1871) in the Art Gallery of Toronto. This picture was painted by Kane after his visit to the West in 1845. The scene is among the islands on Georgian Bay.

Captain MacGregor did not remain long in undisputed possession of this rich fishing ground. His success excited the cupidity of others, and the plea was made that his Detroit connection was placing a valuable resource in the hands of Americans. A group of Goderich men, among whom was the ever-active Dr. William Dunlop, managed through political influence to secure the exclusive rights to the island fisheries and organized a company to carry out their plans. MacGregor, driven from the waters which he had so successfully exploited, sought out new fishing areas at Tobermoray, then at Cape Croker and latterly among islands off the shore of Manitoulin, but none of these could compare with his first discovery. In the early eighties commercial fishing was begun in a large way by C. W. Gauthier of Windsor, who had Detroit financial backing. A gaudy lithograph issued at the time, of which a few copies have survived, shows the fishing fleet and establishment on one of the Duck Islands off the south shore of Manitoulin. The Gauthier venture was at first a success, but equipment was so increased that interest on the investment eventually swamped the promoters.

In one respect only does Gother Mann's description of the Lake Huron shore as a great solitude still hold good. From the long sandy beaches that begin at the entrance of the St. Clair to the rocky tip of the peninsula at Tobermoray, men have transformed the wilderness, cutting off the forests, tilling the arable land and building up communities with all those things required for the satisfaction of their needs. But the lake itself along this Canadian shore is today almost as great a solitude as when the pioneer surveyor came along. The lanes for shipping lie close to the American shore, so that during the season of navigation there is rarely a time when a vessel is not in sight. There are no similar lanes on the Canadian side because there is no direct traffic following its shore. The vessels that enter Goderich harbor come in a diagonal course from the mouth of the St. Mary's River, bringing their huge cargoes of grain from Fort William or Port Arthur. When they leave Goderich, headed again for Lake Superior, they are soon out of sight of the shore. This port alone shares in the bulk trade of the Great Lakes; from the others only a few fishing tugs go and come. From the opening of navigation to its close, no large vessel is ever seen. Viewed from the shore, Lake Huron is still a great solitude.

It was not always so, however. Before the railways provided connections these smaller ports were served by steamers and by the sailing ships which once made the lakes so picturesque. In those days a passenger service was provided from Sarnia and Detroit, and the popularity of the Canadian shore for vacationists was firmly established. The schooners looked after the local business, taking out cargoes of grain and other commodities and bringing in whatever the region might need. But that has long since passed away. The schooners, their captains and their crews have become but a tradition in the little ports. About the docks and in the fishing shanties stories are told of this and that vessel, of her builders, of her captain and crews, and of the storm in which she finally met her end.

The war years after 1939 effected the greatest changes on this eastern shore of the lake that it had known in a generation. Large areas formerly given over to farming were transformed into training camps for soldiers and for airmen. The solitude of the lake was in this instance an advantage. Planes roared out over the water, singly or in groups, and their crews, as they looked to the west, could see no land.

Elsewhere along the shore, camps were instituted for the training of infantry and artillery. There the rattle of small arms might be heard and the boom of great guns firing out over the lake. Men from far distant parts of Canada were brought together to prepare for the ordeal of war on other continents, some to help in the liberation of the land from which came Champlain more than three centuries before to discover this Freshwater Sea.

Chapter 8

Around the Shores of Georgian Bay

Where once the Indian's paddle dipped
To carry Champlain to the Huron lands,
Great vessels bring their wheaten loads
To feed the peoples on far distant strands.
—ANON

I F OUR earth in its primeval days had experienced a few more
convulsions, or a few less (which, one cannot say), there might
have been six Great Lakes instead of five, for Georgian Bay has
area and depth well befitting such rank. The passage between the
tip of the Saugeen Peninsula and Manitoulin Island is a veritable
maze of islands and shoals, while even narrower and similarly
broken is the passage between the northeastern tip of the island and
the main north shore. Perhaps it is because of its closed-in character
that the people who live in Georgian Bay ports and along its shores
constantly think of it as quite distinct from Lake Huron, of which
it is really but a great arm.

Georgian Bay has the distinction of being the first portion of
the Great Lakes to be seen by a white man. Probably it was
Etienne Brulé who first among Europeans looked out to its horizon. The priest Le Caron and Champlain came to its waters in
the summer of 1615, but each was too intent upon other matters to
leave us much description. In succeeding years men pushed out
from the inlets at the foot of the bay and with Indian guides
learned the intricacies of the passages by which one might come to
the mouth of the St. Mary's River. The North Shore route required watchfulness if rocks and shoals were to be avoided, but it
gave shelter from the storms which could arise so suddenly on the

lake itself. Brulé, Grenolle, Nicolet, and Father Isaac Jogues were but a few of those who passed this way during the first half of the seventeenth century, lured on by the tales of far-spreading land and far-spreading waters ahead of them. It was the first lake route to be opened up, and it held few secrets at the end of the first half-century of exploration.

For generations Georgian Bay was an important link in the chain of waters along which the fur trade moved. The *voyageurs* who toiled against the currents of the Ottawa River route and sweated under their burdens as they crossed the seemingly endless portages must have been happy when their canoes at last emerged from the French River. There they left behind them the currents and rapids and entered waters where paddling was pleasure instead of toil. But these Frenchmen did not found settlements on the bay as they did on the St. Lawrence. They came, and having transacted their business they went away. Only the Jesuits tried to establish something permanent when they built their mission of Sainte Marie in the 1640's. They dreamed of a community which would be free from the evils that the white men brought to native minds and bodies, where the Indians would settle down to agriculture, would cease from war, and would be ever under the scrutinizing and protective eye of the priest. Huronia was to be a center of religion from which influences would radiate out to other tribes. But the plans and hopes of the Jesuit fathers were defeated in 1649 when the Iroquois "came down like the wolf on the fold" and scattered the Huron far and wide.

For more than a century and a half thereafter only the fur trader's canoe broke the waters of the bay. At a few small trading posts the Indians turned in their furs and received articles of which their ancestors knew nothing but which to them had become necessities. So swiftly had a race passed from the stone age to that of iron.

Pioneer farmers began to take up land south of Nottawasaga Bay and Owen Sound in the later 1830's, some of them in old

Huronia where their plows brought to the surface relics of the ancient villages. Present-day Owen Sound and Collingwood had their beginnings about 1840; Owen Sound, originally called Sydenham, was described at that time as a cedar swamp with an Indian village on its outskirts, and Collingwood, a little cluster of half a dozen houses, was known as Hurontario Mills, a name still kept in memory by its main street. Midland, where many great ships have been built and whose elevators are today an important link in the grain trade, came into existence only in 1872 when a railway came to Gloucester Bay. Even more recent is Port McNichol, the present terminus of the Canadian Pacific Railway's lake fleet.

Georgian Bay, like Michigan, had its great lumbering era. Beginning on the more southerly shores but in time spreading to the northern regions, there was a rush to exploit the timber and gather in the wealth that it represented. Mills were opened at Collingwood and elsewhere to handle the supply drawn from local sources, and later, great rafts, hauled by tugs, came down from the north shore, two to four million board feet in each tow.

In the 1880's railway builders pierced the rugged country north of Lake Huron. In doing so, they uncovered the greatest deposits of nickel to be found anywhere in the world and along with them other mineral deposits of lesser but appreciable value. In this period, too, the shores of the bay began to see the influx of summer visitors, many of them from the United States, leaving the heat and noise of great cities behind and finding new vigor in the fresh pine-scented air and the brilliant sunshine among the islands and waters and forests of the region. Muskoka, the name given to the country east of the bay, became more widely known than any of its towns.

Dr. John Bigsby, who crossed Georgian Bay in 1823 en route to Lake Superior, has left us some charming pictures of the waters and shores as he saw them at that time. He and his party had come by way of Lake Simcoe and in the last stage by the Nottawasaga River, in the lower part of which they saw scarcely any living thing. It was all a great solitude save for an occasional Indian gliding in his canoe under the shadow of the thickly wooded banks. But when the lake came into view, beautifully blue and stretching to the horizon, *"Huron! Chantons, le lac Huron!"* shouted the French-Canadian steersman, and struck up a spirited song with apparently endless verses:

> *Le premier jour de mai*
> *Je donnerais à m'amie*
> *Une perdrix, oh là! qui vole, qui vie, qui va là!*
> *Une perdrix, oh là! volante dans les bois.*

The morning was serene; lake, sands and foliage sparkled under the rays of the sun. The smooth billows rolled in slow succession to the beach. To the left were the Blue Mountains and to the right a line of broken heights and in the distance, gray and indistinct, the Christian Islands. No wonder that later Bigsby wrote: "I am affected even to tears to think that I never again shall seek the rare insect or fossil, or greet the friendly savage, among the shadowy isles, the purple mountains, and broad waters of Lake Huron." Every hour brought new vistas of beauty and when night came there were yet other attractions:

"The evening had been lowering, but afterwards became partially clear and starry. Our men were asleep at the fire—all, save the cook on duty, who was feeding it with wood and stirring the soup. The cool wind was shaking the birch trees, and the waves were shimmering and rippling among the reefs below. Looking towards the head of Gloucester Bay I saw several solitary red lights wandering over the surface of the lake, which lay here and there in shadow. These were the canoe-torches of Indians spearing the fish attracted by the flame. When they chanced to draw near, the flare of the light, and the frequent streams of cinders dropping into the water red-hot, were reflected beautifully on the dark men and their craft."

Next morning the party started for the old trading post of Bourassa, situated on an island in Parry Sound, the whole intervening shore "as full of fiords and inlets as the coast of Norway." This is a great playground today, drawing to it a summer population of thousands, but it was all solitary when Bigsby went that way. The innumerable islands were so intricate in their relation one to the other that the most experienced guide might be baffled. Evening brought yet another aspect of Lake Huron:

"It was blowing a hurricane in the open lake. We were on the outskirts of the island groups. I shall never forget the hoarse raging of the storm, mingled with the whistle of the bowed reed-beds —so different from the crisp smiles of yesterday. We were glad to pitch our little tent in a tolerably dry hole under a bush, fastening it down with double care, and covering it with a few pine branches to make it warmer, for the low, exposed islet gave us little shelter from the resistless wind."

The third day, with Indians as guides, the journey was continued. The way led toward a basin a mile wide, almost closed by islands and intervening reeds. But the canoe broke through the reeds and threaded its way by rocky passages to pool after pool of calm clear water. A landing was made on a small round island where there was an Indian camp, set in a little meadow in the midst of forest. "Men, women, children and dogs were all about— the men mending nets, the women pounding corn, and the children in busy play until the palefaces appeared." Bigsby was delighted with the well-fed, good-humored looks of the Indians; he made favorable comparisons between them and Glasgow weavers.

Parry Sound was left behind. Twenty miles more brought the fur-trading post of La Ronde, "a melancholy looking log-house, with a cluster of out-houses, sunk for protection behind some sand-heaps and rocks." After that the islets were usually lower, smaller and more naked, advancing farther out into the lake as solitary mounds, hardly emerging above the water at times. The weather was stormy, and the surveyor's canoe crept along behind a succession of island sea walls beyond which the lake was white with breakers exhausting their strength on the naked rocks. When they came to the French River, with its low shores and high woody ridges some miles in the rear, they were viewing the same scene that Champlain must have viewed when he left the river mouth behind and headed his canoe for the Huron country to the south. Until this point was reached the general course of Bigsby's journey had been north-northwest, but thereafter it was a little north of west. The high hills which had been proceeding obliquely to join the lake soon began to form its actual margin in slopes and ridges. Collins Inlet and the Fox Islands brought a further change in the scenery. Dreary cranberry marshes were replaced by the well-wooded district of La Cloche and the long blue line of Manitoulin Island. The bay was merging into the North Shore channel leading to the St. Mary's River.

Penetanguishine can claim not only to have one of the longest names in the province of Ontario but also to have the most ancient lineage of any place on the bay, for it goes back to 1615 when both Le Caron and Champlain landed in its vicinity on their way to the Huron villages. The name means "place of the rolling white sands." All through the period of Jesuit activity among the Huron tribes, men and supplies came and went in its vicinity, but when the Iroquois blight destroyed the mission stations and the Huron nation as well the region again became a solitude.

British rule after the cession of Canada by France brought revival of the fur trade. When Colonel John Graves Simcoe visited Gloucester Bay in October 1793 looking to the defense of the colony, he found a man named Cowan, a fur trader, who had been there for fifteen years. The War of 1812 gave the place a prominence that it had not hitherto enjoyed, its harbor becoming for a brief period the center of British naval activity on the upper lakes. In 1828, following the settlement of the international boundary dispute, the fur traders and *voyageurs* at Drummond Island, which had been declared to be American territory, migrated to Penetanguishine and gave its neighborhood a considerable increase of population. A few years later, however, the only signs of military occupation were a sloop, sunk and rotting in the bay, and a large stone building, called the Fort, which served as barracks for a few soldiers. Near by was a hamlet of twenty or thirty log houses where more than one hundred pensioners of the British army were eking out a very miserable existence.

Memories of the old garrison days are best preserved in the little Church of St. James'-on-the-Lines, "Lines" being an old military term referring to the road which connected this frontier post with the headquarters at the provincial capital, Toronto. The church was built in 1836, chiefly for the use of the garrison, and its one aisle was made wide enough to allow men to march four abreast, separating two by two into the pews. The hinges on the doors are hand-wrought and the bell in the steeple is a ship's bell taken from either the *Tigress* or the *Scorpion,* the two American vessels captured during the last year of the War of 1812. The other bell is in near-by St. Anne's Jesuit Memorial Church. The pews were evidently made by different hands and at different times, so greatly do they vary in design, and many bear the initials of soldiers who probably whiled away a tedious sermon hour in this occupation.

Within the church is a curious memorial tablet, one-half of which is left blank. It is to the memory of a Lieutenant William Glasgott of the Sixty-sixth Regiment who died January 23, 1837. Originally the tablet had the additional words "frozen to death on his return from the village after a night of festivity," but these extra details have been removed. The story has come down that the officer in command left the blank portion as a warning to his young officers not to follow Glasgott's example; otherwise they too might be recorded for posterity as having imbibed unwisely.

Several gravestones in the churchyard bear quaint inscriptions. On that of a child who died of some contagious disease and for whom, when others were afraid, some Roman Catholics performed the duties of bearers, there is this epitaph:

> "Dear Brother, o'er your body here I weep,
> One week after with you I sleep.
> Four kind Papists here me laid.
> The Rev. G. H. the service read."[1]

---

[1] "G.H." was the Reverend George Hallen, who was the first rector of the parish. He died in 1882 after sixty-five years' service as a priest.

Penetanguishine has memories of Sir John Franklin, the Arctic explorer, for it was from this port in 1825 that he began the long 1,500-mile water-and-land journey that would bring him to Cumberland House, the rendezvous of his second Polar expedition. On April 22 he wrote to his wife whom he had left in England dying of consumption: "I am sure you will be rejoiced to learn that we arrived safely at this place, to which you may remember a part of our stores were forwarded from Montreal. The Canadian voyageurs had not reached York Factory at the time of the departure from thence. I therefore left Mr. Back to bring them up. Part of these men have already come up and the remainder we expect today, so that we shall probably commence our voyage this evening or tomorrow. We are first to cross Lake Huron and Lake Superior, and at Fort William, on the north side of the latter lake, we embark in the proper travelling canoes, which are of a smaller size than those we now use.

"Penetanguishine is the most northerly of our naval stations, and the key to Lake Huron. At the close of the war they were preparing to build a frigate of thirty-two guns, but its construction was deferred when the peace was concluded, and the establishment was then reduced. We have found, however, very comfortable quarters in the house of the lieutenant commanding. There are a lieutenant of the army with his wife, and a surgeon and his wife stationed here; these form a social party and cause the time to pass very pleasantly. . . . I do not think, however, that either you or I would relish such a secluded life. If we could convey our library, it would be the very place for me to get through it."[2]

This letter was never sent. Even while he was writing it, Franklin received word that his wife had died on February 22, less than a week after he left England. In a handwriting that betrays his emotion these words were added:

"Seven o'clock P.M. The distressing intelligence of my dearest wife's death has just reached me."

On the following day Franklin and his party set out in two

[2] H. D. Traill, *The Life of Sir John Franklin, R. N.* (London, 1896), 120-121.

canoes on the first lap of their long journey westward and northward.

In the little cemetery at Thornbury village on the south shore a modest stone marks the grave of Captain Charles Stuart, one of the prominent figures in the controversy over slavery before the Civil War. Born in Jamaica, he served for many years in the army of the East India Company, rising to the rank of captain in 1810. Five years later he retired and for the remainder of his days devoted himself to the crusade against slavery in England, the West Indies and the United States.

There is some mystery connected with his retirement from the East India Company's service, which local tradition associates with a protest over punishments inflicted after the Indian mutiny at Vellore. He came to Canada as early as 1817, residing for a year or more at Amherstburg on the Detroit River, where he acted as a magistrate. He returned to England toward the end of 1819 and in the following year published an *Emigrant's Guide to Upper Canada,* which a satirical critic said might be more appropriately entitled the *Pilgrim's Guide to the Celestial Regions,* so heavily was it loaded with moral and religious advice. Six pages were devoted to admonishing women to be modest in their apparel. He was again at Amherstburg in 1821 at which time Dr. John Bigsby found him laboring to establish a colony for refugee slaves from the United States. For the next forty years Captain Stuart worked unceasingly in the abolitionist cause, writing pamphlets, lecturing and organizing, and was associated with Theodore Dwight Weld, James G. Birney and other prominent figures in the antislavery ranks.

His eccentricities must not blind us to his influence in the movement. His looks, dress and manners were peculiar, but his contemporaries paid tribute to his zeal and power. His influence over Theodore Dwight Weld was lifelong and Weld is today recognized as one of the most important men in the abolitionist forces. At late as 1847 Dr. Bigsby met Stuart in England. "I knew him instantly," he wrote; "there was the same carelessness about the outer man, and the same restless zeal for the cause."

Some time after 1850 he retired to the shores of Georgian Bay and established himself on a farm. He carried on an extensive correspondence with the antislavery leaders in the United States and was also active in the Anti-Slavery Society of Canada after its formation in 1851. His home was on a little inlet known as Lora Bay and until recent years ruins of the house were visible. He carried his antislavery principles into the home and would permit no product of slave labor to be brought in. Maple sugar alone was used and linen in place of cotton. He died on May 26, 1865, in his eighty-fourth year.

Georgian Bay had other connections with the antislavery struggle in the United States. In the days when the "underground railroad" was operating to bring fugitive slaves from the South to friendly free states or to Canada, Owen Sound and Collingwood were among the termini of this strange secret system. Many of the escaped slaves made their way to Chicago and there found passage on the grain schooners headed for Canada, "the land of freedom." Sailors were naturally sympathetic and, if necessary, stowed the fugitives in the hold until danger was left behind. Others had their passage paid by friendly Quakers.

From its early days Collingwood had a small colored population, partly drawn from the arrivals in the grain boats and partly from other routes by which the black people traveled. Not far distant was the Queen's Bush settlement with a considerable colored population of runaway slaves. Reverend John McDougall recalled that on his father's little trading schooner in the 1850's the cook and handy man was a Negro named Isaiah, who had made his way to this distant frontier region from the cotton plantations of the South.

Georgian Bay and North Channel place names are closely related to the times in which the early surveys were made and to the background of the men who were in charge of the work. Captain William Fitzwilliam Owen, who came soon after the War of

1812, made sure that his family name would be well remembered, for he bestowed it upon one of the most beautiful and important inlets, Owen Sound, where today a city also brings it to mind. He must have had a high opinion of his brother, the commodore commander of British naval forces on the lakes, for he placed on the charts not only the rank but each of the given names of his relative. Thus we still have Cape Commodore, Edward Creek, Point William, Campbell Cliff and Rich Point.

When Henry Wolsey Bayfield became the chief surveyor, George III was still on the throne of Great Britain and Ireland, and in his honor the whole of the waters, which Owen had thought worthy of being known as a lake by itself, became Georgian Bay. The king's son, Prince William Henry, had an island named after him and the king's son-in-law, the Duke of Gloucester, is today remembered in Gloucester Point and Bay. Bayfield probably felt in duty bound to pay like honor to some of the admiralty officials, and so we have Cape Dundas, Melville Sound, Hope Bay, Cockburn Island, Cape Hurd, Parry Sound, Barrow Bay, Hay Island and Cape Croker.

With the men and events of the War of 1812 so near, Bayfield paid similar honor to the British naval officers who had been prominent in the fighting on the lakes. James, Lucas and Yeo Islands honor Sir James Lucas Yeo who was naval commander in chief in the final year of the war. Barrie Island, Bushby Inlet, Boucher Point, Clapperton Island and Channel, Henvey Inlet, Wingfield Point, Worsley Bay, Grant Island and Thompson Point all bring to mind men who were officers in the Royal Navy and served on the Great Lakes between 1812-1814. Nor did he forget his two able assistants, Philip Edward Collins and Alexander Vidal, for we have Philip Edward Island, Collins Inlet and Vidal Island. As for the Bayfield family, there is Henry Island, Wolsey Lake and Bayfield Sound named after the surveyor himself, Elizabeth Bay after his mother and Helen Bay after his only sister. Julia Bay and Point were named after a young lady at Quebec, but as to the Juliet after whom a quiet cove was named we know nothing. Perhaps she was a lady in some other port.

Chapter 9

Along the St. Clair River

And see the rivers how they run
Through woods and meads, in shade and sun,
Sometimes swift—sometimes slow,—
Wave succeeding wave, they go
A various journey to the deep.

—JOHN DYER

THE shores of Lake Huron, gradually approaching each other in long, low, sandy beaches, almost meet where the St. Clair River begins. The International Bridge swings in a great arch over the "Rapids" through which the lake waters rush for a mile before broadening into Sarnia Bay. Thereafter the blue river pursues its way at a more moderate pace for forty miles until it merges with Lake St. Clair in such gradual fashion that it is difficult to say exactly where the river ends and the lake begins.

Since the time, away back in 1679, when the *Griffin* made its way from Lake Erie to Lake Huron through the connecting waterways, men have never ceased to become excited over the beauty of these waters. "Those," wrote Father Hennepin in 1679, "who will one day have the happiness to possess this fertile and pleasant strait, will be very much obliged to those who have shown them the way."

What Hennepin could not foresee was that this river, through which La Salle's ship was plowing the first recorded furrow, would one day be the busiest marine highway in the world and that through it would flow the commerce of half a continent, bringing down the iron and the copper and the grains of the west and carrying in return the coal and the manufactures of the east. Visitors

148

in an earlier day found their chief interest in the primeval setting—
the broad stream shimmering in the sunlight, the marshy areas
where green rushes waved in the breeze, the deep dark forests bordering the banks and extending far inland. Though the forests
have disappeared, much of the original natural beauty remains;
and for the visitor today interest is added by the little towns, the
myriad of summer homes and above all by the constant procession
of great ships moving up and down the river.

The French were the first to explore the St. Clair and the first
to settle along its banks. Early maps show a long line of narrow
ribbonlike farms below Marine City and again on the shores of
Lake St. Clair. The original survey of Moore Township, below
Sarnia on the Canadian side, shows seventy-two typical river-front
farms quite in the fashion of old Quebec, each with a frontage of
about 750 feet and a depth of a little more than a mile. The homes
of the Campeaus, the Gallarneaus, the Babys, the Gerrards and
other French families must once have presented the same appearance of a river-street that the visitor to the north shore of the St.
Lawrence finds today. Old burying grounds on both sides of the
river show many French names on the gravestones, and the little
Roman Catholic churches whose spires or towers rise at intervals
tell the same story of French influence. But there are not many
French families there today.

The earlier years of the nineteenth century saw the arrival on
both shores of people of other types. Michigan Territory, in common with its neighbor states, was drawing its population both from
the older East and from overseas. Men of shrewd business sense
came to the river and saw possibilities of acquiring wealth in lumbering, shipbuilding and trade. Over the river, in the British province of Upper Canada, officers who had fought in the armies of
the Duke of Wellington or in the navy of Lord Nelson were seeking new homes, and some of them found on the St. Clair River the
desired place for their retiring years. Intermingled with the holdings of this semiaristocratic society were the farms of many more
humble people. But few of the descendants of either class are to

be found there today. They have scattered to all parts of the Republic and Dominion.

Louis Jolliet, coming down from the Sault in 1669 with his Iroquois guide, was the first known white man to traverse the St. Clair River and the waters below it. The two Sulpician priest-explorers, Galinée and Dollier de Casson, reversed his course the next year, paddling through the waters between Lake Erie and Lake Huron and on northward to the Sault. La Salle's *Griffin,* its white sails spread to the breeze, worked its way laboriously against the St. Clair current and was finally hauled through the Rapids to the broad expanse of Lake Huron. That was in 1679. Twenty-two years later Antoine de la Mothe Cadillac, former commandant of the French post of Michilimackinac, undertook to found a permanent settlement somewhere on the "streight" connecting Lake Huron with Lake Erie. His party crossed Lake St. Clair and on the north bank of the river below laid the foundations of a great city, Detroit.

Despite Cadillac's apology that "the trade of war is not that of a writer" his description of the country below Lake Huron might well excite the envy of a modern real-estate promoter.

"The sparkling and pellucid water of Lakes Superior, Michigan and Huron," he wrote, "glide away gently and with a moderate current into Lake Erie, into the Ontario or Frontenac, and go at last to mingle in the river St. Lawrence with those of the ocean. The banks are so many vast meadows where the freshness of these beautiful streams keep the grass always green. These same meadows are fringed with long and broad avenues of fruit trees which have never felt the careful hand of the watchful gardener; and fruit trees, young and old, droop under the weight and multitude of their fruit, and bend their branches towards the fertile soil which has produced them. In this soil so fertile, the ambitious vine which has not yet wept under the knife of the industrious vine-dresser, forms a thick roof with its heavy clusters of whatever it twines round, which it often stifles by embracing it too closely."

Nor was this all. Trees "straight as arrows, without knots, and almost without branches except near the top" grew to enormous size and height. Fish were abundant, "fed and laved in sparkling and pellucid waters." "Swans" were so numerous that the rushes among which they were massed might be taken for lilies. Finally he quotes an Indian from whom he had inquired whether game was abundant. "There is so much," was the reply, "that it only moves aside [long enough] to allow the boat to pass."[1]

Those who came later were likewise moved by the beauty of the region and the luxuriance of forest and meadow bordering the stream. Dr. John J. Bigsby, physician with the party surveying the international boundary after the War of 1812, had ample opportunity to see and describe the river as the vessel moved slowly upstream. "As we float over the smooth waters of the St. Clair," he wrote, "having perhaps just escaped from the turbulence of Lake Huron, it is delightful to gaze upon the succession of dwellings, low and roomy, which its western bank presents, embowered in orchards, the children playing under the far-spreading elms, and the cattle grazing in rich meadows."

James B. Brown, a Scottish visitor who came thirty years later, found on the banks of the upper St. Clair "agreeable slopes, finely wooded, and a good deal cultivated to the margin of the clear smoothly flowing river." This was before the dense forests had been so ruthlessly cleared for firewood, leaving some portions of the adjacent country without sufficient supply for the generations that came later.

European visitors were fascinated too by the Indian life along the river. The encampments on the shores, the canoes on the stream, the campfires at night, all increased the romance of a journey on these inland waters.

"Before I went to my rest yesterday evening," wrote Mrs. Anna Jameson in 1837, "I beheld a strange and beautiful scene. The night was coming on, the moon had risen round and full, like an

[1] Michigan Pioneer and Historical Society, *Historical Collections*, XXXIII (Lansing, 1904), 111-112.

enormous globe of fire, we were still in the channel of the river, when to the right I saw a crowd of Indians on a projecting point of land. They were encamping for the night, some hauling up their canoes, some building up their wigwams; there were numerous fires blazing amid the thick foliage, and the dusky figures of the Indians were seen glancing to and fro, and I heard loud laughs and shouts as our huge steamer swept past them. In another moment we turned a point, and all was dark; the whole had vanished like a scene in a melodrama. I rubbed my eyes, and began to think I was already dreaming."[2]

William Cullen Bryant, the American poet, also left a picture of the Indians on the St. Clair as he saw them on his visit to the lakes in 1846. He had been told by one of the settlers that about twenty miles upstream he would find a Chippewa Indian settlement, and in due time this came into view. "Log houses, at the distance of about a quarter of a mile from each other, stood," he wrote, "in a long row beside the river, with scattered trees about them, the largest of the forest, some girdled and leafless, some untouched and green, the smallest trees between them having been cut away. Here and there an Indian woman, in a blue dress and bare-headed, was walking along the road. Two females came down to the bank with paddles, and put off into the river in a birch-bark canoe, the ends of which were carved in the peculiar Indian fashion.

"A little beyond stood a group of boys and girls on the water's edge, the boys in shirts and leggins, silently watching the steamer as it shot by them. Still farther on a group of children of both sexes, seven in number, came running with shrill cries down the bank. The boys in an instant threw off their shirts and leggins, and plunged into the water with shouts, but the girls were in before them, for they wore only a kind of petticoat which they did not take off, but cast themselves into the water at once and slid through the clear water like seals. The little Indian settlement on the edge of

---

[2] Anna Jameson, *Winter Studies and Summer Rambles in Canada.* 2 vols. (New York, 1839), II, 116. Mrs. Jameson visited Upper Canada in 1837 and while there toured Lake Huron, visiting Mackinac and the Sault and returning by Georgian Bay.

the forest extended for several miles along the river, where its banks are highest and best adapted for the purpose of settlement. It ends at last just below the village which bears the name of Port Saranac [sic]."[3]

Settlers were increasing in number when Dr. Bigsby was there in the early 1820's. While encamped on a woody island in the St. Clair one evening he saw a boat land near by on the Canadian shore and paddled over to see the people arriving.

"It was a large boat," he tells us, "laden almost to sinking with a hearty family of five persons (the parents and three children) with all sorts of lumbering chests and rude furnishings, a long gun, tools, axes, hoes, spades, a dog or two, a few poultry, and a barrel or two of flour and pork. This was the true pioneer family.

"While I loitered about them, not unwelcome, for a couple of hours, they landed and arranged their goods, and went to sleep on matting, snug under the fragrant shelter of pine branches. Two days afterwards I found my friends comfortably housed in an oblong log-hut well caulked with clay. For such expeditious building they must have had help from others."[4]

The abundant and cheap land which might be had in the British province was probably the lure which had brought this family over the river, and the ease with which they adapted themselves to their new surroundings suggests that they were no strangers to frontier life. It was an era in which people were on the march westward, and international boundaries counted for little when placed in the balance against good land.

The army and navy people who made new homes below Sarnia gave to their settlements names that recalled their own war experiences—Corunna and Moore and Sombra; Corunna where so gallant a stand was made during the Peninsular War and where Sir John Moore fell and was buried. Charles Wolfe commemo-

---

[3] W. C. Bryant, *Letters of a Traveller; or, Notes of Things in Europe and America* (New York, 1850), 251-252.

[4] John J. Bigsby, *Op. cit.* 94-95.

rated the episode in the one poem by which he is remembered and which uncounted thousands of British and Canadian children must have memorized in their school days:

> "Not a drum was heard, not a funeral note,
> As his corse to the rampart we hurried;
> Not a soldier discharged his farewell shot
> O'er the grave where our hero we buried.

> "Slowly and sadly we laid him down,
> From the field of his fame fresh and gory;
> We carved not a line, and we raised not a stone—
> But we left him alone with his glory."

When Napoleon was a captive on St. Helena after the battle of Waterloo he must often have watched the white sails of the British ships which constantly cruised off the island. The commander of one of those ships, Captain William Wright, lies buried with other members of his family in the little graveyard not far from his old home on the St. Clair. He had retired from the navy in 1833 and, coming to Canada, resided for a time at Amherstburg where his wife died during the cholera outbreak of 1834. He had earlier arranged for the building of a substantial log house on his property on the St. Clair, which he named Oaklands after the old home of his dead wife in far-off St. Helena. On a May day of 1835 the captain, his seven children, his sister and a multitude of household goods brought from England were landed at his very door from the steamer *General Gratiot*. There he resided until his death in 1869 at the age of eighty-four.

The best remembered of these naval settlers and the most picturesque figure was Alexander Thomas Emeric Vidal. He had first made acquaintance with the St. Clair River region when, as a young lieutenant, he was engaged with Henry Wolsey Bayfield in the survey and charting of the Great Lakes. In 1835 he thought of retiring and, having received a grant of 200 acres on the river front, he built himself a house but was scarcely settled when he was recalled to service and did not see the place again for fifteen years.

By this time the original dwelling had so badly decayed that he decided to build anew. This second dwelling has been described as "almost like a castle." Its timbers were massive and heavy, bolted together as securely as the frame of a ship. In the owner's own room the washstand and chest of drawers which he had used when on service were fastened to the wall with stout iron clamps as if to withstand the force of a gale. Much of the furniture was of walnut cut from his own or adjacent farms, but he preferred oak for a coffin which he kept in his bedroom. Ultimately it housed not himself but his brother's widow.

On his retirement from the navy in 1850, Captain Vidal was gazetted vice-admiral. He returned with his family to England in 1862 and died there in the following year. Though peppery in disposition, as was so commonly the case in his profession, he seems to have been on good terms not only with his aristocratic neighbors but also with the immigrant settlers, and no name among the early residents of the Canadian river front is better remembered today than that of Vidal. But probably few sailors who avoid the Vidal Shoals above the Sault have ever heard of the man whose name is thus commemorated.

They were "nice people," these aristocratic English settlers. They preserved their social traditions and brought to the crude society of the time some measure of culture. They helped to erect churches and themselves set an example in churchgoing. They moved among their more humble neighbors as a sort of squirearchy, received appointments to government posts, commanded the local militia and stood rigorously for law and order. But their real life was behind them, in England and in far-off places where they had served their country.

Over the river, in this same period, men whose lives were not in the past but very much in the present were laying the foundations of business enterprises some of which have continued into our own times. Shrewd and calculating, not always scrupulous in their dealings, they had an aggressiveness that matched the difficulties of a new country. The activities of the Ward family at Marine City would alone form a theme for a volume of business history. Samuel Ward, the first of the name, came to the mouth of Belle River in 1819 with his possessions on his back. In the next year he built a little schooner, the *St. Clair,* shaped curiously like a canal boat with full end and rudder "out doors." With this boat Ward peddled all sorts of merchandise among the settlers along the river front. Later, when the Erie Canal was opened, he loaded the schooner at Detroit for New York and took on board two horses to be used in towing it through the canal. At Buffalo the masts were lowered and the craft proceeded through to Troy. There the masts were raised and the strange-looking schooner sailed down the Hudson River to New York. Ward returned with a full cargo, and the story goes that he felt deeply insulted when charged tolls on the canal, contending that he should have been awarded a premium for taking the first lake vessel through to New York.

Samuel Ward was ready to take advantage of any business opportunity that appeared. One of his early ventures at Newport, as Marine City was then known, was to open a tannery, but when this business failed to reach sufficient volume he promptly tore down the building and began making bricks on the same spot. He brought in artisans to meet local needs, and tradition indicates that he bossed the whole community.

Eber Brock Ward, a nephew of Samuel, came in 1832, first as a clerk to his uncle but later as a partner, and it was he, rather than Samuel, who chiefly made the family name so widely known. His portrait was placed in the State Capitol at Lansing in 1920, his career being summarized in the inscription:

Eber Brock Ward
Born December 25, 1811. Died January 2, 1875

Pioneer of Industry
Vessel owner and operator,
Shipbuilder, iron and steel,
Plate glass manufacturer
and Lumberman

In the field of ships and shipping the Wards were keen and determined rivals of Detroit and Lake Erie interests. Vessel after vessel came off the stocks at Marine City, sailing ships first of all but later steamboats, so that the name of the Wards became known all over the lakes. The first steamboat was built in 1839 and given the name *Huron*. This was originally Samuel Ward's venture but, unfortunately, when he had the hull completed he was without money to buy the engines. At this point Eber B. Ward showed his enterprise, for he secured the money, installed the engines and soon had the *Huron* paying dividends. At least thirty steamers were built and owned by Samuel and Eber B. Ward. If they lost one, they promptly built another; if they saw an opening anywhere for a steamboat they at once supplied it. There was a second Eber Ward, a cousin, who was almost equally active in the same field, building, buying and operating boats, and it is difficult at times to distinguish between the activities of the two men bearing the same name.

The era of the Wards saw flush times on the lakes. The close of the War of 1812 marked the beginning of the great movement of people into the West. Eighty percent of the public land of the United States was waiting to be occupied. The half-century which followed saw one of the greatest migrations in the history of the Republic, tens of thousands of people cutting themselves loose from old associations in the eastern states and beginning a trek to the West.

Several routes led to the new regions. Homeseekers from New England and the Middle States came through New York state to Buffalo and there took boat, or they journeyed through western Pennsylvania and down the Ohio River. Each route received its share of the traffic, but that section of the migration which came to Buffalo taxed the carrying capacity of the lake fleet year after year. In 1835 entries at the port of Buffalo numbered 720 steamboats as well as 920 brigs, schooners and sloops. In that year Henry R. Schoolcraft, Indian agent at Mackinac, could write:

"The Great Lakes can no longer be regarded as solitary seas.

The eastern world seems to be alive, and roused up to the value of the West. Every vessel, every steamboat, brings up persons of all classes, whose countenances the desire of acquisition, or some other motive, has rendered sharp, or imparted a fresh glow of hope to their eyes. . . . Sitting on my piazza, in front of which the great stream of ships and commerce passes, it is a spectacle at once novel, and calculated to inspire high anticipations of the future glory of the Mississippi Valley."

The Panic of 1837 gave temporary check to the exodus westward, as Mrs. Anna Jameson noted when she went to Mackinac in that year, but the movement of people and their belongings was soon again in full swing. The Ward fleet in the forties included the *Oregon* which on trip after trip carried 800 passengers from Buffalo to Chicago, the fare being eighteen dollars for deck passengers. For those who desired it there was not only comfort but even luxury. Schoolcraft, who often journeyed between Mackinac and Detroit, noted as early as 1837 that the new boats were so greatly improved that they resembled a "floating parlor." Americans were soon traveling not only in search of new homes but also for pleasure and recreation. The trip up Lake Huron to Mackinac became one of the most popular, as it is today, and the steamboats provided comfortable cabins, gargantuan meals and even bands which played for the dancers. The insidious polka was already beginning to displace the old square dances.

On an August evening in 1852 the side-wheeler *Atlantic,* built by the Wards only three years before, was proceeding on its course from Buffalo to Detroit. More than 500 passengers were aboard, many of them immigrants from overseas headed for Wisconsin, who, though they had crossed the Atlantic, must still have been amazed at this great fresh-water sea upon which they now traveled. The band had provided a concert during the supper hour and the floor of the main saloon had been cleared for dancing. The light of oil lamps was reflected in the polished rosewood and mahogany of walls and furniture. Those who were not dancing rested in the heavy plush chairs or strolled about the decks. The lake was calm, though there was a little haze.

This was the setting for one of the worst marine tragedies that the lakes have known. Suddenly, without warning, the *Atlantic* was rammed just forward of the port paddle wheel by the steamer *Ogdensburg,* bound for Port Colborne. The *Atlantic* had received a death thrust, the damage extending so far below the water line that the fires were quickly extinguished. Frenzied men and women jumped overboard without waiting to put on life preservers. One lifeboat being lowered too hastily pitched all its occupants into the water. The captain of the vessel was injured and unable to take control of the situation. The immigrants, whose passage money bought them nothing but the right to sleep on the main deck, had less chance of life than the cabin passengers. Though the *Ogdensburg* soon came alongside and rescued those who were on the sinking ship or clinging to wreckage in the water, there was a loss of more than a hundred lives.

The very names given by the Wards to some of their boats indicate what was uppermost in the public mind at the time. Steamboat companies had not yet reached the stage where they named all their vessels after officers and directors. *Atlantic* and *Pacific, Saginaw, Cleveland* and *Keweenaw, Saint Paul* and *Minneapolis, Huron* and *Traveller* are all names that relate to the migrations of the time, and these names were painted in bold letters on the bows of Ward ships.

Whenever and wherever the trade called for it, boats were built and quickly put into service. Four were added in 1851 alone. The *Ruby* was built by the cousin, Eber Ward; the *Arctic, Pearl* and *Caspian* by Samuel and Eber Brock Ward. The *Caspian* had a short life, being wrecked while entering the harbor at Cleveland in 1852. The *Arctic* was wrecked on Lake Superior in 1860, the *Ruby* was broken up at Saginaw in 1865 and the *Pearl* ended her days in 1869. The *Pacific,* which came out as early as 1847, was one of the finest of the earlier boats built by the Wards at Marine City and one of the fastest that they ever owned. Others whose names are recorded were the *Forester, Planet, Forest Queen, Gazelle* and *Sea Bird.* The family name was given to the *Sam Ward*, the *Susan Ward* and the *Eber Ward*.[5]

Three little tributary rivers join the St. Clair along its Michigan shore, and settlements arose at the mouth of each. On Black River was Desmond, which today is Port Huron. On the Pine River was Palmer, now St. Clair, and on La Belle Rivière was Newport, later given the name Marine City. Save for the fact that the shipbuilding industry was so dominated by one family at Marine City, the others were comparable rivals. All about were forests which provided the finest of timber for the frames and planking of wooden vessels. Each place had its own quiet little river where the shipyards were set up and where the completed hulls might be launched in safety. And each had men alert to the business possibilities of the times.

Present-day St. Clair, which once was Palmer, can trace its beginnings to the year 1764, when Captain Patrick Sinclair erected a small fort just south of Pine River. The buildings included barracks for sailors and for soldiers, two blockhouses, and a wharf for drawing out and careening vessels. Around all was a stockade.

Sinclair who is today chiefly remembered as the builder of the fort on Mackinac Island, was then connected with the British Naval Department of the Lakes, a post of considerable importance and responsibility since upon him fell the maintenance and provisioning of all vessels used in the government service and the use of these vessels by the fur traders and merchants. There was nothing larger on the upper lakes at that time than a small schooner, but there were numerous sloops and bateaux and, of course, canoes by the hundreds. The bateau, a long boat worked with oars, was widely used in transporting both freight and passengers and, while more laborious to navigate than the canoe, could take a heavy load and stand a greater degree of rough weather.

---

[5] Eber Brock Ward's activities in shipbuilding, lumbering and manufacturing continued until his death in 1875. His cousin, Eber Ward, was caught in the financial crash of 1873 and lost all his steamboat holdings.

Captain Sinclair's little post on Pine River was well placed for both defense and trade. On the whole he got along well with the Indians, many of whom were still uneasy following the Pontiac uprising when he settled among them. The buildings which he erected had been paid for mainly from his own purse, and to protect himself he obtained from the Chippewa Indians a deed to a tract two and a half miles square fronting on the river. The deed recited as consideration "the love and regard we bear for our friend Lieut. Patrick Sinclair and for the love and esteem the whole of our said nation has for him for the many charitable acts he has done us, our wives and our children." That he was held in equal esteem by his own people is shown by the inscription appearing on a silver bowl which was presented to him by the merchants in the Indian country, testifying their gratitude for the encouragement received from him on all occasions.

Sinclair's possession of property acquired directly from the Indians caused him much legal trouble in later years, since the Royal Proclamation of October 1763 had expressly prohibited such private transactions with the red men. In 1788 his rights to the land were sold by public auction, the buyers being a Detroit firm of merchants and traders. These people later secured a new deed from the Chippewa chiefs, purporting to be a confirmation of the previous transfer but actually conveying an area ten miles along the St. Clair River front by four miles in depth. The government declined to recognize this deal, but the Detroit firm managed to come out of the transaction with five thousand acres in their possession.

While the property at Pine River was in his hands Captain Sinclair made extensive improvements, clearing, setting out orchard trees and adding to the buildings. It has been pointed out that the forest of pine which once stood on Sinclair's property marked, on the east side of Michigan, the southern line of the great pine area of the lower peninsula.[6]

A list compiled by W. L. Jenks, historian of Port Huron, shows

---

[6] W. L. Jenks, "Patrick Sinclair, Builder of Fort Mackinac," *Michigan Historical Collections,* XXXIX (Lansing, 1915), 61-85.

that more than 180 vessels of various types were built at that place in the period between 1838 and 1908. More than half of these were sailing vessels, schooners, sloops, barks, brigs and scow schooners. Steamers numbered more than forty and the remainder were scows, tugs and barges. The years immediately following the Civil War appear to have been the heyday for Port Huron shipbuilders and 1867 the top year of all. In the middle eighties the demand for sailing ships ceased, and after 1890 only steamers were constructed. Several fairly large vessels were turned out at Port Huron in this later period, among them the *Henry Steinbrenner*, the *John B. Cowle* and the *F. B. Squire*, all three of which were of more than 4,000 tons. The *Steinbrenner* was sunk in a collision with the steamer *Berwind* on December 6, 1909, and the *Cowle* suffered like fate in a collision with the *Isaac M. Scott* on July 12 of the same year. The *Scott* was one of the eight vessels lost on Lake Huron in the great storm of 1913.

Many of the sailing ships which left the Port Huron yards were lost in autumn storms. "Capsized on Lake Huron," "Abandoned on Lake Michigan," "Sunk in Lake Erie," are typical obituaries for perhaps half the number. Those built in later years often became tow barges, hauled two and three in a line behind a puffing, snorting lumber carrier, scarcely longer than any one of its consorts. The hulls of some of these old boats lay for decades in harbors about the lakes, resting places for flocks of gulls, until they were finally hauled out to deep water and sunk. Two of those that were built at Port Huron went down not in fresh but in salt water. The schooner *Harvey H. Brown*, built in 1871, was chartered for ocean service in 1898 and was wrecked off the coast of Maine. The *Homer Alverson*, of 760 tons, also went to the seaboard and sank in the St. Lawrence River in 1898. The *Robert Burns*, built at Port Huron in 1848, was said to have been the last full-rigged brig on the lakes when she was lost in the Straits of Mackinac with ten lives in 1869.

The increasing use of automobiles and trucks has driven from the river the boats which in the past provided a local service for passengers and freight. For more than a hundred years they were an interesting section of the marine panorama, and dwellers by the river always had their favorites whose speed and appearance they would defend against all comers. The officers were well known, for they were seen every day, and the crews were largely drawn from the towns and the farms along the river front. There was keen competition for this trade, and the Wards at Marine City fought more than one tough battle with Detroit interests to hold what they regarded as their particular business.

The list of boats used solely for river traffic, if compiled, would be lengthy. As early as 1831 the *General Gratiot* was running between Detroit and Port Huron, to be followed in the next few years by the *General Brady,* the *Huron* and the *Erie.* Captain John Clark was an early commander of the *General Gratiot* and all river boats stopped at his dock at East China, not far from St. Clair, to take on wood. He had a 200-acre farm near by where he kept a large number of pigs, for which the waste from the steamer table provided no small amount of food. It is one of the traditions of the river that when the *General Gratiot* blew her whistle the pigs would rush to the wharf but that they paid no attention to the whistles of other boats.

Crocket McElroy, of St. Clair, who achieved much distinction in his time both in business and in public affairs, was responsible for placing on the river two of the best-remembered passenger boats, the *Mary* and the *Unique.* In its design the *Mary* was a departure from previous models, having the lines of a smart yacht and achieving a speed record which she maintained over all rivals for twelve years. It was a delight to see her go along, with her white hull always freshly painted, overtaking and passing everything in sight. To this day old residents speak of this little boat with a feeling as for an old friend.

McElroy was so proud of his achievement in designing and building the *Mary* that he determined to build an even faster boat. The resulting product was the *Unique,* which appeared first in

1894. The builder had achieved speed, for this boat was able to pass the *Mary,* but the effect had been to weaken the construction and she was not the success that had been anticipated. After a few years on the river the *Unique* was sold and went first to Ogdensburg and later to Philadelphia, finally becoming the property of a wealthy sportsman who transformed the former river boat into a palatial yacht.

On the Canadian side the two boats which served the local trade longest were the *J. C. Clarke,* built in 1864, and the *Hiawatha,* which came on the river in 1874. The *Hiawatha* remained in the river trade as a passenger boat or ferry for fifty years. She then went to the north shore of Lake Huron, but after a few years' service was beached. The *J. C. Clarke* continued in service until 1905, when she burned at her dock at Port Huron. The cylinder head of the old engine was long in view above the surface at the mouth of Black River.

The river trade greatly increased in the summer months when picnics brought passengers by the tens of thousands. It was a gay sight on a summer morning to see one of these loaded steamers, its flags flying, a band playing and children lining the rails as the boat pulled out from the dock. Many a person of middle age must have pleasant memories recalled when the names of these old river boats appear. None who knew them will ever forget the *Idlewild,* the *Darius C. Cole,* the *Greyhound* or the *Tashmoo.* This last steamer ended its days on a June evening in 1936 when, with more than 1,400 people aboard, it struck a rock in the Detroit River. The officers headed the boat for the Canadian shore where it sank in twenty-five feet of water but no lives were lost. The big pilothouse of the *Tashmoo* stands far inland today on the grounds of a summer resort, a curious object in the midst of trees and grassy lawns.

At intervals along the river on both banks there may still be seen the remains of the old wood docks from which, before the introduction of coal as fuel, the boats drew their supplies. Not much is left of them today—only a few oak piles sticking up above the surface of the water. All the planking has long since disappeared but the piles, while rotten above the surface, are as sound below as ever, despite the fact that seventy-five years and more may have passed since they were first driven into the river bed.

The pioneer farmers found a welcome source of revenue in selling the wood which came from the clearing of their farms. During the winter months the cordwood was teamed to the docks and piled ready for the opening of the next season of navigation. Frequently there was a store near by, the proprietor of which combined steamboat fueling with his general trade. The farmer received about a dollar a cord for his wood, payment being in groceries and other needed supplies. The steamers were charged from two to three dollars a cord, depending upon the quality. It was the engineer's duty to see that he received full measure and that the quality was that for which he was paying. Since the storekeeper usually had some second-rate fuel which he was anxious to see vanish from his docks, there were many battles of wit and strategy between the buyer and the seller.

There were two objectionable features in the use of wood fuel, the time required for "wooding up" and the considerable space which the fuel occupied. While delay was less thought of then than now, it was vexatious for both officers and passengers to be held up for hours while the deck hands trundled aboard the necessary supply. When coal began to replace wood on some of the lake boats, wood scows made their appearance. These clumsy-looking craft, capable of carrying from one to two hundred cords, moved about under their own steam. While it was not usually practicable to attach them to the sidewheelers, for fear of injuring the paddle wheels, they solved a problem for the propellers. A steamboat would blow for wood and one of the scows would immediately set out, come alongside and make fast. The wood would then be passed into the gangways as rapidly as possible while the vessel continued on its way. When the required supply was aboard the scow would cut loose and return to its base. These early wood dealers had anticipated a very modern system by which airplanes have been refueled while still in the air.

The summer of 1832 was one of terror for the people **on the St.** Clair. Cholera was brought to the region and left behind a trail of broken homes, scattered families and a fear of the disease that was to linger in men's minds for the rest of their lives.

It was the year of the Indian uprising in northern Illinois under the famous chieftain, Black Hawk. A tall, ungainly man, homely in feature, Abraham Lincoln by name, volunteered for service and was elected captain of his company, though he afterward said that the only enemies he encountered were the voracious mosquitoes. But the government at Washington viewed the frontier uprising seriously and promptly sent a force of 850 men under General Winfield Scott through from New York to Buffalo, from which place they were to be taken by boat to Fort Dearborn at the mouth of the Chicago River. Not more than one-quarter of that force ever arrived fit for service.

Four boats were chartered at Buffalo for the expedition, the *Henry Clay* and *Sheldon Thompson* to carry troops and the *William Penn* and *Superior* chiefly to transport the supplies. The *Henry Clay* was badly overcrowded when it left Buffalo on July 3, and many men had to remain on deck during both the heat of the day and the chill and dampness of the night. On July 4 a soldier became sick, and when the vessel arrived at Detroit that evening, instead of tying up at the dock, it was ordered to anchor just below Hog Island (now Belle Isle). The sick man died during the night and another became ill.

General Scott, deeply alarmed, decided to proceed at once and land any sick on Bois Blanc Island near Mackinac. But the number of those stricken aboard the *Henry Clay* so multiplied that the vessel got no farther than Fort Gratiot at the mouth of the St. Clair River. There, on a bluff just below the fort, the troops were disembarked, the sick being carried ashore in the midst of a drenching rain. A large barn belonging to the fort was turned into a hospital where the army surgeons did their best to give care. But deaths averaged nine a day and such terror was created that there were wholesale desertions, the force of 270 being soon reduced to sixty-eight. Captain Norton, of the *Henry Clay,* had meanwhile turned his boat about and headed for Lake Erie. Six of his crew were sick, and when he put in at Cleveland one was dead and another at the point of death.

The *Sheldon Thompson,* with General Scott on board, halted at Fort Gratiot only long enough to disembark two companies of artillery in order to relieve the overcrowding. These troops were later picked up by the *William Penn.* When the general's vessel arrived at Mackinac one clear case of cholera had appeared and four other men were sick. Three of those who were taken ashore died, and there was also one death among the garrison of the island. But after leaving Mackinac and heading for Fort Dearborn the *Sheldon Thompson* became a veritable plague ship, seventy-seven cases of cholera developing and twenty-one soldiers dying of the disease.

"We have got at last to our place of destination," wrote one of the officers, "but in what a condition! We have traveled six hundred miles in a steamboat crowded almost to suffocation and the Asiatic cholera raging among us. The scenes on board the boat are not to be described. Men died in six hours after being in perfect health. The steerage was crowded with the dying and new cases were appearing on the deck . . . the boat became a moving pestilence, every soldier who was well became a nurse for the sick."[7]

The upper St. Clair received a further accession of cholera victims on July 10 when the officers and men of the Niagara garrison were landed from the *William Penn* at a point thirteen miles below Fort Gratiot. This detachment had been in Detroit for a week, and while there two men who had been aboard the *Henry Clay* had died and five other cases had developed. During the next three weeks there were forty-seven sick among the troops from Niagara and twenty-one deaths.

The little garrison cemetery at Fort Gratiot received more dead

---

[7] J. S. Chambers, *The Conquest of Cholera, America's Greatest Scourge* (New York, 1938), 94-95. This work gives the best account of the several outbreaks of cholera in America during the nineteenth century.

during that summer of 1832 than during all its previous history. When, in later days, the fort ceased to exist and a military plot was established elsewhere, little stones bearing such epitaphs as "A Gunner" or "A Soldier" were mute reminders of the dread cholera era. But other graveyards held their dead also, for the terrorized soldiers deserting from Fort Gratiot carried the disease far and wide. When news of the outbreak spread, any man in uniform was shunned as a possible carrier of plague. Many deserters died by the roadside or in the woods. Relatives in states far distant heard nothing of their deaths. They were merely reported "missing."

If a choice were required of that period on the river of the greatest marine interest, the writer's selection would be the 1880's. Perhaps there is a measure of nostalgia in the choice, proceeding from the memory of boyhood holidays which were chiefly employed in watching the boats go by. But it was a decade in which there was a mingling as never before of the old and the oncoming new. Much of the old was soon to pass away, not a little of it unrecorded and forgotten save in the memories of men who had had a part in it and to many of whom the transition period seemed almost tragedy.

There were probably as many ships on the river in the eighties as there are today, but then there was a far greater variety. Almost everything that the lakes have known, apart from the more recent types of bulk carriers, was to be seen passing up and down. Most numerous were the lumber barges and their tows coming down from Saginaw Bay and upper Lake Huron, their decks piled high with the yellowish pine. Around a bend in the river would appear first of all a steamboat and then one, two, three, and sometimes four schooners, low in the water, all following in dutiful order. Between the masts there was often a line with the crew's washing fluttering in the breeze, bright red shirts looking like flags. At the stern the wheelsman watched from his outdoor post, sheltered from the sun by a little awning or cover. Not one of those lumber carriers could be found if the lakes were searched today.

Sometimes it was a tug which had picked up loaded schooners at the foot of Lake Huron and, stringing them one behind another, was taking them through to Lake Erie. There they would cut loose and head for some port on the south shore. Half a mile away the tug looked so tiny that it was hard to believe it had the power to haul its consorts. But these tugs had powerful engines and their owners gave them good masculine names, *Samson, Gladiator, Champion,* in keeping with their hauling power. Once arrived on Lake Erie, the tugs assembled waiting schooners bound for Lake Huron and with greater effort pulled them against the river current.

How these ships, strung out one behind another, made their way through the tortuous course of the lower St. Clair arouses wonder today. It is doubtful if a more dangerous spot exists between Lake Huron and Lake Erie than at Southeast Bend, and boats passing it today do so with the utmost caution. It is true that the earlier vessels were of less draught and could go freely where the big bulk freighters of today would quickly go aground, but at that the skill of the earlier pilots in bringing their boats safely through such a channel raises wonder.

The wooden propellers were the largest boats seen on the river, many of them pulling a big barge. They were stanch-looking craft. Built of oak and often reinforced by an arch truss, they were capable of withstanding all ordinary gales. The bird-cage type of wheelhouse common on the passenger boats and on some of the lumber hookers was usually discarded for a square-built superstructure atop of which the master took his place when passing through rivers. Commonly there was one stack, but sometimes two abreast or in line. Many of them carried sail which was hoisted on the open lake but seldom seen on the river.

Dwellers along the St. Clair during the eighties were already familiar with the new types of lake boats that were coming from the shipyards. They had seen the *V. H. Ketchum* which, when launched at Marine City in 1874, was, because of its length, in advance of the dock facilities in many ports. They had seen the *Onoko,* the first metal bulk freighter on the lakes, and the *Spokane,* the first steel freighter. The Anchor Line trio of passenger ships, *India, Japan* and *China,* with their bird-cage pilothouses, were already long familiar and admired for their graceful lines. These vessels were the product of Edwin Townsend Evans, who back in 1862 had built the *Merchant,* the first iron freighter that ever sailed the lakes.

Of river boats there was the greatest variety. Small schooners built locally carried lumber and hay and salt, and somehow managed to make their way against wind and current. If the wind was adverse they might anchor in the river for days. When food ran out a small boat would put ashore and replenish the supply at some farmhouse. The "shoepack" was a curious type, with engines and wheelhouse in the after end and the whole forward portion of the vessel clear except for a stumpy mast and a boom for handling cargo. Cordwood, hay, lumber, gravel—all were acceptable to these clumsy-looking craft.

When coal came into general use a new trade developed, small steamboats carrying supplies to the many fueling docks along the Detroit and St. Clair Rivers. Some owners who were engaged in this trade had two vessels with but one crew. When one boat reached the unloading dock the crew was immediately shifted to the other light outgoing vessel and away they went. As Eugene Herman of *The Great Lakes News* remembers, "there wasn't much painting to do but with heavy weather the pumps were kept pretty busy." The last of these independent coal traders disappeared in 1942 when the Pringle Barge Line was absorbed by the Columbia Transportation Company. The Pringle Line dated well back to the era of schooners and lumber hookers.[8]

Rafting was still common in the eighties but has long since ceased and will never be seen again, for the day of exploiting the great forests has passed. Hauled by one or more tugs, the huge mass of logs moved slowly downstream, appearing from the shore like a brown island under way. Steamers avoided it and watched with care for stray floating logs that might injure propeller blades or the paddles of the sidewheelers. When moving at night a raft was

---

[8] *The Great Lakes News,* January, 1943, 3.

a particularly dangerous object to encounter but masters were watchful and took no chances. Occasionally a raft would become broken up and the shores of the river would be littered with logs until men came and gathered them together again.

Far down on the St. Clair, at the "Flats," wealthy Detroiters and others had found a holidaying place where fish and ducks abounded in their season and where relaxation might be found from the cares of business. The "Venice of America" was arising, for here many of the summer homes were built over the water on piles, so that the family and visitors came and went by boat. Near the St. Clair Canal, giving entrance to the lake below, builders indulged in quaint architectural conceits, windmills and towers of variegated design giving the oddest appearance to this low swampy area through which the river lazily wound its way. It was an era when lumber was cheap and the fret saw busy as one may still see when journeying by these summer hotels and cottages built long ago. Hotel hosts were known far and wide, particularly Joe Bedore, with his quaint ways and his quaint sayings. Mrs. Hulda T. Hollands, Michigan poetess, sketched him in words in her little poem "Joe Bedore's Invitation":

> "Hello! my friends. An' how you find yourself?
> All right? Dat's good. You ax what fetch me here?
> I come for feed. My place eez full o' folks,
> Dem ceety folks, what feesh dis time o' year.
> Dey ketch much feesh? Don't ax me dat, my friend.
> Dat's not my beeziness to spile de fun.
> Come on de Flats and sateesfy yourself,
> I let you take my fishpole an' my gun.
> You say nothing—I send my boy wid you—
> He take my scow an' punt you troo de marsh.
> He's good for dat. He ketch you lot o' feesh—
> Nobody knows—jes give him leetle cash.
> Folks feesh dat way? Don't ax me dat, my friend.
> Come on de Flats an' stay all night wid me.
> You hear de bull frog croak, de mud hen sing,
> You bring home plenty feesh. Come up an' see."

Not all the marine tragedies are on the open lakes; the river too has had its share. Through the years there is a long record of ships lost on the St. Clair by collision or by burning. Old residents know where rest the hulls of early sailing ships which were never salvaged. Frames of old tugs lie under the water about the remaining piles of early wood docks and fishermen curse them for the nuisance they are in catching on the baited hook. Timbers taken from old wrecks have gone into farm buildings, and the figurehead of a woman which once graced a schooner's bow today functions in quite another way below Courtright; the woman's hand now holds a rural mailbox.

Fire was one of the dreaded fates of the wooden boats. Despite all the watchfulness that was exercised, it is surprising how many ships were wiped off the marine register in this way. Many were burned at their docks or during the winter when they were tied up without a crew aboard. At the time wooden boats were being displaced, owners who had sufficient insurance may have given a sigh of relief when the flames consumed a worn-out oldtimer.

In all its history the St. Clair probably had no more spectacular fire than that which destroyed the *William H. Wolf* just opposite Marine City in the early morning hours of October 20, 1921. The *Wolf,* when built at Milwaukee in 1887, was the largest ore carrier on the lakes, and it is a tribute to her builders that she was still doing business thirty-three years later. She was 308 feet long and could carry about 3,000 tons.

During September the *Wolf* had been in trouble on Lake Superior, springing a leak while carrying a load of pulpwood and sinking in twenty-two feet of water near the entrance to Keweenaw Waterway. She was raised without much difficulty and was able to deliver her cargo of pulpwood at Port Huron. She then headed down the river in order to go into dry dock at one of the ports below. Opposite Marine City her crew discovered fire in the fore part of the ship. The wind was from the southwest and the vessel being headed into it, the flames spread rapidly. Captain J. P. Hanson decided to beach the boat immediately but, finding that there was another vessel unloading at the point where the *Wolf* would go aground, he promptly headed southeast for the foot of Fawn Island which lies just below the town.

In the forward part of the boat, where the flames were raging, were the captain, the mate and a wheelsman. The mate, said a report on the fire, "went in forward but never came back" and when halfway across the river the wheelsman was also missing, having probably jumped overboard to save his life. With flames and smoke all about him, the captain reached in through the pilothouse window to steer the boat. He was unable to keep it headed on the island and it beached instead on the Canadian shore, the stern in forty feet of water. There it was completely destroyed. The men on the after part of the ship were got off without much difficulty, but when help finally came to Captain Hanson he was clinging to the anchor chains seeking escape from the flames.

The small boys along the river all have the ambition to "go deckin' "—and many of them do. The St. Clair has been and still is a nursery for sailors. Boys amuse themselves by tossing and coiling a line, one of the first things that a sailor must learn. They do it as boys elsewhere practice throwing a lariat. The names of the boats and their qualities are known to every lad on the water front.

Age has this interest as well as youth. The homes of hundreds of lake sailors are in these towns and villages on the river. There they spend the winters between the sailing seasons and to these places many lake captains eventually retire. From the stoops of comfortable bungalows and cottages they look out upon the river and from time to time receive a whistle signal of greeting from some old friend or from younger men who have stepped up to their former commands. Their active life is in the past but their interest in the ever-changing present seldom lessens.

A big freighter swings downstream by St. Clair. Its whistle sounds to any upbound vessel, but it adds another blast of its own, three longs and two shorts or perhaps longs and shorts alternated. Someone in St. Clair hears that signal and knows what it means.

Though to the stranger the tone and key of all blasts may seem alike, it is not so to those who have relatives or close friends on the lakes. They know the whistle that means so much to them and in the middle of the night will be awakened by it though a score of others may have sounded within the hour.

On the water front of Marine City or in the little river park at St. Clair a girl or a mother looks up the river. There is the expected boat. The big carrier swings in as close to shore as possible, and messages are shouted from ship to shore and from shore to ship. There is little time, less than a minute, before the boat is by, and then only the wave of a hand can transmit the heart's message.

Chapter 10

Among Lake Huron's Myriad Islands

Here, where the surfs of the great lake trample,
Thundering time-worn caverns through,
Beating on rock-coasts aged and ample;
Reareth the Manitou's mist-walled temple,
Floored with forest and roofed with blue.

— WILFRED CAMPBELL

LAKE HURON stands first among the Great Lakes in the number of the islands fringing its shores. "Among the thirty thousand islands" is a common description of the waters on the eastern side of Georgian Bay, but no one knows, or perhaps can know, just how many islands there actually are in that area. In a period of low water on the lakes submerged rocks or shoals appear above the surface and if not too inhospitable quickly begin to develop some vegetation. A few years later they may be again beneath the waves. The shore is so fringed with islands and islets that the actual coast line is often completely concealed from view.

The north shore of Lake Huron has the same physical feature. The maze of islands extends out from the mainland for miles, masses of rock whose geological history takes us back to the era in which the molten globe was first changing to a solid state. Through this region there were originally lofty mountain ranges, thrust up by great internal forces, but ages beyond computation have worn them down to the hills and tablelands of today.

In addition to the number, Lake Huron is outstanding also for the size of some of its islands. Even Isle Royale in Lake Superior is scarcely more than one-third the area of Manitoulin, while stretching westward and northwestward from the latter are Cockburn,

Drummond and St. Joseph Islands, all large in area. In the Straits of Mackinac is Bois Blanc Island and in the north channel are La Cloche and Barrie, each of which would be a prominent feature were it set down in any one of the other lakes. The presence of these numerous islands greatly increases the dangers of navigation and hundreds of vessels have come to their end by striking on rocky shores and ledges. But there has been economic value also, for the countless channels are the breeding grounds for the fish which from earliest times have been caught in immense quantities in these waters.

When President Franklin D. Roosevelt spent a week during the summer of 1943 fishing on Manitoulin Island in Lake Huron, thousands of Americans, and some Canadians too, probably became aware for the first time that this is the largest fresh-water island in the world. Physically it is also one of the most curious islands in the Great Lakes, the deep indentations in its shores from north and south almost meeting in certain places, so that early explorers sometimes thought that it was a succession of islands instead of one long body of land. It stretches in a generally east and west direction for nearly one hundred miles, varying in width from two to forty miles. Its inland lakes number more than one hundred, the largest with an eighty-mile shore line, so that the land area is greatly reduced. The whole formation indicates tremendous convulsions of nature at some remote period of geological evolution.

Manitoulin Island is the legendary home of the Great Manitou of the tribes which inhabited the region in the seventeenth century. Though the Indian customarily had many manitous or spirits associated in his mind with nature and its forces, some of them particular as in a rock or a tree, there was a vague conception emerging among some tribes of a spirit superior to all others, even above the manitou of the thunder or of the sun. That he should dwell apart in a region of his own followed naturally and what more suitable home could there be than an island?

To those who passed by it in earlier days there did seem to be a mystery about the place. Dr. John Bigsby, in the 1820's, remarked on its rugged and precipitous scenery, "looking from a distance like a succession of table lands." He was struck also by the swift dip from land to deep water along the north side and speaks of a place where a submerged wall of this kind exists: "Two miles out . . . in the lake there is bottom at six feet, but move one yard northerly and you have a depth of 138 feet, with a muddy bottom."

Many visitors in our own time have spoken of the mystery which seems to hang over the island and of a strange sense of loneliness when on its shore, with a desire to get away; yet no sooner is it left behind than there is an equal longing to return. The spell of Manitoulin draws those who have once been there to come again and again.

The recorded history of the island goes back to the beginnings of French enterprise in America. Though Champlain probably never visited it, he must have learned of it when he was with the Huron Indians in 1615. Etienne Brulé, pioneer *voyageur* and *coureur de bois,* was the first white man to journey by its rocky shores, and every other explorer or missionary who followed in his track must have seen the long irregular coast line with its deep indentations. This was the home of the Ottawa Indians, those shrewd traders who kept aloof from the internecine strife of Huron and Iroquois and in time came to dominate the aboriginal fur markets.

The two Jesuit fathers, Isaac Jogues and Charles Raymbault, passed by the island when they journeyed along the north shore in the fall of 1641 on their way to Sault Ste. Marie, and other missionaries may have landed on the island for brief periods. When the Huron country was devastated by the Iroquois in 1649 a portion of the scattered nation fled to Manitoulin and the Jesuits at first contemplated re-establishing their work on the island. There would have been distinct advantages in such a move. The situation would be closer to the Georgian Bay terminus of the Ottawa River route, it would give ready access to numerous Algonquin tribes living on the north shore and the fishing would go far to meet the needs of food. But in the end Christian Island became the mission center for the Huron who had survived and had not fled to distant regions.

Other Indian tribes later occupied the island, and when the nineteenth century dawned it had a population of Ojibwa, Ottawa and others whose welfare was a matter of concern to the British administration. French and British policies with regard to the Indians were in sharp contrast. The French, in their period of rule, left the Indian to choose his own place of abode and live his life much as before their advent. In this way he was of most value in the fur trade. British policy, on the contrary, was paternal in nature and brought restrictions to bear upon the free and independent aboriginal life. British officials, trained to thoughts of method and order, did not see why the Indians should not be made to live in restricted areas and encouraged to become tillers of the soil. The Jesuits in the seventeenth century appear to have had a similar idea and doubtless British policy was supported by Protestant missionary societies which could see greater opportunities for their work if the Indians were discouraged from roaming about.

British policy was influenced also by the desire to retain the close allegiance of as many Indians as possible and to bring them within the sphere of British rule and control. This was the reason for the distribution of presents, a practice antedating the Revolutionary War. How widespread was the distribution may be seen in the profusion of medals, armlets and other adornments which appear in early pictures of Indians. The United States took over the practice after independence had been achieved, and at Mackinac and other places great numbers assembled to receive the government's bounty. In similar fashion presents were given out in Canada at Walpole Island in Lake St. Clair, at Sarnia on the River St. Clair and at Manitoulin Island.

Some Indians attended the gatherings in both countries, always protesting their loyalty. But the British officials finally announced that only those actually living in Canada would be recognized, and this aboriginal "racket" was checked. Reverend Frederick O'Meara, a Church of England missionary on Manitoulin Island, has recorded that prior to 1844 the number coming to that center for the annual distribution varied from three to nearly six thousand but that in 1844, which was the first time restriction had been applied, only 1,878 Indians appeared. He calculated from this that the total population on the north shore of Lake Huron and adjacent parts of Lake Superior was about two thousand.[1]

The Indians who attended these gatherings were sharply critical of any attempt to reduce the volume or value of the gifts they received, and those who attended on both sides of the line did not hesitate to point out contrasts in national generosity. Henry R. Schoolcraft tells of a Chippewa chief who visited him at Mackinac in August 1837 complaining of the meager supplies he had just received at Manitoulin.

"My father," he said, "I wish to warm myself by your fire. I have tried to warm myself by the British fire, but I could not, although I sat close by. They put on green poplar which would throw out no heat. This is the place where hard wood grows and I expect to be warmed by the heat."

Schoolcraft, experienced in the wiles of his Indian charges, was not taken in by the figures of speech. In the previous year, at the consummation of the treaty of 1836, a most generous distribution of presents had been made at Mackinac, the number of Indians attending on this occasion being greater than the island had ever before known. The Chippewa chief had probably participated in this bounty and hoped to do so again.[2]

Mrs. Anna Jameson, on her tour of the lakes, arrived on Manitoulin Island just a few hours too late to witness the distribution of presents of which Schoolcraft's Chippewa chief had complained, but she was present at the council which followed and saw the

---

[1] F. A. O'Meara, *Report of a Mission to the Ottahwahs and Ojibwas on Lake Huron* (London, 1846), 20-21. Distribution of presents in earlier days was on a lavish scale. During the three years 1813 to 1816 the British spent annually £150,000 in this way, and between 1836 and 1843 the average cost was over $45,000. After 1843, when presents were given only to Indians actually resident in Canada, the expenditure decreased.

[2] Henry R. Schoolcraft, *Personal Memoirs of a Residence of Thirty Years with the Indian Tribes on the American Frontier* (Philadelphia, 1851), 565.

various festivities which accompanied the giving out of the presents. All this she set down in her narrative. The whole shore at the head of Manitowaning Bay was covered with wigwams set up for the gathering, while hundreds of canoes darted about on the water. The schooner which had brought the officials and the presents lay against the green bank, "its tall masts almost mingling with the forest trees, and its white sails half furled and half gracefully drooping."[3]

Mrs. Jameson marveled that the Indians should have come so far, some of them as much as 500 miles, to receive such trifling presents. For each man there was three-quarters of a yard of blue cloth, three yards of linen, one blanket, three pounds of ball, nine pounds of shot, four pounds of powder, three pounds of tobacco, a butcher knife and such small articles as thread, needles and a comb. Each woman received a yard and three-quarters of coarse woolen cloth, two yards and a half of printed calico, one blanket, needles, thread, etc., while for each child there was a portion of woolen cloth and calico. For chiefs who had special claims to recognition there were extras in the way of medals, guns, brass kettles and flags.

The Indians remained on the island for about five days receiving regular rations of Indian corn and tallow. With these they made their soup, boiling the corn to the consistency of porridge and then adding the fat. This, with the fish so easily caught in the bay, was their food at every meal. Mrs. Jameson was told by Captain Anderson, the local superintendent, that it was not so *very* bad when a man was *very* hungry, but she made no experiments with it herself.

At the council which followed the distribution of presents Mrs. Jameson saw the Indians meeting as equals with the representatives of British authority and enjoying to the full their love of oratory. As the chiefs entered the log house where the gathering took place she recognized some whom she had met at Mackinac only a few weeks before. Here was her acquaintance, The Rain, looking quite

---

[3] Anna Jameson, *Winter Studies and Summer Rambles in Canada.* 2 vols. (New York, 1839), II, 277-300.

magnificent, and here also were Cut-Hand, Long-Knife, Forked-Tree, Black-Bird, Little Clam, Yellow-Head and many others.

Nearly opposite her was a famous Potawatomi chief and conjurer, Two-Ears. Hideously painted and fantastically dressed, he had clusters of swansdown hanging from each ear. Close by were three men with disheveled hair, faces blacked with soot and grease, and a generally squalid appearance. These, she was told, were in mourning for near relatives. Even more disgusting was a group whom she had noticed earlier in the day and who were described as cannibals from the Red River. One man had his hair cut short on the top of his head, so that it looked like a circular blacking brush, while it grew long all around and hung like a fringe on his shoulders. They were clad in skins which seemed on the point of rotting off, and their whole appearance reminded her of apes which she had once seen in a menagerie.

The chief superintendent of Indian affairs, Mr. Jarvis, was present and, using the childish language which seemed to be an accepted characteristic of council oratory, informed his "children" that their "Great Father," meaning thereby the Lieutenant Governor, would have been present with them but for the fact that he had just learned of the death of the other "Great Father on the other side of the Great Salt Lake"[4] and that consequently he had been forced to return in order to hold a council with his chief men.

All of this and much more was translated to the stolid Indian audience by Chief Black-Bird, whose name Mrs. Jameson wrote down as "As,si,ke,nack," but who is also known as Assikinack and Assignack. He was one of the most celebrated Indian orators of his time and a man of character and ability. Paul Kane, the artist, met him in 1845 on the occasion of a later distribution of presents at which he was again acting as interpreter.

"On the arrival of the presents," wrote Kane, "the Indians, male and female, accompanied by their children, immediately seated themselves in rows on the grass, each chief heading his own little

---

[4] Word had just come to the province of the death of King William IV and of the succession to the throne of the young Princess Victoria.

band, and giving in their number and names to Sigennok [*sic*], who here appears in his proper element, dividing the goods among them with great impartiality. He is really a very useful man. His voice is heard everywhere above the universal din of tongues, his native eloquence is unceasing, and seems to have the effect of allaying every envious and unpleasant feeling, and keeping all in good humour and proper order."

He owed his name, Kane says, to the untiring volubility of his tongue, but he was acute and intelligent and of great service to the British government through his influence over his fellow Indians. Mrs. Jameson noted the high pitch of his voice and the unusual emphasis as he translated the message of the superintendent to the council.

Many stories have come down of Assikinack's oratorical performances. On one occasion he spoke from sunrise to sunset without intermission, and apparently the Indians who were present stayed through the whole performance. On another occasion, so goes the story, he was on his feet during the greater part of three days, seeking to turn his fellows from their pagan religion to Christianity.

Paul Kane heard an interesting story from Captain T. G. Anderson, the Indian superintendent, of Assikinack's conversion to strict temperance from the drunkenness which had marked his earlier years. One day Captain Anderson found the Indian lying in front of his lodge, so drunk as to be quite insensible, and had him bound hand and foot with strong cords, at the same time placing a sickly weak boy to look after him. For hours he lay in this condition, an object of derision to all members of the village passing by. When sensibility returned Assikinack angrily demanded to know who had bound him, and when the superintendent pointed out the humiliation he had brought upon himself the young warrior vowed never to drink again, a pledge which he kept. Moreover, he became an enemy of all who brought firewater to the tribes and on one occasion led an armed party aboard a Detroit schooner laden with whisky and dumped the cargo overboard.

At the time of Mrs. Jameson's visit the British authorities were trying to induce the Indians of the whole region to settle on Manitoulin Island, a situation which would greatly reduce the costs of administration and at the same time bring them under educational and religious influence. Sir Peregrine Maitland, a veteran of Waterloo, was moving in this direction when he proposed, during his term as lieutenant governor, that the Indians should be collected into villages, in each of which there would be a clergyman of the Church of England and a schoolmaster to look after their welfare. In addition it was proposed to send in blacksmiths, carpenters and farmers who would give instruction in those occupations.

The religious side received first attention, a young divinity student, William McMurray, being sent in 1832 to Sault Ste. Marie. He was a month in reaching his post, and when in the following year he was desirous of ordination he had to follow his bishop for 1,400 miles, finally catching up with him at the Vermont border. Upon his return he was married to Charlotte Johnston, a sister of Mrs. Henry R. Schoolcraft and a daughter of John Johnston, a white trader who had married the daughter of a famous Chippewa chief.

Not much progress was made toward concentrating the Indians until near the end of Sir John Colborne's regime as lieutenant governor. In 1835 Captain Anderson, then an official in the Indian Department, made the suggestion that all the tribes on the north shore and adjacent parts should be brought together on Manitoulin Island, which would be set apart as a great reservation, and that there they should be given instruction in religion, in farming and in trades. Sir John Colborne promptly authorized Captain Anderson to visit the Indians as far west as Sault Ste. Marie and induce them, if possible, to accept the proposal. Anderson was accompanied on his trip by Reverend Adam Elliott, a Church of England clergyman, and between them they achieved a fair measure of success. Quite a number of Indians expressed their readiness to settle permanently on the island.

In the following year active preparations began for the inauguration of the plan, and at the head of Manitowaning Bay a clearing was made and some work done on the log buildings which would house the government officials and others. The situation was an excellent one, the bay affording shelter for vessels of every kind and the land adjacent being fertile. The distribution of presents took place at this point in 1836, being honored by the attendance of Sir Francis Bond Head, the new governor of the province. His journey, made by canoe, occupied five days, and on his arrival he found 1,500 Indians assembled, their lodges scattered along the shore and their campfires blazing. It was a novel experience for this man, fresh from the old settled civilization of England.[5]

Sir Francis is usually regarded as one of the worst choices ever made for governor of the Canadian province, and his course in the political events of 1837 undoubtedly contributed to the armed uprising of that year. But his report on the condition of the Indians and the means of betterment was a sensible and statesmanlike document. Before coming to Manitoulin he had attended the distribution of presents at Amherstburg, and he says that he made it his business to enter every hut and wigwam to see at first hand the aboriginal life. His conclusions were that attempts to make farmers of the red men were doomed to failure, that congregating them for the purpose of civilizing them had implanted more vices than it had eradicated and that the greatest kindness that could be performed toward them was to remove and fortify them as much as possible from all communication with the whites. He thought, however, that the Manitoulin group of islands provided an ideal home for these primitive people. As for the giving of presents to Indians resident in the United States, he regarded it as not only wasteful but an act unfriendly to the Republic. It was in the year following the visit of Sir Francis that Mrs. Jameson came to Manitoulin, and the major portion of Superintendent Jarvis's message to the council which she attended had to do with the proposals for

---

[5] At this council in 1836 on Manitoulin Island Sir Francis Bond Head secured the cession by the Chippewa and Ottawa of 23,000 islands, and from the Saugeen Indians more than a million and a half acres of land on the mainland to the south. See Appendix A, *Journals of the House of Assembly of Upper Canada* (1839), 2.

concentrating the whole body of Indians in these Lake Huron islands.

The political uprising in the province in December 1837 delayed action, but in 1838, under yet another governor, Sir George Arthur, who seldom traveled without a clergyman in attendance, definite steps were taken to carry out the government's policy. In the autumn of 1838 a regular establishment arrived at Manitowaning, traveling in a large bateau from Coldwater on the south shore of Georgian Bay. The party comprised thirty-four people in all— Captain Anderson, the superintendent, Reverend C. C. Brough, the missionary, Dr. Paul Darling and Reverend Benjamin Bayly, the schoolmaster. They were accompanied by their wives and children and by several servants. It was the cold fall season when the journey was made and during the voyage of three weeks the party was exposed to every kind of weather. A daughter of Captain Anderson afterward wrote of her experiences:

"From there being so many women and children on board, it was necessary to encamp early in the afternoons in order to get well under canvas before nightfall, and on account of the number of children to dress and feed; beds, etc., to unpack; tents to be struck and boat to be loaded, the mornings were spent ere we were enabled to proceed on our way. Some days we had only two or three hours in which to travel; for instance, if we arrived at a good camping ground it was advisable to go ashore for the night, as daylight might fail before reaching another. The nights soon became very cold and the ice had to be cut away in the morning in order to get the batteau from her moorings. Our 'Evangeline' had no deck or shelter of any kind; all were exposed to the fury of the biting winds, snow and rain and the freezing spray which frequently dashed over the edge of the boat. It was a marvel how any escaped death."

One child died on the day after arrival on the island and another within six weeks. A schooner which had been sent with winter supplies of food was driven off by the rapidly forming ice and had to return to its port. Scant rations were available for young or old during that winter. Fortunately there was an ample supply of potatoes, and fish could be speared through the ice, though there was no milk for the children and flour was so scarce that only half a slice of bread a day could be given to the little ones. But spring brought sunshine and open water and eventually a schooner with necessary supplies. The crew had wondered if they would find any of the party alive.

The effort to bring the Indians into a more settled life was not altogether a success. There was no market for any produce they might raise and, indeed, at that time no merchant on the island and no mill nearer than Penetanguishine. Some Indians accepted the plan but not nearly so many as had been hoped for. Even the missionary and the schoolmaster became discouraged and left in 1839. It was at this time that Reverend Frederick O'Meara came to the island and crowned a fine record of service by translating both the New Testament and the Book of Common Prayer into the Ojibwa tongue.

The plans so much discussed for establishing a great Indian center in the Manitoulin area never came to fruition. It is true that some Indians did pull up stakes in former dwelling places and move to the island, but these were chiefly from the United States and their motives were mixed. Settlements were set up at Wikwemikong and at Manitowaning, the former being the habitat of those who came from across the border. The government built houses, provided schools and churches and set up mills and shops, but generations of nomadic life were not easily overcome by government edicts or official regulations. In 1840 the population of the two settlements was above 700, a majority of whom were Christians, but this number fell greatly when a group of Potawatomi returned to their old lands around Lake St. Clair.

Laurence Oliphant, that versatile English traveler and writer, visited Manitoulin in 1854 at the time of the annual distribution of presents. He was then Superintendent of Indian Affairs in Canada. Unlike Mrs. Jameson who had witnessed the same scene seventeen years before and had been thrilled by its romantic character, he was quite disillusioned.

"Those who visit the island," he wrote, "are for the most part miserable, poverty-stricken creatures, wretchedly clad in rags and skins as they crawl in and out of their birch-bark wigwams, looking as lean and mangy as the curs that shared with them their grilled fish-heads, which seemed to form the staple of their food."

Oliphant visited some of the wigwams but was nearly choked by the smoke and stench that greeted him. Most of the crude dwellings were close together, the intervening space being filled with stinking fish, snarling curs and papooses in their board cradles. "As they were propped up in a slanting position against a canoe, or anything else that was convenient, and rolled their almost invisible eyes, they looked very much as if they were in training for mummies," he observed.

The Indians actually resident on the island were, he believed, showing improvement as a result of the influence and training of the whites, and there were some among the visiting Indians also who did not fall to the low level of the many. At a place called Petit Courant, where his steamer halted for wood, Oliphant attended a Sunday service in a mission church. "I have seldom been present at a more touching service than I witnessed in that log-hut," he wrote. The congregation was chiefly women, the men being engaged in loading the steamer, and he was struck by the clear melodious voices. The church was perched on a bank at least a hundred feet higher than the level of the lake and from his seat by a window he could look out on a range of blue hills, a thousand feet high, running along the shore of the mainland, the intervening channel studded with islands and in the distance blue smoke curling over the trees, giving indication of an Indian village.

One day in the late 1820's an English officer in the garrison at Malta sat poring over maps of America and in the occupation became fascinated with the picture conjured up by the delineation of the St. Mary's River, connecting the two great lakes Superior and Huron. There and then he resolved that he would visit the region, and the interesting fact is that he not only came but that on the island of St. Joseph he made his home from the year 1835 almost uninterruptedly until his death nearly forty years later.

The story of Major William Kingdom Rains has been told with affection and enthusiasm by one of his descendants.[6] He was born in Wales in 1789, just four weeks to the day after the opening session of the States-General at Versailles, the beginning of the French Revolution. Like that of many another born in the same year, his career was determined by the historic meeting of nobles, clergy and representatives of the common folk called together by Louis XVI. He was but sixteen years old when he received his commission as a lieutenant in the Royal Regiment of Artillery and was placed in charge of a battery. From 1807 to 1813 he fought under the Duke of Wellington in the Peninsular War; then in 1813, in company with other English officers, he was loaned to the Austrian government. A year later he was one of the allied officers who conducted Pope Pius VII to the Vatican, ending the four years' exile to which he had been subjected by Napoleon.

With the coming of peace Major Rains retired on half pay, utilizing his time, however, in the study of engineering; but tiring of this after so many years of stirring military life, he rejoined the army in 1824 and was sent to the British garrison at Malta. There he remained until 1828 when he returned to England and was later married to a Miss Frances Doubleday.

Now came the opportunity of which he had dreamed, of going to Canada and to the region of the St. Mary's River with which his imagination had been stirred. With his wife and two children he sailed from England and with them went also Eliza Doubleday, a sister of Frances. Major Rains first established himself on a farm near Lake Simcoe, a district chosen by many military emigrants of the time. In 1834 he proposed to the government of Upper Canada that he and others associated with him be given a land grant on St. Joseph Island upon which they planned to settle one hundred families. They had in mind also the establishment of "a steam com-

---

[6] Joseph and Estelle Bayliss, *Historic St. Joseph Island* (Cedar Rapids, Iowa, 1938). Mrs. Bayliss is a descendant of Major Rains.

munication through Lake Huron, which will eventually bring not only our own productions but those of the whole of the Michigan Territory . . . through Lake Simcoe to Bay of Quinte." Another argument advanced was that a settlement would "curb the vagrant population in that neighbourhood."

The correspondence which followed shows that Sir John Colborne, the lieutenant governor, thought well of the plan. It is of interest that while he said almost nothing about the proposed scheme of trade communications he thought it would be well to have men in the upper lake region who might act as magistrates and who would exert themselves "to preserve order among the Canadian Voyageurs and half Indians settled at the Sault Ste. Marie." Upper Canada was seething with political unrest at the time, unrest that was to take the form of an armed uprising three years later, and anyone who would aid in keeping order anywhere was sure to stand well in the graces of Colborne, who, like Major Rains, had gone through the Napoleonic Wars.

The free grant which the associates desired was not forthcoming but they were allowed, on the governor's recommendation, to purchase 5,000 acres at a shilling an acre. Major Rains had chosen as partners in the venture his neighbor, Archibald Hamilton Scott, and Charles Thompson, of Toronto. In the spring of 1835 they built a small vessel, loaded it with merchandise and machinery for a sawmill, and sailed away to the island which Rains was now to see for the first time. The sawmill was set up on a beautiful inlet at the southeast end of the island, to which Major Rains gave the name Milford Haven. It was the plan of the promoters to have building materials ready for the settlers who might come, so that there would be no delay in erecting their houses. A store was also opened where they could procure needed supplies. Scott was to operate the mill while Major Rains was to run the store.

But the beautiful dream of a prosperous settlement did not come true. With millions of acres as yet unoccupied in other parts of the province far more easily arrived at and with near-by markets, it was not only foolish for people to go to distant St. Joseph but equally foolish for any government to encourage them to go there. On the island itself at the time the project was inaugurated there were but a few French half-breeds and some Indians, and the market for the sale of their fish and furs was Sault Ste. Marie.

Within two years Major Rains dropped out of the little company. Unwise speculation on the part of an agent had almost completely wiped out the capital which he had possessed on leaving England, about £30,000. He was no longer in a position to back the project. Scott also soon withdrew, selling his shares to his brother, but the third partner, Thompson, continued his interest, turning, however, from colonization ideas to simple trade. A report made to the government five years after the venture began indicated that while no settlers had come, Thompson had in the spring of that year shipped out upward of six hundred barrels of fish and "full one million pounds of Maple Sugar." These commodities went to Chicago and Detroit. The sugar alone had a value of about $75,000.

All of this and much more as well might long since have been forgotten were it not for a more romantic aspect of Major Rains's life. It has already been mentioned that when he left England his sister-in-law, Eliza Doubleday, came also. Some time after their arrival on St. Joseph a triangle arose, not the familiar "eternal triangle" but one of another sort. Both women loved the same man and yet were devoted to each other. What might have happened in an old and ordered society such as that of England one cannot tell, but the difficulty was settled by the Major's establishing a separate home for each and giving his name to the children of both alliances. The utmost harmony seems to have existed and the children grew up together, their mothers, both of whom were well educated, tutoring them in the absence of a school on the island.

A domestic situation such as this was bound to create a measure of notoriety and arouse criticism, some of it not in accordance with the facts. Mrs. Jameson, Victorian to her finger tips, mentions it in her narrative. While passing St. Joseph Island in 1837 on her journey from the Sault she wrote: "There is, in the interior, an English settlement, and a village of Indians. The principal proprietor, Major R——, who is a magistrate and justice of the peace, has two Indian women living with him—two sisters and a family by each! —such are the examples sometimes set to the Indians on our frontiers."

William Cullen Bryant also had something to say about it after he visited the region in 1846. "We passed Drummond's Island," he wrote, "and then coasted St. Joseph's Island, on the woody shore of which I was shown a solitary house. There I was told lives a long-nosed Englishman, a half-pay officer with two wives, sisters, each the mother of numerous offspring. The English polygamist has been more successful in seeking solitude than in avoiding notoriety. The very loneliness of his habitation causes it to be remarked, and there is not a passenger who makes the voyage to the Sault, to whom his house is not pointed out, and his story related. It was hinted to me that he had a third wife in Toronto, but I have my private doubts of this part of the story, and suspect that it was thrown in to increase my wonder."[7]

On the other hand those who had known Major Rains retained memories of a man of education and broad culture, well read not only in the literature of his own tongue but of others as well, fond of music and of beauty in nature. The American scientist Louis Agassiz met him in 1848 at St. Joseph Island and J. Elliot Cabot, who was with Agassiz, left this record in his journal:

"As we landed, a rather rough-looking, unshaven personage in shirt-sleeves walked up and invited us to his house, which was close at hand. We found his walls lined with books; Shakespeare, Scott, Hemans, etc., caught my eye as I passed near the shelves, forming a puzzling contrast with the rude appearance of the dwelling. A very few moments sufficed to show a similar contrast in our host himself. He knew Professor Agassiz by reputation, had read reports of his lectures in the newspapers, and evinced a warm interest in the objects of our excursion. When he found out who the Pro-

---

[7] William Cullen Bryant, *Letters of a Traveller, or, Notes of Things in Europe and America* (New York, 1850), 274.

fessor was, he produced a specimen in spirits of the rare gar-pike of Lake Huron and insisted upon his accepting it, and afterwards sent him various valuable specimens. His conversation, eager and discursive, running over Politics, Science and Literature, was that of an intelligent and well-read man, who kept up, by books and newspapers, an acquaintance with the leading topics of the day, but seldom had an opportunity of discussing them with persons similarly interested. He turned out to be an ex-Major in the British Army, and he showed us a portrait of himself in full regimentals, remarking with a smile that he had once been noted as the best-dressed man in his regiment."[8]

The earlier history of St. Joseph Island is closely linked to the fur trade. Its position was remarked by the earliest explorers and made use of by the traders who came to the St. Mary's River. When England succeeded France in dominion over the interior of the continent her traders followed the same lake and river highways that had lured Frenchmen since the earliest years of settlement on the St. Lawrence. The North West Company located a post on St. Joseph Island in 1792, and the original foundations of the buildings which they erected may still be seen at the spot known as Rains Point.

Four years later the island took on a new importance when the British garrison at Mackinac, forced to leave in accordance with the terms of the Jay Treaty, made it their new post. The officers of the garrison did not even wait for official notice as to where they were to go but sent a detachment to St. Joseph to prevent its possible seizure by the Americans. Two years later the island was formally purchased from the Chippewa Indians, the consideration being "twelve hundred pounds Quebec currency value in goods according to the Montreal price."

Lieutenant George T. Landmann, who had been sent to St. Joseph to superintend the construction of fortifications, arrived on

---

[8] Louis Agassiz, *Lake Superior: Its Physical Character, Vegetation, and Animals, Compared with Those of Other and Similar Regions. With a Narrative of the Tour by J. Elliot Cabot* (Boston, 1850), 27-28.

the island shortly before its transfer, and he has left us an account of the proceedings. All of the Indian tribes to whom the goods were to be delivered assembled on the ground adjoining the old fort, where the merchandise was placed on display. This consisted of blankets, broadcloths of every color, guns, flints, powder, shot, ribbons, a few large silver medals for chiefs, steels for striking fire, some silver brooches, earrings and drops, and a very moderate quantity (fifty gallons) of rum, reduced to one-third its ordinary strength. In addition there were also such curious items as gilt leather trunks, seventy-five pounds of vermilion and a bullock.

The deed was read and interpreted to the Indians, after which the chiefs signed it by drawing the totem symbol of their tribes, and the officers of the garrison attached their signatures, Landmann adding his also as a witness. The Indians, having received a taste of rum, quickly responded to its stimulus. Dancing grew ever wilder in character until finally the commissioners—one of whom was Reverend Richard Pollard, a Church of England clergyman from Amherstburg—finding themselves in the midst of six or seven hundred shouting savages "without much hypocrisy started off, and lost not a moment in securing themselves on board of the vessel, hastily requesting Captain Drummond to protect the property which they had no time to carry off with them."

The original fortifications consisted merely of a blockhouse and stockade, and there was difficulty in building even these because of the haste with which Mackinac had been left behind and the lack of supplies. The post, however, became of immediate importance, situated as it was on the very frontier, and was soon a center for the Indians friendly to the British, who resorted to it just as at Mackinac before the evacuation. Indeed they soon were coming in greater numbers than had ever been known at the former post.

Lieutenant Landmann, though but a youth of eighteen, was in charge of the more permanent military construction which was to consist of a large blockhouse, a guardhouse, powder magazine, provision store, bakehouse and a council house. There was also to be a wharf. It is typical of the casual way in which such matters were often handled by the authorities at Quebec that Landmann received neither plans nor descriptions of the buildings which he was charged to erect. There were times later when it seemed as if the people at Quebec had completely forgotten the existence of the place. In 1801 the commanding officer at the post complained that the blockhouse and other buildings were in such bad condition that rain and snow made their way in everywhere. Nothing had been completed and timber intended for buildings lay scattered about or sometimes even floated away. There were no proper quarters for the officers; they were apparently supposed to look out for themselves. The rations, judging by what Lieutenant Landmann has recorded, were scanty, monotonous and, in the case of the pork and butter, "rancid from having been salted fifteen or twenty years."

The garrison in the later 1790's numbered about forty men under command of Lieutenant Peter Drummond. How primitive were living conditions is indicated by Landmann's description of his own quarters, a log hut twenty feet square, without ceiling or boarded floor, one window closed with oiled paper, a wide space paved in the center for a fireplace and a hole two feet square in the roof to let out the smoke. All in all, except for greater solidity, it was not much better than an Indian wigwam.

Landmann was an adventurous youth and on a visit to St. Joseph in 1800 determined that he would make a new record for the trip between that island and Montreal. Having purchased a twenty-five-foot canoe and engaged a guide and nine *voyageurs,* all picked men, he set out on the long hard trip on July 6. The best time that had been previously recorded for this journey was seven and three-quarter days made by Simon McTavish of the North West Company.

"At starting," he recorded, "I was particularly favoured by the weather; this was of the greatest importance to me whilst coasting Lake Huron from the island of St. Joseph, to the mouth of the French river—a distance of two hundred to three hundred miles— the whole of which, having a fair wind, I performed without landing or striking the small sail, in thirty hours.

"I arrived at Montreal in seven days and a quarter, having passed La Chine without stopping longer than was necessary to procure a guide to descend the dangerous rapids between that place and the city of Montreal. The severe fatigue my men had endured, as well as myself, had consumed a large portion of the flesh which had previously covered our bones, which on our arrival excited general commiseration. Moreover, we were all suffering acutely from sore eyes, occasioned by the smoke of the burning forests; for along an extent of at least seven hundred miles of the country we had passed over, the woods were on fire, and in many parts on both sides of the river, so that every wind covered us with clouds of smoke and ashes, and frequently sprinkled us over with burning cinders and sparks; not only repeatedly setting fire to the contents of our canoe, but to our clothes. On one occasion, the contents of the canoe was on fire in several places, and many of us had red-hot cinders sticking to our clothes; on another, two of our men were so completely in flames, as to render it necessary for them to jump overboard, holding by the canoe.

"Even to this day I have a lively recollection of my sensations while looking ahead of our canoe, thus carried along by a rapid stream into a mass of flames and a shower of fire.

"Notwithstanding all these vexations and painful obstructions, my having accomplished my journey in less time by half a day, than had been taken by the great McTavish, was to me ample compensation: such is the folly of a young man under twenty years of age."

A few civilians came to the island, their log huts forming a little community apart from the military. The North West Company carried on trade with the Indians as did also the South West Company. But after 1808, with the American interdictions on commerce, the fur trade dwindled. From time to time rumors came that all was not well with the relations between England and the United States. Finally, in early July of 1812, word came that war had been declared by President Madison, and Fort St. Joseph, from being a neglected and almost forgotten outpost of British power, at once became a position of highest strategical importance. From it was struck the first blow in the War of 1812 in the capture of Fort Mackinac. With that post in British hands St. Joseph became of lesser importance and only in slight degree did it figure in later military operations. By the end of the struggle the fortifications on the island had gone to ruin.

The Treaty of Ghent having provided for a restoration by both nations of all territory seized or occupied during the war, it was necessary for the British garrison once again to leave Mackinac. As the treaty also provided for an early survey to determine the boundary between Canada and the United States, it was imperative that caution be used in selecting the site for the next post lest it might turn out to be within American territory. Colonel McDouall, the commander at Mackinac, was fearful that this might happen to St. Joseph; consequently he and the officers sent to confer with him on the matter decided in favor of the island commanding the Detour passage which was known to the Indians as Pontanagipy. In honor of Sir Gordon Drummond, one of the British commanders during the war, it henceforth bore his name. The irony of the choice lies in the fact that when the international boundary survey had been completed Drummond Island was declared to be in American territory and St. Joseph remained under the British flag. Thus the state of Michigan includes today a large island bearing the name of a neighboring country's hero.

Pontanagipy or Drummond Island was no such pleasant place as St. Joseph. It was rocky, barren and generally inhospitable, but it occupied a strategic position in relation to both the St. Mary's River and the Straits of Mackinac. Until 1815 little notice had been taken of it, and Major Joseph Delafield, American agent in connection with the boundary survey, said that he had never seen a map in which its correct position was given.

Colonel McDouall had to move rapidly in settling his garrison in its new location. It would have required time to bring the necessary materials and artisans from down below to provide proper accommodation, so he decided to remove some of the buildings from St. Joseph and fit them up as temporary quarters for his men. He was able to make a satisfactory deal with the South West Company by which he acquired several of the buildings no longer needed for their trade. The magazine remained on St. Joseph Island and the small guard left there found quarters in the old bakehouse. As Drummond Island had no pasturage and produced no hay the cattle were also left on St. Joseph.

When Major Delafield visited Drummond Island in 1820 the settlement consisted of one straight street of fifteen or more comfortable two-story log houses, well whitewashed. There were two companies of British troops on the island under the command of a major. The officers' quarters, detached dwellings, were terminated by a small island covered with pines and connected with the mainland by a bridge. Upon the islet was a gay little summerhouse, originally a log hut but beautified by some officer in his spare time and used as a quiet little retreat. The dwellings of the regular residents were grouped together close to a curious inlet about two hundred feet wide, which ran inland for two miles. At its point the Indians had their wigwams and tepees which Delafield found filthy and crowded with squaws and children.

Major Delafield thought that the scenery of Potagannissing Bay on the upper side of Drummond Island was the most beautiful that he had seen upon Lake Huron. This bay, of considerable extent, contained a number of small islands upon one of which there was an Indian settlement. The squaws were timid and on his arrival took to the fields or hid in their huts, but the men brought potatoes to barter for pork. It was September and they were employed in drying corn for winter use, the cobs being spread upon a framework raised about four feet from the ground, under which a slow fire was kept going until the kernels were well dried or partially roasted.

While he was present on the island an independent trader traveling in a large canoe arrived from Montreal, where he had been purchasing goods. "He appeared to be an intelligent man," wrote

Delafield, "and his great strength, health and activity gave evidence of his ability to endure the rudeness of the life he leads. His crew were much the same appearance and in high spirits. His birchen canoe was of the first class and handsomely decorated. Upon the prow was written its name: *Pret-a-Boyre,* Ready to Drink. When we noticed it, by one of the party mentioning the name, the Canadians gave a shout of gratification, and the trader forthwith ordered some drink, upon which the pilot raised a 10 gll. keg of rum and poured some into a one-gallon measure which was handed to the trader who, pouring some into a pint cup, passed it to us. We drank to them and the trader and his pilot did the like, after which the usual courtesies of a politer clime than Lake Huron were exchanged and we parted. They, in full chorus, and in conscious pride of their skill and rapid progress, were soon wafted out of sight and hearing."[9]

Dr. John Bigsby, medical officer with the British section of the boundary commission, found Drummond Island "healthy but dismal, a mere heap of rocks on the edge of an impenetrable medly of morass, ponds and matted woods." The duties of the rank and file of the garrison were so light that they were employed as much as possible at other work, but drunkenness and desertion were common. While Bigsby was on the island an order came forbidding the use of Indians in trailing deserters. He learned that during the preceding summer when five men were missing from the post Indians had been sent out to intercept them and had returned in a couple of days with five heads in a bag.

If the life of the men in the ranks was hard and monotonous, that of the officers was scarcely less so. Bigsby dined at the mess where "nine sharp-set young fellows" sat down with him to a square lump of highly salted beef, a fowl, a suet dumpling and potatoes. This was evidently their regular fare, though at certain seasons they could shoot pigeons and ducks. The life was utterly

---

[9] Robert McElroy and Thomas Riggs (editors), *The Unfortified Boundary. A Diary of the First Survey of the Canadian Boundary Line from St. Regis to the Lake of the Woods by Major Joseph Delafield, American Agent Under Articles VI and VII of the Treaty of Ghent* (New York, 1943), 308-318.

lonely, no visitors coming to the island save a few Indians and once a year an inspector making his usual rounds. Occasionally they went over to Mackinac and fraternized with the American officers, but apart from that they were cut off from white society.

Drummond Island continued as a British post until 1828 when another move had to be made. The International Boundary Commission, after much arguing, had decided that this island should belong to the United States. There had really ceased to be much need of a garrison at this point unless to deal with the Indians, for neither England nor the United States was eager for another western war. Possibly considerations of cost entered into the decision to establish the garrison at a point nearer to the capital of the province where communications could be more easily kept up. So Penetanguishine at the lower end of Georgian Bay was chosen and the garrison and such residents of the island as chose to do so removed to that place in November 1828.[10]

With the departure of the British garrison Drummond Island ceased to be occupied, for there was no necessity of maintaining an American force there as well as at Fort Mackinac. When the British and American officers shook hands after the formal handing over of the island on that November day of 1828, one chapter had been closed and another opened in international relations. For more than forty years each nation had suspected and watched the other; now there was to be no more a British frontier post in these waters and, at a later date, there was no American post either. The unguarded frontier had come to Lake Huron.

---

[10] A list of the French-Canadian *voyageurs* who migrated with the troops from Drummond Island to Penetanguishine in 1828 may be found in Ontario Historical Society, *Papers and Records,* III (Toronto, 1901), 149-166. Narratives of their experiences appear in the same volume, 123-149.

Chapter 11

The Magic Island in the Straits

A little bit of Heaven brought to earth.
    —MRS. ANNA JAMESON

The fine island, 'a fortress built by nature for herself.'
    —COLONEL ROBERT MCDOUALL

THE pointed tips of Michigan's peninsulas almost meet each other at the Straits of Mackinac, the narrow strip of water which connects Lake Michigan with Lake Huron. Forty miles to the east at Detour the waters of Lake Superior mingle with those of Lake Huron. In the very center of the Straits lies the island to which, because of its resemblance to a turtle, the Indians gave the name Michilimackinac, but which white men contracted into its more common form, Mackinac.

This is the Mackinac known now for more than one hundred and fifty years to fur traders and mariners, travelers and tourists, but it is not the only Mackinac in history, for the name has been applied at various periods to three distinct settlements, and often also to the whole region round about. During the period when France was seeking to build up a great empire in the heart of America two places bore the many-lettered Indian name. The earliest was on the north side of the strait, on Point St. Ignace, and for more than thirty years after 1670 it was the center of French influence in this area. The second post of the name, established in 1712, was on the south shore near the present Mackinaw City. After the conquest of Canada this latter site was taken over by the English who continued to occupy it until 1781 when a move was made to the island itself and new fortifications erected. Despite

200

the fact that it was within the area ceded by England at the close of the War for Independence, Mackinac Island continued to be held and occupied by an English garrison until 1796. In that year the American flag was finally hoisted and with but one interruption, during the War of 1812, has remained there ever since.

The strategic importance of these several posts on the Straits is apparent from even a cursory glance at the map of the upper lakes. Here, more distinctly than at any other point, the early trade routes converged. The military importance of Michilimackinac in relation to the economic life of New France increased greatly during the first half of the eighteenth century as the rivalry of England for control of the fur trade was leading both nations toward the struggle that was to determine the destiny of half a continent.

It was with this threat ever in mind that the French raised the fortifications on the south shore in 1712. Fort Niagara was built fourteen years later, another link in the chain of defenses set up on the line of inland waterways. But French ambitions were not equaled by French military strength and when Fort Niagara fell in the summer of 1759, Detroit, Michilimackinac and the West in general were cut off from reinforcements and could only await the outcome of the war.

A few days after the surrender of Montreal an English detachment, consisting of 200 men, set out to take over the western posts from their French garrisons. The party, which traveled in fifteen huge whaleboats, was under command of Major Robert Rogers, a daring New Hampshire officer who had been the leader of a troop of Rangers and Indians during the war. His exploits have furnished the theme for many writers, and it must be admitted that there was enough variety in his career, both of the good and of the bad, and enough vicissitudes, to suffice for several men.

It was autumn when Rogers and his party moved westward from Montreal, and on Lake Ontario and on Lake Erie they were subjected to the force of heavy gales as they skirted the shores in their clumsy boats. At Detroit, Captain Francis Marie Picoté, Sieur de Bellestre, the French officer in command, was inclined at first to be belligerent but sight of a note from the late French governor forced him to yield. Rogers had intended going on at once to Michilimackinac but the rough weather on Lake Huron prevented further progress westward and it was not until the following year that the fort on the Straits surrendered to a detachment of the Sixtieth Regiment, then known as the Royal Americans, under Captain Henry Balfour. The expedition had been twenty days journeying from Detroit to Mackinac.

An unidentified soldier of France, whose manuscript narrative in the Bibliothèque Nationale in Paris bears only the initials J.C.B., has left us an intimate little picture of old Michilimackinac in the closing days of French occupation. All we know of him is that he was in America for ten years after 1751, that he participated in the French and Indian War, and that for a time he was commissary at Fort Duquesne. He appears to have been of an inquiring mind and, having considerable leisure, kept a record of the places where he went and the things which he saw, all of which he described at some length after his return to France.

The writer of this memoir was one of a force under a Captain Péan which in 1754 made a tour of the northern posts. Fort Michilimackinac, at the time of his visit, was surrounded by a stockade with six mounted cannon and a garrison of thirty soldiers. Three years was the usual term of service at such a frontier post but the men were often permitted to remain if they so desired and apparently some of them found the life so pleasant that they served long beyond the regular period. One soldier had been there for twenty years, and another, a Parisian, who had stayed on for thirty years, was sixty years old at the time of the visit. They received no pay but were provided with ammunition for hunting and were allowed to trade with the Indians. On their departure they were permitted to take their bundles of pelts with them. Hunting and fishing added to their larder and they also raised Indian corn.

During the twelve days that Péan's party was at the fort a council was held with the representatives of sixteen tribes. As there were 1,200 Indians present, four times as many as the French force, no chances were taken, the men being kept under arms and the cannon of the fort loaded with grapeshot. All the traditional ritual of an Indian council was enacted, with each side warily watching the other. The French commander informed the Indian assembly that he had been sent by their "Father Ononthro," meaning the Governor of New France, to tell them of his love, but also to reprove them for listening to evil counsel and turning their arms against their French brothers. This message was duly translated into the various tongues of those present, after which the chiefs arose in turn and pledged their allegiance. Tobacco was distributed and the alliance sealed by the giving of strings of wampum. The Indians entertained the French force by presenting some of their ritual dances and supplied them with abundance of fish and game. At the final meeting, after pledges of loyalty had been reaffirmed, presents were given out and the next morning the Indians scattered to their various abodes. The French party under Péan returned to Quebec by the Ottawa River route.[1]

A long succession of explorers and traders, soldiers and missionaries came to the Mackinac region during the ninety years that the fleur-de-lis floated over the historic old posts. Jean Nicolet was the first, voyaging westward in 1634, fulfilling Champlain's commission to seek out and report on the resources of the country that lay beyond Lake Huron. Trained from his youth to the ways of the wilderness, knowing the Indian character and the Indian tongue, he was well equipped for such an adventure. Nicolet was the first known white man to push westward through the Straits and look out upon the waters of Lake Michigan. Medard Chouart Groseilliers and Pierre Esprit Radisson, two of the most intrepid figures in the annals of exploration in North America, were in this region in the decade of the 1650's. Both had come to New France as

---

[1] "Travels in New France," by J. C. B., *Pennsylvania Historical Survey (Frontier Forts and Trails Survey)*, edited by Sylvester K. Stevens, Donald H. Kent and Emma Edith Woods (Harrisburg, 1941), 35-43.

youths and, like Nicolet, had served apprenticeships in the wilds that fitted them for their amazing journeys. Grace Lee Nute, the latest biographer of these two men,[2] to whom she gives the descriptive title "Caesars of the Wilderness," has done much to clear up some of the long-standing mysteries with regard both to their journeys and their writings. Groseilliers had an incurable wanderlust, and coming to a land where new pathways lay unexplored in every direction he was able to indulge his fancy to the full. Much of what Radisson recorded as his own exploits has been discovered to belong to Groseilliers, his brother-in-law, but the two men joined forces in 1659 in a journey to Lake Superior. On this and on further journeys they came to the conclusion that the proper approach to the western tribes and to the regions where furs were most abundant was by way of Hudson Bay. This they urged on their home government but without success. Thereupon they laid all their information before shrewd Englishmen and the formation of the Hudson's Bay Company followed. These two men unconsciously changed the course of history in North America.

The Jesuit missionaries were seldom far behind the explorers and the traders, bringing their religious offices to the most distant regions; sometimes, indeed, they were themselves the pioneers and their reports made to the superior of the order at Quebec added much to the geographical knowledge of the times. Father Claude Allouez was sent in 1665 to Chequamegon Bay on Lake Superior, where Huron fugitives from the Iroquois fury had taken refuge a few years before. After four years he was succeeded by Father Jacques Marquette, who, when his native charges were driven out by their western neighbors, the Sioux, led them to a point on the north shore of the Straits of Mackinac where there was a small fur-trading station. That was the beginning of the mission of St. Ignace and from this frontier post Marquette set out with Louis Jolliet in 1673 on the famous journey that cleared up the mystery surrounding the outlet of the Mississippi River.

---

[2] Grace Lee Nute, *Caesars of the Wilderness: Medard Chouart, Sieur Des Groseilliers, and Pierre Esprit Radisson, 1618-1710* (New York, 1943).

Jolliet's narrative was lost and we are dependent upon Marquette's report for our knowledge of one of the most important journeys ever made in North America. His manuscript rests today in the archives of the Jesuit order at Montreal. Marquette died two years after his return from the Mississippi and was buried under the little chapel at St. Ignace. Two hundred years later the site of the chapel was discovered and also the supposed grave in which this pioneer missionary rested. His statue dominates the slope beneath the fortifications at Mackinac Island and a monument at St. Ignace commemorates his missionary work in this region.

Those who dwelt in St. Ignace of Michilimackinac in the summer of 1679 must have felt themselves far less remote from civilization when La Salle's *Griffin* came on its first (and last) voyage and cast anchor in the quiet waters. "Before her," writes Parkman in one of his charming descriptions, "rose the house and chapel of the Jesuits enclosed with palisades; on the right, the Huron village, with its bark cabins and its fence of tall pickets; on the left, the square compact houses of the French traders; and, not far off, the clustered wigwams of an Ottawa village. Here was a centre of the Jesuit missions, and a centre of the Indian trade; and here, under the shadow of the cross, was much sharp practice in the service of Mammon. Keen traders, with or without a license; and lawless coureurs-de-bois, whom a few years of forest life had weaned from civilization, made St. Ignace their resort.... The *Griffin* fired her cannon, and the Indians yelped in wonder and amazement. The adventurers landed in state, and marched, under arms, to the bark chapel of the Ottawa village, where they heard mass. La Salle knelt before the altar, in a mantle of scarlet, bordered with gold. Soldiers, sailors and artisans knelt around him—black Jesuits, gray Recollets, swarthy voyageurs, and painted savages; a devout but motley concourse."[3]

When the Baron Lahontan was at Michilimackinac in 1688 he saw the arrival of the Abbé Cavelier, elder brother of La Salle, and

---

[3] Francis Parkman, *La Salle and the Discovery of the Great West* (Boston, 1887), 140.

other survivors of the unfortunate Louisiana expedition in which the great explorer lost his life.

"They give out," he wrote, "that they are sent to Canada, in order to go to France, with some Dispatches from M. de la Salle to the King: But we suspect that he is dead because he does not return along with them."

At the time of Lahontan's visit the Huron and Ottawa had each a separate village, though he tells us that the two communities were separated only by a single palisade. The Ottawa, however, were beginning to build a fort on a hill not far distant, being prompted to this by a recent murder in which four young Ottawa had killed a Huron. Evidently they were fearful of reprisals. Of the Jesuits and their work he wrote somewhat disparagingly: "In this place the Jesuits have a little House, or College adjoining to a sort of a Church, and inclosed with Pales that separate it from the Village of the Hurons. These good Fathers lavish away all their Divinity and patience to no good purpose, in converting such ignorant Infidels: For all the length they can bring them to is, that sometimes they'll desire Baptism for their dying Children, and some few superannuated Persons consent to receive the Sacrament of Baptism, when they find themselves at the point of Death."[4]

Mackinac itself Lahontan regarded as of great importance both for trade and for defense. It was free from Iroquois attacks, its fisheries provided an abundance of food and it was on the direct line of trade with the Indian tribes to the west.

Transfer of the French possessions in America to the new rule of England brought about the most serious Indian uprising in the history of the continent and brought tragedy to the post of Michili-

---

[4] Lahontan's writings, first published as early as 1703, have passed through numerous editions and translations. A more favorable view than that usually expressed is taken by Stephen Leacock, who edited an edition published in 1932. "The great value of Lahontan's writings—or of ninety-nine-one-hundredths of it," says this editor, "lies in its exactness, in the picture which it produces of the actual facts, the actual conditions of the life, the wars, the dangers and the hardships of the colony of New France. Lahontan wrote with a lack of conscious effort, with no anxious striving for style or effect."

mackinac. The times were such as might well unsettle the Indian mind. For many years their aid had been sought by each party in the wars and their services turned by white men against other white men. Tribes which had been former allies of France distrusted the English, realizing that the change would probably greatly alter their way of life. These English were not like the French. Where they came they enforced their rule. Their traders were wont also to drive hard bargains.

The discontent which prevailed throughout the West in the two years immediately following the conquest was skillfully promoted by Pontiac, the principal chief of the Ottawa. He was virtual head of a loose confederacy then existing between the Chippewa, Potawatomi and his own people, but his power and influence extended far beyond these tribes. Parkman says of him: "Courage, resolution, address and eloquence are sure passports to distinction. With all these Pontiac was pre-eminently endowed, and it was chiefly to them, urged to their highest activity by a vehement ambition, that he owed his greatness. He possessed a commanding energy and force of mind, and in subtlety and craft could match the best of his wily race. But, though capable of acts of magnanimity, he was a thorough savage, with a wider range of intellect than those around him, but sharing all their passions and prejudices, their fierceness and treachery. His faults were the faults of his race."[5]

In May 1763 came the uprising which bears the name of its instigator and leader. A surprise attack on Detroit failed because the English received warning that trouble was brewing and made adequate preparations. But every other garrison west of Niagara fell in that summer. The whole of the gains made by the British in the West as a result of the war just closed were threatened for a time.

At Michilimackinac British traders had quickly appeared following the transfer of ownership, just as they appeared at all other

---

[5] Francis Parkman, *The Conspiracy of Pontiac and the Indian War after the Conquest of Canada.* 2 vols. (Boston, 1887), I, 183.

posts handed over by France. One of the first to arrive was Alexander Henry and it is to his narrative that we owe much of our knowledge of the tragic events of 1763. He had received a cool greeting when he first arrived at the post two years earlier, and twice in succession his house had been invaded by threatening bands of Indians. On the second occasion he was saved from more serious trouble only by the timely arrival of a British detachment. But month after month there continued to be disquieting rumors and disquieting incidents. Hints were thrown out by French-Canadians and by Indians themselves that trouble was brewing but Captain Etherington, the British commandant, seemed blind to what was happening and rebuffed those who brought warnings.

This was the situation on the morning of the second of June, 1763. At Mackinac the dull monotony of barracks life was to be relieved, for officers and men had been invited to witness a game of ball to be played between Chippewa who had recently arrived and some bands of the Sauk Indians whose lodges were close by. No one suspected danger. The gates of the fort were left wide open and on the cleared space outside the palisade Indians, French-Canadians and the men of the garrison were intent upon the swift thrilling moves of the game being played. It was the Indian form of lacrosse, and players and spectators alike were worked up to a high pitch of excitement.

Suddenly, and seemingly as but a move in the game, the ball was tossed high in air and landed almost at the gate of the fort. In an instant what had been sport became war. The players rushed in a wild throng, snatching from the squaws who had been seated near the entrance hatchets which the women had concealed beneath their blankets. One trader, several officers and about two-thirds of the soldiers were murdered on the spot. Captain Etherington and Lieutenant Leslie, one of his junior officers, were seized and led off to the woods, presumably for a like but delayed fate.

Alexander Henry was in his own house when the massacre occurred, not having witnessed the game. He sought refuge with a near-by French-Canadian family and was concealed by them for a time, but repeated visits of the Indians and inquiries regarding him forced his protectors to give him up. For a month he and the surviving members of the garrison and community were constantly in danger, particularly at those times when their Indian captors were crazily drunk, but finally relief came from Fort Edward Augustus on Green Bay and negotiations procured their release. On July 18 the survivors of the massacre embarked for Montreal.

For more than a year there was no British garrison at Michilimackinac, nor indeed anywhere in the lakes region save at Detroit. But in September 1764 Captain William Howard arrived with two companies of the Seventeenth Regiment and other troops, and with him came also several traders. Captain Howard immediately took steps to rebuild and strengthen the fort, the new post being close to the former site on the south shore. For sixteen years this continued to be the military and trading center for the Northwest area and then a transfer was made to Mackinac Island.

The outstanding figure in the history of old Michilimackinac in this period of English occupation was Major Robert Rogers who became commandant in 1766. It was there he set on foot his plans for the expedition that was to cross the continent to the Pacific and search for the western end of the Northwest Passage, that dream of so many men before him. Rogers came to his post in the little schooner *Gladwin*, accompanied by his wife, one of the first Englishwomen to arrive in this distant region. The incidents of the next two years would fill a volume: the intrigues of Rogers and his quarrels with the commissary, Lieutenant Benjamin Roberts, ending with the arrest of Rogers and his trial by court-martial in Montreal on charges of treason, holding correspondence with enemies of his King and misappropriation of government monies. His acquittal but opened the way to further romantic and adventurous chapters in a career which, in its own way, has scarcely a rival in American history.

Captain Patrick Sinclair is the man who was responsible for the removal of the military post from the south side of the Straits to the island in its center. He was the first lieutenant governor of the Michilimackinac Territory under the new scheme of government of the Indian country set up by the British following the passing of the Quebec Act in 1774. Four western districts were established, the others being Detroit, Vincennes and the Illinois, and his fellow administrators were respectively Henry Hamilton, Edward Abbott and Matthew Johnson. Boundaries of the several territories were undefined but there was little risk, because of distance, of any clash of jurisdictions. For Michilimackinac Territory the seat of administration was to be the former French post on the south side of the Straits.

Sinclair was a native of Caithness, the most remote and northerly county on the mainland of Scotland. This inhospitable corner of old Scotia, with its bleak skies, frequent gales and chilling rains, gave to America not only Patrick Sinclair but also Arthur Saint Clair, the first governor of the Northwest Territory. They were born in the same year and within twenty-five miles of each other. Of Sinclair's early years little is known but in 1758, at the age of twenty-two, he purchased a commission in the Black Watch Highland Regiment. He was in America by 1760 and was with General Amherst when Montreal surrendered. But soon after he became connected with the Naval Department of the Lakes, where his duties were to supervise the shipping so as best to serve the needs of both the garrisons and traders. In this capacity he appears to have been the pioneer in making lake surveys, for in a petition dated 1769 he says that he is the only person to have aided navigation on the lakes "by taking exact soundings of them and the rivers and Straits which join them with the bearings of the headlands, islands, bays, etc."

In the spring of 1769 Sinclair returned to England, was promoted to a captaincy in 1773 and a year later retired from the army. He had friends in influential places who knew that he had made expenditures on behalf of the government for which he had received no recompense and they probably influenced his appointment in April 1775 as lieutenant governor and superintendent at Michilimackinac. He sailed at once for America but upon arrival at Baltimore was taken into custody by the revolutionary party, the movement for independence being now well under way. He was later allowed to return to England but came out again in the fall of 1777, landing at Philadelphia where he was advised by Sir William Howe to go to Quebec and from there attempt to reach his post. Communications between Philadelphia and Halifax and from Halifax to Quebec were so interrupted during this period that it was not until June 1779 that he arrived at the ancient capital on the St. Lawrence and four months later that he eventually came to the fort on the Straits. Four and a half years had passed since he received his commission.

The post to which Sinclair had been assigned was one of extreme importance at this time, but the buildings and defenses from which his sway was to extend were scarcely worthy of being called a fort. They were in about the same condition as in the days of French rule. Sinclair's predecessors in command of the garrison had on several occasions complained that their "rickety picket" was commanded by sand hills and that when gales were blowing the waves sometimes reached the actual line of the stockade. The place was not only incapable of defense but also afforded no protection to vessels. The Revolutionary War was progressing actively in the West under George Rogers Clark of Kentucky, who had already swept down upon Kaskaskia and Vincennes and might next strike at Detroit, thus isolating the post to the northwest. Four days after his arrival Sinclair sent off a message to Captain Brehm, aide to General Haldimand, governor of Canada, suggesting the removal of the fort to the island and adding the warning: "For God's sake be careful in the choice of an engineer and don't send up one of your paper engineers fond of fine regular polygons."

It took seven months for an answer to come from Haldimand but Sinclair was not idle in the interval. He secured from the Indians the little island in the Straits, henceforth called Mackinac, paying for it eighteen months later £5,000 New York currency. He waited for authority from no one but set to work clearing the ground and preparing materials for the buildings. Haldimand's reply, when it came, was entirely favorable and gave Sinclair authority to act as his own engineer, which must have pleased the man mightily. Work was prosecuted vigorously and by the summer of 1781 the garrison and headquarters were removed to the island. Construction was continued under Sinclair's direction until 1782, by which year nearly $300,000 had been spent. At that time Haldimand questioned some of the expenditures made at the post for presents to the Indians and Sinclair retired, later returning to England. There seems to have been no stigma upon his reputation for he was made a colonel in 1793, a major general in 1803, a lieutenant general in 1810, and when he died seven years later, at the age of eighty-four, he was the oldest officer of his rank in the army.

The fortifications which Sinclair erected are practically those which the visitor to Mackinac Island sees today. Originally there were four blockhouses, but that at the southeast corner was later removed. The walls have also been widened and raised higher and the roadway by which the cliff is ascended has been made of easier grade, for which all who visit the old fort must be grateful. But little change has come to the place in the more than a century and a half that it has looked out over the lovely waters of the Straits. Sinclair had planned to name the fort after Governor Haldimand but the latter insisted on the historic name being retained, which we must place to his credit. As the oldest center of civilization west of the Allegheny Mountains it would have been a pity had it been altered.

The change from mainland to island of fortress and garrison was accompanied by the removal also to the new location of much of the old community. Michilimackinac pulled itself up by the roots and was replanted. The old life continued in a new environment, the fur trade, always the master interest of the community, going on to a larger activity than anything that the past had recorded. From 1781 there came to Fort Mackinac the *voyageurs,* the traders, the Indians and always that fringe of almost unclassifiable persons who frequented every frontier community.

Mackinac was an English fort and it had an English commander and an English garrison, but the old French life and color could no more be eradicated there than it has been on the banks of the St. Lawrence after that section of America has had English rulers for nearly two centuries. Nor did anyone wish to change it. There was more French than English spoken and the little Jesuit church was the center of religious life for most of the community. Spring, above all, was the season of joy, for then the hand of winter fell from the island and with the returning leaves and flowers the *voyageurs* also came, bringing from long distances the furs that had been taken during the hunting season.

Shouts and songs heralded the arrival of the canoes, heading toward the landing beach day by day and coming from all directions. What greetings as the canoes grated on the soft sand and were unloaded of their valuable burdens! What inquiries about this one or that one, what boasts as to prowess in hunting! No modern carnival could vie with the place in color. Along the water front the fur traders were busy day and night, opening up the bundles of furs, computing their value, paying off the *voyageurs,* selling them new outfits and trinkets. And every place that had hard liquor was doing a whirlwind business. The hardships and toils, the dangers and privations of past months were quickly forgotten. Spring was here and the *voyageurs* were at Mackinac.

The Indians added their touches of color and interest. Along the beach, in a manner so often described by later travelers, their tepees went up as if by magic and they settled down to enjoy the excitement and have their share, too, of the good things that were to be had. With paint and feather they paraded wherever the white men congregated and their whoops and yells broke in on the old French songs or on the sound of the fiddle, that indispensable instrument at all social occasions, whether at Mackinac or any other French community.

"No wilderness," says one writer, "was so far away that the little

French fiddle had not been there. The Indian recognized it as a part of the furniture of every fur-trader's camp. At night, as the wanderers lounged around the blazing heap of logs, the sepulchral arches of the forest resounded with the piercing strains of tortured catgut, accompanying the gayly-turbaned voyageurs, as in metallic tones they chanted favorite melodies of the river, the chase, love and the wassail. In the village no christening or wedding was complete without the fiddler; and at the almost nightly social gatherings, in each other's puncheon-floored cabins, the fiddler, enthroned cross-legged on a plank table, was the king of the feast."[6]

So life went on with little change for fifteen years. Tidings must have come to Patrick Sinclair in the earliest days of the progress of the revolutionary forces in the East. Sometimes news of a more threatening nature came to him as the western campaign became menacing. But he was busy, and happy we may be sure, building the fort from which he was free to exclude all useless "polygons." In October 1782 he was at Quebec, ready to meet the questions that had been asked regarding his expenditures, and in 1783, when the representatives of England and her colonies were meeting in Paris to conclude the war and sign a treaty of peace, Sinclair was on the Island of Orleans in the St. Lawrence, still awaiting a decision from his superiors. It was not he who received the tidings at Mackinac that the island had passed from the hands of England to the newly independent states. It would have been a hard blow to give up the fort which was so much his own creation and to see the flag of his country descend and that of another take its place. He was spared the humiliation and he would have been spared it had he continued much longer as governor. For thirteen years the British held not only Mackinac but Detroit and other posts, despite the fact that they were within the boundary of the new United States.

Major Henry Burbeck was in charge of the two companies of American regulars who finally arrived at Mackinac on the first of September, 1796. Ever since the treaty of 1783 the British government, knowing that Mackinac would probably have to be

---

[6] Reuben Gold Thwaites, in *Wisconsin Historical Collections*, XIV (1898), 9.

given up eventually, had been seeking out a new center from which they might still control the fur trade. As early as February 1792, before John Jay had undertaken his mission to England, Lieutenant Governor John Graves Simcoe of Upper Canada had written from Montreal:

"Should it ever be thought an object to establish a settlement at the head of the Lake or change the present post at Michilimackinac, the Island of St. Joseph appears to be the best situation for that purpose, it is in the direct route of the canoes from the French River, and on the north side the ship channel to St. Mary's, which passes through Lake George, the narrows leading into which are not more than 200 yards wide."

The British had placed troops on St. Joseph Island as early as June 1796, so that when the Americans at last arrived at Mackinac the garrison of the place was able to retire immediately to a new post where the ground had already been cleared and where, soon after, fortifications were erected. To hold the Indian trade, invitations were sent to chiefs of the tribes to come to St. Joseph in 1798 where they would receive presents as in the past. The Indians having responded to the invitation, previous negotiations were completed by which the whole island passed into the hands of the British. Fort St. Joseph, when erected, was the most westerly military post of the army establishment in Canada.

Major Burbeck's report indicates that little had been done since the departure of Captain Sinclair toward improving the fort or even keeping it in proper repair. The wave of governmental economy which had entangled Sinclair had probably handicapped his successors, for all the woodwork, picketing and platforms had to be rebuilt by the incoming American garrison. However, the gardens were found in good order and a grassy park surrounded the fortifications. A year later, when General James Wilkinson came on a tour of inspection, the government house was described by one of his party as "elegant." Winthrop Sargent, secretary of the Northwest Territory, had visited the place in the meantime and had set up civil government, appointing justices of the peace and other necessary officers. At the time of Wilkinson's visit the village at the foot of the hill was said to consist of eighty-nine houses, two stores and the little Roman Catholic church.

The War of 1812 was the first of the conflicts waged in America which actually reached the Mackinac region. The old fort on the south shore had not felt the shock of attack during the French and Indian War, though it suffered a backwash of the war in the Pontiac uprising. Nor did old Fort Michilimackinac on the mainland nor Patrick Sinclair's creation on the island have any part in the conflict between England and her revolting colonies. It was a different story, however, when the second war with England came. Mackinac was then the center of the stirring events already narrated in this volume. For three years, from July 1812 to July 1815, the fort and island were in English hands, and when the invaders finally left, following the Treaty of Ghent, it was to go to near-by Drummond Island, at the very mouth of the St. Mary's River.

While the English were in possession of Mackinac they built a new fort at the summit of the island, naming it Fort George, but when the Americans returned they named it Fort Holmes in honor of Major Andrew Holmes, who was killed in the attempt at its capture in July 1814. It was later abandoned as a fortification and of those who visit the island today comparatively few climb to where the remains of old earthworks, restored by the Mackinac Island State Park Commission in 1936, serve as a reminder of the most warlike days the place ever knew—indeed many visitors to Mackinac do not even know that Fort Holmes ever existed.

The period following the War of 1812 was the heyday of the island as far as the fur trade was concerned, and since the fur trade dominated all else, it was the busiest time the island ever knew, and in many respects the most picturesque. An American garrison occupied the fort above the harbor, fur-trading establishments were expanding and the schooners which had given passenger service to Detroit or to the Sault were being challenged by the steamboats which soon came to the place, trailing clouds of light wood smoke behind them. The world outside began to hear about Mackinac in the pages of writers who visited the place and were enchanted with its beauty and romance. Little hints of the Mackinac that was yet to be were appearing.

When the *Walk-in-the-Water*, the first steamer on Lake Erie, extended her trips to Mackinac in June of 1819 she had a distinguished passenger in the person of Major General Jacob Brown, whose services in the War of 1812 had earned for him both the thanks of Congress and a medal struck in his honor. When peace came he continued in command of the northern division of the army and the purpose of his journey in 1819 was to inspect the more distant posts on the lakes.

At Mackinac the general was received with military honors and the soldiers of the garrison were put through various maneuvers, with the ladies and gentlemen who had arrived on the steamboat and all the citizens and Indians in the village attending as spectators. Captain Jones, one of General Brown's staff on this journey to the northern posts, grew almost lyrical in his journal as he wrote of the beauty of the place. "I never have seen a finer water prospect, either for extent or variety of natural scenery," says his diary. All things seemed to be combined to show what Nature could do. "Heavenly weather" prevailed and the apple trees were in blossom, yet at night a little fire was pleasant. It reminded the captain of October weather in Virginia.[7]

Before the departure of the *Walk-in-the-Water* for Detroit it was deemed courteous to return in some measure the hospitality of the garrison and of the little frontier village. Accordingly, the deck and cabins of the steamboat were thrown open to the villagers and many Indians also had been invited to share an excursion on the adjacent waters. Let us permit Captain Jones himself to picture the scene:

"On one side of the deck, ladies and gentlemen were gaily lead-

---

[7] A journal of the tour kept by Captain Roger Jones is preserved in the Library of Congress and is printed in the Buffalo Historical Society *Publications*, XXIV (1920), 295-323.

ing down country dances, and on the other side, the painted, fantastic Indians, decked in all their tinsel and savage costume, were equally happy, whilst they enjoyed their native dance.

> "Ever and anon, a half-concealed, half-naked, tawny thygh
> Was half uncovered, to white women's lowering eye."

During the week that followed, General Brown visited the Sault and went also to Green Bay by the schooner *Tiger.* Arriving back at Mackinac on July 9, the return journey to Detroit was made in record time, and we are told that the *Tiger* covered the stretch between Fort Gratiot and Detroit, sixty miles or more, in eight hours and ten minutes.

Charming pictures of social life on the island in the period of General Brown's visit have been left for us by Elizabeth Thérèse Baird who lived there as a young girl.[8] Mrs. Baird, "a woman of charming personality, proud of her trace of Indian blood and having a wide acquaintance with the principal men and women of early Wisconsin," saw much of the country in its early days, and a retentive memory enabled her to pass on information of rare value to historians.

Mrs. Baird's narrative tells us much of the island life in the winter season, when, with the Straits icebound, it was almost cut off from communication with the outside world. The population being predominantly Roman Catholic, much attention was paid to the church holidays which had both a religious and a social side, bringing neighbors and friends into pleasant contact.

"Some weeks before Christmas," she tells us, "the denizens of the island met in turns at each other's homes, and read the prayers, chanted psalms, and unfailingly repeated the liturgy of the saints. On Christmas eve, both sexes would read and sing, the service lasting till midnight. After this a *réveillon* [midnight treat] would be partaken of by all:

---

[8] Elizabeth Thérèse Baird, "Reminiscenses of Early Days on Mackinac Island." *Wisconsin Historical Collections,* XIV (1898), 17-64.

"The last meeting of this sort which I attended was at our own home, in 1823. The cooking was done at an open fire. I wish I could remember in full the bill of fare. We will begin with the roast pig; roast goose; chicken pie; round of beef *à la mode; pattes d'ours* (bear's paws, called so from the shape, and made of chopped meat in crust, corresponding to rissoles); sausage; head-cheese; souse; small-fruit preserves; small cakes. Such was the array. No one was expected to partake of every dish, unless he chose. Christmas was observed as a holy day. The children were kept at home, and from play, until nearly night-time, when they would be allowed to run out and bid their friends a 'Merry Christmas,' spending the evening, however, at home with the family, the service of prayer and song being observed as before mentioned. All would sing; there was no particular master,—it was the sentiment that was so pleasing to us; the music we did not care so much about."

When the Christmastide had passed, all the young people looked forward to New Year's Day. This was the occasion for giving presents. "On the eve of that day great preparations were made by a certain class of elderly men, usually fishermen, who went from house to house in grotesque dress, singing and dancing. Following this they would receive gifts. Their song was often terrifying to little girls, as the gift asked for in the song was *la fille aînée,* the eldest daughter. The song ran thus:

> "*Bon jour, le Maître et la Maîtress,*
> *Et tout le monde du loger.*
> *Si vous voulez nous rien donner, dites-le-nous;*
> *Nous vous demandons seulement la fille aînée!*"

As they were always expected, these visitors were sure to be well received. On this last evening of the year the children were sent off to bed at an early hour but at dawn on the happy New Year's morning they one and all went to the bedside of the parents to receive their benediction, an old custom doubtless brought long before from the province of Quebec.

Mrs. Baird's own Indian ancestry gave her a particular interest in the many tribes who came to the island. Her childhood had been passed with the Indians constantly about her, and she had deep sympathy for their weaknesses in the face of the temptations placed in their path by the white man.

"Many of their habits were startling," she recalled. "It was their custom while in towns to saunter about the streets in a very indifferent manner; and if they chose, to take a look at the interior of any house they might be passing. Men, women, or children, would spread their blankets to the top of their heads, to exclude the light, and then peer in through the windows to their heart's content. This was done at any home and no one dared to resist the intrusion. Indians never herald their approach. They never knock at a door; but stalk in, and squat themselves on the floor. You always heard a man come in, as his step was firm, proud and full of dignity. The women, however, made no sound."

Every year, at a particular season, the Indians who still held allegiance to the British passed in great numbers through the Straits headed for the place of distribution of presents. On their journey to Canada and on their way home once more they would stop off at the island, bringing with them on their return the broadcloth and ribbons, the beads and silver ornaments which they had received. Chiefs would appear, wearing high hats encircled by silver bands one and two inches wide. On their arms would be great silver bands worn both below and above the elbow, while earrings and brooches added to their splendor. In lean years, when the Indians sometimes ran out of provisions on their way to Canada, they would exchange the silver ornaments received in previous years for bread and potatoes. There was always a ready market for this British silver which was sure to be purchased far below its real value.

Such a place as Mackinac, a center of trade and travel, was bound to include in its population people who would be remembered long after by those who had known them. There was Dr. David Mitchell, of whose family Mrs. Baird left interesting memories. He was a British army surgeon who had married an Indian woman of the Ottawa tribe by whom he had several children. The daughters were sent to Europe and the sons to Montreal for their education. When the American troops came to Mackinac in 1796 Dr. Mitchell removed at once to Drummond Island, but the wife, daughters and two sons remained behind, engaging in the fur trade and adding to an already ample fortune. Mother and daughters visited with Dr. Mitchell during the summer but never stayed on with him in the winter.

The Indian wife, in addition to her other duties, maintained a farm of considerable size, hay being the principal crop, though grains and potatoes were also produced. In addition she had a fine vegetable garden, surrounded by a high whitewashed picket fence, and this she was accustomed to visit almost daily during the seasons of growth and harvest, coming in a two-wheeled calash which she drove herself. "When the old lady arrived," says Mrs. Baird, "the men would hasten to open the gate, then she would drive in, and there, in the large space in front of the garden beds, in the shade, the man would fasten the horses, while 'my lady' would walk all over the grounds giving her orders."

Mrs. Mitchell knew no English and her speech was such a combination of French, Ottawa and Chippewa that there were few who could understand her, though she is described as having got along admirably in company, by her expressive face and by signs making up for speech difficulties. Her dress, says Mrs. Baird, was as peculiar as her conversation:

"She always wore black,—usually her dresses were of black silk, which were always made in the same manner. A full skirt was gathered and attached to a plain waist. There were two large pockets on the skirt, and she always stood with her hands in these. About her neck was a black neckerchief; on her head she wore a black beaver hat, with a modest plume at one side. There were ties, but nowhere else on the bonnet was ribbon used. The bonnet she wore day and night. I do not think she slept in it, but never did I know of anyone who had seen her without it. She was quite large, tall and heavy. She was an intelligent woman, with exceptional business faculties, although devoid of book-learning. Her skill in reading character was considerable. Such was the 'Mistress of the manse.'"

We have glimpses also of John Tanner, that strange tragic figure in the Mackinac and Sault region. Kidnaped as a child by Indians, he grew to manhood among the Chippewa, married and had a family. Later he returned to civilized life and in the summer of 1820 came to Mackinac with his Indian wife and three children, one of them an infant but a few days old. The family was an object of curiosity even in that community which saw so many unusual people. Tanner discarded his Indian dress on his arrival at Mackinac, but he was not happy, nor was the wife. At intervals he disappeared, once to Kentucky and again to the Red River country. Later he became interpreter for the government agency at the Sault. Mrs. Jameson heard of him when she was there in 1837 and was interested in his story which had even before this attracted attention in England. William Cullen Bryant also mentions him in the account of his trip to the St. Mary's Falls in 1846. As the steamboat proceeded up the river the poet had pointed out to him a white chimney standing behind a screen of fir trees "which, we were told, had belonged to the dwelling of Tanner who himself set fire to the house the other day before murdering James Schoolcraft."[9] Bryant, coming fresh from the East, must have felt that he was on the very edge of civilization when he found the place excited over a murder but a few days old. He was like Dr. John Bigsby who, in 1823, at the Sault, realized how near he was to the frontier when one day he met in the street a handsome white woman "who wore a broad silver plate on her head on account of having been scalped."

In all its history Mackinac had few more interesting personages as dwellers than Henry Rowe Schoolcraft, the Indian agent for the

---

[9] James Schoolcraft, a brother of Henry R. Schoolcraft, the former Indian agent at the Sault, was shot from ambush on July 6, 1846. For many years it was believed that the murderer was John Tanner, since the latter disappeared at the same time, but today it is doubted that Tanner was responsible.

region from 1822 to 1841. He resided at the Sault until 1832, but thereafter on the island. He had accompanied Governor Cass on his northwest expedition in 1820 and thereby made his first acquaintance with the northern country in which he was to spend nearly a score of years. Shortly after the return of the expedition he was invited to become secretary of the commission appointed to meet and confer with the Indians at Chicago in the following summer. This gave him further acquaintance with the West and its Indian dwellers. Appointment to the post at the Sault followed.

In the score of years which he spent in the northern region, Schoolcraft acted as diplomat in the negotiation and conclusion of almost a dozen treaties with various tribes. The most important was that of 1836 by which all the Indian lands north of Grand River and Thunder Bay in Lake Huron were transferred to the United States government. This purchase was particularly auspicious for the new state of Michigan, clearing the title to one-third of the Lower Peninsula and to extensive territory to the north of the Straits.

But Schoolcraft was more than a mere Indian agent. He had the instincts of a scholar and being set down in a region where an ancient civilization was being replaced by a new, he set himself to the task of gathering all available information about the country and its primitive peoples. His extensive writings form a legacy for all who have had occasion since his time to study the life and thought of the aborigines among whom he lived and whose affairs were his particular concern. Moreover, his studies of the Indian legends and lore became the basis of one of the best known poems in American literature, Henry Wadsworth Longfellow's *Hiawatha.*

Travelers of distinction from the East and from overseas found welcome hospitality in the old agency house at Mackinac Island. It stood near the foot of the bluff, not far from the well-known Island House, until it was destroyed by fire in the winter of 1873-1874. Mrs. Jameson wrote of it when she was there in 1837:

"On a little platform, not quite half-way up the wooded height which overlooks the bay, embowered in foliage, and sheltered from the tyrannous breathing of the north by the precipitous cliff, rising almost perpendicularly behind, stands the house in which I find myself at present a grateful and contented inmate. The ground in front sloping down to the shore, is laid out in a garden, with an avenue of fruit trees, the gate at the end opening on the very edge of the lake."

From other descriptions of the Schoolcraft house we learn that a stockade ten feet high protected it from the street, and entrance to the garden was through a tall old-fashioned gateway opening on the avenue that led to the house. It was a rambling old building, additions having been made from time to time as need required. The larger rooms on each side of the main entrance had chimney pieces, candelabra on the mantels and brass andirons on the hearth-stones. It was a confusing house for a stranger. You might open a door expecting to step outside but instead it would lead off into some fresh group of little rooms. In the central portion of the house dormer windows indicated a second story and over the front door was the plate bearing the words "United States Agency."

The year 1836 was an especially busy one for Schoolcraft. In that summer the Indians gathered at the island to receive the payments due to them by the great treaty of that year. Looking back, he wrote in his diary: "... busy business summer, replete with incident and excitement on the island, closes this day by the termination of the several classes of payments made under the treaty. So large an assemblage of red and white men probably never assembled here before."

More than four thousand Indians were encamped in that summer along the beach and were subsisted for a month, while, before their departure, each separate village received two thousand dollars' worth of flour, pork, rice and corn. Money payments amounted to $220,000 and merchandise of a value of $150,000 was systematically divided among those present. "The Indians," wrote Schoolcraft, "went away with their canoes literally loaded with all that an Indian wants, from silver to a steel trap, and a practical demonstration was given which will shut their mouths forever with regard to the oft-repeated scandal of the stinginess and injustice of the American government."

One evil which persisted despite all that Schoolcraft could do to combat it was the sale of liquor to the Indians. Its deplorable effects upon them were noted by many visitors on the island where it was so freely sold. Mrs. Jameson tells of an evening when at twilight she stood by the gate of the Schoolcraft home and listened to "the sound of the Indian drum mingled with the shouts and yells and shrieks of the intoxicated savages, who were drinking in front of the village whiskey-store." An Ottawa chief whom she knew, The Rain by name, drew near, "one of the noblest figures I ever beheld, above six feet high, erect as a forest tree." He stood deep in thought, apparently undecided whether he should join the drunken crowd or go home to his lodge. She watched him, then to her sorrow saw him draw his blanket about him and stride away in the direction of the village "with an air of defiance and a step that would have become a prince."

Francis Parkman visited Mackinac in 1845. A youth of twenty-two, he had already determined that his life work should be to write the history of the great struggle between France and England for possession of North America. In his diaries he was busily setting down details that would give life and color to those projected narratives, and of Mackinac he wrote, in notebook form:

"The place is the picture of an ancient Canadian settlement, the little houses in Canadian style, some of them log, with roofs thatched with bark, the picket-fences of rough sharpened stakes that surround them all, the canoes and Indian huts on the shore give them a wild and picturesque air. Wild-looking half-breeds in abundance, a group of squaws and children wrapped in their blankets, sat on the steps of a store, one little Canadian, three-quarters savage, had a red shawl tied around his head, red leggins, gay moccasins and a blanket coat. Another, who looked out from beneath his straight black locks with a wild and particularly vile expression, was staring at the steamer."

And this little incident also:

"Last night the Indians in the lodges on the beach got drunk. I heard them singing for a long time in a mournful, maudlin fashion, repeating the same words, and varying the song with what seemed to be boasts or narratives of exploits. The same monotonous music rose from half a dozen lodges that stood in line together."

Margaret Fuller, journalist and social reformer, "high priestess of American Transcendentalism," followed in the path of Anna Jameson in 1842, visiting Mackinac and the Sault and extending her trip into Illinois and Wisconsin. Like Mrs. Jameson she was fascinated by the Indians whom she saw on the banks of the St. Clair River as her steamer moved toward Lake Huron, and could not help contrasting their freedom with the materialism of the New England emigrants, her fellow passengers, who had brought with them "their habits of calculation, their cautious manners, their love of polemics."

"It grieved me," she wrote, "to hear these immigrants, who were to be the fathers of a new race, all, from the old man down to the little girl, talking, not of what they should do, but of what they should get in the new scene. It was to them a prospect, not of the unfolding nobler energies, but of more ease and large accumulation."

But her soul was cheered by the first sight of Mackinac, where "man seemed to have worked in harmony with Nature instead of rudely invading her as in most Western towns." And here were more Indians. She wished that there might have been a Sir Walter Scott present to describe those "weather-beaten, sullen but eloquent figures," but she herself made much of them in her *Summer on the Lakes,* published a year later.

For a week and more she reveled in the sights and sounds, and, to a lesser degree, in the smells of her Indian friends. It was the time of year when members of the Chippewa and Ottawa tribes came to receive their annual gifts from the Great White Father at Washington and she found more than two thousand encamped on the beach with more arriving every day. At break of dawn she was out among the rude lodges, finding activity everywhere, "children creeping out from beneath the blanket door of the lodge, women pounding corn in their rude mortars, young men playing on their pipes." But this music was practiced only, she learned, to allure a mate. There was no music for the wife or mother.

When afternoon came the prospect, as she looked down upon the beach, was even more attractive. "The Indians were grouped and scattered among the lodges; the women preparing food, in the kettle or frying-pan, over the many small fires; the children, half naked, wild as little goblins, were playing both in and out of the water. Here and there lounged a young girl, with a baby at her back. . . . Some girls were cutting wood, a little way from me, talking and laughing, in the low musical tone, so charming in the Indian women. Many bark canoes were upturned upon the beach; others coming in, their square sails set, and with almost arrowy speed, though heavily laden with dusky forms, and all the apparatus of their households."

She went to the Sault for a few days and on her return found the Indians leaving for their forest haunts. It was not as pleasant as it had been to watch them come in. The departing canoe was a beautiful object but the beach was a litter of old rags, dried boughs, fragments of food and marks of the campfires. Her reflections were less pleasant also. She had observed that her Indian sisters were degraded. The married women she found almost invariably coarse and ugly, with an awkward gait and backs bent by carrying burdens. Only their eyes retained some beauty, and in their manners there was a decorum and delicacy. They would not stare, however great their curiosity, but only cast sidelong glances.

Her idealistic conception of the red man had begun to weaken during those days on Mackinac. Whatever the Indian might be in a state of nature, he had fallen far by contact with the white man. "Our people and our government have sinned alike against the first-born of the soil," she wrote, and began to wonder whether this new state was better than the dog feasts and bloody rites of the past. Only Mackinac itself could ease her mind. There were still the pleasant evenings, looking over old-fashioned gardens or over the beach and the waters under the clear moonlight. But all good things have an end and at two o'clock one morning the *Great Western* came snorting in and Mackinac was left behind, a dream within a dream.

When the middle thirties had arrived, the importance of Mackinac in the fur trade was visibly declining and already there were indications of what the island would eventually come to be. Schoolcraft saw it when he wrote in 1835: "The rage for investment in lands was now manifest in every visitor that came from the East to the West. Everybody more or less yielded to it. . . . Among other plans, an opinion arose that Michilimackinac must become a favorite watering place, or refuge for the opulent and invalids during the summer; and lots were eagerly bought up from Detroit and Chicago."

Mrs. Jameson also foresaw the coming change. The year prior to her visit there had been a number of strangers holidaying on the island. "This year," she wrote, "there is only one permanent visitor—a most agreeable little Irish-woman, with the Irish warmth of heart and ease of manner. She has brought her children here for the summer, and has her piano, her French and Italian books, and we have begun an acquaintance which is likely to prove very pleasant." Mackinac, in Mrs. Jameson's opinion also, was destined to become a "watering place for Michigan and Wisconsin fashionables."

William Cullen Bryant also experienced the charm of the place when he was there in 1846 on his way to the Sault and wondered if it would not be spoiled in days to come. The steamer halted but a short time on the upbound trip and he had only a moment at Mackinac, "a moment to gaze into the clear waters, and count the fish as they played about without fear twenty or thirty feet below; a moment to look at the fort on the heights, dazzling the eyes with its new whiteness; a moment to observe the habitations of this ancient village, some of which show you roofs and walls of red-cedar bark confined by horizontal strips of wood, a kind of architecture between the wigwam and the settler's cabin."

He was able to see more of the island when his steamer returned. He appreciated its possessing beauty. But the place was crowded with strangers. "I remember," he wrote, "hearing a lady say that she was tired of improvements, and only wanted to find a place that was finished, where she might live in peace. I think I shall recommend Mackinac to her. I saw no change in the place since my visit to it five years ago. It is so lucky as to have no back country, it offers no advantages to speculation of any kind; it produces, it is true, the finest potatoes in the world, but none for exportation."

But doubts were present also in the poet's mind: "It may, however, became a fashionable watering-place, in which case it must yield to the common fate of American villages, and improve, as the phrase is. I cannot see how it is to escape this destiny. The world has not many islands as beautiful as Mackinac. I can not but think with a kind of regret on the time which, I suppose is near at hand, when its wild and lonely woods will be intersected with highways and filled with cottages and boardinghouses."

A century has passed since Bryant was at Mackinac Island and if he were to return today he would be startled to find how little change has taken place. The highways are few and wind about the island in no such straight lines as he must have anticipated but accommodating themselves to the twists and turns that Nature herself has enforced. The quiet is not disturbed by the blasts of auto horns, for there are no automobiles on the island. Only the regular *clop, clop* of horses drawing the ancient carriages in which visitors are driven disturbs the stillness of the forest-bordered roads. The odor of pine and cedar is all about.

The poet would see new landing places for the steamboats and he would see pleasant old houses, painted white and set behind picket fences that were not there in 1846. If his first glance were toward the fort he would find it almost unchanged, still gleaming white in the sunshine. Going a little off the main street he would find the old John Jacob Astor fur warehouse, not doing business as of old but now preserved as a memory of an earlier chapter in the island's history. It would seem like old days to see the white cross-crowned church and the quaint inscriptions on the gravestones in its shadow. The little frame stores on the winding main street might appear strange and he would wonder what was meant by the word "Movie" over a doorway. He would miss, surely without regret, the old "whiskey-stores" and most of all he would miss the Indians' tepees along the beach and the Indians themselves.

Seen from the deck of an approaching vessel the island rises mistily at first and then more clearly as a mass of green foliage set in the blue water of the Straits. Anna Jameson said she must despair of properly describing it unless her words were "of light, and lustrous hues and breathing music." Harriet Martineau said that it was the "wildest and tenderest bit of beauty" she had ever seen.

Palatial steamboats, their decks crowded with passengers, move today through the same waters that rippled beneath the canoes of Jean Nicolet and Father Marquette and the many others who came this way long ago. Island residents come down to the dock to meet the incoming steamer just as villagers elsewhere go to the station to see the evening train go through. On the main street the ancient vehicles stand ready for fares. Where did all these outdated carriages come from? How did they escape spending their old age in the Dearborn Museum at Detroit?

For two months in the year Mackinac is thronged with visitors. Its hotels accommodate the annual gatherings of organizations of every kind. Businessmen meet to discuss their problems. College fraternities and sororities hold their conventions and the streets are lively with youth. Politicians gather in this pleasant atmosphere to draft platforms and plan campaigns. At night the lights gleam out from the long, slim freighters passing to and from the ports on Lake Michigan. The roar of their whistles echoes among the cliffs. The commerce that once was furs is today coal and iron ore and limestone and grain. Mackinac has seen it all, the canoe, the bateau, the little schooner, the larger sailing ships, the wooden steamers, the steel freighters, each with its cargo. It once waited months for a letter to arrive; today the outside world is brought closer than the neighbor next door. But the spirit which seems to brood over this little island once so sacred to the Indians remains unchanged.

Mackinac Island Park Commission Photo

LOOKING OUT UPON THE STRAITS

View from the walls of old Fort Mackinac. Through these waters went Nicolet in 1634, the first known white man to enter Lake Michigan. Today a vast commerce moves through the Straits.

Mackinac Island Park Commission Photo

A CORNER OF OLD FORT MACKINAC

This blockhouse is one of three remaining. From within the stockade a beautiful view is obtained of the Straits connecting Lake Huron and Lake Michigan.

Mackinac Island Park Commission Photo

WITHIN OLD FORT MACKINAC

No officers' commands are heard today or sounds of men drilling. The historic old post, established by Patrick Sinclair in 1781, is today but a reminder of the past. Its museum contains interesting relics of garrison days.

Mackinac Island Park Commission Photo

OLD FORT MACKINAC

This view is taken from the little park at its foot. The statue of Father Marquette, who with Jolliet discovered the Mississippi River, is in the foreground.

Part III

FOUR LAKE HURON STORIES

Chapter 12

A Victorian Lady Visits Lake Huron

The ways through which my weary steps I guide
In this delightful land of faëry,
Are so exceeding spacious and wide,
And sprinkled with such sweet variety
Of all that pleasant is to ear or eye,
That I nigh ravish'd with rare thought's delight,
My tedious travel doe forget thereby,
And when I'gin to feel decay of might
It strength to me supplies, and clears my dulled
    spright.

—SPENSER

THE advent of the steamboat on Lake Huron opened up a new world of mystery and beauty and wonder for visitors from the eastern states and from abroad. Mackinac and Sault Ste. Marie, hitherto regarded as on the outward edge of civilization, soon became the objective points of a new "fashionable tour," taxing the capacity of the vessels that plied north from Detroit. It was an era of romanticism, and the Indian and the *voyageur* and the fur trader all became part of a popular conception that was often far removed from reality.

Every variety of experience and prejudice and prepossession was represented in those who came on this northern tour. We may wish that Charles Dickens, when he was in America in 1842, had included the upper lakes in his journeyings. His only contact with these inland waters was between Sandusky and Buffalo, aboard a small steamer with high-pressure engines which made him think of "lodgings on the first floor of a powder mill." But there were many other English visitors, some of whom left records

233

of their experiences and impressions. Harriet Martineau, "a woman who could not exist without a cause to cherish," came in 1834 when a certain condescension toward Americans was still prevalent, but she showed herself one of the most open-minded of the many who pictured the republic for their fellow countrymen. Captain Frederick Marryat and Anna Jameson both traveled northward in 1837 and left quite differing impressions on Henry R. Schoolcraft, the Indian agent at Mackinac, whose home was opened to all such visitors from the outside world.

"It seems to me," he wrote, "that Englishmen and Englishwomen look on America very much as one does when he peeps through a magnifying glass on pictures of foreign scenes, and the picturesque ruins of old cities and the like. They are really very fine but it is difficult to realize that such things are. It is all an optical deception. It was clearly so with Marryat, a very superficial observer; Miss Martineau, who was in search of something ultra and elementary, and even Mrs. Jameson, who had the most accurate and artistic eye of all, but who, with the exception of some bits of womanly heart, appeared to regard our vast woods, and wilds, and lakes, as a magnificent panorama, a painting in oil."

Schoolcraft had been advised in advance that he would find in Marryat "one of Smollet's sea-captains." "Stick Mackinac into him with all its rock-osities," was the suggestion made by a friend.

"He turned out a regular sea-urchin," Schoolcraft recorded, "ugly, rough, ill-mannered and conceited beyond all bounds. Solomon says 'Answer not a fool according to his folly,' so I paid him all attention, drove him over the island in my carriage, and rigged him out with my canoe-elège to go to St. Mary's. I saw a good deal of the novelist. His manners and style of conversation appeared to be those of a sailor, and such as we should look for in his own Peter Simple. He aimed to be knowing when it was difficult to conceal ignorance."

Mrs. Jameson, who visited in the Schoolcraft home in 1837, left only pleasant memories behind her. "We thought her a woman of beauty and warm affections and attachments," wrote her host.

"The freedom from restraint in her motions was an agreeable trait in a person of her literary tastes and abilities. She took a very lively interest in the Indian race and their manners and customs, doubtless with views of benevolence for them as a peculiar race of man, but also as a fine subject of artistic observation."

So they came, visitors from overseas and from the older states, some with strange and weird ideas of the Indian and this north country in which he made his home. Schoolcraft received them all and in his memoirs records what he thought of them and what they thought of the people in this frontier region.

Anna Jameson came to America in 1836, not, as did so many English visitors, for the purpose of writing a book about the country, but to see if it were possible to live happily with her husband, Robert Jameson, who held a judicial position in the colonial administration of Upper Canada. The union was an example of marriage at leisure and repentance in haste. She first met Jameson in 1820, a good-looking and seemingly agreeable young barrister, by whom she was alternately attracted and repelled but whom she finally married in 1825. A week or two was sufficient to show that they were unsuited to each other. She turned to literature for consolation and, beginning with the anonymous *A Lady's Diary,* she continued until her death in 1860 to turn out volume after volume, much of it in the field of art criticism.

Jameson went out to Dominica in 1829 to a judgeship and four years later was made attorney general of Upper Canada. He urged her to join him at the little provincial capital, York, now Toronto, but when she arrived there on a cold winter day he was not even on hand to welcome her and it did not take long to show that there was no more hope than in the past for married happiness. However, with a writer's instinct, she realized that there was material for a book if she could but see something of the new country. Out of that thought came her journey around the north shore of Lake Erie and up Lake Huron. Her travel experiences during the summer of 1837 are all told in *Winter Studies and Summer Rambles,* published in New York in 1839. She had an intense curiosity regarding the Indians, of whom she had probably read much in the romantic literature of the time. Her curiosity was fully answered during the tour of the lakes.

It was still a considerable adventure for a woman unused to the frontier and delicately reared as was Anna Jameson to go unaccompanied as far north as Sault Ste. Marie. Nathaniel Hawthorne wrote of her in his notebook: "She must have been perfectly pretty in her day, a blue, or grey-eyed, fair-haired beauty." Fanny Kemble spoke of her as fair, small, delicately-featured, "with a skin of that dazzling whiteness which generally accompanied reddish hair such as hers was." She had found the provincial society at York intolerably dull, "a small community of fourth-rate, half educated, or uneducated people where local politics of the meanest kind engross the men and household cares the women." Nowhere had she met with so many discontented, repining women as in Canada. But once she left that stifling official atmosphere behind her, a new world began to open. *Winter Studies and Summer Rambles,* in so far as it relates to this journey, is a cheerful, joyous record of a brief period in her life to which she must often have looked back with satisfaction.

She traveled overland from York to the little village of Chatham on the Thames River, stopping on the way to visit the famous Colonel Tom Talbot, the founder of the growing settlements along the north shore of Lake Erie. At Chatham she boarded a steamer that took her by way of the Thames River and Lake St. Clair to Detroit. "A wretched little boat, dirty and ill-contrived," she described it. The upper deck, to which she fled from the close hot cabin, was merely an open platform without railing. There she installed herself with chair, table, pencil and paper, sketching and writing, though always in danger that a sudden gust of wind would turn her large umbrella into a parachute and carry her and all her accouterments overboard.

All about her and on the deck below were Scotch, Irish and American emigrants who had journeyed westward through Upper

Canada on their way to Illinois. A family group from Vermont interested her particularly. The head of the family, over sixty years of age, his shrewd face burned a deep, brick-red color, the sinews of his hands like knotted whipcords, had with him fifteen children by three wives. The latest wife, a careworn-looking little woman, probably thirty years younger than her husband, spent her whole time dispensing to her brood their rations of lard, Indian corn bread and pieces of sassafras root.

The decks were everywhere encumbered with a confusion of wagons, oxen, horses and barrels of flour and sacks of grain. It was a hot summer day and even on the open lake there was scarcely a breath of air, but at sundown a fresh breeze came and with it the first view of Detroit—spires and towers against the sky, steamboats and schooners and little canoes on the river, noisy docks, busy streets, all "bathed in the light of a sunset such as I have never seen, not even in Italy."

Detroit itself proved less pleasant than anticipated—perhaps the hotel accommodation was crude—but on the morning of July 19 she went aboard the *Thomas Jefferson* to voyage to more distant shores. She had been in Detroit only a few days but a "cortege of amiable people" was at the dock to say farewell. Mrs. Jameson had a genius for making friends, a charm that drew people to her all her days, and so General Schwarz and his family were there, and the sister of the governor, and certain other ladies and gentlemen whose talk was so pleasant that she regretted she had not seen more of them.

The *Thomas Jefferson* provided as good accommodation as was then to be had. It was a comparatively new steamboat, built at Erie in 1834, having upper-deck cabins and carrying sails to assist the engines in favorable weather. In contrast to the steamer in which she had come to Detroit the cabins of the *Jefferson* were beautifully furnished and carpeted, with draperies of blue silk. Beneath the awnings on the upper deck were rocking chairs where the passengers might take their ease.

The captain told her that the year before he had never gone up Lake Huron with less than four or five hundred passengers. But times were bad in the summer of 1837—that was the year of the panic—and so there were less than two hundred on board. Among them she met Mr. Fletcher Webster,[1] a son of the "Godlike Daniel," who was going out to Illinois to look after his father's lands in that state. The statesman himself had been in Detroit when she arrived there, "appealing to the people against the money transactions of the government," but illness prevented her from seeing or hearing him. This she greatly regretted, since she would so much have liked to talk to him.

Another fellow passenger was the Right Reverend Samuel A. McCoskry, rector of St. Paul's Episcopal Parish in Detroit, who a year before had become Bishop of the Diocese of Michigan. Mrs. Jameson had heard him preach on a Sunday in Detroit and had been "childishly surprised" to find that instead of the traditional English bishop, an old gentleman in a wig and lawn sleeves, this bishop was a young man of very elegant appearance, "wearing his own fine hair" and in a plain black silk gown. He was no less a surprise as a fellow traveler. She had greatly admired his pulpit utterance and she found his conversation quite as good as his preaching. He was then on his way to visit some of the more remote missions of a diocese that was eight hundred miles long and four hundred miles wide. She learned many things from the bishop, one being that in his opinion two-thirds of the misery which came under the notice of a popular clergyman arose from the "infelicity of the conjugal relations." Mrs. Jameson could have given the bishop some information on that subject—perhaps she did, for serious reflections upon the topic follow immediately in her journal. As for the bishop, he too was to know personally such "infelicity," for he ended his clerical career in disgrace following an unfortunate infatuation for a young girl of Detroit.

Life on the *Thomas Jefferson* was truly delightful, a little world,

---

[1] The Twelfth Massachusetts Regiment of Civil War days was known as Fletcher Webster's. At Second Bull Run he gave his life for the flag his father loved.

a miniature social system in itself. She had brought as reading Miss Sedgwick's tale *The Poor Rich Man and the Rich Poor Man,* and also *The Travels and Adventures of Alexander Henry.* But far more absorbing were the people about her. First of all there were her more aristocratic friends, Mr. Fletcher Webster and the bishop. Also on board was General Hugh Brady, an officer of high distinction of whom she wanted to ask a thousand things, but she found him of a "silent and modest temper" and so had to content herself with admiring his fine military bearing as he paced alone up and down the deck. In another class were the missionaries and the missionaries' families, military officers on their way to northern garrisons, and a few traders. But most numerous were the emigrants with their faces turned to the West—Germans and Norwegians, and Irish "with good-natured potato faces, and strong arms and willing hearts." Yet perhaps the *Thomas Jefferson* had no more interesting person on its passenger list than Mrs. Jameson herself.

She found pleasure, as has every traveler since, in viewing the blue water and ever-changing scenery of the St. Clair River. At Palmer's Landing (St. Clair) fourteen men were kept busy for four hours bringing aboard wood as fuel for the boilers. She learned here of several amusing metaphors which were in common use in the lakes region.

"Will you take in wood?" was an invitation to take refreshment, liquid or solid.

"Is your steam up?" meant "Are you ready to go?"

Every minute brought some new picture to be described in her journal or set down in her sketchbook: the river shores widening into little bays, the dense forest always close at hand, the bateaux of the Canadians or the canoes of the Indians gliding along winding channels or shooting across the river; now and then a schooner, its white sails gleaming against the green mass of foliage, then gracefully curtsying and passing along; wild fowl disporting among the reedy marshes, and here and there a great black loon, diving and skipping, or skimming over the waters.

It was night when the river was left behind, and when morning came the steamboat was crossing Saginaw Bay. Like many another traveler since, Mrs. Jameson sought her berth while on this troubled bit of water but later in the day was able to note the totally unbroken character of the forests along the Huron shore of Michigan. Thunder Bay lighthouse seemed "terrific in its solitude." When night came the boat was still on the fresh-water sea.

Morning brought Mackinac Island and it required pages of her journal to record first impressions. "Mackinac! That fairy island," she wrote later, "which I shall never see again! And which I should have dearly liked to filch from the Americans, and carry home to you in my dressing box, or, *perdie,* in my toothpick case." She was so thrilled by the view that the steamer might have carried her away had not the good bishop awakened her from her dream and hurried her to the pier. She found a little inn kept by a half-breed woman "who spoke Indian, bad French and worse English" but who immediately placed before her guests an excellent breakfast of whitefish, eggs, tea and coffee. Then, with sketchbook in hand, she went to the beach where, amid more than one hundred wigwams, every phase of Indian domestic life was before her. Women were busy with their cooking, pounding Indian corn in primitive mortars. Close to shore, men were spearing fish. Details of costume were quickly recorded, the blue or scarlet leggings, the deerskin moccasins, the necklaces, the silver earrings, the curious bark cradles in which the babies were carried. All of these and a hundred other features of Indian life were to fascinate her during her stay on the island.

Mr. Schoolcraft invited her to be a guest in his home, a privilege which was enhanced by the presence of Mrs. Schoolcraft, granddaughter of a great Chippewa chief and warrior. More than one writer has paid tribute to the beauty of character of this woman, the daughter of John Johnston, a trader at the Canadian Sault, and his Indian wife. Mrs. Schoolcraft's grave is in the old burial ground of St. John's Church at Ancaster, not far from Hamilton, Ontario. On the large flat stone it is recorded that Jane, wife of Henry R.

Schoolcraft, Esq., was born at St. Mary's Falls on January 31, 1800, and that she died May 22, 1842, while visiting her sister Charlotte, the wife of the Reverend William McMurray, rector of the parish. The lives of all these people are closely linked with the early history of the Sault region.

Mrs. Jameson became deeply attached to Mrs. Schoolcraft and when she finally left the island it was in the company of her hostess. Sault Ste. Marie was their objective and the two days' journey was made in a little Canadian bateau, rowed by five *voyageurs* who occupied the ends of the little craft, where also was stowed baggage and provisions. The clear space in the center was reserved for the passengers. With sail hoisted, the rowers took their ease and navigation of the craft was left to the youngest of the group, a half-breed lad of eighteen, who announced that he was captain. When the breeze fell at evening the men all pleaded fatigue and curled up under their blankets, leaving the care of the boat to the boy, who kept himself awake by singing hymns in which Mrs. Schoolcraft joined him. At midnight the bateau was tied to a tree but kept a little offshore to avoid the mosquitoes.

"Whenever I awoke from uneasy, restless slumbers," Mrs. Jameson wrote, "there was Mrs. Schoolcraft, bending over her sleeping children, and waving off the mosquitoes, singing all the time a low, melancholy Indian song; while the northern lights were streaming and dancing in the sky, and the fitful moaning of the wind, the gathering clouds, and chilly atmosphere foretold a change of weather."

The Sault provided a wide variety of interests and experiences and, above all, abundant opportunity to see the Indians. She was taken to see old Mrs. Johnston, the Indian mother of Mrs. Schoolcraft, and after a dinner which she described as the best dressed and the best served that she had seen since she left Toronto, there followed a visit to the wigwam of Mrs. Johnston's brother, set on the verge of an old Chippewa burial place. Though it was but the typical Indian dwelling, formed of poles stuck in the ground and covered with mats and skins, within there was a measure of comfort and tidiness and, as Mrs. Jameson particularly noted, no disagreeable smell. The place was not far from the head of the rapids and the temptation to adventure through in an Indian canoe was first strong and then overpowering.

"The canoe being ready," she wrote, "we launched into the river. It was a small fishing canoe, about ten feet long, quite new and light and elegant and buoyant as a bird on the waters. I reclined on a mat at the bottom, Indian fashion, in a minute we were within the verge of the rapids, and down we went with a whirl and a splash—the white surge leaping around me—over me. The Indian with astonishing dexterity kept the head of the canoe to the breakers, and somehow or other we danced through them. I could see, as I looked over the edge of the canoe, that the passage between the rocks was sometimes not more than two feet in width, and we had to turn sharp angles—a touch of which would have sent us to destruction—all this I could see through the transparent, eddying waters, but I can truly say, I had not even a momentary sensation of fear, but rather of giddy, breathless, delicious excitement. The whole affair, from the moment I entered the canoe till I reached the landing place, occupied seven minutes and the distance is about three quarters of a mile."

Mrs. Jameson would gladly have stayed long at the Sault, so fascinated was she by the frontier life all about her. She said a regretful good-by to friends, and in company with the Church of England missionary, Reverend Mr. McMurray, and his wife, began the long return journey to Toronto. Her plan was to go by the North Shore and Georgian Bay route to Penetanguishine and then overland to the little provincial capital. Her experiences were more adventurous than on earlier stages of the journey and she was given abundant opportunity to see the Indians while on Manitoulin Island.

The party left the Sault in a small well-built boat manned by four Canadian *voyageurs* whose names are recorded: Pierrot, described as a most comical fellow; Masta, a great talker; Content, the steersman and captain; and Le Blanc, who always led the singing. They received a fixed daily allowance of fat pork, Indian meal and tobacco. Whenever possible the sail was hoisted, the little craft making good speed and proving seaworthy even in rough water, though its pitching was not always pleasant for the passengers. From one such experience Mrs. Jameson has left us what may be regarded as a most concise and accurate description of the progress of seasickness: "We became all at once very silent, then very grave, then very pathetic, and at last extremely sick."

At La Cloche the party met the first and only signs of civilization during the voyage. The North West Company had a trading station at this point, a small village made up of the large log house used as factory and headquarters, the huts for the work people and the ruder dwellings of the Indians. Table was laid for supper in the great hall when they arrived but the party did not halt. They took away with them, however, a large dish of broiled fish and a can of milk.

On the following morning as the bateau was headed toward the barely discernible shore of Manitoulin Island, away in the distance there appeared something like the black hull of a vessel which gradually grew more distinct, with masts rising against the sky. It proved to be a great heavy-built schooner going up the lake against wind and current. A man was standing in her bow with an immense oar which he pulled slowly as he walked backward and forward, though the vessel seemed to lie still like a great black log. As the bateau came nearly alongside they hailed the stranger with the question: "What news?"

And the answer was that King William IV of England was dead and that the young Princess Victoria reigned in his stead. "We sat silent looking at each other," wrote Mrs. Jameson. "Meantime, many thoughts came into my mind—some tears too into my eyes—not certainly for that dead king but for that living queen so young and fair—

> " 'As many hopes hang on that noble head
> As there hang blossoms on the boughs in May.' "

Special good fortune favored Mrs. Jameson on Manitoulin Island for she arrived at the government post just at the time when the annual distribution of presents was made to those Indians who were in allegiance to the British government. Nearly four thousand had assembled, of various tribes and many of them from far distant points. With pencil and sketchbook she was busy during the next few days setting down details of face and figure and costume while in her journal was recorded the lengthy ceremonial of a council between the chiefs and the representative of the Great White Father over the seas. She watched women putting the birchbark on the framework of a canoe, she saw a man who was said to have devoured his wife and two children during a winter of famine and was shunned by the other Indians, she looked cautiously and hesitantly at scalps suspended as decorations to warrior dress and confessed that she never could see without a start "the scalp of long fair hair." She talked with the missionaries who were present, Father Crue, the Roman Catholic, "always on the go—up the lake and down," and the Methodist missionaries. "Zealous men" she found them, and lamented that the Church of England was not represented in this region.

On the sixth of August she bade good-by to the McMurrays, who were returning to the Sault, and made preparations for the second stage of her journey which was to be by canoe and in company with Mr. Jarvis, the chief superintendent of Indian affairs. There were twenty-two in the party: twenty-one men and herself. Two canoes, each twenty-five feet long and four in width, were required, and Mrs. Jameson suffered few discomforts.

"My blankets and night gear being rolled up in a bundle served for a seat and I had a pillow at my back," she wrote. "I had near me my cloak, umbrella and parasol, my note-books and sketchbooks, and a little compact basket always by my side, containing eau de Cologne, and all those necessary luxuries which might be wanted in a moment."

She was fascinated by the skill of the Indian steersman, Martin.

In a cotton shirt, arms bared to the shoulder, loose trousers, a scarlet sash richly embroidered with beads, with his long black hair waving, he stood in the stern, twisting and turning himself with the agility of a snake, wielding his long paddle, first on one side and then on the other, graceful and picturesque in every movement. His fellow paddlers, young, good-looking, were clothed much the same, a shirt and trousers, the usual gay sash and a kerchief twisted round the head. We may be sure that they were depicted in the sketchbooks.

She found that the *voyageurs* measured the distance by *pipes*. Regularly there was a pause of about five minutes for a smoke and she calculated that *trois pipes* was twelve miles. She loved the canoemen's singing, very animated if not always harmonious and timed by their paddles. One always led, but in these there was a diversity of taste and skill. "If I wished to hear *En roulant ma boule roulant* I applied to Le Duc. Jacques excelled in *La belle rose blanche,* and Louis was great in *Trois canards s'en vont baignant.*"

They landed one day on the "Island of Skulls," an ancient sepulcher of the Huron; skulls and bones lay scattered about among the stones that had once been heaped over them. They rounded the cape which Alexander Henry had called the Pointe aux Grondines, with its constant swell and perpetual sound of water breaking on the rocks. They passed within a few miles of the mouth of French River out of which Champlain's canoe had come on a summer day over two hundred years before, and one day they saw through a misty atmosphere the outline of Christian Island, long ago the refuge of the war-scourged Huron. One of the canoemen, Dupré, told Mrs. Jameson that there were still to be seen on the island the remains of "une grande cathédrale."[2] Finally at nine o'clock one night the canoes entered the bay at Penetanguishine and the tour of the lakes was completed. Mrs. Jameson was given a room with a

---

[2] On Christian Island there are still remains of the massive stone mission station erected by the Jesuits in the summer of 1649 following the dispersal of the Huron Indians by their Iroquois enemies. To the illiterate mind of the canoeman the religious association of the ruins evidently suggested the idea of a cathedral.

bed but sleep came unwillingly. She wished that she were again, as for a week past, making her bed on a rock.

From Toronto she wrote to her friend Mrs. Schoolcraft at Mackinac: "As long as I live the impression of your kindness, and of your character altogether, remains with me; your image will often come back to me, and I dare to hope that you will not forget me quite."

Of her return journey she wrote: "It was all delightful; the most extraordinary scenery I ever beheld, the wildest! I recall it as a dream."

And of the Indians she observed: "The propinquity of the white man is destructive to the red man; and the further the Indians are removed from us the better for them. In their own woods they are a noble race; brought near to us, a degraded and stupid race. We are destroying them off the face of the earth."

Chapter 13

William Beaumont: "Backwoods Physiologist"

His work remains a model of patient, persevering investigation, experiment and research, and the highest praise we can give him is to say that he lived up to and fulfilled the ideals with which he set out, and which he expressed when he said: "Truth, like beauty, is 'when unadorned, adorned the most' and, in prosecuting these experiments and inquiries, I believe I have been guided by its light."
—Dr. William Osler

O N June 6, 1822, Dr. William Beaumont, the army surgeon at the post of Mackinac, received a hurried call to the huddled water front at the foot of the hill. In the fur company's store a gun had been discharged accidentally and powder and duck shot had entered the body of an eighteen-year-old French-Canadian, Alexis St. Martin, causing a frightful wound which would probably have resulted in death almost anywhere else in that northern country, for there were not more than one or two other doctors within hundreds of miles. But Alexis St. Martin lived, thanks to the care and treatment which he received from Dr. Beaumont, and their names should be long remembered, one as the human guinea pig for unique physiological experiments, and the other as the observant and careful scientist whose thinking and reasoning upon these experiments form a point of departure for modern gastric research.

Alexis St. Martin was a badly damaged young man when the army surgeon first saw him. The reader may be spared anatomical details, all of which were duly recorded, but even Dr. Beaumont, with all his surgical experience in the War of 1812 where, his diary tells us, he had once "cut and slashed for 36 hours without food or sleep," promptly gave the youth twenty minutes to live, after doing what he could to relieve his sufferings.

But the young French-Canadian, with his background of hardy ancestors off in the province of Quebec, had unexpected vitality and strength. When the doctor returned after a short interval he found St. Martin not only alive but showing surprising improvement, and on the following day, after more lead and bone fragments had been removed and the wound given treatment, there was more than a chance that the man would live. And live he did, until June 24, 1880, and married and raised a family. But our chief interest in St. Martin is the fact that despite all Dr. Beaumont's efforts the wound failed to close entirely. Ultimately a portion of the stomach lining formed into a sort of valve which could be pushed back and the interior of the organ exposed to view. Opportunity was thus afforded for careful and systematic observation of a stomach at work and, fortunately for science, there was a man with the necessary training and interest present to make such observations. Every dyspeptic should honor the name of William Beaumont and incidentally remember also Alexis St. Martin.

The young man's recovery took a considerable time. For ten months he required constant medical attention and this long period of suffering so affected his general health that he was, as Dr. Beaumont records, "altogether helpless and suffering under the debilitating effects of his wounds—naked and destitute of everything." The civil authorities had looked after the man's support for a time, but seeing the prospect of having him on their hands indefinitely they finally declared him a "common pauper" and ordered that he should be deported to his native province of Quebec, a distance of more than 1,000 miles. This was in the spring of 1823.

Dr. Beaumont had no official responsibility for St. Martin's health or future but he knew that the man would not survive the long journey in an open boat. When no other solution appeared he took the sick man into his own home and during two years looked after him in every way, dressing his wounds daily, clothing him, lodging him and out of his meager salary of forty dollars a month providing such necessaries and comforts as the man required. At the end of that time St. Martin was able to walk and do some light work about the house but was still unable to earn his own living.

We may assume that during those two years Dr. Beaumont had observed much in his patient's condition that stirred his scientific interest. Day by day, through the orifice in the man's side, he could see food entering the stomach and in various stages of digestion. He must often have speculated during this period upon the processes of digestion of which so little was known at that time. Finally came the resolve to carry out the series of experiments which he so minutely recorded and the results of which form one of the glories of American medicine.

As early as 1824 Beaumont had sent a report of the case to his friend Surgeon General Joseph Lovell at Washington and it had appeared in the Philadelphia *Medical Recorder* under the title "A Case of Wounded Stomach," though authorship of the paper was mistakenly attributed to Lovell. This was a record of earlier observations noted while the French-Canadian was making recovery.

By May of 1825 Beaumont had resolved that he would enlarge his observations by varying the foods which his patient received and by varying also the conditions under which he received them. But scarcely were these experiments under way before an order came from Washington directing the surgeon to report at Fort Niagara. Here was a problem—what to do about St. Martin. It was quickly solved—St. Martin was taken along, first to Niagara, then to Burlington and later to Plattsburg. These repeated moves interfered sadly with the investigations but whenever opportunity afforded, the experiments were continued. The following January saw the appearance of a second article dealing with the case, a report in the *Medical Recorder* concerning four experiments which had already been carried out. The form of Dr. Beaumont's research is explained in the following portion of Experiment Number 1 which is recorded as having taken place on the first day of August 1825:

"At 12 o'clock M., I introduced through the perforation, into the stomach, the following articles of diet, suspended by a silk string, and fastened at proper distances, so as to pass in without pain— viz:—a piece of high seasoned *a la mode beef;* a piece of *raw, salted, fat pork;* a piece of *raw, salted, lean beef;* a piece of *boiled, salted beef;* a piece of *stale bread;* and a bunch of *raw, sliced cabbage;* each piece weighing about two drachms."

St. Martin continued his usual employment about the house and after one hour Beaumont pulled the string and its attached foods through the hole in the stomach to see what had happened. The cabbage and bread were about half digested, the pieces of meat were unchanged. So back went everything into the man's interior again.

At two o'clock the whole process was repeated. By this time the cabbage, the bread, the raw fat pork and the boiled beef were all gone from the string; the other pieces of meat were scarcely affected.

Another hour went by. A third examination showed the *à la mode* beef partly digested but the raw beef was only slightly changed. When a fourth examination showed no further prog- ress, and since St. Martin was by no means enjoying the experience, the experiment was discontinued. Beaumont records that the lad complained of "considerable distress and uneasiness in the stomach, general debility and lassitude, with some pain in the head," which proves that even the hardened stomach of a French-Canadian *voyageur* found difficulty in handling such a mixture as had been attached to the silken cord. The next day St. Martin was still in pain.

"I thought it advisable to give medicine," Dr. Beaumont records, "and, accordingly, dropped into the stomach, through the aperture, half a dozen calomel pills, four or five grains each. . . . The effect of the medicine was the same as when administered in the usual way, except the nausea commonly occasioned by swallowing pills."[1]

Alexis St. Martin has sometimes been accused of ingratitude be-

---

[1] William Beaumont, *Experiments and Observations on the Gastric Juice and the Physiology of Digestion* (Plattsburg, 1833), 125-126.

cause he did not remain continuously with his benefactor and submit himself to observation. But there is ample evidence in Beaumont's notes to show that the man underwent much physical distress and suffering during the course of the 238 experiments which are described, not to mention such severe aftertreatments as generous doses of calomel and other drugs which were widely in use in those days but which physicians of today use sparingly if at all. Moreover, St. Martin had to undergo considerable mental suffering, for who would wish to be popularly known in his community as "the man with a lid on his stomach"?

One day the French-Canadian disappeared. He went east to his native province of Quebec, married, had two children and again earned his living as a *voyageur*. For four years there was no report of him; then officers of the American Fur Company who were friends of Beaumont and knew of his experiments engaged St. Martin and promptly sent him and his family to Prairie du Chien, a post on the upper Mississippi, where Beaumont was then stationed. One can imagine the surprise which awaited St. Martin when on his arrival he learned who was surgeon at the post.

There had been no change in the wound and the experiments were at once resumed. St. Martin was given a variety of foods and the comparative digestibility of each was carefully observed and recorded. The effect upon digestion of such stimulants as tea, coffee and liquors was also investigated and a series of experiments was carried out by removing gastric juice from the man's stomach and having the digestive process proceed in little glass jars containing various foods. Beaumont found that digestion went ahead outside the body just as it did inside but that the process was slower. A foundation was being laid by these experiments for the modern study of practical dietetics.

Day by day Beaumont made use of the unusual opportunity which had come to him to extend the bounds of medical knowledge. Other men before him had encountered cases of a similar character but it is his peculiar glory that he alone had the scientific zeal and the patience to utilize such an opportunity, persevering in his task despite many obstacles, not the least of which was the difficulty of retaining St. Martin. Finally, in 1831, the French-Canadian announced that he was going back to Quebec, his wife being lonely and homesick for her own people. We can realize how completely St. Martin had recovered his health when we read that the journey to Quebec was made in an open canoe via the Mississippi and Ohio Rivers, Lake Erie, Lake Ontario and the St. Lawrence River. The family arrived in Montreal in June, having traveled more than 2,000 miles.

During one further period, from November 1832 to November 1833, Dr. Beaumont again had contact with St. Martin, in Plattsburg and at Washington, but after that time all efforts to secure further co-operation were fruitless. The French-Canadian traveled about at times, displaying his wound to doctors and medical societies, making considerable money in this way but saving none of it, and he ended his days poor and almost a drunkard.

Dr. William Osler was on the staff of McGill University at Montreal when St. Martin died on June 24, 1880, at the village of St. Thomas de Joliette in Quebec. He immediately communicated with the local physician and with Father Chicoine, the parish priest, endeavoring to secure the privilege of an autopsy and, if possible, possession of the man's stomach. But the family had evidently had enough notoriety and kept the body at the home until it was so badly decomposed that it could not be taken into the church and had to be left outside during the burial service. Furthermore, they had the grave dug to a depth of eight feet to offset any attempt to resurrect the body. St. Martin had outlived his benefactor by seventeen years. He could attribute almost sixty years of his own long life to the care given him by Dr. Beaumont.[2]

Modest though he was with regard to his achievements, Beaumont realized the importance of placing his findings before the medical profession, and in 1833 published his *Experiments and*

---

[2] William Osler, *An Alabama Student and Other Biographical Essays* (London, 1908), 167-169.

Observations on the Gastric Juice and the Physiology of Digestion.
St. Martin was taken to New York where an artist made colored
drawings of his wound while Beaumont himself retired to the little
town of Plattsburg, New York, where he had once practiced his
profession, and there put the finishing touches to his work.

The printing was also done at Plattsburg and there went out to
the world the little volume which is one of the treasures of American medical history. It was an octavo of 280 pages, paper and type
rather indifferent, just the sort of book that any small-town printing office might produce. But collectors of Americana seek eagerly
for it today and libraries which possess copies preserve them in
their treasure rooms.

The book caused no great stir in America. Congressmen who received complimentary copies expressed their individual thanks but
by a vote of 129 to 56 refused a trifling grant of $10,000 to aid the
author in his research. One thousand copies had been printed of the
first edition but not enough were sold to cover the cost of printing.

Dr. Osler points out that in the very year in which Beaumont
first published his observations in book form, in another work, Dr.
Dunglinson, a man of wide learning, was still discussing the theories of digestion that had been current for centuries past and which
had been so succinctly enumerated by William Hunter, eighteenth-
century surgeon and anatomist, when he wrote:

"Some physiologists will have it that the stomach is a mill, others,
that it is a fermenting vat, others, again, that it is a stew-pan; but,
in my view of the matter, it is neither a mill, a fermenting vat, nor
a stew-pan; but a stomach, gentlemen, a stomach."

Osler lists no less than eight distinct contributions to medical
science arising from the observations of Beaumont. Apart from
the purely physiological and anatomical findings, he emphasizes
the establishment by direct observation of the profound influence
of mental disturbances on digestion and the study of the digestibility of different articles of diet in the stomach, "which remains
today one of the most important contributions ever made to practical dietetics." And he quotes with hearty approval Beaumont's

statement: "The system requires much less than is generally supplied to it. Dyspepsia is oftener the effect of over-eating and over-drinking than of any other cause."[3]

While Beaumont's fellow countrymen were slow to appreciate the importance of his work, the discoveries quickly caught the attention of scientists in Europe. As early as 1826 his first publication in the *Medical Recorder* had been translated and copied in German journals. A Scottish medical journal followed with a translation back into English of the German reprint and in 1828 a French journal also reviewed some of Beaumont's work. A German edition of the book was printed at Leipzig in 1834, and an English edition as well as a second edition in America in 1847, but Beaumont realized nothing from them.

Dr. George Rosen has recently pointed out the very characteristic manner in which Beaumont's observations and discoveries were received in the different European countries. In Germany, where recognition came first, interest centered chiefly upon the scientific problems growing out of this first study of physiological processes in a human being, German physicians being almost entirely uninfluenced by the researches. The English, more practical-minded, attempted to find clinical use for the discoveries, to adapt them to actual medical practice. The French, who took notice of the discoveries latest, used them as a point of departure for further investigation, proceeding to create artificially in animals the same conditions which had come to St. Martin by accident.[4]

Dr. Beaumont's real monument is the great volume of medical literature which has proceeded from his initial discoveries and which grows year by year. The contents of his book have been described as "the greatest contribution ever made to the knowledge of gastric research." He had made "such an exact study of the physical and chemical properties of the gastric juice that with the

---

[3] *Ibid.*, 174-176.

[4] George Rosen, *The Reception of William Beaumont's Discovery in Europe* (New York, 1942), 84-86.

exception of the discovery of pepsin, the closest research of modern times has added but little to the work done by him."[5]

It is pleasant to recall that as early as 1825 the Medical Society of Michigan Territory, at a meeting in Detroit, made Dr. Beaumont an honorary member. This was the first recognition which he received from his own profession. Today the Wayne County Medical Society at Detroit has a room specially devoted to preserving the record of Dr. Beaumont and his work. In it hangs the composite oil portrait executed by Deane Keller. Dean Cornwell's fine painting "Beaumont and St. Martin" has been made familiar by its extensive use in the advertising of a large American pharmaceutical firm. In this picture Dr. Beaumont is shown in reflective mood as he collects gastric juice through the gunshot wound of Alexis St. Martin—"the wound that never healed."

The visitor to Mackinac who climbs the steep slope to the height where the buildings of the old fort still stand will find a huge boulder which bears the inscription:

"Near this spot Dr. William Beaumont, U. S. A., made those experiments upon St. Martin which brought fame to himself and honor to American Medicine. Erected by the Upper Peninsular and Michigan State Medical Societies, June 10, 1900."

Near by is the cottage which he occupied while surgeon to the garrison and in which he so self-sacrificingly cared for the young French-Canadian over a period not of months but of years. No honor would seem to have been too great for this man whose work has so benefited humanity but, as is so often the case, recognition came late.

William Beaumont probably received no more than a common-school education before being apprenticed to a practicing physician in the manner of the times. But his mind had a scientific bent and even as an apprentice he kept notes of the cases that came under his eye, and from his youth he kept a diary. His services during the War of 1812 brought him a permanent post in the army when men

---

[5] V. C. Vaughan, "William Beaumont," *Dictionary of American Biography* (New York, 1929), II, 108.

much older were discharged. At Mackinac, remote from contact with other men of his profession, came the opportunity which he seized and utilized to the benefit of all men since.

After 1834 Beaumont was stationed at St. Louis where he was permitted to carry on a private practice. But he had an enemy in the person of Thomas Lawson, then Surgeon General at Washington, who made every effort to humiliate him, and in disgust Beaumont resigned from the army in 1840. Thereafter his record is that of a private physician in St. Louis. He rendered noteworthy service during the cholera outbreak of 1849 and died in St. Louis on April 25, 1853. In the Barnes Hospital in that city a special memorial room contains his portrait and that of his wife, Deborah Green Beaumont, whom he married in 1821 and who not only shared his frontier life after that date but must also have contributed mightily to the success of his experiments.

Chapter 14

"Piratical Doings on the River St. Clair"

In all the trade of war no feat
Is nobler than a brave retreat.
—SAMUEL BUTLER (1612-1680)

THE title of this chapter was the chief headline in the *Western Herald,* a newspaper published at Sandwich, opposite Detroit, when it went out to its readers on July 10, 1838. Editor Henry Grant literally "went to town" on happenings so sensational in a pioneer community and before his pen halted had filled four columns of his little journal. He was to fill many another column with reports and rumors of disturbances along the border during the following months.

Upper Canada, now the province of Ontario, had an armed uprising in December 1837. It was led by William Lyon Mackenzie, editor and proprietor of a Toronto newspaper, and also, perhaps of greater contemporary interest, the grandfather of Canada's wartime prime minister who bears his name. Since many Canadians even to this day have strange ideas as to the background and nature of the so-called Rebellion of 1837, it is not to be wondered at that Americans of the time, less than two generations removed from their own Revolution, were also confused. Interpreting the disturbances in the neighboring British province—and in Quebec also—as a struggle for emancipation from the "British yoke," they were ready and willing to lend a hand.

The uprising in Upper Canada was not a rebellion against England but was a hearty frontier protest, backed by arms, against numerous abuses prevalent in the government of the colony and against the people who were responsible for those abuses. The back-

257

ground was a strange mixture of religious and social animosities, economic difficulties and constitutional quarrels, all well seasoned with Jacksonian Democracy and British radicalism, brought in by the immigration of the times.

Upper Canada, which came into existence in 1791 by the separation of that part of Quebec lying between the Ottawa River and Lake Huron, had received as its first inhabitants a portion of the Tory or Loyalist migration from the United States. These people settled chiefly along the St. Lawrence River and in the Niagara district. The government of this new colony consisted of an appointed governor, an appointed council and an elected assembly. The governor's immediate advisers formed an inner circle known as the executive council.

Abuses soon developed, some of them recalling American pre-Revolutionary days. The assembly found itself in conflict with the two councils and with the governors, almost all of whom were veterans of the Napoleonic wars, highly conservative and fearful of such ideas as democracy or republicanism. Uniformly they were suspicious of the United States and of the numerous American settlers who, after 1800, crossed the border in search of cheap land. The War of 1812 quieted discontent for a time but it soon broke out afresh and in greater measure. From 1818 to 1836 Upper Canada was in political turmoil with curious swings from conservatism to radicalism and back again in the composition of its assembly.

Religious differences added to the bitterness of the times. An attempt was made to establish the Church of England in the province and give to it complete control of education. This was fought by the noncomformist bodies, particularly by the Methodists. The appropriation of large areas of land for the support of the proposed church establishment was another grievance, since these undeveloped tracts obstructed settlement, delayed road building and in other respects handicapped the settler. And always there was the democracy of the new western states standing out in contrast to the aristocratic administration of Upper Canada with its little inner governing circle commonly known as the Family Compact.

By 1834 the reform element had definitely formulated their grievances and set forth their platform which called for an elected legislative council and a somewhat vague suggestion of a responsible ministry along British lines. The rebellion came suddenly and was quickly put down but the reform ideas had not died. Impressed by the seriousness of the affair, England promptly sent out the young Lord Durham to diagnose the political sickness and prescribe a remedy. In his report, which has been called the Magna Charta of modern British colonial policy, he set forth not only the sources of the trouble but with great wisdom pointed out a solution. Upper Canada's difficulties could be ended, he said, only through the grant of a wide measure of self-government. This advice was accepted and during the next decade Upper Canada peacefully achieved the goal which had been sought by arms in 1837.

Moreover, this development in self-government led in due time to the union of four Canadian provinces as the Dominion of Canada, and the Canadian type of government became a model in the formation of other British dominions overseas. But greatest of all, these ideas became a factor in the creation of the British Commonwealth of Nations, the strength of which, however loose the constitutional ties, has been wonderfully displayed in the trying days of war.

The uprising of 1837 was over in a short time and in Upper Canada caused little loss of life. Mackenzie and his followers were quickly scattered and some of them fled into the United States. There, during the next year, they sought to stir up trouble between the two countries and succeeded fairly well in doing so. The boom times of the early thirties had been dissipated by the panic of 1837, and in the year that followed, the unemployed could be numbered in tens of thousands. These out-of-works formed fertile ground for mischievous ideas, and young men ready for a lark were drawn by the hundreds into the "Hunter's Lodges" which mushroomed along the American border from the eastern end of Lake Ontario to the foot of Lake Huron. This organization with its

signs and passwords and flummery of ritual was the chief agency
in provoking trouble, but, as usually happens, there was a fringe
of unorganized ruffianry also ready to take advantage of the disturbed times.

It was with the depredations of such a gang that Editor Grant
dealt in his issue of July 10, 1838, and this was how he began his
story: "For some time past there has existed in the minds of a considerable portion of the inhabitants on the Western Frontier, a
suspicion that the Pirate-Rebels were hatching mischief in Michigan. It was known that the scoundrels were skulking about the
villages of Newport, Palmer and Port Huron, as also in the adjoining forests, in small parties. On Friday, the 22nd, se'nnight, information was obtained, by means of scouts, that an attempt was to be
made, within a few days, to effect a landing on the Canadian side
of the River St. Clair. This information was immediately conveyed
to the Magistrates, a meeting was called, and although some, even
there, were scepticle on the subject, it was resolved to call out the
Moore Militia. Though, at this season, all the settlers were most
actively engaged in attending to their agricultural duties, and, in
general, had no idea of danger, they, in the most prompt and loyal
manner, instantly obeyed the call, exchanging the hoe for the
musket, and with hearty good will, hurried to the banks of the
river."[1]

Now, with the good yeomen of Moore Township assembled, let
us see what happened. On the morning of June 28 a small sloop,
belonging to "a scoundrel named Bowerman living on the Canadian shore," landed an armed party near the general store kept
by Mr. C. Gouin, about opposite present-day Marine City. He was
not at home so they plundered his stock of goods and then proceeded to deal likewise with some commissary stores which were
under charge of a Captain McDonald. Eight barrels of flour and
fifteen bushels of oats were loaded on the sloop and for good

---

[1] Mrs. Ann Anderson, of Corunna, has a copy of the summons to arms issued by
the officer commanding the Moore Militia. It was received by her father, Donald
Collum, and bears the signature of Captain William Wright, a retired naval officer
whose home was near present-day Courtright.

measure the Captain and Mr. Angus McDonald, of Sombra, were also taken along. Then the sloop headed for Palmer, which today is the town of St. Clair.

The American authorities were keeping an eye on the "piratical doings," and Deputy Marshall Cornwall crossed from Palmer to Sutherland's Landing opposite to assure the commander of the Moore Militia that he would do all he could to preserve the peace. The steamer *General Gratiot* would soon be up from Detroit, he said, and would be sent in pursuit of the sloop. But the Moore Militia, having exchanged their hoes for guns, were aching for a fight and decided to make a dash across the river. With them was a party of twenty-four Chippewa Indians from the Rapids above, and, seeing some log canoes handy, the expedition set out forthwith, seven Indians and seventeen militia volunteers. An armed invasion of the United States was under way.

The "pirates," as the editor constantly describes them, at once lowered their sails, put out big sweeps, and headed the sloop for the Michigan shore. Behind them raced the clumsy dugout canoes, the Indians in the lead shouting wildly. This was too much for the crew of the sloop. They hastily landed and took to their heels. But war, even war on the River St. Clair, raises delicate questions, about seized property, for example. Captain John Clark, late of the steamer *General Gratiot,* was on hand and, being a man of seasoned experience in marine matters, he gave immediate judgment. The sloop, having been abandoned in American waters, was now the property of the United States, as was also the arms and ammunition aboard. But the stolen goods would be restored to their rightful owners in Canada. All of which was doubtless in accord with marine law. So the sloop was hitched on behind the *General Gratiot* with a towrope and taken off to Detroit.

The Moore Militia, their honor sustained, now marched on the Canadian side to the home of a ne'er-do-well named Nugent. Here they arrested six men whom they connected with the robberies. One of these, Horace Cooley, had been in prison not long before on a charge of carrying messages between the "Patriots" in Michigan and the discontented element that existed in Upper Canada.

But other things are recorded as having happened on that June day of 1838. Some miles back from the St. Clair, on Bear Creek, there lived a Captain William Kerry who had been prominent in the measures taken to defeat any "Patriot" aggression. In company with three other farmers he was on his way to the river front, and at night the party put up at the home of a Mrs. Lick. About midnight there was a knock at the door and a stranger asked for a drink of water. One of Kerry's party noticed that there were four men lurking by the fence, so he roused the others. Kerry went to the door and was instantly shot dead. Thereupon the four men took to their heels, but they left behind two guns, a valise and some clothes marked "W. P." From this it was concluded that one of the party was William Putnam, a rather notorious character during the troubles of 1837.

The *Herald* gives us a further glimpse of the affair in its issue of October 2. Bowerman, the leader in the robberies, had been arrested along with others and after trial before the Court of King's Bench sitting at Sandwich he and Horace Cooley were found guilty of burglary and sentenced to be hanged on October 27. The sentence sounds severe but in Upper Canada the rigorous old English laws had not yet been modified, though they were not always enforced to the letter. So the *Herald* remarked: "We do not expect the sentence to be carried out."

In settlements which were removed from the frontier the inhabitants were kept in suspense for weeks by rumors of invasion along the St. Clair River. Elijah Woodman, at London, wrote in his diary on June 28 (the day of Kerry's murder): "News arrived that the rebel army was coming and would be in London on the 4th of July to take dinner. All was confusion and bustle. Families began to move, goods and all."

Three days later, on a Sunday, there was another alarm. "The court house square was covered with regulars and militia all under arms. All the bridges leading into the town were put into preparation for defence and if obliged to retire were arranged to be cut

Courtesy of Wayne County Medical Society

DR. WILLIAM BEAUMONT
This composite portrait, painted by Deane Keller, has an honored place in the Beaumont Room of the Wayne County Medical Society at Detroit.

GENERAL GEORGE GORDON MEADE

From 1857 to 1861 he was in charge of the United States Lakes Survey and did extensive work on Lake Huron. Called to active service in the spring of 1861, he was in command of the federal forces at the Battle of Gettysburg, July 1–3, 1863.

Courtesy of Wayne County Medical Society

DR. WILLIAM BEAUMONT

This composite portrait, painted by Deane Keller, has an honored place in the Beaumont Room of the Wayne County Medical Society at Detroit.

GENERAL GEORGE GORDON MEADE

From 1857 to 1861 he was in charge of the United States Lakes Survey and did extensive work on Lake Huron. Called to active service in the spring of 1861, he was in command of the federal forces at the Battle of Gettysburg, July 1–3, 1863.

away. At ten o'clock in the evening sixteen waggon loads of prisoners, seventy-two in number, drove up to the door of the jail. This filled the jail to overflowing."[2]

Editor Grant was never short of news for his little paper during that year 1838. The "pirates" and "brigands" between Detroit and Lake Huron furnished him with abundant copy and inspired copious comment on their activities. The climax came on the night of December 3-4 when "Patriots" to the number of more than one hundred, having crossed the river in a small steamboat, made an attack on the village of Windsor opposite Detroit. A number of the invaders were killed and a bloodthirsty militia officer, Colonel John Prince, shot four prisoners in cold blood, an atrocity which became the subject of debate even in the Imperial Parliament at London, England.

Not all the invading force made its way back to Detroit. Many scattered into the surrounding country and a number were taken prisoner on the margins of Lake St. Clair. In all, forty-four were rounded up and after being assembled in the Sandwich jail were taken in wagons to London for trial by court-martial. There, during Christmas week of 1838, they were examined, several of the group giving evidence against their fellows. In the end all save one were condemned to death and six were hanged early in January. In April, sixteen others were sent to Quebec to be transported to the penal settlement in Van Diemen's Land, while the remainder were ordered to leave the country. Of all this the *Herald* kept its readers well informed.

The Battle of Windsor, as people in that area still like to speak of it, marked the close of the 1837-1838 border troubles. The United States authorities were vigorously alert by this time in combating activities which were creating a nasty international situation. Lord Durham had come to Canada as governor general and was

[2] Elijah Woodman's diary and other papers are in the library of the University of Western Ontario. He was with the "Patriots" who invaded at Windsor in December 1838. He was arrested, tried and condemned to death, but the sentence was modified to transportation overseas. Sent to Van Diemen's Land in 1839, he died in June 1847 aboard ship while being returned to Canada. He was a native of the state of Maine.

assiduous in cultivating good relations with the United States, efforts which were reciprocated.

Amid all the border turmoil it is pleasant to notice in the *Herald* an account of the founding in this very year of the Sarnia and Plympton Library. Residents of the village collected books to the number of one hundred and put them in circulation. John Dougall, a Windsor merchant, sent others. Probably this was the first public library to be opened in the whole St. Clair River area. "What a glorious example is here presented for imitation by the several towns along our extended frontier," wrote Editor Grant. "Even the capital of the Western District may blushingly look up to the public spirit of the people of Port Sarnia and confess its own delinquency."

Brigandry of another type appeared along the St. Clair River in the early 1840's in the operations of "The Missouri, Illinois and Eastern Trading Company." This was the high-sounding title given to an organized gang of horse thieves whose activities extended over several states of the Union and also into the Canadian province of Upper Canada. Their operations were chiefly in the area between Indiana and northwestern Pennsylvania on the south side of Lake Erie, while in Upper Canada they worked along the old Talbot Road between the Detroit River and Niagara. Later they found it necessary to take a more northern route in Canada, and one of the collecting points was in the dense forest east of the St. Clair River. At times Detroit was a safe market and the gang had a steam scow, ostensibly for carrying cordwood, which, it was asserted, had space for a number of horses in the hold. This craft, with its innocent-looking load, displayed astonishing speed on certain occasions.

The operations of the concern were carried on by means of stations in remote areas, at each of which they would buy a few horses from near-by settlers, paying cash. But the real use of the stations was to pass on the animals stolen elsewhere. It was a sort of "underground railroad," except that it was horses, not fugitive slaves, which were being transferred.

Raymond Baby, a settler on the St. Clair River front, had his fine span of blacks lifted one September night and, suspecting where they had disappeared, he took prompt action to recover his property. He found that where his farm lane joined the river road the team had divided, one horse going north and one south. "They will rendezvous at the Niagara River," he remarked and forthwith set out for Sarnia. The distance from there to Niagara was a good 200 miles, but by using relays of horses and stopping only for brief rests he made the journey in three days.

The border authorities were informed of his loss and a patrol was sent to the shores of Lake Erie. Several days later a strange-looking boat was observed half a mile offshore. A posse was sent to the place and awaited developments. The "traders" were discovered in the very act of unloading horses from their scow and already had half a dozen ashore. But they were vigilant. When the officers swept down on them they hastily pushed off, and their scow was soon a mile or more out in the lake. Happily for Raymond Baby, his blacks were among the horses already landed. At a later date the Canadian authorities proceeded vigorously against the thieves, captured their leader, a man by the name of McDougal, and in May 1848 he was sentenced to eight years in the provincial penitentiary. Similar vigorous action in the states where the thieving had been going on broke up the operations of the gang, or at least sent them to more distant fields.

The Fenian Brotherhood provided the international border with both plenty and variety of excitement during the spring and summer of 1866. This organization, aiming at Ireland's independence and ready and willing at any time to give the lion's tail a twist, elaborated plans for an attack upon Canada as a step toward an Irish republic. Bonds were sold to raise funds, men were enlisted and drilled and the Brotherhood seems to have believed that the Canadians would rise against their English "oppressors" as soon as the Fenians placed foot upon Canadian territory. In this they were sadly disillusioned. They found themselves no more popular north of the boundary line than their "Patriot" predecessors had been in 1838.

There were Fenian threats in the spring of 1866 and an order went from the newly chosen capital, Ottawa, calling out 10,000 of the militia for active service. The call was "oversubscribed" by forty per cent—everybody seemed to want to have a whack at the Fenians. The government felt very happy about it and for a time kept them all on service, having a suspicion that something might happen on March 17, St. Patrick's Day. But the good saint's day came and went with no alarms and by the end of March the government sent the militia home, except for the companies that were at frontier posts. These continued their watch.

The invasion came on the first day of June on the Niagara frontier and was short-lived, the Canadian volunteers quickly driving the Fenians back over the border. United States authorities arrested hundreds but eventually paroled most of them and told them to go back to their homes. The attack upon Canada was a fiasco. As a doggerel verse said of one of the leaders:

> General O'Neil went up to Pigeon Hill
> The brave Canucks to slaughter,
> But he came home in a U. S. Hack
> Much quicker than he oughter.

The Canucks have always been rather proud of the manner in which they disposed of this invasion, but fear at the time was widespread. Some of the incidents resembled comic opera. There were few daily papers; indeed many people did not even see a weekly newspaper, but rumors of all kinds spread widely and rapidly and were usually credited. It is to be remembered that the Civil War in the United States, so recently over, had itself brought several alarms for the Canadian people, and it was well known that hundreds of recently discharged northern soldiers were in the Fenian organization.

Probably nowhere outside the Niagara district was the excitement more intense than at Goderich on Lake Huron. As the only good port on the Canadian shore it seemed a likely objective of Fenian designs, and if once captured would form an admirable base from which to carry on further operations. A considerable force of the county militia was therefore assembled; heavy chains were strung at night across the mouth of the harbor, and a vigilant watch was kept. Manual exercises, battalion movements and company drill kept everybody busy during the day, while at night the sentries stationed on the high banks above the harbor called one to the other in turn, thereby ensuring that no one was asleep. Word came of the attack at Ridgeway on the Niagara frontier and its successful repulse, but Major A. M. Ross, who was in charge of the Goderich force, cautioned his men to continue their vigilance.

There seemed to be justification for such watchfulness when word came a few days later that a suspicious-looking vessel, believed to have several hundred armed men on board, had left Chicago and was headed for Lake Huron. Precautions were redoubled. Small boats with parties of armed men patrolled river and lake; sentries were increased, and it was announced that should a crisis occur the town fire bell would be rung and the big Russian cannon on the heights, a trophy from the Crimea, would be fired.

A few days later, just as troops and town people were at dinner, the fire bell clanged violently and the big Crimean gun boomed out, probably for the first time since the English troops had laid their hands on it a decade before. The sentries on the bank had sighted a vessel which they could not identify and it seemed to be headed straight for Goderich harbor. Militiamen jumped from the table, grabbed their guns and cartridge pouches and ran wildly to their stations on the hill. Civilians crowded the streets, many of them expecting to find themselves in the very midst of a battle in the next few minutes.

As the vessel continued its course straight for the harbor, excitement was intense. The black smoke indicated that it was burning coal and was therefore no local lake vessel since they were still burning wood. Soon it was seen that there were men in uniform on the deck, quite a number of them in fact, and there were arms also in view. But fears were lessened when the steamboat glided quietly into the harbor, came to a dock and was made fast.

Major Ross promptly ordered a sergeant's guard to go down the hill and inquire into the character and mission of the arrival. Then the mystery was cleared. It was an American revenue cutter, and it had on board no less a personage than General William Tecumseh Sherman. Nor was Sherman the only person of distinction aboard. General Edward Ord was there and other officers of rank. The party was returning from a tour of inspection of the posts on the upper lakes and had just dropped in on Goderich as a little break in the trip. They had no idea what consternation their approach caused.

Major Ross was prompt to offer the courtesies due to such distinguished visitors. In the evening they were entertained by officers of the garrison at a sumptuous dinner, the cooks in the hotel putting forth their best efforts to mark the occasion. On the part of the townsmen there was intense interest in seeing a man whose name had become so widely known in the war years, and many people came in from the countryside round about when news spread of his presence in the town.

But there was a comic side to the incident, which came to light later. In General Sherman's party was a Chicago newspaperman with a good sense of humor. He had a pretty good idea of what had happened in Goderich, and as he narrated it for his paper the story lost nothing. He informed his readers that for some time before the cutter reached harbor it was observed that there was unusual activity ashore, troops moving from place to place and sentries marching up and down the top of the heights. As General Sherman's party had been out of touch with what was happening in the East they could not conjecture what all the military activity meant and were only enlightened when they touched shore.

The correspondent reserved his best touch for his account of the meeting between General Sherman and Major Ross. As the gang plank was thrown out, he wrote, "General" Ross stepped forward to shake hands with General Sherman, remarking in a most serious manner: "General Sherman, I am under lasting obligation to you, sir, for not firing a salute when you entered the harbor; for had you done so the whole of my command would have immediately taken to the woods."

In due time a copy of the newspaper containing this account of the meeting reached Major Ross's eye. Perhaps it was his Scottish ancestry which obscured the humor for him, for he took the matter seriously, writing to General Ord at Detroit and asking for his version of the incident. General Ord must have had difficulty in keeping a straight face as he replied with apparent equal seriousness that he knew of no such conversation and regretted that Major Ross should have been caused any annoyance.

As for Sherman, he knew nothing of the joke until some years later when, returning to Goderich as a summer visitor, he was told the story by one of the men who had been on guard at the top of the hill when the vessel on which the general was traveling tied to the dock. He remarked that, old soldier as he was, it was one of the best jokes to which he had ever listened.

General Sherman figured in yet another episode as he journeyed toward Detroit. At Sarnia, as at Goderich, militia had been assembled in considerable number and were patrolling the St. Clair River watching for any sign of an attack from the Michigan shore. The commanding officer at Sarnia was Colonel James Shanly, of the London Field Battery. He had infantry and he had guns, but by some mischance ammunition for both had failed to arrive, a situation by no means pleasant to contemplate. It was at this juncture that General Sherman and his party arrived in Port Huron, where Fort Gratiot was still an occupied post. Colonel Shanly at once sent a message across the river inviting the distinguished visitor to inspect the Canadian troops, and the invitation was as promptly accepted.

Shanly, as an old soldier, saw to it that nothing was lacking to give tone to the occasion. General Sherman was met on landing by the officers of the several battalions and escorted to headquarters where refreshments were served. He was then taken to the parade ground where every man was on his mettle. There had been constant drilling for weeks past, and as Sherman looked at those healthy young farmers his own thoughts must have reverted to the boys like them who had served under him in the recent tragic years. The lines were as straight as though the men were toeing a visible mark. The bayonets glistened in the sunshine and the response to orders was smartly uniform.

Sherman, mounted on Shanly's own fine horse, rode slowly along the lines, observing closely the appearance of each unit. On the flank was Shanly's Field Battery from London, which, we may be sure, was behind no other in smartness. "Fine" was Sherman's remark as he turned to its commanding officer. He had missed just one thing—the battery had no ammunition.

Before leaving, the general was invited to say a few words to the officers who were now assembled before him. In reports which have come down we have the substance and perhaps the exact words which he used.

"Colonel Shanly and officers of this garrison," he said, "I have to thank you for this very pleasant half hour you have given me on Canadian soil. And for the honor you have done me, sir, in asking me to land here to review this contingent. If I had not been informed that this fine force I see before me is composed of volunteer militia, I should certainly have supposed it to be a contingent of the army of the British line. Your excellently equipped field artillery is quite equal to anything in that branch of the service I have ever had under my command."

Here he paused, and then added: "We have just got over our little trouble on our side of the line. Yours seems about to commence. Well, I am quite sure when you come into action you will give a good account of yourselves."[3]

---

[3] See letter of Captain J. B. Perry, in *Mail and Empire* (Toronto), May 24, 1923.

Sherman may or may not have comprehended that in his acceptance of the invitation to visit Sarnia and inspect the troops there concentrated he might be doing the Canadians a good turn. His visit and his remarks were given publicity and had a most salutary effect upon Fenian designs. A force that attracted the attention of William Tecumseh Sherman was not to be taken lightly. The needed ammunition arrived in a few days, and after that there was no fear in Sarnia of what might come. No attempt was ever made by the Fenians to cross the St. Clair River.

Chapter 15

The *Pewabic* and the *Asia*

O pilot! 'tis a fearful night
There's danger on the deep.
　　　　　　　—THOMAS HAYNES BAYLY

ON THE evening of August 9, 1865, the passenger steamer *Pewabic*, at that time one of the finest vessels on the lakes, was sunk on Lake Huron in a collision with her sister ship the *Meteor*. Though now so far in the past, it continues to be one of the most widely known and best remembered of the many shipping tragedies on the lake. The circumstances in which this fine vessel and many of those aboard her were lost were so unusual that the tragedy has become almost a tradition, while popular interest has been revived from time to time by efforts made to recover the valuable cargo which went down into almost thirty fathoms of water.

There were no separate lanes for upbound and downbound traffic in those days; had there been such lanes there would have been no collision. When, half a century later, vessel owners were urging the adoption of this safety plan for Lake Huron, there must have been frequent reference to the fate of the *Pewabic*. That two ships, in clear weather and on calm waters, seeing each other's lights well in advance, should come into collision seems almost incredible. Everything happened in a few brief minutes—recognition by both ships that they were in danger, the crash as they met, the swift disappearance of the *Pewabic*.

The *Meteor* and the *Pewabic* were engaged in the trade between Lake Erie and Lake Superior ports. They were substantial vessels, with comfortable accommodations, and were popular with the passenger trade. The surrender of Lee and the closing episodes of the

Civil War were but a few months past and already there was a heavy traffic westward, the beginnings of that great movement which would bring many new states into existence. Pictures of the *Pewabic* show a vessel of fine lines, with extensive deck cabins, a type of vessel that even yet may be found doing local trade here and there on the lakes. With no such aids to navigation as are available today, such vessels weathered the storms and many survived to a good old age.

On the evening of the collision the *Pewabic* was downbound on Lake Huron, and at dusk was about seven miles off Thunder Bay Island and abreast of Alpena. Many of the passengers had already retired; others were dancing or listening to the music in the cabin. A few remained on deck. Toward nine o'clock the lights of an approaching vessel were plainly seen and were recognized as those of the *Meteor*. It was evident that the vessels would pass near each other. No alarm was felt, however, since it was not unusual when meeting for the downbound steamer to get from the upbound the Detroit daily papers.

There was a small group of passengers near the bow of the *Pewabic*. Among them was Silas H. Douglas, first professor of chemistry at the University of Michigan, and members of his family, including a small boy, Samuel Douglas, who more than sixty years later wrote his recollections of the disaster.[1]

"We were sitting on the port side of the deck," he recalled, "and as the *Meteor* approached she suddenly seemed to change her course and, as it seemed to us, to pass us on the starboard side. The crash came almost in an instant. The bow of the *Meteor* struck about 25 or 30 feet from the *Pewabic*'s bow, cutting a deep gash in the side of the latter vessel, and causing her to fill and sink in an almost incredibly short space of time.

"We all ran to the stern of the boat on the starboard side, my father and the women in advance. When we reached the stern my father, realizing that the vessel might go down at any minute,

---

[1] Samuel T. Douglas, "The Pewabic Disaster," *Michigan History Magazine*, XVI (1932), 431-438.

ordered the women to jump into the lake, and he did likewise. We were all equipped with the ordinary cork life-preserver, used at that time. Running around the stern of the boat to the port side I saw that the *Meteor* had swung alongside the sinking *Pewabic,* and as it seems to me today the sides of the vessels were not more than six or eight feet apart. As I jumped I touched one of the hands outstretched, my body striking the side of the *Meteor* and I fell between the two boats. So close were the vessels together that I could almost touch the sides with my hands.

  "I was in the water from one half to three-quarters of an hour, but finally the hurricane deck of the *Pewabic,* wrenched off as she made her final plunge, was floating some distance from where she went down. It was to this that my efforts were directed and I was finally pulled on to this raft by the steward of the *Pewabic,* John Lynch. My father, sister, brother and myself were all rescued at different times. A number of passengers were saved by jumping from the deck of the *Pewabic* to the deck of the *Meteor*. After passing through the horrible night of rescue, the saved passengers were taken on board a passing propeller called the *Mohawk,* bound for Detroit."

Despite the curious circumstances of this disaster and the loss of between seventy-five and one hundred lives, memory of the *Pewabic* would probably have faded with the years had it not been for the fact that her cargo included more than 250 tons of almost pure copper, dug from a lode in the Lake Superior region, and for the persistent belief that on the night when she went down there was a large amount of money—$40,000, it was said—in the strongbox of the purser's office. Lost treasure exercises a strange fascination over men's minds, and there was treasure indeed in the copper alone if only it could be salvaged. Years afterward a diver descended and tried to reach the old vessel. He never came to the surface. Another tried and he too paid with his life. In all seven or more men perished in attempts to reach the depths where the *Pewabic* lay.

Finally, in 1917, in the midst of the First World War, when copper was at a high premium, Benjamin F. Leavitt, inventor of a new

type of diving suit, made surveys and soundings and again located
the wreck. With his improved apparatus, successful descents were
made to a depth greater than had ever before been achieved on the
lakes, and about seventy tons of the copper were recovered. Many
little personal objects were also brought to the surface. Padlocks,
revolvers, little jade ornaments, a jewel box containing two
watches—these all recalled that night of terror. Coins, black after
half a century in the water, and remnants of water-soaked paper
that might have been currency were all that remained of the
treasure.

Captain George Perry McKay was in command of the *Pewabic*
on the night when she was lost. No one would seem more destined
for a sailor's life than he, for he was born in 1838 aboard the steamer
Commodore Perry while she was lying in Swan Creek on the
Maumee River. He began his sailing career on the little schooner
Algonquin of which his father was then master. When this vessel
had been laboriously hauled over the portage at Sault Ste. Marie
during the winter of 1839 there was nothing else on the upper lakes
but the Indian's canoe and the bateaux of the *voyageurs.*

From 1861 to 1882 Captain McKay commanded some of the
finest steamers on the lakes, among them the *General Taylor,* the
Mineral Rock, the *Pewabic,* the *Peerless* and finally the *Sparta*
which he brought out in 1874. When he died in the summer of
1918 he was the last remaining link with the first navigation of
Lake Superior. A year or two before his death a newspaper re-
porter asked him to describe the sinking of the *Pewabic.*

"There was no storm the night the *Pewabic* sank," he said. "It
was clear weather and just beginning to get dark. I was on the
main deck near the engine room when I saw the lights of the
Meteor approaching us. I went up to the pilot house. The *Meteor*
drew closer. She was trying to avoid us. I gave orders to stop the
starboard engine and hold the steering wheel hard. We shifted
wheels three times to clear the *Meteor.* Then came the crash. The
Meteor didn't sink. The *Pewabic* did.

"The passengers on the boat rushed up from the saloon where

they had been dancing. Some were trapped in their staterooms. I helped them all I could, and succeeded in getting some of them over to the *Meteor,* which was beside us unhurt. Our boat was sinking rapidly, and the upper cabins were being forced off by the expulsion of the air and drifting out into the lake. The crew of the *Meteor* were manning the lifeboats and going to rescue the people in the floating cabins. The *Pewabic* sank slowly, and when the water reached the deck where I was working I seized a rope thrown from the *Meteor,* tied it around me, and as the vessel sank beneath me was hoisted to the deck of the Meteor."

Fifty-three years after the loss of the *Pewabic* the old *Meteor* came again into the public eye like a ghost from some far-off past. In 1918, when every nerve was strained to the war effort, the urgent need of all steel tonnage on the lakes for the carrying of ore, coal and grain created a demand for wooden tonnage to handle the general trade. Harbors and creeks, the graveyards of old-time ships, were searched for anything that might carry coal to intermediate ports, and once again the lakes saw vessels which in years past had been among the best known on those waters.

The most interesting of these, and probably the oldest vessel brought into service, was the barge *Nelson Bloom.* She was none other than the old *Meteor.* After having been partly destroyed by fire in 1872 she had ceased to be a passenger steamer, was converted into a barge and for many years was used as a lumber carrier. But she had ceased to be useful even in that capacity and somewhere about the lower lakes had been left to rot out her days. War gave her new life and a new, even if temporary, notoriety. Vessel men told and retold the story of the loss of the *Pewabic.* Newspapers pictured the old ship and gave exaggerated accounts of the great treasure which she had sent to the bottom of Lake Huron. It may be that in those last months before his death in August 1918 the old *Meteor* came under the eye of Captain McKay. If so, what strange memories the vessel must have awakened in his mind!

Go where you will on Georgian Bay and let the talk turn to vessels wrecked or lost, the name of the *Asia* will soon be heard. Georgian Bay has swallowed up its scores of vessels and broken up hundreds more on its rocky shores, but no other disaster on its waters has equaled in loss of life that which accompanied the disappearance of this small steamer. There was little attention in those days to passenger and crew lists, and no one can say with certainty how many people were on board the *Asia* when it left Owen Sound on the night of September 13, 1882. But it is known that more than one hundred perished. Only two escaped death. During the four days from the time of the vessel's departure until an Indian's sailboat brought the two survivors of the disaster to Parry Sound, families represented on the ship were left in harassing uncertainty as to the fate of their relatives and friends.

The *Asia* was a wooden vessel, 136 feet in length and with a 26-foot beam. She was built at St. Catharine's in 1873 and met early misfortune in 1881 when she was sunk in Lake George. Raised and repaired, she ran for a time between Sarnia and Duluth, but in the summer of 1882 was transferred to the Georgian Bay trade to take the place of the *Manitoulin,* which had burned a few months before. Captain J. N. Savage was in command, John McDonald was first mate and John McDougal was purser.

It was the time of the year when men and supplies were moving to the lumber camps. Barrels and boxes of provisions were piled even on the hurricane deck of the little steamer, while on the main deck were a number of horses. But to avoid undue handling there was little freight in the hold, and the vessel was top-heavy when she left the dock. Men in rough clothes lay sleeping wherever they could find a corner, their heads pillowed on ancient valises or grain bags containing their few effects. Every cabin above was occupied by passengers, most of whom had gone to their berths before the *Asia* cast off its lines and headed out into the sound.

It was a rough night even under the shelter of the Saugeen Peninsula and the steamer rolled considerably. Every few minutes a wave would strike the hull and send a shiver through its framework. The crew kept the vessel out of the trough of the seas, though in her top-heavy condition this was difficult. Most of the passengers were seasick and unconscious of any danger threatening them.

At seven o'clock in the morning the course was changed to run straight across the bay for French River. This was about opposite the entrance between the Manitoulin Islands and the mainland, and at once the full force of the gale broke upon the little vessel. Soon she was wallowing in the trough and in danger of capsizing. Orders were given to throw overboard much of the cargo but still the ship would not respond to her helm. A gigantic wave smashed in a portion of the hull and water swept through the cabin. A clergyman who was on board went among the people, seeking to calm the dull terror which had seized upon many. D. A. Tinkis, one of the two survivors, has left us a vivid picture of the last few minutes aboard the doomed vessel.[2]

"The aft gangway," he said, "leading from the promenade to the main deck was jammed with men, women and children who could get neither up nor down. At every pitch of the ship this mass would writhe and twist like a serpent while the waves broke over them from above. The horses in the meantime had broken loose and at every roll they were thrown from one side of the main deck to the other. The cabin was already broken in at several points but still the craft floated. At last about 11:30, she pitched up at the head and went down stern first, the cabins breaking off and the boats floating off as she did so."

Tinkis was in one of the wooden lifeboats when the *Asia* made her final plunge, but it was quickly swamped. "As she was about to sink," he recalled, "I sprang over and swam for the captain's metallic lifeboat. There were great combs on every wave, and these, loaded with floating debris, broke over my head every time

---

[2] James McCannell, of Toronto, has in his possession the original marine "protest," or report, filed under Canadian law. In this document Tinkis related his experiences. At various times later he was interviewed by newspapers and gave more detailed accounts of the loss of the *Asia*.

I came up on the crest. My hands and head were both cut and bleeding, but I reached the lifeboat and managed to clamber in. We were driving fast before the sea and soon lost sight of wreckage and other boats as well."

Christine Morrison, a young girl, the other survivor of the wreck, jumped as the deck became awash. Caught by a wave, she was carried close to the captain's boat and was hauled in by the mate, who was her cousin. At one time there were more than twenty people in the boat but it was repeatedly upset and after each overturn there were fewer survivors. When dusk came there were only six left alive, but there was also the body of a French-Canadian deck hand who had died an hour or two before.

Night was coming on. The wind had lessened in violence but the sea was still high. Suddenly there was a flash in the distance, which was recognized as that of the Byng Inlet light. The welcome gleam gave hope, and led by the mate those in the boat began singing the old revival hymn "Pull for the Shore, Sailor." But there were no oars and the boat was half-full of water and darkness was all about. Voices grew feeble and the song died out. Later they sang together "In the Sweet By-and-By."

We have a record of those who were in the boat at this time. In addition to Tinkis and the young girl, those still living were Captain Savage, Mate McDonald, a man named Little and a man from Gore Bay named McAlpine. One by one these others succumbed to the exposure and shock of the day. McAlpine died at eight o'clock, Little went next and the mate who had led the singing died at eleven. Sometime after midnight the captain seemed to be falling asleep, and when Tinkis shook him he murmured, "All right, I'll be up in a minute." A wave struck the boat at that moment, and when Tinkis looked again the captain was dead.

The boat was half full of water, but as each one died Tinkis placed the body under the seats to prevent it from being washed out. For the two that were left there could be no sleep or rest. To give way to the almost overpowering drowsiness meant death. Probably it was their youth which enabled them to hold to life where strong men had given way, for both were under twenty years of age. All through the dark and lonely night the boat drifted they knew not where, but at daylight land was in sight, one of the innumerable islands on the eastern shore of Georgian Bay. Tinkis recognized the place as near Point au Baril. Between ten and eleven o'clock the boat drifted to land, but the two were so exhausted that they could scarcely stand. It was now Friday and neither had had any food or rest for over thirty hours. All that day and the night that followed they remained where they had landed, threatened with starvation unless help came.

On Saturday morning about eleven o'clock a sail appeared. By this time both were nearly delirious. Tinkis was able to attract attention by raising his coat on a pole and a small sailboat, piloted by an Indian, drew to shore. He had food with him, fat pork and "choke dog," which to the two survivors must have been the most welcome meal of their lives. In return for Tinkis' gold watch the Indian agreed to take them to Parry Sound, but when within two miles of that place he decided to camp for the night, so that not until Sunday morning was their safety known. Rumors of the disaster had reached Parry Sound on Saturday and a tug had been sent out which actually passed the Indian's boat, but as the two survivors were lying in the bottom they were not seen.

Tinkis lived until 1910, residing at Manitowaning and Little Current. Miss Morrison, who in 1896 became Mrs. Albert Fleming, died only in the summer of 1937, fifty-five years after the terrifying experience through which she had passed on the stormy waters of Georgian Bay.

The loss of the *Asia,* the most costly in lives of any wreck in the history of Lake Huron, made lasting impression on the country round about, and year by year newspapers published about the Bay, even to the present, recall the story of that wild storm of 1882. It also produced one of the few ballads of Lake Huron, written by some unknown resident of the Georgian Bay district and printed in a local newspaper soon after the tragedy:

The Wreck of the Asia

Loud raged the dreadful tumult,
  And stormy was the day,
When the Asia left the harbour,
  To cross the Georgian Bay.

One hundred souls she had on board,
  Likewise a costly store;
But on this trip, this gallant ship
  Did sink to rise no more.

With three and thirty shanty men
  So handsome, stout and brave,
Were bound for Collin's Inlet
  But found a watery grave.

The men cried "Save the Captain,"
  As the waters round him raged;
"Oh, no," cried he, "Ne'er think of me
  Till all on board are saved."

The cabin boy next passed away,
  So young, so true, so brave;
His parents weep while his body sleeps
  In Georgian's watery grave.

I'll ne'er forget McDougall,
  Which was his honored name;
He immortalized his noble deeds,
  And hands them down to fame.

And likewise Billy Christie,
  With his newly-wedded bride,
Were bound for Manitoulin
  Where the parents did reside.

"Oh, had we only left this boat,
　　Last eve at Owen Sound!
Oh, Willie dear, why came you here
　　To in these waters drown?"

But in the deep they're fast asleep,
　　Their earthly trials are o'er;
But on the beach, their bones will bleach
　　Along the Georgian shore.

Of all the souls she had on board,
　　Two only are alive;
Miss Morrison and Tinkiss,
　　Who only did survive.

Miss Morrison and Tinkiss
　　Their names I'll ne'er forget;
Protected by a life-boat
　　Which five times did upset.

Around each family circle,
　　How sad the news to hear,
The foundering of the Asia
　　Left sounding in each ear.

Part IV

THE SHIPS AND THE MEN WHO SAIL THEM

Chapter 16

The Surveyors and Their Charts

Skill'd in the globe and sphere, he
  gravely stands,
And, with his compass, measures seas
  and lands.

—Dryden

Navigation of the Great Lakes had its historical beginning when Champlain in the summer of 1615 coasted through the maze of islands along the eastern shore of the Georgian Bay. So intent was he upon reaching the country of the Huron Indians that he left us but the briefest record of his "Freshwater Sea." After him came many others who penetrated to the most remote parts of the lake regions, usually with some particular motive, chiefly trade or the extension of the Christian religion.

These early voyagers on the Great Lakes had no charts by which they might guide their course, but of such aids there was less need than in later days. The Indian's birchbark canoe was their only craft, and because of its small size and delicate construction they seldom ventured far from shore. When winds were adverse or darkening clouds were threatening, a landing was quickly made, and since travel was by day there were few unseen dangers. For more than two centuries the canoe was the chief means of travel on the lakes. As late as 1820, when Governor Lewis Cass of the Michigan Territory undertook an exploration of the interior Northwest, he and his party set out from Detroit for Mackinac in three large canoes, though in this very year there was a steamboat crossing Lake Huron.

In a later period of navigation on the lakes information bearing upon dangerous localities was largely acquired by masters through the mishaps of others. Word quickly passed about in the ports of any new menace to the safety of vessels navigating particular shores. Crude maps sometimes appeared with such dangers to navigation marked upon them. But in this period masters had to be dependent chiefly upon their intimate acquaintance with the coasts and waters where they took their vessels. Champlain had this in mind when he wrote in his *Treatise on Seamanship:* "Let the master have a good memory for recognizing landfalls, capes, mountains and coast-lines, tidal currents and bearings wherever he has been." That admonition was given three hundred years ago, but it has lost none of its value despite all that has been done to lessen the risks of navigation on the Great Lakes and their connecting rivers.

Defense and diplomacy rather than trade and commerce were behind the first surveys of Lake Huron and its connecting waters. Gother Mann, a British military engineer of considerable experience, was commissioned in 1788 by Lord Dorchester, the governor general of Canada, to make a report on the coasts and harbors of Lakes Ontario, Erie and Huron. Behind this order was the delicate situation then existing between Great Britain and the new United States, arising out of the retention by Britain of certain frontier posts which were properly within American territory.

The treaty which closed the War for Independence gave to the States the large area of western territory extending from the Appalachian Mountains to the Mississippi River and stipulated that the British were to withdraw from the ceded territory "with all convenient speed." As a designation of time this was a very loose phrase, and it was actually thirteen years before the occupation was completely terminated. For various reasons, some stated and some less openly exposed, the British continued to hold Niagara, Detroit, Sandusky, Mackinac and other posts until the summer of 1796. The difficulty was finally cleared up by John Jay, first chief justice of the United States, in the famous treaty which bears his name.

Historians still differ over the reasons for this British policy, though it is now generally accepted that it was a combination of fur-trade interests, concern for old agreements with the Indians in this territory and the desirability of maintaining some means of enforcing American obligations in the treaty. As to the relative importance of these factors, opinions differ. "Great Britain and the United States," says one writer, "violated the Treaty of Paris from the very beginning. Each side entered upon this unhappy course quite independently, and then tried to cast the blame on the other. The result was a bitter controversy."[1]

During the thirteen years of British occupation of the posts there were conferences and correspondence, protests and threats, the new republic unable to enforce its demands and the British government too much occupied with European affairs to give much attention to this North American situation. The British administrators in Quebec during the period of controversy were Sir Frederick Haldimand and Lord Dorchester. They were sorely tried by the lack of definite instructions from the home government. Dorchester reached the limit of his patience in 1787 and bluntly put the question to his superiors: Were the frontier posts to be held or surrendered? If held, it would be necessary to reinforce them and repair the fortifications, all of which would require money. He waited a year for an answer and was then told that he might place the disputed posts in a "temporary" state of defense. The amount to be expended was left to his judgment.

This was the occasion for sending Gother Mann on a tour of the lakes to examine the state of the fortifications and also to gather such other information as might be useful in case the dispute led to hostilities. Captain Mann had come to Quebec three years before as commanding royal engineer. He was a capable officer who later went far in the service, rising in 1810 to lieutenant general and inspector general of fortifications and going on to be commander of the Corps of Royal Engineers in 1819. As a reward for his

---

[1] A. L. Burt, *The United States, Great Britain and British North America from the Revolution to the Establishment of Peace after the War of 1812* (New Haven, 1940), 82.

services in Canada he later received, in the bountiful manner of the day, a grant of 22,859 acres in one of the townships of Quebec.

Mann's survey in 1788 extended as far westward as Sault Ste. Marie, but Lake Huron, because of its extent and its numerous islands, occupied much of his time. We do not know the name of the vessel which was used on this lake but it may have been the schooner *Dunmore* of Detroit. In anticipation of a possible surrender of the post at Detroit a site was selected on the Canadian side of the river from which the British might continue to control the valued Indian trade. The place selected became Fort Malden (Amherstburg). After Detroit was given up in 1796 the great assemblages of Indians coming each year to receive their presents made the fort on the Canadian side of the river an important center for both trade and diplomatic relations with the red men.

Continuing his journey northward, Mann mentions the shallow nature of Lake St. Clair and the bar which he found across the outlet of the river above, a bar pierced at only one point by a narrow channel of but seven-foot depth. Of the St. Clair River he wrote: "From the general prevalence of northerly and northwesterly winds, and the strength of the current, it is often a difficult and tedious operation to get up from Detroit; and vessels are not unfrequently a fortnight or more in accomplishing it. The whole of the East shore of this River, as well as the West shore, serves good land and very proper for settling upon; and when that event shall have completely taken place the Navigation will be much aided thereby for the banks of the river being cleared vessels may then in contrary winds be tracked most of the way up to the Rapid, there being in general two and a half and three fathom water within fifty feet of the shore. The River is for the most part about three quarters of a mile broad except at the Rapid, where it is somewhat narrower, but the shore here does not offer any advantage to recommend it for a Post."[2]

[2] The entrance to the St. Clair River from Lake Huron ("the rapids") is narrow and the current is swift. Sailing vessels always experienced difficulty in working their way into the open water of the lake above.

The suggestion that vessels might be towed upstream by a line to the shore, a method in use on European canals and on swift, narrow streams in America, was probably never attempted on the St. Clair River. Until the era of the steam tug which could pull three, four and even more schooners against the current, the upward course from Lake St. Clair to Lake Huron was tedious and often dangerous, calling for careful handling of the vessel to avoid going aground.[3]

Gother Mann's observations on Lake Huron considerably increased the information then available concerning its shores and waters. The whole lengthy coast line of Georgian Bay was examined and many of its inlets and river mouths were charted for the first time. Matchedash Bay was given special attention as it was the northern terminus of the Indian trail leading from Toronto on Lake Ontario. Five years later Colonel John Graves Simcoe, the first lieutenant governor of Upper Canada, projected a military road connecting these two points, and during the War of 1812 it became an important route for supplies. On one of the islands off Nottawasaga Bay the exploring party came upon some massive masonry ruins. These were portions of the fortified mission station established by the Jesuits in 1649 when the place became a refuge for Huron Indians after the onslaught of their Iroquois enemies a few months before. Mann named the place Isle au Maison Pierre; today it is known as Christian Island. More than a century and a quarter had passed since the island mission had been abandoned by the Jesuits, and Mann's party was probably the first to visit and record the presence of these ruins since the missionaries left the place.

Cruising up the western shore of Georgian Bay, with its numerous inlets and its bold headlands at Cape Croker and Cabot Head, the surveying party rounded the tip of the Bruce or Saugeen Pen-

---

[3] In 1832 General Winfield Scott, hurrying troops and supplies to Chicago for the Black Hawk War, had several sailing vessels laden with such supplies towed by steamboats up the St. Clair to Lake Huron in order to hasten the date of their arrival at Chicago. These steamboats were not "tugs," although for the moment they were serving the function of a tug.

insula. Here is a region of small islands through which the channel for vessels is today well charted and marked, but in Gother Mann's time it must have been most confusing. "To go round is rarely attempted," he wrote. "Of those who have ventured several have perished." But his party suffered no mishap and the voyage continued down the eastern shore of the lake to the mouth of the St. Clair. There was little to note on this long coast line. It was without harbors other than the mouths of small rivers, which were not easy of approach and were liable to be clogged by silt brought down in the currents.

"A great solitude, little known or frequented except by some Indians," was Mann's quite correct description of this region in 1788, and the same description would have applied also at that time to the western shore of the lake.

Nearly thirty years passed before there were further systematic surveys of the lakes. Since the time of Gother Mann's expedition, both England and the United States had been involved in the great European struggle arising out of the French Revolution, England as an active participant from 1793 on, and the United States finally going to war with England after years of fruitless effort to remain neutral. The War of 1812 educated both nations to the importance of the Great Lakes but England alone made any immediate move to chart the waters or provide otherwise for the safety of navigation. In 1815, immediately following the peace, Sir Edward William Campbell Rich Owen was appointed commodore commander in chief of British naval forces on the lakes and he in turn appointed his younger brother, Captain William Fitzwilliam Owen, to the post of chief hydrographer. These men were experienced naval officers, still in their early forties, members of a family with a naval tradition, and under their vigorous direction an amazing amount of work was accomplished. Several surveying parties were promptly sent out, so that at the close of 1815 Sir Edward was able to supply the Admiralty with more than fifty charts covering waters all the way from the Island of Montreal to the St. Mary's

River. The foundation had been laid for work that still goes on.

Captain Owen was occupied during 1815 in various surveys extending from the St. Lawrence River to Georgian Bay. September was already well advanced when he began work on Lake Huron, and autumn gales made the work hazardous. His assistants on this survey were Lieutenant Alexander T. Vidal and Shipmaster John Harris. Vidal later settled on the St. Clair River while Harris became the treasurer of one of the western districts of Upper Canada (Ontario). The schooner gunboat *Huron* was used during the closing months of the year, particular attention being given by the surveyors to the eastern shore of Lake Huron and to Georgian Bay. Owen was so impressed by the size of the great bay, Champlain's "Freshwater Sea," that he named it Lake Manitoolin.

Captain Owen had the reputation of being exceedingly peppery at times. On one occasion he arrived at Sheerness aboard H. M. S. *Columbia,* a clumsy old craft, the crew of which was about to be paid off. In the absence of the commander in chief of the port an officer of lower rank was on duty and was inclined to be insistent that all due respect be paid to him. Owen, who knew that the commander was absent, ignored the practice of sending a lieutenant ashore to report, and the acting commander quickly signaled his displeasure. When this failed to bring an answer he came out in person to see who was responsible for the situation. He received a surprise when at the gangway he encountered Rear Admiral Owen, much his superior in rank. Owen is said to have exceeded himself in forceful language in telling off the port official.

However bold he may have been in affairs of the navy, Owen appears to have been more timid in matters of the heart. When he was in Canada after 1815 he met a Miss Herkimer and his admiration led to a proposal of marriage. But this he made through Amelia Harris, the wife of John Harris, his assistant surveyor. What happened is best told in the entry made by Mrs. Harris in her diary, long years after:

"October 1 [1864] Mrs. Sadlier called. I knew Mrs. Sadlier as

Miss Herkimer 47 years ago. She was then a pretty young girl. I carried her a proposal of marriage from Captain Owen, afterwards Admiral Owen, which she declined as she said she had so many engagements on hand already. She was engaged to a midshipman who had gone to England. If he failed she was engaged to old John Kirby, and if that failed Robert Kerr was the third on the list. She married a Capt. Sadlier, I think of the 37th, and is now a widow with £800 a year and looking young enough to have another engagement."[4]

When Captain Owen went down to Quebec in July 1815 to secure an assistant surveyor, he brought to the Great Lakes a man whose individual contribution to the safety of these waters was greater than that of any other who came before or after him. Henry Wolsey Bayfield was a young naval lieutenant only twenty years of age when Owen met him at Quebec aboard the *Wanderer,* on which he was then serving. He had entered the navy when not much more than a child and the ship which he joined had been in action off Portsmouth six hours after he first climbed to its deck. The navy caught them young in those days, so young that they never knew any other life. Bayfield had received only elementary schooling before going to sea, but he took every opportunity to improve himself. From two of his messmates who were college men he borrowed books, and in every spare moment applied himself to study. His notebooks were models of neatness; indeed, it was the orderly character of his notes which first attracted Captain Owen's attention. Leaving active service aboard ship was not relished by Bayfield at the time but he could look back later and see that his meeting with Owen at Quebec had been the first step in his advancement, for he ended his naval career as an admiral.

When Captain Owen returned to England in 1816, Bayfield was

---

[4] Captain Owen ended his days in Canada. He was engaged for some years in surveys of the Bay of Fundy and Nova Scotia and had his home on Campobello Island, a place since become widely known as the summer home of President Franklin D. Roosevelt. Because of his connection with the island the Admiral (as he later became) was familiarly known as "Campobello Owen." He was a member of the Legislature of New Brunswick for some years and died at Saint John in 1857.

made admiralty surveyor. For nine years thereafter he was engaged continuously on the surveys of the Great Lakes, two years on Lake Erie, four on Lake Huron and three on Lake Superior. The excellence of his work during this pioneer period of the lakes survey has aroused the admiration of every man who has followed him in like duties. No small part of the operations had, of necessity, to be done in the winter, holes being chopped through the ice in order to determine depths. The hardships of such a life were considerable but do not appear to have adversely affected Bayfield, for he lived to be ninety years of age. Captain J. G. Boulton, who at a later date resurveyed many of the same waters, has said of him: "The Admiralty Survey Service has produced good men from Captain Cook onwards, but I doubt whether the British navy has ever produced so gifted and zealous a surveyor as Bayfield."[5]

Bayfield's charts, based upon his work during the 1820's, were the sole aids of their kind available to mariners until well toward the middle of the century. Bayfield had indicated the coast lines with remarkable accuracy but it remained for later surveyors to fill in the depths of water and the presence of reefs and shoals. For many years masters of ships learned of these by personal experience, often costly, or from the experience of others. And there were many other things that had to be learned in the same way, dangerous currents, for example, and the presence of old wrecks. But ships were still small and many a locality that would be shunned by vessels today could at that time be approached in perfect safety.

While Bayfield was busily engaged upon the upper lakes, another survey of these waters, of a quite different character, was also under way. This was the determination of the boundary line be-

---

[5] Bayfield's work was not confined to the Great Lakes. In 1827 he was appointed to the survey of the St. Lawrence, from Montreal through the straits of Belle Isle to Cape St. Lewis on the Labrador coast, together with all navigable streams, also Anticosti, Mingan, the Magdalens, Prince Edward Island, Cape Breton and the coast of Nova Scotia westward to Halifax, including Sable Island. His charts, issued subsequently by the British Admiralty, were found to be singularly accurate in all particulars. He was a resident of Quebec from 1827 to 1841 and later resided at Charlottetown, Prince Edward Island, where he died on the tenth of February 1885.

tween the United States and the British possessions. The boundary question was nearly forty years old, dating back to the peace conference at Paris following the Revolutionary War. There the American commissioners, Benjamin Franklin, John Jay and John Adams, had secured for their country clear title to all the territory between the Appalachians and the Mississippi. It is true that in doing so they sidetracked the understanding with France that there would be no separate peace, and they even ignored the instructions of Congress, but they made such a smart bargain with England that their diplomatic sins were quickly forgiven. There was little difficulty about this since no one believed that France was looking out for other than her own interests.

The major portion of this new international boundary lay in waters which in days ahead would be traversed by the shipping of both countries. But since there were so many other problems facing the young republic it was not until after the War of 1812 that any attempt was made to fix the lines. The Treaty of Ghent, signed on Christmas Eve of 1814, provided for the appointment of commissioners to settle disputed boundary questions and led to the surveys which were made on the northern lakes and rivers during the next few years. Peter B. Porter was the American commissioner and John Ogilvy the original appointee of Great Britain. Some disputed points remained unsettled until the Webster-Ashburton Treaty of 1842 but in general there was an excellent spirit shown by both sides.[6]

It was no simple task that had been assigned, since some of the waterways were thick with islands and the main channel which would be used by future shipping did not always coincide with the middle of the waters under examination. It was agreed that the boundary line should give to each country the largest possible share in the waterways and that the islands should be divided between them as equally as possible. Each commissioner nominated a secretary, an astronomical surveyor and an assistant surveyor, then by lot the chief secretary was chosen. This fell to Stephen Sewall of

---

[6] Ogilvy died in 1819 and was succeeded by Anthony Barclay.

THE LOST "ASIA"

When this vessel foundered on Georgian Bay in September 1882, more than one hundred lives were lost. There were but two survivors of the disaster.

HAPPY DAYS ON GEORGIAN BAY

The old passenger steamer *Atlantic*, rebuilt from the burned *Manitoulin*, which carried so many Sunday School picnic parties that it became known as the "Gospel Ship." It was itself destroyed by fire in 1905.

WAITING THE WORD TO GO

Typical lake carriers in early spring ready to begin the sailing season as soon as word comes that the ice is gone

Montreal, while Major Donald Fraser became assistant secretary. In 1820, Sewall having retired and Fraser having become secretary, Dr. John Bigsby became his assistant. It is to Bigsby that we owe our chief knowledge of the work of the survey on the lakes, for he kept a private journal and later published an interesting account of his experiences.[7] His appointment was probably influenced by the fact that he was a physician. The surveying parties had already learned that however health-giving the open waters of the lakes might be, their borders were in some places as dangerous to newcomers as pesthouses. On Lake Erie and on Lake St. Clair there were areas where rotting vegetation made the air foul and where malaria awaited its victim. Mr. Ogilvy, the British commissioner, was taken ill on Bois Blanc Island in the Detroit River in September 1819, and died at the neighboring village of Amherstburg after a ten-day illness. David Thompson, the British astronomer, fell sick in the same month and eventually had to be removed to his home on the St. Lawrence where he was laid up during all of the following winter. Two of the British boatmen died of fever, and all of the American party were sick for a time.

Henry R. Schoolcraft, who met Bigsby, described him as having "a very bustling clerk-like manner, which does not impress one with the quiet and repose of philosopher." Schoolcraft thought that Bigsby regarded the Americans in the more remote lake districts as mere barbarians, but there is nothing in his writings to indicate that he had any such superior attitude. On the other hand, he appears to have had a genuine interest in those whom he met, and he has left us a whole series of interesting pen portraits of people and places encountered in the course of his work. At Amherstburg he spent an evening with that strange figure in the annals of the antislavery movement, Captain Charles Stuart, who was devoting his time to the Negro refugees in this southwestern corner of Upper Canada.

Here also he made the acquaintance of a French family, aristo-

---

[7] John J. Bigsby, *The Shoe and Canoe or Pictures of Travel in the Canadas, Illustrative of Their Scenery and of Colonial Life.* 2 vols. (London, 1850).

crats who had fled from their native land during the Revolution. The Chevalier and Madame de Brosse had been at the court of Versailles in the days of Louis and Marie Antoinette, but the political tempest had exiled them to this remote part of America. Their cottage on the bank of the river was but a jumble of added parts, each under its own roof, yet within all was refinement. Portraits of French nobility, pictures by Watteau, a piano and other musical instruments, books and objects of art, all indicated the culture that had been brought to this isolated frontier region.

"The moment I entered the sitting-room," wrote Bigsby, "I felt myself in France. I was among the fanciful articles and feminine knickknackery with which Madame de Genlis has made the un-travelled English familiar. There was no carpet, but little rugs instead, in favorite spots, before two short hair-seated sofas covered with yellow plush, with four arm chairs to match close by. The tables were of the native walnut, and very beautiful. They were more or less covered with books and culled flowers and the one in the middle of the room had a large Limousin plate, painted over with blue and white saints, and holding fans, seals and medallions. For dear Versailles' sake, well remembered through a vista of chequered years, Madame had preserved, or somewhere picked up, a somewhat shattered cabinet of marqueterie."

There were others who, for one reason or another, had come to this remote district and concealed their identity. One such person whom Bigsby met on the St. Clair River was known locally as "the Banished Lord." His speech and bearing revealed clearly that he was an Englishman of education and breeding, though how he came to be in this part of America was a mystery. His home was on Bear Creek where he dwelt alone, his young wife having died soon after coming to this unwholesome district. His small farm was in fairly good order and he was suffering no hardships. Bigsby saw him a second time at Fort St. Clair, accompanied on this occasion by his little ten-year-old daughter, "a handsome freckled, sunburned lass, somewhat delicate in appearance but full of spirit." The child needed to have a tooth extracted, an operation which

Bigsby performed, at the same time advising the father that he should send the child to a good school in Toronto or Kingston, advice which he took in good part.

Through the pages of Bigsby's narrative there runs a constant procession of people whom he met and with whom he conversed. He was highly pleased with the "agreeable manners and extensive information" of Dr. William Beaumont, the American army surgeon who at Mackinac Island had been given the unique privilege of witnessing the actual processes of digestion through the wounded side of the French-Canadian Alexis St. Martin. He "longed" to join a young man named Hunter who claimed to be a descendant of Pocahontas and was making a journey to the Mississippi. He was struck by the unusual appearance on the frontier of Rev. Mr. Morse, "very distinguished for his exertions in the cause of missions," who was dressed wholly in black, with small-clothes and silk stockings, a white neckcloth and a broad-brimmed hat completing an outfit not often seen in the West.[8]

Bigsby would be forgotten today were it not for his writings, but there was another man in the survey party, little known at the time, whose fame has grown with the years. This was David Thompson, who has been properly described as "one of the greatest land surveyors that the British race has ever produced."

"In the sheer length of his journeys," says his biographer, "few western explorers have equalled the record of Thompson, for he travelled in all not less than fifty thousand miles. Much of this was through country untrodden by the feet of white men; nearly all of it was in regions as yet unsurveyed. . . . Throughout his life Thompson was inspired by a restless impulse to push forward

---

[8] Rev. Jedidiah Morse, Congregational minister and "Father of American Geography," had been commissioned in 1819 by the United States government to study the condition of the Indians and to make a report. He was also secretary of the Society for Propagation of the Gospel among the Indians. In dress and manners he was "a gentleman of the old school." His geographies, the first of which was published in 1784, went into many editions and for more than a generation virtually monopolized the field in the United States. His friend Timothy Dwight said of him that he was "as full of resources as an egg is of meat." Samuel F. B. Morse, artist and inventor, "the greatest figure in the history of the telegraph," was a son of Rev. Jedidiah Morse.

the exploration and mapping of the West until not a corner of it remained unknown."[9]

Bigsby has left us an intimate glimpse of Thompson as he remembered him: "Our astronomer, Mr. Thompson, was a firm churchman; while most of our men were Roman Catholics. Many a time have I seen these uneducated Canadians most attentively and thankfully listen, as they sat upon some belt of shingle, to Mr. Thompson while he read to them in most extraordinarily pronounced French three chapters out of the Old Testament, and as many out of the New, adding such explanations as seemed to him suitable."

The exactitude of Thompson's observations has excited the admiration of every surveyor who has had occasion to examine his work. Certain districts which he covered a century and more ago have never been resurveyed but appear on the maps of today just as he set them down. His travels covered areas extending from the rocky regions southwest of Hudson Bay, over the broad prairies, through the Rocky Mountains and to the valleys beyond. He was unnoticed and unknown in his own day and his grave in Mount Royal Cemetery at Montreal is still unmarked. The government of Canada, however, has raised cairns with appropriate inscriptions at three points in the West where his work was outstanding, and on the shore of Lake Windermere in British Columbia there stands a David Thompson Memorial Building, honoring his contribution to the exploration of that far western province of Canada.

It was the great westward movement of population during the 1830's and the commerce incidental thereto that first impressed official Washington with the need of more detailed surveys of the Great Lakes. Tens of thousands of people were seeking new homes in the West, and steamboats from Buffalo and Detroit headed for Chicago were crowded with these people and their belongings. There were many dangerous places on the course, and accidents to

---

9 C. N. Cochrane, *David Thompson the Explorer* (Toronto, 1924), 166-167, 170.

vessels were frequent. Congress, which had heretofore been inclined to view the Great Lakes as local waters and the safety of their navigation as the concern of the bordering states, was now forced to accept a national responsibility. Surveys which were begun in 1841 extended over a period of more than forty years, while corrections and revisions continue to the present day.

The Great Lakes survey had a distinguished chief between 1857 and 1861 in the person of George Gordon Meade, who at that time held the rank of Captain of Topographical Engineers. When Meade was recalled to military duties at the end of August of 1861 he did not dream that two years later his name would be on the lips of every citizen of the United States. For it was General George Gordon Meade who on the first three days of July of 1863 commanded the Federal forces at the Battle of Gettysburg. He saw Longstreet's men smash into his lines at the Peach Orchard, the Wheat Field and at Devil's Den. He saw Pickett's men, 15,000 of them, come out of the woods on Seminary Ridge and march in straight lines toward his center on Cemetery Ridge. He saw those same gray lines, broken and in disorder, make their way back again in the last hour of the battle. He was so close to the fighting that his old horse "Baldy," already five times wounded in previous battles, had a bullet remaining in his body after Gettysburg, though at that he outlived his master.

Meade, after the close of the Mexican War, had been attached to the Lighthouse Service, but in 1856 was transferred as first assistant to the officer directing the survey of the lakes. In the following year he himself took charge of operations. He brought to his duties precision of mind and a strictly scientific attitude, and during his four years of service he was able to make important and valuable improvements in the methods employed. His term coincided happily with the appearance of new and more accurate instruments and with appropriations by Congress which were more in keeping with the national importance of the work. Meade was thereby enabled to survey the whole of Lake Huron and to bring to completion the work begun in 1856 on Saginaw Bay. He also surveyed the northeast end of Lake Michigan and shortly before being called back to army duties in 1861 he had started work on Lake Superior.

By the early eighties the work begun in 1841 was regarded as completed and likely to serve all needs for many years to come. But this idea was soon dispelled. The surveys made up to this time had charted the lake waters to a depth of about eighteen feet, which was viewed as ample since the largest vessels at that time had a draft of but twelve feet. But soon the growth of commerce, the deepening of harbors and channels and the construction of longer and deeper locks at Sault Ste. Marie brought larger vessels than the lakes had hitherto known. This, in turn, made necessary a revision of previous surveys, and in 1900 Congress made the necessary appropriations. The open lakes were now to be charted to a depth of thirty feet and the river channels to twenty-five feet.

This work begun at the turn of the century may be regarded as still under way. With the steady growth in the size of the bulk freighters, the increase in the number of such vessels on the lakes and the extension of harbors, there can be no end to the constant checking and revision of the charts needed for the safe navigation of the lake waters. Year by year in the reports of the Lake Carriers' Association and in other publications, one may read summaries of the operations during any particular season. In 1941, for example, survey work was being done on all five of the Great Lakes and in their connecting waters. Two particular undertakings may be mentioned. On Lake Michigan an area between Ludington and Little Sable Point had to be swept to determine if the wreck of the *William B. Davock,* lost in 1940, was a menace to navigation. No trace of the wreck was found. On Lake Superior an area of thirty square miles in the vicinity of Superior Shoal was examined. At this strange locality, far from shore, one pinnacle of rock was found to be but twenty-one feet under water and three others close by were at depths ranging from twenty-seven to thirty-five feet. Perhaps this shoal accounted for some vessels which in the past mysteriously disappeared, leaving no trace behind them.

The field work of the hydrographic engineers consists chiefly of sounding and sweeping. Soundings are made by lowering at half-minute intervals a heavy fish-shaped weight from a boat traveling at a speed of two to three miles an hour. Between soundings the weight is lifted a short distance off the bottom so that if there is a high spot at any point the weight will strike it. If the lake bottom is regular, soundings are quite sufficient for charting purposes, but where the bottom is irregular and there is no certainty of a depth adequate for safe navigation the sweep is used. This is a long horizontal wire submerged by heavy weights and supported on the surface by floats. When drawn through the water it is at a definite depth. If any portion of the submerged wire strikes an obstruction the float immediately above will be disturbed and the tipped flag on the float will indicate the exact location. Soundings are then made at this place to determine what is the nature of the obstruction. It was work of this type which was required in looking for the wreck of the *Davock,* mentioned above.

The task assigned to the Lake Survey is of huge proportions. The water area to be charted is 96,000 square miles, about two-thirds of which is within United States jurisdiction. The length of the shore line is over 8,000 miles, of which about 4,700 is American. A comparative idea of its extent may be gained by comparing it with the Atlantic, Pacific and Mexican seaboards of the United States, excluding Alaska and all islands, which is about 5,000 miles.

The work of the marine surveyor differs considerably from that of the land surveyor. While the latter deals with areas, the former is first of all concerned with depths. It is his job to find out where vessels may go with safety and where they may not go and to record his findings on charts that will be kept constantly under correction as new data is assembled. The marine surveyor must also take account of the features and relief of the shore line and note all compass errors due to magnetic deviation caused by the presence of mineral deposits.

The land surveyor has one advantage over the marine worker. When a land area has been measured and mapped, the job may be regarded as finished, subject only to such errors as may later be detected and corrected by the use of better instruments or more accurate calculations. But the work of the marine survey can never be regarded as final and must be subject to constant revision. There is no guarantee that because a certain depth of water has been found at a particular locality the same depth will be found there a year later. Currents may quickly create shoals that will menace shipping. Moreover, account has constantly to be taken of the numerous changes resulting from commercial and industrial enterprises along the shores and in the rivers and harbors. It is quite as essential to his business that the master of a vessel shall know the location of a new steel plant or a new coal dock and the approaches thereto as that he know his way along the courses on the lake waters.

The first charts issued by the United States Lake Survey appeared in 1852 and were three in number, all having to do with Lake Erie. Thirty years later, when the original survey was regarded as finished, a series of seventy-six charts had been issued and were available for navigators. It sounds curious to read that for a time appropriations were reduced to a few thousand dollars. Only a few years passed, however, before the original charts were made obsolete by the decision to begin the new survey with greater depths. Today in addition to six general charts of the Great Lakes there are more than 120 special charts of portions of the lakes, of their connecting waters and of harbors. Fourteen of these special charts are related to Lake Huron, the Straits of Mackinac and the St. Mary's River.

The headquarters of the Lake Survey is at Detroit, where the charts are also prepared. Their production requires accurate preliminary field work by hydrographic surveyors who carry on their operations between April and October. The winter season is occupied in reducing their notes and making the drawings necessary to change these notes into a map of permanent record. In producing a chart all the pertinent information in the files is first gone over and a drawing made on paper mounted on an aluminum plate. This drawing is photographed on a pane of glass to whatever scale may be required. The glass negative, after it has been developed and while it is still wet, is so stained as to produce an amber image of the drawing on an opaque background. The engraver then goes to work, engraving the drawing through the photographic film, using the stained image as a guide. When revisions are necessary, the part requiring change can easily be painted out and new work engraved through the paint. When the engraving process is completed the glass negative is transferred to a sensitized aluminum plate by the photolithographic process, and the aluminum plate is finally treated so that it will have an affinity for the ink used in printing.

Five colors are used in printing the charts, each color having a particular purpose. Black is used for the general outlines, blue to accentuate particular water depths, buff for land, brown for land contours and red to accentuate lights and buoys. A separate plate has to be prepared for each color so that there are five impressions, the black being made first. Corrections which are slight but nevertheless vital to those using the charts are frequently made by hand directly on each copy. Bulletins sent out from the Lake Survey office monthly during the season of navigation keep masters of vessels informed of all changing conditions and also supply information on the highly important matter of lake levels, providing thereby a basis for the draft to which the freighters may safely be loaded.[10]

---

[10] This description of the process is condensed from *The United States Lake Survey* (Detroit, 1939), a pamphlet issued by the Corps of Engineers of the United States Army.

Chapter 17

Georgian Bay Ships and Sailors

... spread the sail,
Heave oft the lead, and mark the soundings well;
Look to the helm, good master; many a shoal
Marks this stern coast ...
— WILLIAM FALCONER

GEORGIAN BAY was the cradle of Great Lakes shipping. When Champlain journeyed on its waters in the summer of 1615, seeking out the Huron Indians so essential to the French fur trade, the business of the lakes had begun. Dugouts and birchbark canoes were then the only means of transportation and continued to be so for a long period. In due time traders saw that canoes could be made larger so as to carry heavier burdens. Bateaux, manned by husky oarsmen, also came upon the scene. Small sailing ships, built chiefly for local trade, led on to the era of the schooners, and these were later supplemented by fleets of wooden steamers which provided perhaps the most distinctive period of Georgian Bay shipping. Last of all came the steel bulk carriers, bearing through all the lakes the ore, the coal, the grain, and such other commodities as East takes from West and West from East.

The evolution in shipping on Georgian Bay is typical of that in other portions of the lakes region but, nevertheless, has had its own individuality. The port of Collingwood made early connections with Lake Michigan, sharing in both the grain trade and the transportation of immigrants headed for new homes in the western states and territories. Georgian Bay boats carried the surveyors and scientists who prospected the resources of the Canadian West.

They carried men and supplies for the building of the Canadian Pacific Railway and were pioneers in opening up the Lake Superior trade. Fleets of wooden vessels were built in Georgian Bay shipyards and manned by men from the bay region. When steel supplanted wood, shipyards quickly turned in the new direction; and some of the largest carriers on the Great Lakes have come from these ports. Though the passenger trade that was once so large has dwindled, the grain traffic has continued and under the impetus of war demands has grown beyond all previous records. The same influence has brought about a new era in Georgian Bay shipbuilding.

When, a century or more ago, settlers began to find homes on the south shore of the bay, many of their needs were supplied by little sailing vessels which took the farmer's surplus grain and pork, giving in exchange hardware and tools and materials for clothing, commodities that could not be supplied locally. This trade extended to Manitoulin Island and to the North Shore where the Indians were the chief customers. Reverend John McDougall, an early missionary in the Canadian West, has recalled that as a boy he made many a trip with his father to the lake's northern shore where loads of fish and furs and maple sugar were taken on board for delivery at Detroit and Lake Erie ports, and sometimes taken as far east as Toronto. These little sailing ventures were frequently "family" affairs, such as may still be found among the French on the St. Lawrence River, a father and son or other relatives owning a small vessel in common. Some of these craft had a cabin specially fitted up for the display of goods. There was little cash and most transactions took the form of barter.

Sailing vessels of larger size had appeared on the bay as early as 1837, for Mrs. Anna Jameson describes vividly the sight of the "huge black hull of a vessel, with masts and spars rising against the sky" from which was shouted the message that King William IV was dead. But she does not tell us its name. Shipbuilding began at Owen Sound as early as 1848 when the schooner *Ann Mackenzie* was launched, followed not long after by the *Elizabeth*

Broder and the *Belle McPhee*. The *Ann Mackenzie* after a period on the bay went east to Quebec, then to England, and later, it is said, to South America, after which records cease. The *Broder* met her end on the rocks of Manitoulin Island and the *Belle McPhee* was wrecked on the south shore of the bay near Thornbury.

When railway development came in the middle of the century some lake ports, those on the north shore of Lake Erie, for example, lost much of their importance. But this was not true of the Georgian Bay ports. For them the coming of the railways brought new and increased business. The Northern Railway, which came to Collingwood in 1855, was a link in the grain trade with New England, and the number of schooners putting in at that port grew rapidly. Grain elevators arose, primitive affairs at first, by which a few hundred bushels an hour could be scooped from a vessel hold and dumped into small railway cars. When a new and larger elevator was built in 1871 it was described as an "enormous" affair, having a capacity of 160,000 bushels and equipped to unload 3,000 to 3,500 bushels an hour.

The early grain trade was largely in corn, brought from the western states, for the Canadian West had not yet become a factor in the continent's production. It was a profitable business, encouraging owners to take pride in their vessels. Gilded name plates and fanciful figureheads, polished masts and white sails all enhanced the beauty of the slim schooners gliding gracefully toward harbor. Their names, too, added a touch of romance: *Rising Star, Erie Belle, Flying Cloud, Gold Hunter, Flying Mist* and *Golden West*. In size they varied greatly, from little vessels carrying no more than 3,000 bushels to such a large vessel as the *F. W. Gifford* which could carry 32,000 bushels.

Early pictures of the harbor at Collingwood show a forest of masts rising from the schooners anchored and waiting their turn at the elevator. On September 16, 1871, so it is recorded, the leg of the new elevator was dropped into the hold of the schooner *Potomac,* just arrived from Chicago with a cargo of 16,000 bushels of corn. Fifty years later to the day, on September 16, 1921, the steel steamer *Clemens A. Reiss,* also just arrived from Chicago, began to discharge its cargo of 258,780 bushels of corn and Captain Tom Conlin was presented with a silk hat in honor of the event. But the big *Lemoyne,* itself the product of a Georgian Bay ship-yard, in 1938 carried 534,000 bushels of corn on one trip, the equivalent of more than thirty-three *Potomac* cargoes. Such are the changes in shipping that need and invention have brought about.

The steamboat era on the bay was inaugurated in the late forties when the little steamer *Gore,* a craft of less than 200 tons, made regular trips between Owen Sound and Collingwood. Reverend John McDougall tells of traveling from Coldwater to Collingwood on this boat in 1851. The *Gore* was followed by the *Kaloolah* (later renamed *Collingwood*) and the *Rescue,* both of which had historic connection with the opening up of the Canadian West. The *Collingwood* left the port whose name she bore in July 1857 with the members of the expedition under Henry Youle Hind sent by the government of Canada to explore the resources of the Red River country. The steamer passed through the Sault Canal on July 27 and anchored outside the bar at Fort William four days later. It was the first Canadian registered boat to go to Lake Superior.

The *Rescue,* in its turn, was the first vessel to carry the Canadian mails to Lake Superior. In the 1850's the great territory beyond the lakes was exciting the interest of eastern businessmen, and in 1858 a company known as the North West Trading and Coloniza-tion Company was formed. The new steamer *Rescue* was pur-chased in Buffalo and fitted out for the passenger and freight trade. A contract was made to carry the mails for the Red River country, and on July 12, 1858, with Captain James Dick on the bridge, the vessel began her first trip. She arrived outside Fort William on the fifteenth and the next day proceeded to Grand Portage. There the mail, consisting of three letters and two newspapers, was turned over to be taken to its destination by Indians.

In the fifties and sixties the tide of emigration to the western states was running heavy, and thousands of homeseekers, many of them Scandinavians, passed through Collingwood on their way to Minnesota and Wisconsin. Railway companies, prompt to seize business of this nature, chartered a fleet of sidewheelers for the trade, and beginning in the spring of 1855 a triweekly service was maintained with Chicago. Among the early vessels on this run were the *Lady Elgin, Queen City, Niagara, Keystone State* and *Buckeye State.* The service was widely advertised in the press of both the United States and Canada and was maintained for several years. The loss of the *Niagara,* one of the fleet, in September 1856, was the first marine tragedy of any size to affect the Georgian Bay ports. The steamer left Collingwood with a full load of merchandise, 100 cabin passengers and 200 deck passengers, many of them immigrants. Shortly after leaving Sheboygan fire was discovered and fifteen people lost their lives. Survivors gave harrowing accounts of the panic on the burning vessel.

The *Frances Smith,* which was launched at Owen Sound on April 30, 1867, just two months before the Dominion of Canada came into existence, is still remembered with singular affection on the bay. She was a sidewheeler, 190 feet in length, and named after the wife of the owner, Captain W. H. Smith. She was built by Melanchton Simpson at a time when that shipbuilder was at the height of his reputation. Mill machinery had not yet reached the point where it could do most of the timber work on a vessel and every plank in her hull was hand-sawed. Husky French-Canadians were brought in to drive home the spikes. The engines were of the walking-beam type and originally there were two stacks. Cabins and staterooms were commodious and furnished as well as those of any steamer on the lakes.

For two seasons the *Frances Smith* operated as a day boat between Owen Sound and Collingwood, but in the fall of 1868 she ran on a shoal near Byng Inlet, a place afterward known as Frances Smith Shoal, and was forced to remain there for the winter. In later years she ran between Owen Sound and the Sault and still later between Owen Sound and Prince Arthur's Landing, the present-day Port Arthur on Lake Superior. In the early 1890's the name was changed to *Baltic,* and during the World's Fair in Chicago in 1893 the vessel did a profitable passenger trade. The end came, as with so many other wooden boats, when she burned at Collingwood on September 5, 1896. After the machinery had been removed the hull was towed out of the harbor and let go in a northwest wind which carried it to shore, there to join other vessels whose day had passed. The burned and charred timbers were visible for many years, all that remained of a boat that had once been the pride of its ports.

Vessel after vessel was brought to the bay, or, in later years, built in its shipyards to meet the growing trade. The *Algoma,* a sidewheeler, originally the *City of Toronto,* was placed upon the Georgian Bay-Lake Superior route in 1864, her ports of call during the next nine years including Batchewana, Michipicoten Harbor and Island, St. Ignace, Nipigon and Fort William. The *Algoma* has been described as of "the old decorative Victoria-and-Albert type, with impressive figurehead, three rigged masts and all the trimmings." The fare from Owen Sound to the Sault and return, including meals and berth, was $10; from Owen Sound to Fort William and return was $24. A sister ship to the *Algoma* was the *Cumberland,* which was later lost on Isle Royale.

The ill-fated *Waubuno,* which had been built at Port Robinson in 1865, was brought to the upper lakes by James H. and William Beatty, pioneers in the Canadian shipping business. She was a sidewheeler about 150 feet in length and 40 feet beam. In 1867 she was chartered by the Canadian government to carry the expedition sent to open a route between Lake Superior and the Red River country. But in general she made trips to and from any port where freight was to be had, sometimes to lumber camps along the north shore, occasionally to Thunder Bay on Lake Superior where the Hudson's Bay Company post was about the only sign of civilization, but periodically calling in at Parry Sound where William Beatty, one of her owners, was trying to found a model temperance settlement.

Of all the early vessels on the bay none had a more romantic past than the famous Confederate blockade runner of Civil War days, known as the *B* (often called the Let-her-B). This boat, after lying idle for some years in Halifax harbor, was brought to the lakes as the *Chicora*. She still had the gun tracks of earlier days on her decks and her long rakish hull was unbroken save by the pilothouse, two funnels in line and the two tall masts which carried sail. On her ship's bell was the letter B, placed there by the builders. She made a trial trip to Lake Superior in September 1868 with a number of distinguished guests aboard and from 1869 to September 1875 was regularly engaged in the trade with the upper lake. After 1875 the *Chicora* went to Lake Ontario, where for many years she was well known in the Toronto-Niagara run.

The Georgian Bay Navigation Company, organized in the early seventies, included Thomas and John J. Long, two shrewd Irish businessmen who were long identified with upper lakes shipping. This company bought the *Gladys,* product of a Marine City shipyard, and renamed it *Northern Belle.* After twenty-two years' service it was burned at Byng Inlet in 1898.

Another group, organized as the Canada-Lake Superior Transit Company, entered the field about 1878 with the steamer *City of Winnipeg* (formerly the *Annie Craig*) and the *City of Owen Sound.* The *City of Winnipeg* was burned in Duluth on July 19, 1881, and the *City of Owen Sound* was wrecked on Clapperton Island during the last trip of the season of 1887. She was later raised and rebuilt as the *Saturn* but was finally lost on Lake Huron.

To replace these losses the iron steamer *Campana* was brought from salt water. Originally called the *North,* she had been built at Glasgow for the South American cattle trade but when purchased in 1881 was running between England and South Africa. It was necessary to cut the vessel in two at Montreal in order to get the hull through the canals. This was the first time that such a practice had been followed. The *Campana* was a twin-screw steamer, the first to come to the upper lakes. When she arrived in Collingwood on November 14, 1881, she had the appearance of an ordinary tramp steamer. During the winter, however, cabins were added, and in the following spring she was ready for the busy Lake Superior trade, carrying large quantities of supplies for the builders of the Canadian Pacific Railway north of Lake Superior and in the more distant West.

Between 1879 and 1882 the Georgian Bay Navigation Company (changed in name at this time to Great Northern Transit Company) experienced a series of vessel losses that would have discouraged most men. The *Waubuno* foundered in November 1879, and twenty-four lives were lost. The *Manitoulin,* purchased to replace the *Waubuno,* burned in May 1882, again with loss of life, and the *Asia,* which had been chartered from the Northwest Transportation Company at Sarnia, went down in Georgian Bay in September 1882, more than one hundred of her passengers and crew perishing. But the company persisted and added other vessels—the *Emerald,* the *Simcoe,* the *Northern Queen* and later the *Atlantic, Pacific,* and *Majestic.*

The enterprise of the men associated with the Great Northern Transit Company brought a new order in Georgian Bay shipping. To list all the steamers which came into the trade would be tedious. Changes in ownership were frequent; indeed, buying and selling vessels seemed to have some of the same charm that has long been associated with horse trading and in all probability there were some deals that rivaled horse trading in their slickness.

The steamers belonging to the Great Northern Transit Company were popularly known as the White Line, because of their color. When the North Shore Navigation Company entered the field as a rival in 1890 its vessels, for a similar reason, were promptly christened the Black Line. Beginning operations with the *City of Midland,* a product of the Simpson shipyards at Owen Sound, the new company's fleet grew by addition of the *City of Collingwood* and *City of Toronto,* also built by Simpson, the *Britannic,* the *City of Parry Sound* (formerly the *Favourite,* built at Meaford) and the *City of London.*

Rivalry for business between the Black and White Lines was so keen that at times passengers traveled at rates below cost, and it was said that shippers were almost paid to send their freight by one or the other line. The speed of individual vessels was a constant topic for debate and dispute, and when two rival steamers found themselves near each other and headed for the same port a race was inevitable. A Manitoulin Island editor in 1892 gave this description of such a contest involving two particularly keen rivals:

"Capt. Pete Campbell of the *Pacific* came in Wednesday with three niggers and a Sheguiandah cheese on the safety valve and the keel carefully greased to prevent friction. The story they brought was that they had beat the *City of Midland* by five minutes and 37.12076 seconds between Collingwood and Owen Sound. You could see the Cap's smile half way to Strawberry shining like the church steeple and his chin whisker was sticking out at an angle of 90 degrees with excitement, while his hat was tied on with a stout piece of hawser, and in each boot was a flat iron to keep him from blowing off the hurricane deck. Few and short were the words he said and his story was briefer than a guinea pig's tail. Then the *Pacific* steamed out, making 22 knots and smoking at every seam. Two hours after the *City of Midland* hove in sight, throwing the foam from her bow six feet into the air and twenty feet on each side of her like great white wings, belching forth rolling masses of smoke and looking thoroughly business-like in her neat black coat. Her story was also brief, and Capt. Bassett once more started on the trail of the *Pacific* with blood in his eye. All the paint was burnt off her smokestack."

The ruinous competition between the two lines came to an end in 1899 when they were amalgamated, the merger bringing in also the Beatty Line at Sarnia with its two fine wooden steamers, *United Empire* and *Monarch*. The ships were now all part of the fleet of the Northern Navigation Company of Ontario with headquarters at Sarnia. Even before this amalgamation much of the traffic that had formerly passed through Collingwood was directed to Owen Sound, the southern terminus of the Canadian Pacific Railway Company's fleet, and in 1900 the Collingwood steamboat connections with Lake Superior ceased. Forty-three years had passed since the little steamboat *Collingwood* had carried the Hind expedition to the head of the lakes and it was the *City of Collingwood* which closed this chapter of lakes shipping history. For fourteen years during the period, steamers from this port gave the only service to Fort William and Port Arthur, a contribution of no little importance to the opening up of the Canadian West.

The entry of the Canadian Pacific Railway into the lakes shipping business was an important development for Georgian Bay. In 1883 the rails had been laid between Port Arthur and Winnipeg and taken over from the contractors. To provide the necessary connections with the East, three Clyde-built steamers were brought across the Atlantic, the *Algoma,* the *Alberta* and the *Athabaska.* Two of these, the *Alberta* and the *Athabaska,* are still in service, more than sixty years after their arrival in fresh water. For a long time these vessels were the finest boats on the Great Lakes and they can still hold their own with boats launched long after they first came into the trade. They were built with Georgian Bay and Lake Superior requirements particularly in mind and were practically ocean ships of canal draught. Because of their length it was necessary to cut them in two at Montreal and move them to Buffalo where they were joined together and taken to Owen Sound. Service was inaugurated on the upper lakes in the summer of 1884.

On November 7, 1885, Donald Smith (afterward Lord Strathcona) drove the last spike to mark the completion of the Canadian Pacific Railway, the great project to link the East and West of Canada. The place selected for the ceremony, Craigellachie in British Columbia, was scarcely more than a name. Mr. Smith and the distinguished company who were present did not know that at the very moment when the historic spike was being driven one of their three fine ships, so recently placed in service, was pounding to pieces on the rocky shores of Isle Royale in Lake Superior. The wreck of the *Algoma* was a major disaster involving the loss of forty-eight lives.

The vessel had left her dock at Owen Sound on Thursday, No-

vember 5, with eleven passengers and a load of merchandise for
Port Arthur. She passed through the Sault lock early Friday and
by midnight was thought to be about fifty miles from port. The
vessel carried sails on her two masts and had all her canvas spread
while crossing Lake Superior. A northeast gale was blowing,
with rain and sleet and occasional snow. At four o'clock on Saturday morning Captain John Moore, realizing that he must be near
Isle Royale, decided to head back into the open lake and take in
sail. The alteration of course was scarcely completed when the
stern of the vessel struck the rocky shore, smashing the rudder
and making the ship unmanageable. At six o'clock, amid darkness and snow, the whole forward portion of the *Algoma* broke off
and disappeared. A small group of survivors clung to the sloping
afterdeck. A few of the crew had been able to reach land, less
than a ship's length away, in one of the lifeboats to which they
had lashed themselves, but for the others there was no alternative
to remaining crouched on the wreck which might at any moment
slide off into the deep water. They were there all day Saturday
and all Saturday night, but when the weather moderated on Sunday morning they managed to reach shore on an improvised raft.
Those who remained alive were taken off the island by the sister
ship *Athabaska* on Monday afternoon.

Midland, younger by a generation than either Collingwood or
Owen Sound, has rivaled them both as a shipbuilding center and
as a grain port. The locality was once known as Mundy's Bay,
named after an early settler, Asher Mundy, who took up land as
early as 1818. But there was no settlement until the announcement
came that the place would become the terminus of the Midland
Railway. When the railway did come in 1872 there was a little
village awaiting it. Lumbering was the chief activity in those
days, and sawmills hummed in and around the edges of the harbor,
one of the finest on the Great Lakes, thousands of acres in extent
and almost perfectly protected.

Midland may not have known it at the time but it was an important day when young "Jim" Playfair, a youth of twenty-three, came from Toronto to work for one of the lumber companies at the princely salary of twelve dollars a month. That was in 1883. Five years later he entered into a partnership with his friend D. L. White, which developed through the years into one of the largest shipping interests on the Great Lakes. One of Playfair's first ventures was the purchase of an old boat, the *W. B. Hall,* which he renamed the *St. Andrew.* This he had overhauled and lengthened and with it entered the grain trade between Fort William and eastern ports. The capacity of the vessel, 35,000 bushels, was tiny compared with that of carriers which later came under his control.

Playfair and White organized the Midland Navigation Company, the Great Lakes Navigation Company, the Midland Shipbuilding Company and various other concerns. Around the turn of the century they branched out into iron ships, the *Midland Queen,* with a capacity of 100,000 bushels, being built for them in England. This vessel, while carrying munitions and foodstuffs overseas, was sunk in 1915 in the English Channel by a German submarine, one of the first vessels to meet such a fate. Subsequent to the purchase of the *Midland Queen* and to meet the requirements of the growing grain trade, the *Midland King* and *Midland Prince* were added, these being the product of Collingwood shipyards. Additional vessels were acquired or built but all were later merged with other lines and a new company was organized, the Great Lakes Navigation Company, whose fleet included both vessels purchased and others built in the Midland yards. The *Alva* was the earliest acquisition and was renamed the *Glenfinnan.* Thereafter many of the boats added to the fleet had the syllable "Glen" as the beginning of the name—*Glenlivet, Gleneagles, Glenisla,* etc. But in 1926 this second fleet also entered a merger, that which became Canada Steamship Lines Limited.

Midland is but a small town and its shipyards as a stranger sees them give little indication of their capacity for turning out big steamships. It would never be suspected that as long ago as 1926 this place turned out what was until 1942 the largest bulk freighter on the Great Lakes. Originally *Glenmhor,* its name was changed to *Lemoyne* before its first trip. Almost immediately, carrying records began to tumble.

Built under the direction of James Playfair, this vessel was 633 feet long, 70 feet beam and 33 feet depth. Her length was eight feet greater and her beam six feet more than any other ship then on the lakes. On her maiden trip in August 1926 the *Lemoyne* took on at Sandusky 15,415 net tons of soft coal; a month later at Fort William she took on the largest cargo of wheat ever loaded up to that time on the Great Lakes, 518,000 bushels, equal to 15,540 net tons. At the end of the season of 1943 the big ship was still holding no less than seven cargo records, including soft coal, wheat, corn and mixed grains. Several of these records had remained unbeaten for many years. Only in 1943 was the *Lemoyne's* record for cargoes of iron ore finally exceeded by several of the new carriers of the Pittsburgh Steamship Company's fleet which entered the lake trade in the season of 1942.

James Playfair must have had a most justifiable pride in this great ship, the product of his own shipyards. From his youth he had been interested in boats, and he was an enthusiastic yachtsman. For many years he was the owner of the palatial yacht *Venetia,* 225 feet in length. During the First World War she was turned over to the British Admiralty and was celebrated for having sunk a German submarine.

A circumstance which aroused curious interest for many years was the fact that Mr. Playfair, a stanch member of the Presbyterian Church in Canada, was the owner of the property on the little river Wye upon which stood the remains of old Fort Ste. Marie, the home during the 1640's of the Jesuit mission to the Huron and probably the most sacred spot in Canada to devout members of the Roman Catholic Church. Subsequent to his death it was acquired by the Society of Jesus and has become a shrine to which the greatest reverence is paid.

Georgian Bay captains were as well known as their ships, and their records are a part of the tradition of its waters. Men like Campbell, Foote, McNab, McCannell, MacGregor, McLean, McIntosh, Bassett and others piloted their vessels to the Sault and to Fort William at a time when lighthouses were fewer than today and when gas and spar buoys were unknown. They had their charts and they had the lead line but beyond these aids they had an intimate knowledge of the waters they traversed and courage and initiative to bring them through. Snowstorms and fogs were as perilous in their day as now, and it is significant that more of these Georgian Bay steamers ended by the fire route than by foundering or piling up on some shore.

Peter M. Campbell, "Black Pete," as he was commonly called, was one of the best known and most skillful navigators of the eighties and nineties. The Manitoulin editor who made joking reference to his beard touched on one of the most distinctive points of his facial appearance. Whiskers which fringed his face, worn heavier on the chin and with the upper lip shaved, gave him the appearance of a Dunker elder. The name "Black Pete" had no reference to his character or manners, for he was one of the most popular and colorful figures in the bay shipping. He was one of the directors of the White Line and skipper of several boats built for its trade. The particular episode in his sailing career which is best remembered and which displayed his courage and resourcefulness was the burning of the steamer *Manitoulin* of which he was master.

The *Manitoulin,* a propeller, was built at Owen Sound during the winter of 1879-1880 for the Great Northern Transit Company's trade between Collingwood, Owen Sound and the Sault. She was in her third season when the end came. The vessel left Collingwood on Wednesday, May 17, 1882, heavily laden with freight for northern points and with a considerable passenger list made up of commercial travelers, merchants returning from buying trips in the East, and prospective settlers going to the North Shore or to Manitoulin Island.

The weather was fine and all went well until the second day

when, as the *Manitoulin* was moving up Manitowaning Bay, about four miles from the village of the same name, fire was discovered. It was at the noon hour, and a majority of the passengers were at table when the alarm first came. Captain Campbell, hurrying below, found the whole engine room in flames. Realizing that his ship was likely to be completely destroyed in the next few minutes, he gave immediate orders to head the vessel for the shore, which was little more than a mile distant, and to drive the engines full speed.

Although it took only six minutes to bring the *Manitoulin* to shore, the vessel was a mass of flames when the hull grated on the beach. Had the captain's commands been obeyed there might have been no loss of life; but many frenzied passengers jumped overboard and eleven were lost. Lifeboats had been swung out in case the steamer grounded some distance from land, and lines had also been placed down over the bows to lower away passengers. But neither was needed, for the steamer came ashore in water so shallow that it could be waded.

George Playter was first mate of the *Manitoulin* and later commanded several Georgian Bay steamers. The pilothouse was burning over his head when the race with the flames ended, and he and Captain Campbell were the last to leave the vessel, the latter going over the side with a child in his arms. Chief Engineer William Lockerbie, when his assistants had been driven from their posts by smoke and flames, stayed at the engines and tried desperately to give the vessel greater speed. Reaching through the flames, he got hold of the throttle lever with his left hand, but as it was set with a hand screw he was unable to get it completely open. At the last moment he escaped by the starboard gangway and crept along the main wale strakes from fender to fender, dropping into the water when the vessel struck shore.

Residents of Manitowaning who had witnessed the tragedy hastened out with boats to offer help. The steamer had burned to the water line, and cargo, mails and the personal effects of passengers were entirely destroyed. The hull was afterward taken away and

rebuilt, coming out in 1883 as the *Atlantic* under Captain Robert
D. Foote, his first command. The vessel ran weekly on the north
shore route, leaving Collingwood each Saturday and returning on
Thursday. Friday being a free day, the boat was often chartered
for Sunday-school picnics and eventually came to be popularly
known as the Gospel Ship, perhaps through someone's memory of
the old revival hymn:

> "The Gospel Ship is now a-sailing
>   Bound for Canaan's happy shore.
> All who wish to sail for Glory,
>   Come and join us, rich and poor."

J. G. ("Josh") Belcher was purser of the *Atlantic* and knew
everyone in the district. It was said of him that he was as much an
attraction as the ship itself on these outings, for he made himself
agreeable to young and old alike. Captain Robert Foote went on
to larger ships and became one of the best-known captains in the
passenger trade on the upper lakes. The *Atlantic* eventually suffered the same fate as her predecessor. On November 10, 1903, she
was discovered to be on fire while off Red Rock on the Parry
Sound route. The vessel was abandoned and sank in sixty feet of
water, but no lives were lost. That was the end of the Gospel Ship.
Men and women around the bay and even far distant must have
had memories of the past recalled when they read of its loss.

One of the most picturesque figures on the upper lakes in his
day was Captain F. X. La France, who lived in Owen Sound for
many years and remained there after his retirement. He was in
command of the passenger steamer *Carmona* in the later eighties
and was also master of the *City of Midland* of the old Black Line.
He was a man of distinguished appearance, with mustache and
goatee of the Napoleon III type. In bringing his boat to dock, it
was often his custom to stand on the bridge in front of the pilothouse and by motions of his arms signal to the wheelsman behind
him. He always had an audience watching this performance and it

was hard to say which derived the greater enjoyment, the people on the dock or the old captain so aware of the attention he was attracting.

These lake captains had an intimate knowledge of the shores of Lake Huron and Lake Superior. With their small steamers they could enter places of refuge that would be impossible for the larger carriers of today, and they were acquainted with places which to most lake captains are now but names on the charts. Yet not all of them came through safely. Elsewhere in this volume is recorded the *Asia's* fate. There was also the *Waubuno,* which disappeared mysteriously with all on board on November 22, 1879, and though the hull was discovered later in comparatively shallow water, no one knows what fate overtook the vessel. Since almost every life preserver came ashore among the wreckage, none apparently having been used, it was conjectured that whatever happened came suddenly. But not one body was ever found.

The *Waubuno* was on the Collingwood-Parry Sound run at the time, a course that lay along the east shore. Ordinarily there were no risks in such a trip, the only really exposed portion being a twenty-mile stretch between Hope Island and Lone Rock, and even this could be avoided by heading for Moose Point and running into the sound by way of the south channel. But the boat was small and its engines none too strong for the gale that was blowing on Friday, November 21, so Captain Burkett remained at the dock in Collingwood though his full load of freight was aboard and most of the passengers were impatient to be on their way. Those who had gone to the local hotel to spend the night were fortunate, for when the weather seemed to moderate, the captain, thinking the worst was over, pulled out of harbor at four o'clock on Saturday morning without waiting for those not aboard the ship. A few dock men saw the boat depart but the only person who saw her afloat after leaving harbor was the lighthouse keeper at Christian Island, the old Jesuit sanctuary of Huron-Iroquois days. He saw her lights as she went north. Several hours later some lumbermen working near Moon River heard a whistle which they thought was that of the *Waubuno,* but they paid little attention to it.

First intimation of tragedy came when the steamer *Magnetawan,* belonging to a rival line, arrived in Parry Sound on Monday. This vessel had left Collingwood some hours after the *Waubuno,* but finding the weather thick and a heavy sea running, Captain O'Donnell went into the shelter of Christian Island. At that late date in the fall, sailing schedules were broken, so no suspicions had been aroused by the delay of the *Waubuno.* Even when the *Magnetawan* reported, it was thought that the other steamer had probably remained somewhere in shelter or might have gone aground in some shallow channel. A tug was therefore sent out to look for her. Very quickly a lifeboat was found, and wreckage, and later a part of the *Waubuno's* paddle box with the name painted on it. There could be no doubt of the fate that had befallen the vessel but there was still the possibility that passengers and crew might have escaped and made their way to one of the myriad islands along the shore. But search which extended over days found no one living or dead; there was only wreckage on every island.

It was too late in the year to look further for the vessel, but in the following March an Indian reported that he had found the hull bottom side up in a little bay behind Moose Point. The Indian's story was found to be true, but how the wreck had come to this place is still a mystery. There was no indication that the boat had struck a rock; it appeared rather that it had capsized.

In afteryears portions of the machinery were found on the Haystack Reefs, some miles to the northwest, and in 1898 a fisherman's net brought to the surface a hand truck and some chains that were evidently off the lost vessel. But no portion of the main deck was ever found, and it is possible that it was broken off by the machinery when the vessel capsized and that all the bodies were beneath it. Twenty-four lives in all were lost. The hull still lies in the little bay near Moose Point to which it drifted, and in years when lake levels are low some portions of it project above the surface.

November 22, 1879, was the day on which the *Waubuno* disappeared, and on November 22, 1906, a like fate overtook the little steamer *J. H. Jones*. Again there were no survivors and it can only be conjectured what led to disaster. The *Jones* left her dock at Owen Sound on a Thursday afternoon. It was the last trip of the season and there was a full load of freight and a passenger list of seventeen. At the last moment a number of barrels of oil were rolled from the dock to her deck, and it has been suggested that these breaking loose may have caused the disaster.

It was stormy on the bay and fishermen near Griffiths Island saw the little steamer go north rolling heavily in the waves. The last man to see the boat was Captain William Chapman, the lighthouse keeper at Cape Croker. The first port of call would be Lion's Head, but the *Jones* never arrived there. Those who were most competent to express an opinion believed that she had gone down soon after passing Cape Croker.

The owners of the boat felt no special anxiety until Sunday, believing that Captain Crawford might have decided to run straight for Manitoulin Island. But when no word had come by Monday there was real anxiety. Messages were sent to various ports but no one had seen or heard of the *Jones*. Tuesday brought the first word. A message from Penetanguishine said that wreckage of the vessel was coming ashore on the west side of Christian Island, and a letter sent by the Methodist missionary on the island reported that two lifeboats, the pilothouse and portions of the cabin of the *Jones* had been discovered. Other wreckage included life preservers of this vessel. Searching parties patrolled the beach for days but no bodies were ever found. The *J. H. Jones* had gone as mysteriously as had the *Waubuno* twenty-seven years before.

It is pleasant to turn from such late season tragedies to other years when, with better fortune, all the boats came safely to their ports and the crews to their homes and families. In Collingwood, which was, and still is, a "sailor town," when the season closed and the last boat was in, there came an event always looked forward to—the wind-up supper on the flagship of the line. As there were two lines, there were two such suppers. That of the Great Northern Transit Company (the White Line) was usually held aboard the *Pacific,* of which Captain Peter M. Campbell was skipper for many years. Around a long table set in the main cabin gathered the officers of the several ships in the fleet, railway officials, the mayor and city council and other special guests. The cooks of the steamer excelled themselves for such an occasion, and there was a round of speeches in which the office paid tribute to the navigators and the navigators expressed their high opinion of the office. Usually Mr. Thomas Long presided and could be relied upon to give some account of the history of the company, beginning with the day when he and his associates purchased the little steamer *Gladys* at Marine City and renamed her the *Northern Belle.*

When the North Shore Navigation Company came upon the scene it too instituted an annual wind-up dinner. As there was but one boat at first, the *City of Midland,* the dinner was held in its cabin, but when the fine new *City of Collingwood* was added in 1893 her more spacious dining room was used. Here the chairman would be James Scott, the president of the company, or Martin Burton, its vice-president. As at the rival dinner, the story of the company would be retold and tributes paid to directors and crews. But all of this is in the past. Not since 1900 has Collingwood had the fleets of passenger boats that once were so much the life of the town. The glory has departed. But it is still a sailor town. In the big storm of 1913 on Lake Huron twenty-six Collingwood men perished. Probably no other port on the Great Lakes suffered as severely.

These Georgian Bay towns are marine-minded. They build ships and they furnish sailors by the hundreds for the lake fleets. Their newspapers give first place to marine news and feature stories of the lakes. At Collingwood the Huron Institute has one of the finest collections of ship models, boat pictures and material relating to Great Lakes shipping to be found anywhere. Editor David Williams was one of its founders and is its presiding genius today.

Wartime demands have greatly increased the grain trade through Georgian Bay and Lake Huron ports. Over seventy per cent of the Western Canadian grain brought to Canadian ports in 1942 went to the bay, Midland alone handling over 32,000,000 bushels, Port McNichol 25,000,000 and Owen Sound more than 17,000,000. The greater volume of this was for export to Great Britain. New life also came to the shipyards which had languished in the years before the war. Ships for carrying supplies across the seas and ships for war service were turned out at an amazing rate. Some day the whole story of this wartime development will be told. It may prove to have been the beginning of a new era in that important industry.

Chapter 18

The Great Storm of 1913

*White are the decks with foam; the winds aloud
Howl o'er the masts, and sing thro' ev'ry shroud:
Pale, trembling, tired, the sailors freeze with fears;
And instant death on ev'ry wave appears.*

—HOMER

SUNDAY, November 9, 1913, is the blackest day in the history of navigation on the Great Lakes. The gales which swept the lakes region on that day sent ten stout ships to the bottom, drove more than a score of others ashore and took the lives of 235 sailors. No other storm of such destructive character has ever been recorded on these inland waters.

"Heavy gales" signals were flying in more than a hundred ports as early as the preceding Friday morning, but when November comes around and shipmasters must count every minute before the close of navigation, long chances are taken. Scores of bulk freighters were on the open waters when the storm began. Those most fortunate found shelter. But eight ships went down on Lake Huron and two more on Lake Superior with not a single survivor to tell the story of what had happened.

The storm had its beginnings on Lake Superior early Saturday morning though there had been unsettled conditions there for some hours before.[1] Lake Huron received the full force of the gale on Sunday and it was chiefly there that loss of life and ships took

---

[1] Captain Noble of the steamer *Cornell* ran into bad weather conditions as early as midnight of Thursday, November 6. While fifty miles west of White Fish Point, with the wind light from the southeast, he suddenly encountered an unusually heavy northeast sea, and shortly afterward the wind backed to northerly, blowing a gale which lasted until Monday night. The *Cornell* sustained heavy damage and was kept off the shore with the greatest difficulty.

place. In the lower lakes region the storm was accompanied by rain and a heavy fall of moist snow. Throughout large sections of Michigan and Ontario telephone and telegraph communication was completely out before Sunday evening, and it was several days before these services were restored. Trains and electric cars were stalled by the wet snow which in some places was four feet deep. The water rose from four to five feet above normal at the foot of Lake Huron and in the St. Clair River, and it was estimated that damage amounting to $100,000 was done at Port Huron alone. The Fort Gratiot lighthouse at the foot of the lake was badly undermined by the huge waves which came tumbling about its base, and the Huron lightship, about two miles up the lake, was torn loose from its anchor and dragged with its crew to the Canadian shore.

Newspapers published on Monday morning had extensive accounts of the damage done by the storm on land and expressed fears for vessels that might have been caught in the open waters, though as yet there were no reports of disaster. But such word came quickly. On Monday morning Captain Plough of the Lakeview lifesaving station above Port Huron searched the tossing waters with his glass and suddenly saw, far out, what appeared to be the hull of a vessel, without masts or stack, rising and falling with the movement of the waves. He at once telephoned to Captain Tom Reid of the Reid Wrecking Company at Sarnia and a tug was sent out to investigate.

Captain Reid found the strangest wreck that he had ever seen in all his long experience on the lakes. A big steel freighter had turned turtle and was now floating bottom side up. The bow was about thirty feet out of water but the stern was submerged so that it was not possible to tell the length of the vessel. The visible portion of the hull was coated with ice and there was no mark by which its identity could be established. Captain Reid circled about it for hours and even took a diver out with him, but the lake was too rough for a descent. The hull differed not at all from scores of others and the name plate, if it remained, was below

Photo by James McCannell

LAKE CARRIERS OF TODAY

The steamer *Sullivan Brothers,* upbound above Port Huron, as seen from the deck of the downbound steamer *Royalton.* Beyond the *Sullivan Brothers* may be seen the stack of another steamer.

Photo by James McCannell

THE "COL. JAMES M. SCHOONMAKER"

When built in 1911, this vessel, 617 feet in length, was the largest bulk freighter in the world. Elaborate provision was made for guests, the entire forward deckhouse being set aside for this purpose. But the comfort of the crew was not overlooked as is shown by the two-story quarters at the stern.

Pittsburgh Steamship Company Photo

THE LARGEST ON THE LAKES

Five vessels, of which the *Benjamin F. Fairless* is one, added to the Pittsburgh Steamship Company's fleet in 1942–1943, are the largest ore carriers on the lakes. Each has an estimated capacity of 18,600 tons.

A GREAT LAKES OIL TANKER

About seventy vessels, specially built for the trade, are engaged in transporting oil about the Lakes. The *Britamolene,* shown above, is a typical example of these vessels.

Photo by James McCannell

THE "GOVERNOR MILLER"

One of four bulk carriers added to the Pittsburgh Steamship Company's fleet in 1938, each 610 feet long and driven by steam turbine engines. These vessels were built for the iron-ore trade.

Photo by James McCannell

THE "COLONEL JAMES PICKANDS"

This vessel, which entered the lake service in 1926, is the second of its name, the earlier being a wooden steamer of 1,529 tons built at Cleveland in 1886. The *Pickands,* one of the Interlake Steamship Company's fleet, is 600 feet over-all, 60 feet beam and 32 feet depth.

Photo by James McCannell

THE "SOUTH AMERICAN"

One of the modern type of passenger boats which during the summer months operate on the upper lakes.

East Michigan Tourist Association Photo

THE "CITY OF CHEBOYGAN"

One of the Michigan State Highway Department's fleet of ferry boats used in the transport of passengers and automobiles across the Straits of Mackinac from Mackinaw City to St. Ignace.

the surface. It was a mystery ship and a mystery ship it remained for the next six days.

News of tragedy soon came from another quarter. Robert Turnbull, a farmer living near Grand Bend on the Canadian shore, had for many years made it a practice to visit the lake shore each day. He had a great love for the water, and rain or shine he strolled along the beach. On the Tuesday after the storm he looked out from the high cliff near his farm and at its base saw the body of a man drifting in and out with each successive wave. The arms were extended from the elbows and gave a curious impression of pleading for help.

With considerable difficulty he pulled the body up on the sand. Help was summoned and members of the Turnbull family and others soon recovered another body. Two others were also found farther along the beach. All bore life preservers with the name *Wexford*. A broken lifeboat was further evidence that this vessel had been lost.

With telephone lines down and roads made almost impassable by the heavy snowfall of Sunday and Monday, it was with difficulty that word could be carried to the nearest railroad and telegraph point. A railroad conductor brought the news to Sarnia that bodies were coming ashore "up the lake." Within the next few hours other messages came from ports farther north along the Canadian shore that bodies were being washed in, three and four at a time, and that they had on them life preservers from the *Regina,* the *James Carruthers,* the *Charles S. Price* and other vessels. For more than a week bodies continued to come ashore, from the ships that have been mentioned and from others for which some measure of hope had been at first entertained. In all more than sixty of the dead were found along the Lake Huron beach.

As soon as the weather permitted, mournful little processions began to move from farmhouses along the lake shore, wagon after wagon bearing the bodies to Zurich, Goderich, Thedford and other towns where inquests were held. These places were thronged with relatives and friends seeking information as to the fate of those known to have been on the boats that were believed to be lost. At Thedford, a small place thirty miles east of Sarnia, the bodies were taken to the local undertaker's establishment, the usual small-town combination of furniture store and funeral parlor. All about were tables, chairs and beds and on the floor the bodies of drowned sailors. Men and women, some dry-eyed, some in tears, gazed intently at the faces which were revealed when the blankets were lifted one by one.

A young woman, her face swollen with weeping, her lips bloodless, moved about the temporary morgue, looked at each body intently and shook her head. She was the wife of Howard Mackley, the second mate of the *Charles S. Price*. When his boat was passing Detroit early on Sunday morning he had posted a letter to her, and when the *Price* was abreast of his home at St. Clair he pulled the whistle in the customary salute. She was there waiting to wave a greeting. His boat went on up the river and she watched it until it had passed from sight.

There were six bodies in the undertaker's rooms. The undertaker took her gently by the arm and led her to a barn near by where on the concrete floor lay five others just as they had been picked up from the sand. She shook her head—none of them was her husband. But she saw one body which she recognized. The man was still wearing a cook's apron.

"It's Mr. Jones, the steward," she gasped. "The boat is lost."

She had been aboard the *Price* not long before and knew the steward. Later she was able to identify one other from the same vessel. But the body of Howard Mackley was never found.

Milton Smith, of Port Huron, an engineer on the *Price,* left the boat at Cleveland just before it sailed on its last trip. Men hesitate to leave their mates at a time when risks have become greater and he was sorry to be quitting. It was particularly hard to say good-by to his friend Arz McIntosh of St. Clair, because McIntosh, a wheelsman, was having trouble with his eyes and wanted to quit too. But he needed the money for a possible operation and he "guessed he would stick it out for another trip."

Smith went to Thedford to assist in identifying the bodies off the *Price.* The first he looked at gave him a shock. It was John Groundwater, chief engineer on the vessel he had so recently left, the man under whom he had worked.

"That's big good-natured John," he said. "How the boys all liked him."

"Are you sure it is him?" asked Coroner Clarke.

"As sure as I know that my name is Smith," was the reply.

"Well, this man had one of the *Regina's* life preservers wrapped around his body," said the coroner.

And in that fact lies the only clue to what may possibly have happened to these two ships in the storm and darkness of that November Sunday night. Did the *Regina* and *Price* collide, perhaps even hold together in some strange way for a few minutes, so that men passed from one deck to the other and seized any life preserver that was handy? No one knows or will ever know.

Smith looked down at the body of Herbert Jones, the steward, still with his cook's apron. "There he is," he said, "just as he looked hundreds of times when he was about to prepare a meal or just after he had prepared it."

Strangest experience of all was that of young John Thompson, of Hamilton, Ontario, who read in a Toronto paper that his body had come ashore from the *James Carruthers.* He hastened to his home and was astonished to find a coffin in his father's house and preparations being made for a funeral.

A sister of young John, who lived in Sarnia, on learning that bodies were coming ashore from the *Carruthers* and believing that her brother was aboard this vessel, sent word to the family in Hamilton. The father hastened to Goderich and was shocked to find a body which bore every resemblance to his son even to the tattooed initials "J. T." and a remembered scar. He had little hesitation in claiming it, and at Hamilton others also identified it. The return of the son alive was almost as great a shock as the report of his death. He had left the *Carruthers* and had been aboard another vessel at the time of the storm. The body which the father had claimed was sent back to Goderich.

Not all the bodies which came ashore were identified. The graves of five "unknown" sailors may still be seen in the Maitland Cemetery at Goderich. A dark red polished obelisk, with an anchor carved on the top, bears on one side the inscription: "A memorial to the unidentified seamen whose lives were lost in the Great Lakes Disaster of Nov. 9th, 1913." On the other side is the single word "Sailors."

What deeds of heroism and sacrifice marked the last minutes of men aboard the sinking ships can only be conjectured. Mrs. Walker, the stewardess of the *Argus,* perished with that vessel's crew. Her body came ashore wrapped in a heavy coat belonging to one of the engineers and about it the captain's own life preserver. But when the body of Captain Paul Gutch was washed up on the sand it was without a life preserver.

During these anxious days the hull which had been discovered floating upside down near Port Huron was still there. At first it was believed to be the *Wexford,* since wreckage and bodies from that boat were the first to be reported. Later there was reason to believe that it might be the *Regina* or the *James Carruthers.* By Friday there was a strong suspicion that it was the *Charles S. Price* of the Mahoning Steamship Company's fleet. This was confirmed on Saturday, the fifteenth, when William Baker, a Detroit diver, went down and worked his way around the hull, clutching the railings above him until he found the nameplate. There was no indication of a collision and Baker found that the buoyancy of the hull was due to the imprisoned air which was gradually escaping in two streams of bubbles. There was no other vessel under the bow as some had conjectured might be the case. The *Price* finally sank from sight on the morning of November 17, eight days after she had turned over.

The location of the hull was about ten and a half miles from the Fort Gratiot light, east and a little north. When it was examined in June 1915 the bow was only twenty-four feet under water and a possible menace to shipping. A year later the bow was raised to the surface when it was found that all the machinery had dropped out, perhaps while the hull was floating. Deckhouses and superstructure were also broken off clean so that nothing was left but the distorted hull. In 1917 Canadian interests purchased the wreck for $30,000 but it has never been raised. No trace has ever been found of any of the seven other vessels which were lost in the same section of the lake.

The loss on Lake Huron, both of lives and vessels, was so far in excess of that on all the other lakes combined, that the storm of 1913 has since been thought of chiefly in terms of Lake Huron.[2] On Lake Superior the steamer *H. B. Smith,* of 10,000 tons capacity, and the *Leafield* of 3,500 tons were lost with both crews, forty-one in all. The barge *Plymouth* disappeared on Lake Michigan with seven lives while Lightship No. 82 at Point Abino near Buffalo went down with its crew of six. The steamers *L. C. Waldo, Major* and *Turret Chief* were constructive total losses on Lake Superior as was the steamer *Louisiana* on Lake Michigan, but their crews escaped death after experiences that none would ever forget. Three lives were lost however, when the steamer *Nottingham* was wrecked near Parisian Island on Lake Superior.

The storm of November 9 practically demoralized lake shipping

---

[2] The loss of life and vessels on Lake Huron was as follows:

TOTAL LOSSES

Name of Vessel	Length in Feet	Carrying Capacity Gross Tons	Value	Lives Lost
Charles S. Price	524	9,000	$340,000	28
Isaac M. Scott	524	9,000	340,000	28
James Carruthers	550	9,500	410,000	19
Wexford	270	2,800	125,000	17
Regina	269	3,000	125,000	15
John A. McGean	452	7,500	240,000	23
Argus	436	7,000	130,000	24
Hydrus	436	7,000	130,000	24
CONSTRUCTIVE TOTAL LOSSES				
H. M. Hanna Jr.	500	8,500	315,000	
Matoa	310	3,104	117,900	

for the remainder of the season. The Lake Carriers' Association ordered that every vessel on its roll should carry a flag at half mast until navigation ceased for the year. Vessel owners were appalled to think that the products of the best shipyards in America were unable to withstand the force of this storm. And this was true also of British shipbuilding, for the *Wexford* and the *Leafield* were typical British tramps which had sailed salt water and weathered gales in all parts of the world before they came to fresh water.

What happened aboard the various steamers is pure conjecture, though three of them were seen not long before their disappearance. Captain A. C. May headed the big 550-footer *H. B. Hawgood* out of the St. Clair River into Lake Huron early Sunday morning. At noon he saw the *Price* just north of Sand Beach, "making bad weather." Soon after he decided not to take further chances and so turned his vessel, heading back toward the foot of the lake. He met the *Regina* fifteen miles south of Harbor Beach and at three-thirty saw the *Isaac M. Scott* five or six miles north of the Fort Gratiot Light. No one else saw these vessels after that time. Soon Captain May himself ran into trouble, for, shaping his course by the Huron lightship which had broken from its anchorage and gone on the Canadian shore, he too went aground about two miles above the mouth of the St. Clair River.[3]

Masters of vessels which survived the storm were unanimous in declaring that they had never before witnessed such rapid changes in the direction of the wind and such gusts of speed. The duration of the storm was also without a precedent. For sixteen hours there was a continuous gale, the wind averaging sixty miles an hour and even going beyond that intensity. At times the wind was blowing in one direction and the waves, often as high as thirty-five feet, running in another. A tremendous strain was placed upon both the hull and the engines of any vessel caught in such a situation.

---

[3] This also happened to the steamer *Matthew Andrews,* loaded with iron ore, which came safely down Lake Huron on that stormy Sunday afternoon. Captain Lampoh saw the lightship through the snow and decided to anchor for the night. But the lightship was not where it should have been and his boat went on the Corsica Shoals, fortunately with but slight damage.

Captains reported seeing three huge waves strike their vessels in quick succession. How dangerous this could be was learned in the sinking of the steamer *S. R. Kirby* on May 8, 1914. This boat, regarded as entirely seaworthy, sank almost without warning in midday during a comparatively moderate storm. The investigation revealed that a great wave had come over the port bow, submerging the deck and by its weight tipping the stern high in the air. Before the *Kirby* could right herself a second wave came, and as the boat stood poised with the after hull out of the water a third wave seemed to catch her from beneath. She heaved upward, stood motionless for thirty seconds and then suddenly plunged to the bottom.

Something was learned also from the experience of the men aboard the *Howard M. Hanna Jr.* which went ashore and broke up at Point aux Barques on the Sunday evening of the 1913 storm. Her master, Captain W. C. Richardson, was unable to keep the steamer's head to the sea and she was subjected to heavy rolling and pounding in the trough. Half an hour before she struck the shore her smokestack went overboard and she lost her rudder. The lifesaving crew at Point aux Barques saw the distress signals and were able to rescue all the crew, thirty-two men and one woman. Many other vessels which went ashore had similar if not as severe experiences.

The fate of the *Charles S. Price* caused more concern than that of any other vessel. Here was a boat, built but three years before, thought capable of withstanding any storm and equipped with every known device to ensure its safety. It had not been thought possible that a bulk freighter, with its wide flat bottom, could possibly turn turtle, yet some combination of circumstances had brought this about. Undoubtedly very unusual conditions obtained in the lake regions during that November Sunday of 1913, especially on Lake Huron.[4]

---

[4] Twenty-seven years later, between November 11 and 13, 1940, a storm of similar cyclonic character struck on Lake Michigan. Two freighters were lost, the *William B. Davock*, with its entire crew of thirty-three, and the *Anna C. Minch* with its crew of twenty-four. As in the storm of 1913 no one knows what happened.

Apart from the *Wexford* all of the boats lost on Lake Huron were comparatively new. Five of the eight had been built within the last six years. The *James Carruthers,* the largest of all, 550 feet in length, had been so short a time on the lakes that it was scarcely more than broken in. The Georgian Bay town of Collingwood had turned out en masse on May 22 to see it launched, and it had made but a few trips before it was lost. It was carrying a cargo of 340,-000 bushels of wheat on its last trip.

Three other vessels, the *John A. McGean,* the *Isaac M. Scott* and the *Charles S. Price,* were all recent additions to the lake fleet, having appeared in 1908, 1909 and 1910 respectively. The *Scott* and the *Price* were each 524 feet long, the *McGean* was smaller, 424 feet long.

The *Argus* and *Hydrus* were but ten years old, products of 1903, one of the great shipbuilding years on the lakes. They were in the 400-foot class, owned by the Interlake Steamship Company of Cleveland. The *Regina,* of Canadian registry, had been built in 1907. She was a smaller boat, 269 feet long and with a carrying capacity of 3,000 gross tons.

The *Wexford,* short and squat, usually needing a coat of paint, had been a familiar craft to sailormen for years. She was somewhat similar in build to the *Bannockburn* which was mysteriously lost on Lake Superior in the fall of 1902. She had been built in a British shipyard as long ago as 1883 yet she was regarded as perfectly seaworthy. She had gone through many a storm on salt water but Lake Huron swallowed her up.

Chapter 19

"The Stately Ships Go On"

*The winds and waves are always
on the side of the ablest navigator.*
—GIBBON

WHATEVER may have been true of earlier days, rugged in-
dividualism has no place in the navigation of the Great
Lakes today. The safety of vessels and cargoes depends
upon the existence of clearly defined rules and the strict observance
of these rules by masters. "It is risk of collision and not the collision itself that masters of ships are under duty to avoid" is an
admonition of the Lake Carriers' Association which applies in
principle to many other situations in which the master of a vessel
may find himself.

The deepwater sailor is inclined to look down his nose at the
men who sail the Great Lakes. It seems so simple to navigate
waters where land is almost always in sight and where voyages
are counted in days rather than weeks or months. But the deepwater man changes his mind if he finds himself in the lake service
or if his ocean-going vessel has to bring a cargo to some lake port.
He quickly learns that vigilance such as he has had to exercise only
at times must here be constant if accidents are to be avoided. He
finds himself moving through narrow and crooked channels in
rivers, amid such a congestion of shipping as he has seen before
only in some busy harbor. Nothing surprises the salt-water man
more than to observe the skill with which the masters of great bulk
freighters move their vessels about crowded lake harbors under
their own steam, working their way into narrow slips where an
ocean-going vessel would have a team of tugs hauling it to its place.

The number and size of freighters on the Great Lakes has so greatly increased in the last forty years that lake shipping is greater today in volume than shipping on any other inland waters in the world. The little town of Amherstburg on the Detroit River has been properly described as "the spot that sees more through traffic than any other on the globe."[1] Day and night vessels move in constant procession so that at times as many as a dozen or more may be in view. But almost as great a marine traffic could be recorded at Port Huron where the ships enter or leave the St. Clair River, and a total scarcely less impressive could be made of the ships which pass near Detour at the mouth of the St. Mary's River. Over a period of from seven to eight months of each year this inland traffic proceeds swiftly, efficiently and with surprisingly few accidents. To dwellers near these marine highways the deep-throated roar of the whistles, as vessels signal one to another, is so familiar a sound that they become as oblivious to it as the dweller by a busy railroad does to the sound of passing trains.

Yet not one of those blasts is without meaning. The most common purpose of the signals is to indicate the course that is being followed. When two vessels are approaching each other from opposite directions it is the duty of the downbound vessel to inform the other upon which side it will pass. The practice in narrow channels is to pass to the right or starboard if possible, just as is done by the drivers of automobiles on land. But this is sometimes impossible or unwise, so the whistle gives the necessary information. One blast means "I am directing my course to starboard," that is, to the right, while two blasts mean "I am directing my course to port," meaning to the left. It is the duty of the other vessel to reply at once, repeating the signal if it is in agreement.

Sometimes, however, there may be good reason for the master of an upbound steamer to disagree with the signal which he re-

---

[1] During the season of 1942 vessels passing this town numbered 14,004 upbound and 14,163 downbound, a total of 28,167. In 1941 the number was even greater, the total being 29,770. A careful check is kept on all boat passages by the Westcott Marine Reporting Agency, which is located at the Livingstone Channel Lighthouse at the head of the Livingstone and Amherstburg Channels.

ceives. He may be aware of some condition not known to the downbound vessel which may endanger one or both. In such a case his duty is to sound at once a danger signal of five or more short and rapid blasts. Then, if the vessels are near to each other, he must slow down to a speed barely sufficient for steerageway, and if necessary stop his engines completely or even reverse.

The men in the pilothouse pay closest attention to the signals they receive and send. By day the signal of an approaching vessel can be seen before it is heard by watching the steam escaping from the whistle. At night special lights on the foremast become illuminated while the whistle is sounding, giving additional warning to the approaching vessel. In some cases the arrangement of the lights serves as identification of the line to which the vessel belongs.

Apart from merely passing, there are many other situations for which rules are provided. When one vessel overtakes another in a narrow channel and desires to go by, it is the responsibility of the overtaking vessel to select the time and place for passing and to indicate its intended course by the proper signals. The only duty resting upon the overtaken vessel is to maintain her speed and course and not encroach upon the course of the other vessel.

There is no place on the Great Lakes where this particular section of the rules is of more importance than on Lake St. Clair and the lower portion of the St. Clair River. The channel upward from the Detroit River across Lake St. Clair is narrow and shallow and ordinarily a score or more of big bulk freighters are traversing it, some upbound, some downbound. Deeply loaded vessels move through this channel and may at times have less than a foot of water beneath their keels. As the lake sailor says, they move along wherever the ground is a little damp. These broad, flat-bottomed freighters, navigating in such shallow water, exert considerable suction and, in the lake phrase, tend to "sidle up" to each other, producing a risk of collision.

Another form of suction is produced when a vessel is running at full speed close to a submerged channel bank. The stern is drawn by what is called "bank suction" toward the adjacent side of the channel while the bow is thrown the other way, imperiling any near-by vessel. Despite all the care that is exercised, accidents arising from these causes are reported almost every year.

Those unacquainted with the navigation of the lakes are often incredulous when told that a great 600-footer may at times be moving ahead with but a few inches of water under its keel. Reduction of speed aids a deeply loaded vessel in passing over such shallow stretches since it is a recognized fact that the keel of a vessel is nearer the bottom when in motion than when at rest. Slowing down thus facilitates passing a shallow spot.[2]

The safety of ships on the open lakes has been greatly increased by the adoption of separate lanes for upbound and downbound traffic. This plan, first tried out in 1911 on Lake Huron, has since been extended to Lakes Michigan and Superior. It has never been enforced by government regulation but observance is the general practice of vessels. The master who fails to keep to his own lane and thereby endangers his own or another vessel has to show good reason for his action. Stress of weather is the only excuse allowed for not following the assigned course.

In the year preceding the first trial of separate courses on Lake Huron four collisions along the Michigan shore had resulted in a loss of eighteen lives and of $400,000 in ships and cargoes. Many masters were opposed to the inception of the plan or gave but grudging support, resenting dictation from shore offices as to the course they should follow. By 1914, however, the wisdom of separate lanes was conceded, and former opponents became warm supporters. The Canadian Lake Protective Association declined to associate itself with the plan in 1911 but, following a collision in 1915 between the *Wahcondah* and the *Choctaw,* the Dominion Marine Association adopted the regulation for all vessels enrolled

---

[2] Tests which were made in 1923 showed that the average bulk freighter on the lakes when traveling at ten miles an hour would "squat" in the water more than a foot, traveling along in an elliptical depression created by the propeller's pull of water from beneath and around the ship and its expulsion to the rear. See the Great Lakes Protective Association, *Report* (1924), 17-20.

in its membership and further suggested separate courses on Lake Superior from Whitefish Point to Port Arthur and Fort William.

It is true that there have been collisions on the open lakes since the separate lanes were introduced but in general these have been due to fog. On May 16, 1919, the *D. R. Hanna* came into collision with the *Quincy A. Shaw* six miles off Thunder Bay light. Shortly after the accident the *Hanna* turned turtle and sank in deep water. The weather was calm at the time and the crew of thirty-two was taken off by a fish tug and landed at Alpena. Ship and cargo of grain constituted a total loss of one and three-quarter million dollars. Later in the year a diver located the wreck, bottom side up in ninety feet of water.

Four years passed before there was another such accident; then, on May 20, 1923, the steamer *Edward U. Demmer,* upbound with 7,000 tons of coal, was sunk in the same locality, following a collision with the *Saturn.* Those aboard the *Demmer* later testified that the fog at the time was so dense that they did not even know the name of the vessel which had run into them. A great vague shape had suddenly come out of the fog, smashed into their ship and as quickly disappeared. The *Demmer* filled rapidly and the crew of twenty-five took to the lifeboats. The *R. L. Agassiz* picked up twenty-four and the *James B. Eads* came along in time to rescue a deck hand who was alone in a lifeboat half-filled with water. A year later the *Glenorchy* was sunk off Harbor Beach when in collision with the *Leonard B. Miller.* There was heavy fog at the time and the conflicting testimony as to the place where the two vessels met made it difficult to fix the blame.

On Lake Huron the courses are seven miles apart, the lane for upbound vessels being nearer to the western or Michigan shore. If the regulations are observed and boats are not allowed to stray during fog or under the influence of currents, the risk of collision is slight. The real danger lies at those points where the lanes of traffic converge, near Detour at the mouth of the St. Mary's River and at the lower end of Lake Huron, above the mouth of the St. Clair River. At this latter point there is a lightship, one of the last of its type on the Great Lakes, and there are range lights to guide vessels safely into the river.

The vicinity of Detour is a much more dangerous locality, particularly when fog prevails. The axial line up and down the river at this point is practically north and south. Detour Point extends down somewhat like a hook into the lake and is marked by a light and fog whistle. It is surrounded by shoal rocky reefs of which one, called Detour Reef, extends in a southwesterly direction for some distance. Less than a mile farther out in the lake is the converging point both for boats following the two courses on Lake Huron and for those going to or from the Straits of Mackinac. It is a place where the utmost caution in navigation is required.

The frequent mention of fog indicates the threat which it offers to safe navigation on the lakes. There is no sound more mournful than that of the whistle sounding its warning from a shore which lies completely hidden in the mist. He would be a hardened sailor who had grown comfortably accustomed to it. Scarcely less disturbing to those aboard a vessel anchored or moving ahead cautiously is the three-blast signal coming minute by minute from some other vessel, perhaps only a few hundred yards away but of which nothing can be seen. A heavy fog will sometimes tie up as many as thirty or forty vessels in the St. Clair River or above the canal at the Sault. As the mist begins to clear there is a bedlam of signal blasts and then the ships begin to move off in stately procession, each master anxious to make up lost time.

Forest fires in the past endangered sailing conditions by the clouds of smoke which would drift out over the water. Lake Huron was at one time particularly notorious for this menace to navigation. Today, with greater vigilance in detecting and fighting forest fires, the danger has been much reduced, though not completely absent. Fog is usually dissipated within a few hours by the sun but smoke may hover for days over a body of water and when mixed with fog is worse than either alone. Though the danger from the smoke of forest fires has decreased, another hazard exists in the clouds of thick, black smoke of passing vessels which may suddenly obscure the view ahead from the pilothouse. Pilots and wheelsmen dread this happening, even though it may last only three or four minutes, since in the crowded waterways obscured vision for that brief time may easily bring about a collision.

River currents are more or less regular in their speed and direction, and navigators became well acquainted with all places where their influence has to be taken into consideration. On the open lake, however, there are frequent changes both of speed and direction of currents, due to changes in the wind. Records compiled at the coast guard station at Thunder Bay on Lake Huron showed that ninety-five per cent of all the groundings or strandings in that vicinity were the result of vessels being carried off their course by the currents during thick weather. The prevailing current at this point is from the north, and its greatest flow is about seven miles east of Thunder Bay Island. But this current is not always from the north and sometimes it is not even in the same direction as the wind blowing at the time. There was a good illustration of this a few years ago when a coast guard at Thunder Bay observed an ice floe traveling directly into the teeth of a moderate northwest gale at a pace faster than he could walk. It is only by long experience in their profession that masters gain knowledge of such unusual influences affecting the navigation of their vessels.

There is seldom a season in which ice conditions are not a handicap. From the middle of February on, every vessel owner and every sailor is interested in reports on the thickness of ice in the Straits of Mackinac, the St. Mary's River and on Lake Superior. Early opening of navigation on these waters means the probability of more round trips with greater profit for the owners and more wages for the men. But no one can make any prediction as to a whole season. It may open early and be closed before the usual time by ice forming in the St. Mary's River. On the other hand the season may open late and end with mild weather, so that even in December boats move freely through the channels.

The year 1917, a war year with high pressure on shipping, was one almost unprecedented in the matter of bad ice conditions. It was the middle of June before vessels could sail without risk of damage from this source. To make matters worse the weather turned bitterly cold on the upper lakes at the first of December and in the harbors ice-crushing boats had to be brought into use to permit the loaded freighters to get away. In all, there was less than six months' fair sailing weather during the entire season, and in the early months heavy fogs further handicapped navigation.

The season of 1923 was likewise unfortunate for vessel owners. At the middle of April, the normal date of opening of navigation, there was two solid feet of ice in the rivers and channels of the upper lakes. Toward the end of April the Pittsburgh Steamship Company sent two freighters as icebreakers to clear a channel to Calcite and up the St. Mary's River. The *J. B. Neilson* finally reached the Sault on April 30 and the *Henry Cort* followed later. Icebreakers and heavy tugs were still in use above the Sault as late as May 20. This was a year, however, in which the closing months compensated for the delayed start. During November there was an absence of gales and the record volume of 121,000,000 tons of ore, coal, grain and stone was successfully moved during the year.

Three years later, in 1926, conditions at the close of navigation were so unusual that they are still talked about when mariners get together. The season had opened badly, the first cargo of iron ore reaching a Lake Erie port on May 6. The port of Buffalo was not open until May 9, and at one time no less than seventy-eight freighters which had left harbor were fast in the ice fourteen miles out in the lake. But even worse conditions appeared as the sailing season neared its end. Beginning in the middle of November there was a succession of gales accompanied by the lowest temperatures recorded in years. On December 4 there were sixty downbound and twenty-five upbound vessels fast in the ice in the St. Mary's River with the temperature twelve degrees below zero. Other downbound vessels continued to pile in behind so that the river was like a crowded harbor, and at night the miles of lighted ships looked like the streets of a city. When a huge icebreaker finally cleared a passage more than one hundred loaded ships passed out into Lake Huron.

This had been bad enough but the trouble continued. One day later a freighter became fast in the ice. Before it could be released eighty others had been held up and it was not until December 12 that they were freed. Some vessels, finding themselves unable to get to open water, wintered at the Sault. In all, nearly 250 freighters were affected by the severe weather conditions.

It is more pleasant to record such a season as that of 1931 when navigation ended chiefly because there were no more cargoes to be moved. During that winter it would have been possible for vessels to continue operations on the lakes until the end of February. Real winter weather was not experienced until the first week of March, and there was little ice, even on Lake Superior.

It is even more pleasant to write of the season of 1942, so vital to the war effort of the United States and its allies. The bulk freighters were running by the middle of March and vessels continued to move until the first week of December. Never before in the history of the Great Lakes was there such a quantity of iron ore brought from the mines around Lake Superior. More than 92,000,000 tons scooped from the northern ranges came to the docks along Lake Erie, the Detroit River and Lake Michigan to be turned into airplanes, guns, shells, fighting ships and all other things made of steel with which war is conducted. One vessel, the *L. E. Block* of the Inland Steel Company's fleet, made thirty-eight round trips during the season of navigation and traveled 61,985 miles. Captain Howard H. Kizer had reason to be proud when he tied up his big ship at the close of the year. And Chief Engineer Alan Seelye, who had kept the engines turning during the busy season, must have had similar pride. The *Block* had carried 583,625 gross tons of ore during the year, her largest individual cargo being 16,359 gross tons.

All previous records of individual ore cargoes were broken during 1942 under the spur of war necessities. Captain C. E. Robinson took the big Canadian freighter *Lemoyne* out of Superior, Wisconsin, on July 9 with a cargo of 17,080 gross tons of iron ore to be delivered at Hamilton, Ontario. The second largest ore cargo in 1942 was that transported from Duluth to Conneaut, Ohio, by the *Leon Fraser,* one of the five new carriers added to the Pittsburgh Steamship Company's fleet in 1942. Her record cargo amounted to 16,863 gross tons.[3]

---

[3] Participation of the *Lemoyne* and other Canadian vessels in the United States ore trade was one of the changes brought by war. Thirty-five Canadian vessels, belonging to eight steamship companies, carried 2,662,582 tons of iron ore during 1942 for United States industry. About two and a half million tons of American ore was carried to Canadian steel plants as well as half a million tons of Canadian ore.

Chapter 20

Lake Vessels Past and Present

Build me straight, O worthy Master!
Stanch and strong, a goodly vessel
That shall laugh at all disaster,
And with wave and whirlwind wrestle!
—LONGFELLOW

THROUGHOUT the preceding chapters there have been many references to the vessels which have sailed on Lake Huron and to the men who manned them. It may be well in this closing chapter to give some account of the evolution of the ships on the Great Lakes. No one type has been peculiar to Lake Huron but the story of the changes that have been seen upon its waters will serve to explain and illustrate those which have been general upon the lakes. It is a far cry from La Salle's *Griffin,* with its forty-five tons' burden, to the great bulk freighters of today with their carrying capacity of more than 18,000 tons, but Lake Huron has seen them both and all the changes that lie between. Over a period already much beyond two and a half centuries the panorama of lake shipping has been unfolding. Canoes and bateaux, sailing ships and wooden steamboats, iron and steel freighters, whalebacks, tankers and self-unloaders have all come, and some of them have gone never to return. Today there remain chiefly those types which by sheer functional efficiency are able to meet the demands of modern business, for, however beautiful or however worthily constructed, a vessel is tested solely by its ability to perform the task for which it has been designed.

Though we have only the crude picture of the *Griffin* appearing in early editions of Father Hennepin's narrative and drawn by some artist in Europe who presumably never saw America, we may properly assume that the vessel which La Salle constructed in 1679 near Niagara was of a type with which he was already familiar, and there seems reason to believe that it was a Dutch galiot which took form before the wondering gaze of the Indians and that finally sailed away to the upper lakes never to return.[1] This type of ship could navigate in comparatively shallow water and at the same time it possessed considerable cargo space. Both were desirable features, for La Salle already knew of the shallows on Lake St. Clair, and one of his ideas in building the vessel was that it should bring profitable cargoes from the regions to the north.

The *Griffin* led the way into the upper lakes, but with the exception of one small vessel on Lake Superior, built in 1735 by De la Ronde, no other is known to have followed during all the French regime. Only canoes and bateaux were available to carry men and goods over these bodies of water with their long heaving swells and their sudden storms that could so easily engulf small craft. When Canada passed to England in 1763 it might have been expected that there would soon be merchant ships on these upper lakes, but such was not the case. Little time elapsed after 1763 before the English colonies along the Atlantic coast were moving toward independence, and it was not long before this independence movement took the form of hostilities. To prevent the colonials from intriguing with the Indians in the lakes region and further to curtail trade with the colonies, the British administration ordered that all goods should be carried on government ships. Vessels that were privately owned were to be laid up or absorbed in the naval service.

Such a situation proved almost intolerable to merchants engaged in legitimate business, though there is some evidence that the regulation may at times have been ignored or evaded. John Askin, for example, trading between Michilimackinac and Detroit, makes

---

[1] The type of vessel followed in the building of the *Griffin* has been discussed by George A. Cuthbertson in his *Freshwater* (Toronto, 1931), 44-45, 227.

several references in his letters to private vessels carrying his goods around the year 1778, though in that same year a vessel belonging to him was taken into the King's service. Petitions asking better consideration for trade needs were sent to Sir Frederick Haldimand, governor of Canada, but he was adamant. In 1784 not half the goods destined for Detroit ever got beyond Niagara. The Detroit merchants were furious over the losses which they were sustaining and renewed their petitions to Colonel Barry St. Leger, who had been placed in command of the troops after Haldimand's departure. He consulted with the home government and eventually the building and operating of private vessels were permitted, though still under certain restrictions. Shipbuilding began at once.

The first to be constructed was the *Beaver,* a little one-masted vessel of about the same tonnage as La Salle's *Griffin.* She was intended for trade on Lake Superior, but when it was found impossible to haul her through the rapids at the Sault she remained in use on the waters below. Her place was taken by the *Otter,* somewhat larger in size, which was built above the rapids in 1785 by the North West Company. A year later the company added the *Industry,* a sloop, and gave an order also for the building of a schooner which was christened the *Detroit.* The *Nancy,* whose exploits in the War of 1812 have already been narrated, was another product of this period, being built at Detroit in 1789. The *Swan,* built there also in 1792, was used four years later to bring United States soldiers to that place when it was formally taken over from the British. And there were others as well.

The War of 1812 gave a tremendous impetus to shipbuilding on all the lower lakes, so that when it came to an end a considerable number of vessels were available for commerce and there was much better knowledge of the type of ships suited to traffic on the lakes. The close of the war opened a new epoch in the development of the United States, and in this development lake shipping played a notable part. Between 1812 and 1820 six new states were added to the Union, two of these, Indiana and Illinois, being a part of the Old Northwest. The population of the western country increased rapidly in this period and since the chief means of communication with the new states was by water, a trade soon developed that taxed every vessel. Until the coming of the railroads it was the lake and river vessels which carried the larger portion of the westward migration.

Closing scenes of the War of 1812 were still fresh in men's minds when the first steamboat built west of the Niagara River made its appearance. This was the *Walk-in-the-Water,* constructed at Black Rock in 1818 for a group of merchants and intended to provide service between Black Rock and Detroit. Its builder was Noah Brown, a distinguished New York marine architect. The vessel was 135 feet long, 32 feet beam and had a depth of 8½ feet. Compared with the graceful types of today, the *Walk-in-the-Water* was an awkward-looking craft. Between her two masts was a tall ungainly smokestack. The paddle boxes stuck out on each side, adding further to her clumsy appearance. Passenger quarters were below deck and divided into separate compartments for men and women.

The vessel was launched on May 28, 1818, and sailed on its first trip westward on August 23. As the engines were not sufficiently powerful to breast the current of the Niagara River, the boat was hauled to the river entrance on Lake Erie by twenty yoke of oxen, a process in common use and popularly known as a "horned breeze." According to the *Niagara Patriot,* the steamboat was well down on the horizon inside of two hours after its departure. Several stops were made en route to replenish the wood fuel supply, a little cannon on the forward deck booming out to announce the arrival. No one as yet had thought of a steam whistle. At Cleveland, and particularly at Detroit, great crowds assembled to see this marine curiosity. To the Indians along the Detroit River it was wonderful magic that a boat could move swiftly without sails, and the story goes that some of the whites suggested to the aborigines that the vessel was pulled along by huge sturgeons harnessed beneath the water.

The *Walk-in-the-Water* ran for three seasons. In June 1819 she went as far north as Mackinac and at a later date made a trip to Green Bay. The end came on the night of October 31-November 1, 1821, when the little steamer went ashore near the mouth of Buffalo Creek after a stormy night on Lake Erie. The vessel had cleared from Buffalo on the preceding afternoon but ran into a storm soon after leaving port. Seams in the hull began to open and so much steam was required for the pumps that the engines could not be used to their full capacity. An attempt was made to anchor but the cables snapped. Shortly before daylight the vessel grounded, and by good fortune all on board were able to reach land. The engines were later salvaged and placed in a new boat, the *Superior,* which made her first trip in the spring of 1822. In 1825 the *Henry Clay* and several other ships were added. It will be remembered that these vessels were used in 1832 in transporting troops and supplies westward for the Black Hawk War.

The steamboat had come, but that did not mean that the sailing ship was ended. On the contrary, the next seventy-five years after the appearance of the *Walk-in-the-Water* was the great era of the sailing ship on the lakes. Hundreds of schooners were built in American ports and hundreds in Canadian ports. On all the lakes they were the chief carriers for nearly half a century. The opening of the Welland Canal in 1829 influenced the design of such as would have to pass through its locks, and there was evolved what was known as the "canaler," with blunt, straight stem, flat stern with almost no cutaway and a short bowsprit which could be raised to a vertical position when passing through the canal.

Schooners which restricted their trade to the upper lakes had no need to follow such design, and they were as a rule more graceful vessels. Since they were generally the product of small shipyards there was an absence of standardization and builders or owners could exercise their fancy. Many of these lake schooners were beautiful craft and would stand comparison with the creations of the best designers. Their rigging included at least one feature that was peculiar to the Great Lakes. From a yard immediately below the crosstrees on the foremast, a large square sail was spread reaching almost to the deck, while from the yard to the truck of the topmast was spread a three-cornered sail known as a raffee topsail. These raffee topsails seem to have originated on the lakes, for there appears to be no parallel on other waters.

As late as the period of the Civil War ninety per cent of the tonnage on the lakes was sail and less than seven per cent steam. One result was the presence of a large fleet of tugs, some of them the most powerful in the world, able to haul as many as eight and ten vessels behind them. But steam was rapidly superseding sail by the seventies, and farseeing sailors could even then recognize that the ships they loved were doomed to go. In the period of westward migration the schooners carried thousands of emigrants and their belongings to western ports whence they proceeded to the new states. It is recorded that the topsail schooner *Illinois,* going up Lake Huron in 1834, was so laden with farm implements and household effects belonging to her passengers that to economize space the wheels were taken off wagons and hung in the shrouds.

The steamboats made early provision for both cabin passengers and emigrants going into the West. The *Superior,* built in 1822, had a regular steerage hold with bunks, tables, bins for baggage, and cooking stoves. But provision for first-class passengers was more elaborate. The *Thomas Jefferson,* on which Mrs. Anna Jameson went up Lake Huron in 1837, had upper-deck cabins and was furnished as well as a first-class hotel. Henry R. Schoolcraft, after journeying in 1838 from Mackinac to Detroit in the new steamer *Illinois,* could write:

"The style of the lake steamboats is greatly improved within the last few years, and one of the first-class boats bears no slight resemblance to a floating parlor, where every attention and comfort is promptly provided. He must be fastidious, indeed, who is not pleased."

John R. Godley, an English visitor in the early forties, bore like testimony to the newer lake boats. "There are steamers almost every day running between Buffalo, Detroit and Chicago," he wrote. "I went on board one, and found her a magnificent vessel, of 780 tons, and 300 horse-power, i.e. about the size of the Dublin and Liverpool mail-boats, with three tiers of cabins above water, so that one is sure at least of plenty of air." Godley was not as certain of the stability of these steamers. "I should think she must be top-heavy," he added, "and not calculated to stand much sea: there is sometimes very heavy weather on the Great Lakes."[2]

Laurence Oliphant did not mention the name of the steamer on which he traveled on Lake Huron in 1855 but said of his experience: "To a person who had never made a voyage upon the American lakes in the steamboats which traverse them, the first effect is very singular. The whole passenger accommodation is upon deck. Sometimes there are cabins opening off the saloons; but in the boat we were in, the berths were screened off simply by curtains suspended to bars, which projected a little beyond the berth, so that there was just room enough allowed for the process of dressing. Few persons, however, thought it necessary to make use of these, and the great majority of toilets, therefore, took place in the saloon."[3]

Oliphant might have traveled in that year on the *Western World,* which marked the peak of the shipbuilder's art and craft in that period. This vessel was 348 feet long and from outside to outside of her paddle boxes had a beam of 72 feet. These paddle boxes were 39 feet in diameter, the equal of anything on salt water. The age was one of ornamentation, and such carving and gilding had never before been seen on any vessel plying the lakes. But she had a short life, since the panic of 1857 finished what the competi-

---

[2] John R. Godley, *Letters from America*, 2 vols. (London, 1844), I, 143-144.
[3] Lawrence Oliphant, *Minnesota and the Far West* (Edinburgh and London, 1855), 66.

tion of the railroads had already begun. The *Western World* lay for a time at a Detroit dock, her paint fading and her iron rusting. Then in 1863 she was towed over to Buffalo, her engines removed and the hull turned into a dry dock. Not for many years was there so large a passenger vessel in the lake trade.

Smaller vessels continued, however, to do profitable business. In the same year that the *Western World* was broken up, six other passenger boats were advertising trips to Lake Superior. The *Meteor, Illinois, Northern Light* and *City of Cleveland* were described as having "good brass and string bands" for the pleasure of their patrons. The steamer *Traveller* offered a ten-day cruise covering 2,000 miles at $35 from Cleveland and $33 from Detroit. Servants and children over three years old were charged half price. The *Iron City,* also running to Lake Superior, offered as a special attraction a visit to the Pictured Rocks and the iron and copper mines.

The appearance upon the upper lakes in the early seventies of the iron ships, *India, China* and *Japan,* of the Anchor Line, marked a new era in the passenger trade. At about the same time a new Canadian company also entered the field. In 1870 J. H. and H. Beatty, who had been operating boats on Georgian Bay, established a line out of Sarnia with the sidewheeler *Manitoba* and a leased propeller, the *Acadia.* These boats ran to Lake Superior.

A few years later they built the *Ontario* and *Quebec* which, when introduced, were the largest Canadian boats in the Lake Superior trade. Next they added, by amalgamation with another company, the *Sovereign* and *Asia,* but the *Asia* was later removed to Georgian Bay where she foundered in 1882 with heavy loss of life. To replace her the *United Empire* was built at Sarnia in 1883 and the *Monarch* was added in 1890. Both became popular passenger boats. The *Monarch* went on Isle Royale in the late fall of 1906, but the *United Empire* survived as a passenger boat until 1915 when she was partly burned and was afterward turned into a barge. This old Sarnia company, dating from 1870, was incorporated in 1900 in the Northern Navigation Company which thereafter added first the

Huronic, then the *Hamonic* and finally the *Noronic,* the last still one of the finest passenger boats on the lakes. The *Huronic* has in recent years been used only as a freighter. All three vessels became part of the fleet of Canada Steamship Lines in 1926.

For sheer magnificence, nothing before or since has rivaled the steamers *North West* and *North Land* which came upon the lakes in the nineties. They were owned by the Northern Steamship Company behind which was James J. Hill and the Great Northern Railroad. They provided a connecting link between this western railroad and lines which ran eastward from Buffalo.

No one who ever saw these vessels is likely to have forgotten them. Three hundred and eighty-six feet in length, standing high out of the water and with their hulls painted white, they were as striking in appearance as anything the lakes have ever known. Three huge smokestacks were painted yellow with a black band at the top. Palatial scarcely describes their interior fittings. Passenger quarters were finished in costly woods. The dining room sparkled with silver and cut glass. Money was not spared to provide anything that might add to the comfort of passengers or enhance their feeling of importance in traveling on such a vessel. President McKinley came from Washington to be a guest on the first trip of the *North West.* These were the gay nineties, and the Hill vessels lived up to the reputation of that era. But they were not a financial success—perhaps they were not expected to be. Their season was short—early June to late September—and maintenance costs were enormous.

The end of the two ships was not in keeping with their palatial character. The *North Land* was swept by fire at Buffalo in June 1911 and sank at the pier. She was raised but not reconditioned. When the First World War came her engines were removed and she was cut in two to be taken to tidewater where it was planned to reunite the parts. But the forward section foundered while being towed across Lake Ontario. The after section became the freighter *Maplecourt.* The *North Land* in 1919 was also cut in two and towed to Quebec where it was intended that she should be used in ocean traffic but this never came about and in the immediate postwar depression she was reduced to scrap.

When these vessels first went up the Detroit and St. Clair Rivers the great swells which they raised wrecked boathouses and small docks, leaving a trail of destruction along the shores. It was said that the compensation which was made for the numerous claims was regarded as excellent advertising for the boats. The shore residents made their docks more secure and tied their boats higher after the first experience.

The design of freighters on the Great Lakes has always been influenced by the commodities which they carry. Grain and lumber were the two chief cargoes in the schooner era and scores of these earlier sailing vessels passed on into a period when they became barges, towed three and four at a time behind a puffing wooden steamer. The stanch build of these early schooners and barges gave some of them extraordinarily long life. In 1912 there were still between 250 and 300 of the old lumber carriers on the lakes. None then carried ore, though at times they were used to carry coal. As late as 1918 the schooner *Alice* was sold for use in the lumber trade between Texas, Cuba and Puerto Rico. She was the last of a famous fleet owned by Captain Ole Hansen, which at one time had comprised twenty-one schooners, and of which the *Alice* had been the flagship.

The navigation season of 1920 was disastrous for these older wooden vessels. The lumber barge *Goshawk* foundered on Thunder Bay in June. She had been built at Cleveland in 1866 and for more than a quarter of a century was one of the vessels in the Blodgett fleet of lumber carriers. The *Schoolcraft,* built in 1884, took fire on Lake Ontario on December 3, while on her last trip of the season. Thirteen of the crew took to the lifeboats but Captain Thomas Sughrue stayed at the wheel until he beached his ship. Other old-timers which disappeared in 1920 were the *Byron Whitaker* which was burned; the *Mary A. McGregor* which went on the Magnetic Shoals in Georgian Bay; the *James H. Shrigley,* lost on Lake Ontario, and the barge *John F. Eddy* which foundered in Lake Erie.[4]

Earlier forms of the modern carriers were already appearing on the upper lakes in the 1870's. The *R. J. Hackett,* which came out in 1869 as an ore boat, was really the first bulk freighter on the lakes. She was 211 feet long, had a beam of 33 feet and her engines were placed aft. A year later the *Forest City,* two feet longer but of similar beam, was built as her consort, and for the next twenty years propeller and consort were the prevailing practice. There was justification for this consort system in the days of wooden shipbuilding since there was already in existence a fleet of sailing ships whose destiny in the evolution of lake trade was to be that of hauled carriers. When the *V. H. Ketchum* came on the upper lakes in 1874 her builders were tending toward the type of freighter which is common today. Pilothouse and captain's cabin were well forward, engines and boilers as far aft as possible, thereby leaving large open deck space. Instead of the ungainly arch trusses which were a feature of so many early steamboats the *Ketchum* had its oak hull braced and trussed entirely below the main deck. She was 223 feet long, with 41-foot beam and a depth of 16 feet.

In the early seventies ships could carry from 350 to 1,000 tons of ore, but with loading and unloading facilities as yet undeveloped it took three weeks or more to make a round trip from Cleveland to Marquette. The *Chamberlain* with a capacity of 1,000 tons and the *Martin,* of 1,200 tons, were the largest vessels on the lakes in 1874.

The *Onoko,* built at Cleveland in 1882, is remembered as the first metal freighter, though as early as 1844 the iron vessel *Michigan* had been built for the United States Navy at Erie, Pennsylvania. The *Spokane* was the first steel bulk freighter, entering the upper lakes trade in 1886. A year later came the second steel steamer,

---

[4] When the Great Lakes Protective Association was formed at Cleveland in 1909 it included in its membership nineteen wooden steamers and six wooden barges. Gradually these disappeared, some lost, some sold into a less strenuous trade. The last to go was the *Chickamauga* which foundered off Harbor Beach on September 12, 1919, in a moderate gale. "She had come to the end of her voyage and died of natural causes," said the annual report of the Association for that year.

the *Cambria,* which was for many years an ore carrier for the Pittsburgh Steamship Company. Later, as the *Lakeland,* she was successively a package freighter, then engaged in the coal trade and finally a carrier of automobiles. The *Lakeland* sprang a leak on Lake Michigan in December 1924 and foundered a few miles off Sturgeon Bay. She had been on the lakes for thirty-seven years.

By 1888 ore was the largest article being carried in bulk. Dock facilities had been improved, but it was still the older type of ships which were engaged in the trade. The carrying capacity of individual vessels had not been materially increased. But many channels had been deepened, and within a few years the United States was to enter upon a period of great industrial expansion. The time was ripe for an advance of some nature in the design of ships carrying the bulk commodities.

The whaleback or "pig," as it became known in the slang of the sailors, was the most radical departure in ship design since the time when the first iron vessel appeared upon the lakes. It was Captain Alexander McDougall, born in Scotland and reared in the Georgian Bay district, who designed and built these vessels which, when they first appeared, excited such ridicule and criticism that their inventor found it a difficult matter to secure financial backing to construct them. The design was worked out while he was captain of the *Hiawatha* and towing the barges *Minnehaha* and *Goshawk* up and down the lakes. At that time he wrote:

"I have thought out a plan to build an iron ship cheaper than wooden vessels. I want to get a ship that wind and water alone cannot destroy—a boat that could be made from the flat, smooth plate and fine straight frames as they come from the rolling mill, a boat that could be made with a few large tools and built on a sand bar close to eight feet of water into which to launch it side wise; a boat square in cross section able to carry the greatest cargo on the least water."[5]

---

[5] See Duluth *News-Tribune,* November 16, 1941.

Many a lake captain had probably dreamed the same dream as he stood his watch and in the darkness of night considered in what way vessel design might be improved. McDougall's fame rests in the fact that he carried his dream into reality. He began by making models in which the ideas that had come to him were incorporated. But no models such as his had ever been seen before. His ships were to have flat bottoms so that they would carry the most cargo on the least depth but they were to have a rounded top so that water could not stay on board.

He took his model to shipowners and shipbuilders but got no encouragement. "You call that damn thing a boat?" said one. "What it looks more like is a pig." And "pig" the ships became forthwith. Since none would accept his design, McDougall determined to build such a vessel himself, with his own money and on his own land at Duluth. That was in 1888 and when the queer-looking craft was launched and finished he had it towed to Two Harbors and loaded with 1,200 tons of ore for Cleveland. The trip was a success but perhaps not since the first voyage of the *Walk-in-the-Water* had anything in marine design aroused more comment.

The first whaleback was not given a name but a number, *101*. It is said that the number commemorated a bet offered by a skeptical acquaintance at ten to one that the craft would never arrive at its port. A year after the *101* had gone into the trade, a model of the same type was built, the *102*, twice as large as the first. It was then that a group of New York men, after seeing the models and examining the record of the boat already built, decided to back the enterprise. A site for a shipyard was found in West Superior and on Christmas Day of 1889 work began on the construction of a dry dock. By the early summer of 1890 a whaleback was under way which became the *Colgate Hoyt,* named after one of the New York backers. Others followed in quick succession, and in 1893 ten steel whalebacks were constructed at once.

At this time preparations were being made for the World's Fair at Chicago and it was suggested that a boat of the whaleback type might be designed to carry the Fair crowds. The result was the building of the *Christopher Columbus,* 362 feet long, 42 feet wide, 24 feet deep, with five decks. She was a great success and during the period of the exhibition carried more than 1,700,000 passengers.

In the ten-year period after 1888 Captain McDougall built forty-six of these vessels. One was built in England for the run from Liverpool to the Black Sea and the Danube and was in use for more than twenty years. In 1891, with its builder as pilot, the *Charles W. Wetmore* loaded with wheat at Duluth and carried it to England. Later the *Wetmore* made a trip round the Horn carrying construction materials to the new city of Everett, Washington, and continued in the Pacific trade for several years.

For a long time the whalebacks were familiar vessels on the lakes, but they have gradually disappeared until today there are but few surviving. They have been supplanted by the modern bulk freighter which for efficiency of operation and maximum carrying capacity is as yet unchallenged. The old *Alexander Mc-Dougall,* named after the inventor of the type, is still afloat and so is the *John Ericsson.* The *South Park,* which came out in 1896 as the *Frank Rockefeller,* and which had been carrying automobiles until the outbreak of war, was driven on the rocks near Manistique by a storm in 1942. During the following winter it was reconstructed as a tanker and came out in 1943 as the *Meteor.*

While the whalebacks were uniform in their general design, the most noticeable feature being the rounded top, there were some variations otherwise. Some had the pilothouse aft, close to the stack, while others had it placed well forward. Usually a steamer hauled one or more barges of like construction. They were not graceful and the brown color which they were painted gave them a dull appearance. But they had a look of strength and their record on the Great Lakes showed that they could stand heavy weather.

The turn of the century inaugurated the era of the modern type of bulk freighter. Many men had a part in this development—

Photo by W. G. Trestain

THE ENTRANCE TO LAKE HURON

The International Bridge linking the United States and Canada towers above the Rapids where Lake Huron empties into the St. Clair River. The passenger steamer *Hamonic* is seen passing upbound beneath the bridge. Within three minutes it will be on the open waters of Lake Huron.

eration back, the tanker plays an important part in present-day lake commerce. The growth of the bulk traffic in petroleum products has in recent years brought to the lakes a considerable fleet of these vessels, nearly 70,000,000 barrels being moved in 1941 by the sixty-seven ships then engaged in the trade.

The first real tanker appeared on the lakes in 1910. This was the *Imperial,* of Sarnia, which had been built in England. It was 200 feet long and of 796 gross tons capacity. A year later it was joined by the *Impoco,* 243 feet long and having more than double the capacity of the *Imperial.* These two Canadian boats were followed in 1912 by the first American boat, the *Renown* (later the *Beaumont Parks*), and in the same year a third Canadian boat was put in service. This was the *W. S. Calvert,* formerly an old barge built at Chester, Pennsylvania, in 1874. The name was subsequently changed to *En-Ar-Co.*

It was not until 1918 that a second American tanker was added, this being the *William P. Cowan,* 420 feet long. Although more than fifty additional tankers have been added in the years since 1918, only one has exceeded the *Cowan* in dimensions. This was the *Red Crown* built in 1937, which had a length of 454 feet and 7,500 gross tons capacity. At the beginning of 1920 there were seven Canadian and three American tankers on the lakes. At the end of 1931 American tankers and barges had increased to eleven and the Canadian fleet to seventeen. Ten years later there were thirty-three American and thirty-four Canadian vessels in the trade, but the American tonnage was considerably higher.

The self-unloader is not a new type of carrier but rather a modification of the standard bulk freighter to handle particular commodities, chiefly limestone and coal, and to be able to discharge cargo at any place where the vessel draft is sufficient. The first of this type was the *Wyandotte,* built in 1908 to carry limestone from the lower peninsula of Michigan. Since then the fleet has increased to more than thirty. One steamship company alone owns ten or more such vessels. The massive steel framework, placed directly behind the forward housing and towering high above the deck, detracts from the beauty of the ship but conveys an impression of great strength and efficiency. The ease with which the standard bulk freighter may be put to other uses is illustrated by the numerous conversions into self-unloading coal and stone carriers, and also into large-capacity automobile carriers.

The turret boats, to which reference has been made, came to the lakes after 1900 and before they passed from the inland waters had found a place in the history of lake shipping. They were British-built and had been in ocean trade before coming to the Great Lakes. The feature of their construction which attracted attention was that from about the water line the hull curved, or "tumbled home" as a sailor might say, to the main deck on which the hatches and deckhouses were located. The object in building this type had been to cut down on the gross tonnage while still carrying a capacity load. Tolls through the Suez Canal and at many ocean ports were charged on the basis of gross registered tonnage, and the turret type of construction reduced this tonnage and in turn the port and canal tolls.

Seven of these boats were brought to the lakes, the *Turret Chief, Turret Court, Turret Cape, Turret Crown, Turret Bell, Turret Bay* and *Scottish Hero*. They came to various ends, some wrecked, some scrapped and one or more sent back to salt water. No others of the type came later to the lakes, and none were ever built on fresh water.

No record of shipping on the upper lakes would be complete if it omitted to mention the package freighters which in the past perhaps more than in the present carried miscellaneous cargoes between the chief ports. This class of steamers included some of the most beautiful vessels that have sailed the lakes. In their day the Lehigh Valley Transit Company's fleet, with their four masts, engines amidships and rakish funnels, were not surpassed in gracefulness by anything on fresh water. They were like ocean vessels in appearance.

Navigation on the Great Lakes is a definite profession. The men who come to the command of these big lake carriers or who have charge of the engines reach that goal after a long apprenticeship and by giving proof of their knowledge of seamanship or engineering. The man who takes one of these vessels through the lakes and rivers, in calm or storm, in fog or ice, may easily have in his charge a ship and cargo valued up to a million and a half or two million dollars. He has also the responsibility for a crew of from thirty to forty men. It is his job to make as many trips as is possible during the season of sailing. To do this he must see that his boat is loaded in the least possible time, that he avoid as many delays en route as he can and that at the terminal his ship shall be quickly unloaded and another trip begun.

Men come to the command of these vessels or to the post of chief engineer by no easy route. They begin at the bottom and can look forward to many years of hard physical work before being entrusted with the chief responsibility. In the navigating crew a man may feel that he is rising when he is finally put at the wheel and steers the ship. Later he may become a third mate and rise through second to first grade. And there he may stay for the rest of his life. Not every man who has first mate's papers will feel that he is competent to command a ship. And the same is true of the men who work aft in the engine room.

There is excellent provision made today for the young man who wishes to follow this profession. During the winter, when the boats are laid up in harbors, schools are conducted where seamanship and engineering are taught by men who themselves are Great Lakes captains and chief engineers. These winter schools have been promoted by the Lake Carriers' Association since 1916. When the twenty-fifth year of these instructional classes was completed in March 1941 the number of men studying navigation who had received their first or original pilot's license was more than 800 while the number of marine engineering students who had received original licenses was but a little under 1,000. All told a total of 2,724 sailor students had, following their classroom instruction, successfully passed examinations for the various licenses sought.

In other ways much is done to promote a high standard in the profession, to assist men to advance and to provide for the welfare of sailors. A savings plan which was instituted in 1911 provides the men with an easy means to conserve a portion of their earnings while on shipboard, instead of carrying large sums of money about with them. In 1917 the deposits so made totaled half a million dollars, in 1920 the million mark was reached and in the war years this has gone to nearly three million dollars annually. Ship safety committees, designed to safeguard members of the crew against personal injury, have been highly effective, particularly for new men becoming acquainted with the routine of a vessel. Assembly rooms, where men may gather in their off time ashore, and a lending library system maintained at the Sault Canal are other welfare features. Proof that the men appreciate this library service is shown by the fact that their voluntary contributions to the carrying-on of its work have been as high as four and five thousand dollars in one year. Since 1909 death benefits have been paid to the beneficiary of any seaman sustaining fatal injuries in the performance of ship's duty.

Aboard ship life follows a definite routine. On American vessels the watches are four hours in length followed by eight hours off, making an eight-hour day. This means that the crew includes three mates, three wheelsmen, three assistant engineers, and so down the scale both fore and aft. On Canadian boats the six-hour watch is still adhered to, with the result that men have to work a twelve-hour day. Crew's quarters on lake vessels are clean, comfortable and sanitary. They offer a striking contrast to the accommodation on ocean vessels which occasionally come to the lakes.

A visit to the dining room and galley of one of the big freighters would be a revelation to most land folk. Officers and most of the crew eat together, the captain at the head of the table. White linen and silver give a homelike appearance. The menu would do credit to a good hotel, not elaborate but varied and wholesome.

The firemen and deck hands are served in a separate dining room, but the menu is exactly the same as that provided elsewhere. Since men come off watch at times between regular meal hours, one watch at ten o'clock at night, a buffet lunch is always available— hot coffee, stew, pork and beans, bread and butter, cheese and cake. No man need ever be hungry on these boats.

The kitchen from which three full meals are served daily is a busy place. A glance into its huge refrigerator at the beginning of a trip would show sides of beef and pork, baskets of fruit and quantities of vegetables. Further supplies may be taken on as the vessel passes through the locks at Sault Ste. Marie, and more will be received at the head of the lakes. Shipping companies are quite aware that the cook and his staff can do much to maintain spirit and morale aboard ship, particularly in the hard days that come as the sailing season nears its end. The larder is never stinted.

Where men are thrown together as closely as they are aboard ship and that over a whole season, there develops a pride in the vessel, its past record and its current performance. The ship comes to possess a personality, it has its good points and it may also have its bad points, but from the "old man," as the captain is usually called, down to the humblest deck hand there is the feeling of being a part of something that has life and individuality. Where men sail together year after year in the same vessel, it becomes a sort of second home. They understand the ship, they know and trust one another, and there is attained some measure of that spirit and morale of which Kipling was thinking when he wrote:

> When crew and captain understand
> each other to the core
> It takes a gale and more than a gale
> to put their ship ashore.

Epilogue

W AR HAS come again to Lake Huron. These peaceful waters which for more than a century and a quarter have formed a part of an "unguarded frontier" are today embraced in a battle front that knows no bounds, a battle front that girdles the globe and that extends almost from pole to pole. The roar of guns is heard on four continents and on all the seas. But the war also extends to the most remote hamlets of North America and to inland waters where ships of war have not been seen in far more than a man's lifetime.

War came to Lake Huron with the first shot that was fired in 1939. Though few people realized at the time that a whole world would become involved, Canada was almost instantly in the struggle, and the United States found the allied nations looking to it for supplies of every kind. There was immediate need of quickening the nation's industrial and transportation systems. More iron ore must be brought to the steel mills, more grain carried, more coal moved about the lakes to those places where it was needed. And, as a sequel to all of this, more ships and bigger ships had to be built.

Industry in both the United States and Canada rose to the challenge. So, too, did transportation. Pearl Harbor brought the United States into the war and all that had been done in the past for national well-being was then eclipsed by that which was done for national security. Today on the Great Lakes every vessel that can bear cargo is enlisted for service. Great shipyards on these shores have laid down vessels of a size and capacity not heretofore known and have placed them in commission in record time. From other shipyards have come armed vessels which on the Seven Seas are aiding in the struggle for human liberty.

Sixty years ago Bay City, at the head of Saginaw Bay, was one of the chief lumber towns on all the Great Lakes. Today it has achieved fame through its wartime shipbuilding record and the "upside down" and "roll over" methods which its shipbuilders are using in construction. To build the hull of a welded vessel upside down and then roll it over for completion and installation of machinery might seem feasible for a small ship, but these Bay City people are doing it with war vessels more than three hundred feet in length and doing it successfully.

In the autumn of 1905 two brothers, H. J. and F. W. Defoe, with an associate, G. H. Whitehouse, established a small boat-building concern at the mouth of the Saginaw River, where they constructed small pleasure craft. At the close of the last war they secured a contract to build eight 100-foot harbor mine planters. These were delivered in 1921, and from that time on the partners continued to build small steel vessels of various types.

When the present war came and the United States government was embarking upon a huge shipbuilding program, the Defoe Company received as its first contract an order for twenty-five coastal patrol vessels of the type known as PC's. Succeeding orders increased this number to fifty-five and contracts were also received for the building of four mine sweepers and four big ocean-going rescue tugs for the British government. These tugs left Bay City manned by British crews and flying the British flag. One of them, the *Destiny,* launched at Bay City on July 2, 1941, has been credited by the British Admiralty with having towed a disabled ship 1,650 miles from Gibraltar to England, through fog and heavy seas, without charts and with only a pocket atlas for guide.

Of greater interest, however, are the destroyer escorts, a new type of vessel, designed since the war began, and intended for convoy duties. The DE's, as they are called, are larger than the British corvettes, but they are smaller than a regular destroyer. The Navy's idea was that they would relieve destroyers for more important duties, the DE vessels being sufficiently fast and sufficiently powerful for convoy duty.

The Defoes had already built many smaller vessels upside down, chiefly to facilitate the work of the welders. The "upside down" plan had been successfully used in the building of submarine chasers, but would it work in the case of a 300-foot destroyer escort? The first DE built by the Defoes was constructed on the conventional plan of an upright hull throughout the building period. But after that the change was made. Easter Sunday of 1943 will remain a red-letter day in the annals of Bay City. For the first time in history a steel-welded ship, more than 300 feet in length and weighing more than 600 tons, was rolled over. Then on June 22 an even more striking demonstration of the method was given. On that day, in quick succession, the destroyer escort *Rich,* named after a young fallen hero in this war, was launched, and immediately in its place the hull of another vessel was rolled over right side up from an adjacent cradle to the cradle just vacated by the *Rich.* Less than an hour was occupied in the two processes. Since then the "roll over" method has become almost a commonplace as far as Bay City is concerned. During 1942 the Defoe yards turned out thirty-six fighting ships, their value exceeding $46,000,000.

These destroyer escorts are the largest warships ever built on the Great Lakes, and Bay City is justly proud of its record in their construction. It has no desire today to be known as having once been one of the roughest, toughest lumber towns on the lakes. That was a long time ago, and since then there has arisen a pleasant city of 50,000 population with diversified industries and a sound healthy civic life. There are more than 3,500 people working in its shipyards today and the honor roll on the walls of the plant records 600 former employees who are in the armed services.

Around the shores of Georgian Bay, Canadian shipbuilders are doing a job similar to that of their American cousins. Collingwood, Midland and Owen Sound have all in the past been shipbuilding towns, but during the 1930's the industry languished.

The war has brought expansion and a record volume of activity to these ports as well as to places of lesser importance on the Canadian shores of Lake Huron.

The Midland shipyards, known all over the continent in the days of James Playfair, had been idle since 1928 until reopened in January 1941. They had been purchased in 1940 by interests controlling similar plants elsewhere on the Canadian shores of the lakes. Howard Johnson, a young English naval architect and shipbuilder, was placed in charge. Though he had to begin at the bottom and not only rebuild the yards but also train shipbuilders, he has made the Midland plant one of the most efficient in Canada.

The corvette, a new type of vessel bearing a very old name, has been the chief product of the Midland yards, but in addition trawlers have also been turned out. These and the earlier corvettes were for the British Admiralty but present corvette building is entirely for the Canadian navy, the expansion of which during this war has been rapid. From Midland have also come numbers of subchasers, lifeboats, landing barges and other craft. Subchasers have also been built at Penetanguishine, Honey Harbour and Sarnia.

Collingwood has long been a shipbuilding town. In the earlier days wooden vessels were turned out in numbers, but after 1900 steel ships of large size took their place. Like Midland, Collingwood had suffered eclipse during the depressed thirties, but war has given a new impetus to an industry for which this port is well equipped. Here, as at Midland, corvettes have been the chief production, one of those taking the water late in 1943 bearing the name of the sister town Owen Sound. It was a gala day for Owen Sound when this vessel paid an official visit before starting on its way to salt water. It was the first time that a warship of any kind had ever entered Owen Sound harbor.

The corvette as a type has been changed and much improved in design as successive vessels have come from the yards on Georgian Bay or elsewhere about the lakes. With its protective guns and machinery for handling depth charges, the corvette is adequately equipped to do battle with the enemy on the high seas, but its principal duty, like that of the American DE boat, to which it corresponds, is the protection of merchantmen in convoy. The corvettes have a sturdy bulldog look and are built to meet heavy weather. Their record of performance in the war has been highly creditable.

Owen Sound has not in the past been as prominent in ship-building as either of its sister harbors, but since 1940 its yards have been active in the construction of steel-welded tugs, some of them for the British Admiralty and others for the government of Canada. These tugs, equipped with Diesel engines, have been built to meet heavy weather conditions wherever they may be put in service. One other Owen Sound marine activity is the production of propellers for vessels built in other yards. Made of manganese bronze, some of those turned out have had a diameter of twenty feet.

Away on the distant shores of Lake Superior, from April to December, long slim carriers have tied up to the ore docks and within a few hours have been loaded and sent on their way eastward. The lines are being cast off as the last ton is poured into the hold. The deck crew fastens down the hatch covers, making all secure against any gale they may encounter. Ahead on the horizon the smoke of other steamers may be seen. All are racing for the Sault Canal. There a new lock has been added since the war began, built in less than fourteen months though it was estimated that it would take twenty. It is named after General Douglas MacArthur.

Once through the locks the big freighters race again, for ports on Lake Erie or Lake Michigan or Lake Ontario. There equipment waits to provide speedy unloading and a swift return to northland docks. Mountains of ore pile up, for the winter months are ahead when none can be moved. Other ships, their hulls white with dust, bring cargoes of limestone from the quarries along the Michigan shore of Lake Huron. It too is a resource vital to the war effort. On their upbound trips many of the ships bear coal, but if the need for ore seems pressing they go up light, their bows projecting high above the water. From the time when the ice has cleared sufficiently to allow these vessels to move northward until the December days when the St. Mary's River is again clogged, there is not a minute to be lost. Battling with fog and snow and ice as the season draws to a close, deeds of endurance and heroism are done of which the world hears nothing.

To the record of the ships and the sailors may well be added that of the managerial skill which keeps this vast system of inland marine transportation at top speed despite difficulties of all kinds. The job of moving the ships and their cargoes so as to meet wartime industry's every need is done quietly and those who perform it are not conspicuous, but without their management there would have been no such records as the war years have produced. It was wise planning which in 1942 brought from Lake Superior that all-time record of 92,000,000 gross tons of iron ore, 4,000,000 tons in excess of the goal originally set; a coal movement on the lakes of over 48,000,000 tons, exceeding all previous records except 1941, and an all-time record for the movement of limestone of over sixteen and a half million tons.

The navigation season of 1943 is near its close as these lines are being written. The ice is already thickening on the more sluggish sections of the St. Mary's channel. Vessels passing through the locks at the Sault bear an icy coating laid on by the winds and waves of Lake Superior. Lighthouse tenders are removing the keepers from more remote stations and lifting some of the buoys and other aids to navigation. Many vessels have made their last voyage of the year to Lake Superior and are downbound with their final cargo. A few days more and navigation on the upper lakes will be officially closed.

Who can measure the value of these Great Lakes in the economic life of the two nations that use them in common? Were the Great Lakes to dry up, much of the industry which they now feed would simply cease to exist. And by what yardstick can we measure the value of these waterways at this time when the world is at war and the cause of human liberty at stake?

All that has been said of Lake Huron in its relation to the war effort of the allied nations can be said also of the other Great Lakes, and in even greater measure, for Lake Huron differs from the others in being chiefly a channel for industry rather than a terminal for its raw materials. Yet, in the measure of its people's spirit it differs not at all from the others. The shipbuilders at Bay City or on Georgian Bay, the fishermen who go out from the lake shores, the farmers of Michigan or of Ontario, the sailors who will soon be returning to their homes in these little lake ports, all are doing their part to achieve the victory which they hope will bring with it a new and a better world.

ACKNOWLEDGMENTS
AND
BIBLIOGRAPHICAL NOTE

A WORD OF THANKS

I AM deeply indebted to friends who have assisted in the preparation of this volume by supplying information or reading critically one or more chapters. Dr. Milo M. Quaife, general editor of this series of volumes on the Great Lakes, has constantly advised and has read each chapter. His suggestions and criticisms, based upon intimate acquaintance with the field of the work, have been most helpful. Any excellences the book may have owe much to him; the imperfections are my own.

Friends who have assisted by supplying information include Mr. W. E. Turnbull of Dashwood, Ontario, Dr. David Williams of Collingwood, Mr. Harry G. Ellsworth of Port Colborne, Mr. J. W. MacLeod of Kincardine, Mr. Eugene Herman of Cleveland, Mr. Lewis H. MacLeod of Bayfield, Mr. James McCannell of Toronto, Mr. Harry A. Hopkins of Port Huron, Mr. Howard Fleming of Owen Sound and Mrs. James Playfair of Midland. The Cleveland and Detroit Public Libraries have courteously answered various queries.

Colonel P. S. Reinecke of the United States Lake Survey office at Detroit supplied interesting information regarding the surveys of the lakes and the preparation of the official charts.

Captain Malcolm Johns of the steamer *A. B. Uhrig* kindly read the chapter entitled "The Stately Ships Go On," as did also some of his officers. Captain H. H. Kizer of the steamer *L. E. Block* supplied information regarding the outstanding carrying record of that vessel during 1942.

The Macmillan Company of Canada and the author, Dr. E. J. Pratt, gave permission for the use of a quotation from the poem *Brébeuf and his Brethren*. Messrs. Farrar and Rinehart of New York courteously gave like permission for use of a quotation from Stephen Vincent Benét's *Western Star* (Copyright 1943 by Farrar & Rinehart, Inc.) and the Ryerson Press of Toronto for a quotation from the poems of Wilfred Campbell.

For photos which have been used in this book I tender my thanks to Mr. A. G. Atkinson of Bayfield, the Art Gallery of Toronto, the Royal Ontario Museum of Archaeology at Toronto, the Detroit *News,* the Michigan Department of Conservation, the Park and Harbor Commission of Mackinac Island, the East Michigan Tourist Association, the Wayne County Medical Society, Detroit, Mr. Deane Keller of the Department of Fine Arts at Yale University, Mr. Harry G. Ellsworth of Port Colborne and particularly Mr. James McCannell of Toronto.

To Miss Lillian R. Benson, who typed the manuscript and made many helpful suggestions as to its form, I owe grateful thanks.

F. L.

BIBLIOGRAPHICAL NOTE

SOURCES for the history of Lake Huron are many but scattered. Champlain provided the first, when he recorded his journey in 1615 to the country of the Huron in the course of which he came upon Georgian Bay. The daily newspaper is the latest when it tells of a gale or wreck or gives us statistics of the grain entries at Goderich or the limestone shipments from Alpena. Life around and upon any single lake has been so varied and covers such a length of time that not only the obvious but many obscure sources must enter into the writing of its record.

In the preparation of this volume much has been drawn from such well-known publications as the Michigan Pioneer and Historical Society *Collections,* the *Papers and Records* of the Ontario Historical Society, the Wisconsin Historical Society *Collections,* the *Michigan History Magazine* and the *Wisconsin Magazine of History.* Two rich sources for the history of shipping in the last generation are the reports of the Lake Carriers' Association and of the Great Lakes Protective Association. Year by year, through these annual volumes may be traced both the trade developments on the lakes and changes in the ships which carry that trade. Nor should one overlook the files of that chatty little publication, *Great Lakes News,* which Eugene Herman has been publishing at Cleveland for nearly thirty years.

The writings of travelers comprise a source from which much has been drawn, though usually in small portions. In the French period the writings of the Jesuit missionaries and of such figures as Lahontan and Hennepin and the obscure soldier who merely signed himself J. C. B. tell us of conditions of the time, but it was not until the nineteenth century, with its greater ease and safety of travel, that detailed narratives appeared in number. From that period we have such works as Mrs. Jameson's *Winter Studies and Summer Rambles,* Margaret Fuller's *Summer on the Lakes,* William Cullen Bryant's *Letters of a Traveller,* Paul Kane's *Wanderings of an Artist,* George T. Landmann's *Adventures and Recollections* and Laurence Oliphant's *Minnesota and the Far West.* Typical of many lesser known narratives of this period are Thomas Nye's accounts of his journey between Montreal and Chicago in 1837 and Samuel A. Storrow's report to Major General Brown on his inspection trip to Michigan in 1817.

The survey of the international boundary after the War of 1812 brought to its service two men who took note of what they saw on Lake Huron and recorded it in interesting fashion. Dr. John Bigsby's *The Shoe and Canoe; or Pictures of Travel in the Canadas,* published in 1850, is a reliable and interesting account of the scenery and of the social conditions in the twenties. Bigsby's work has recently been supplemented by publication of the contemporary diary kept by Major Joseph Delafield while acting as agent of the American Boundary Commission. C. N. Cochrane's *David Thompson the Explorer* tells in brief the story of that remarkable personage who was also associated with the boundary surveys, and Captain J. G. Boulton has provided a sketch of Admiral Bayfield in the *Transactions* of the Literary and Historical Society of Quebec, No. 28.

James Cleland Hamilton's little volume, *The Georgian Bay,* published in 1893, is accurate but too brief to be of much value. The great storehouse of Georgian Bay lore is to be found in the scrapbooks compiled over many years by the Huron Institute at Collingwood, and in the publications of that society. The shipping of Georgian Bay and of Lake Huron generally found an historian in the late Captain James McCannell whose writings in the Ontario Historical Society *Papers and Records* and in newspapers published about the Georgian Bay are authoritative. The files of the Collingwood *Enterprise-Bulletin,* the Owen Sound *Sun-Times* and the Midland *Free Press* are rich in marine material. Norman Robertson's *History of the County of Bruce* gives some account of the Saugeen Peninsula.

Mackinac Island has had such a varied and picturesque history that the literature dealing with its life and people is extensive. Many articles on its earlier history are found in the Wisconsin Historical Society *Collections* and in the Michigan Pioneer and Historical Society *Collections.* Henry R. Schoolcraft's *Personal Memoirs* and other writings tell us much about the Indians with whom he dealt both at Mackinac and at Sault Ste. Marie. Dr. Beaumont's famous experiments, made while he was on the island, are best told in his own book, published as far back as 1833, but he himself has become the subject of a voluminous periodical literature. A recent study is George Rosen's *The Reception of William Beaumont's Discovery in Europe.*

St. Joseph Island has found its biographers in Joseph and Estelle Bayliss, whose *Historic St. Joseph Island* is a model in the writing of local history. It is to be regretted that the late W. F. Lawler of Detroit was cut off while engaged in his study of Michigan Islands, only fragments of which had appeared. Much information on the St. Clair River is contained in the *History of St. Clair County* edited by W. L. Jenks, and the writer must express his indebtedness also to the writings of the late William E. Phillips of Sarnia, whose death in 1943 removed one of the most enthusiastic students of Great Lakes shipping history. His newspaper and magazine articles, published over several years, contain a wealth of marine data.

The late Brigadier General E. A. Cruikshank and Mr. C. H. J. Snider have laid all students of the War of 1812 under obligation by their writings on the Great Lakes operations during that struggle. The development of the sailing ship on the lakes is comprehensively dealt with by George A. Cuthbertson in *Freshwater*. He has also written of the war period and of its effect upon shipbuilding.

The development of the Michigan shore of Lake Huron has been the subject of numerous articles in the Pioneer *Collections,* in the *Michigan History Magazine* and in the writings of such scholars as George N. Fuller *(Economic and Social Beginnings of Michigan)* and Ida A. Johnson *(The Michigan Fur Trade),* both publications of the Michigan Historical Commission. Finally may be mentioned the writer's own collection of material on the Great Lakes, notes, clippings, pictures, etc., assembled over many years through personal interest in the subject.

INDEX

INDEX

A. H. Ferbert, the, 360 f.n.

Abbott, Edward, administrator at Vincennes, 210

Acadia, the, passenger steamer, 352

Agassiz, Louis, visits St. Joseph Island, 191

Alberta, the, passenger steamer, 313

Alcona County, Mich., 113

Alexander McDougall, the, whaleback, 358

Algoma, the, C.P.R. steamer, 313-314

Algoma, the, former *City of Toronto,* 309

Algonquin, the, schooner, 275

Algonquin Indians, 34, 43, 177

Alice, the, schooner, 354

Allouez, Father Claude, 204

Allumette Island, Ont., 43

Alpena, Mich., 104, 106, 114

Alpena County, Mich., 113

Alva, the, later *Glenfinnan,* 315

American Fur Company, 68, 69, 70, 251

Amherstburg, Ont., 81, 145, 184, 288, 295, 336

Andaste Indians, 20, 30, 36, 49

Anderson, Mrs. Ann, 260 f.n.

Anderson, Capt. T. G., 180, 182, 183, 185

Ann Mackenzie, the, schooner, 305, 306

Anna C. Minch, the, 333 f.n.

Annie Craig, the, later *City of Winnipeg,* 310

Anti-Slavery Society of Canada, 146

Arctic, the, Ward vessel, 159

Argus, the, 331 f.n., 334

Arpin, Alphonse, 59

Arthur, Sir George, Lieutenant Governor of Upper Canada, 185

Asia, the, 277-282, 311, 352

Askin, John, 68, 346-347

Assikinack, Chippewa chief, 181, 182

Astor, John Jacob, 68, 69

Athabaska, the, C.P.R. steamer, 313-314

Atlantic, the, Georgian Bay steamer, 311, 319

Atlantic, the, Ward vessel, 158-159

Au Sable Point, Mich., 97

Au Sable River, Mich., 97

Augustus B. Wolvin, the, first 500-footer, 359

Aux Sables River, Ont., 122

Baby, Raymond, 265

Baird, Mrs. Elizabeth Thérèse, 218-220

Balfour, Capt. Robert, 202

Baltic, the, former *Frances Smith,* 309

Bannockburn, the, 334

383

Barclay, Capt. Robert Heriot, 81

Battle of Lake Erie, 71, 81-82, 98

Battle of Windsor, 263

Bay City, Mich., 105; wartime shipbuilding at, 366-368

Bayfield, Henry Wolsey, 125, 154, 292-293

Bayfield, Ont., 125, 147

Bayfield River, Ont., 125

Bayly, Rev. Benjamin, 185

Beatty, James H., 309, 352

Beatty, William, 309, 352

Beaumont, Deborah Green (Mrs. William Beaumont), 256

Beaumont, Dr. William, 247-256, 297

Beaumont Parks, the, tanker, former *Renown,* 361

Beaver, the, 347

Bedore, Joe, 171

Bee, the, gunboat, 122

Belcher, J. G., 319

Belle McPhee, the, 306

Benjamin F. Fairless, the, 360 f.n.

Bigsby, Dr. John, 139, 145-146, 151, 176, 198, 222, 295-298

Birney, James G., 145

Black Hawk War, 99, 166-167

Black Line, the, *see* North Shore Navigation Company

Black River, Mich., 100

Bois Blanc Island, Mich., 97, 166

Boulton, Capt. J. G., 293

Bourget, Ignace, Bishop of Montreal, 57

Brady, General Hugh, 239

Brébeuf, Father Jean de, early life, 42; character, 42; in Huron

Brébeuf, Father Jean de—*Cont.* country, 32-33, 41, 44, 115; canonization of, 40; martyrdom of, 50-52

Bressani, Father Joseph, 48

Britannic, the, 311

British Landing, Mich., 77

Brock, General Isaac, 71, 76

Brough, Rev. C. C., 185

Brown, Major General Jacob, 217, 218

Brown, James B., 151

Bruce, William, 65

Bruce Peninsula, Ont., *see* Saugeen Peninsula

Brulé, Etienne, 18, 20, 22, 177; his travels, 19, 30; his death, 20

Bryant, William Cullen, 70, 152, 191, 222, 228

Buckeye State, the, 308

Bulger, Capt. A. H., 91, 92

Bullock, Capt. Richard, 82

Burbeck, Major Henry, 214

Burlington Bay, Ont., 35, 36, 82

Burton, Martin, 323

Butler, Colonel Anthony, 86

Byron Whitaker, the, lumber carrier, 354

Cabot, J. Elliot, 191

Cabot Head, Ont., 122, 289

Cadillac, Antoine de la Mothe, 65-67, 150

Cadot, Father Jean-Joseph, 56

Calcite, Mich., 114

Caledonia, the, North West Company brig, 77, 84

Calhoun, John C., 72-73

Cambria, the, passenger steamer, 106

Cambria, the, later *Lakeland,* 356

Campana, the, former *North,* 310

Campau, Louis, 69

Campbell, Capt. Peter M., 312, 317, 323

Canada Company, 119-120, 123-125

Canada-Lake Superior Transit Company, 310

"Canadian Boat Song," authorship of, 121-122

Canadian Lake Protective Association, 338

Canadian Pacific Railway, 305, 311, 312, 313

Cape Croker, Ont., 289

Carhagouha, Huron village, 22

Carmona, the, 319

Cartwright, John, 29

Carver, Jonathan, 65

Caspian, the, Ward vessel, 159

Cass, Governor Louis, 286

Cavelier, Abbé, brother of La Salle, 205-206

Chabanel, Father Noël, canonization of, 40; martyrdom of, 53

Chamberlain, the, first metal freighter, 355

Champion, the, tug, 169

Champlain, Samuel de, 17-27, 131, 177, 286; discovers Lake Huron, 17-19; his achievements, 23; monuments to, 24; tribute of Paul Le Jeune, 24; concern for religion, 24, 41; early life, 25-26

Champlin, Stephen, 91-92

Chapman, Capt. William, 322

Charles S. Price, the, 327, 328, 329, 330, 331 and f.n., 332, 333, 334

Charles W. Wetmore, the, whaleback, 358

Charts, 302-303

Chaumonot, Father Joseph-Marie, 32-33, 115

Chazelle, Father Pierre, 57, 58

Cheboygan, Mich., 97, 106

Cheboygan River, Mich., 97

Chickamauga, the, 355

Chicora, the, former *B,* 310

China, the, 170, 352

Chippewa Indians, 80, 102, 103, 128-129, 178, 207

Choctaw, the, 338

Cholera, 166-168

Christian Island, 53, 60, 140, 177, 245, 289, 322

Christopher Columbus, the, whaleback, 358

City of Cleveland, the, 352

City of Collingwood, the, 311, 313, 323

City of London, the, 311

City of Midland, the, 311, 312, 319, 323

City of Owen Sound, the, 310

City of Parry Sound, the, former *Favourite,* 311

City of Toronto, the, (Black Line), 311

City of Toronto, the, later *Algoma,* 309

City of Winnipeg, the, former *Annie Craig,* 310

Clark, George Rogers, 211

Clark, Capt. John, 163, 261

Clark, General William, 83

Clay, Henry, 71, 72, 93

Clemens A. Reiss, the, 307

Clement XIV, pope, 56

Clements, W. L., 105

Cleveland, the, Ward vessel, 159

Colborne, Sir John, Lieutenant Governor of Upper Canada, 117, 118, 183, 189

Colgate Hoyt, the, whaleback, 357

Collingwood, the, former *Kaloolah,* 307, 313

Collingwood, Ont., 83, 109, 139, 146, 304, 306, 312, 322, 323; wartime shipbuilding at, 369

Colonel James M. Schoonmaker, the, 359

Columbia, the, British warship, 291

Conboy, Dr. F. J., 88

Confiance, the, former schooner *Scorpion,* 91

Conlin, Capt. Tom, 307

Connon, Thomas G., 59, 60

Constellation, the, passenger steamer, 111

Cooley, Horace, 261, 262

Copper mines, 20, 29, 30

Cornell, the, 325

Cornwell, Dean, 255

Corunna, Ont., 153

Cove Island, Ont., 131

Coyne, James H., 37

Croghan, Colonel George, 84, 85, 86, 88, 99

Cumberland, the, 309

DE boats, 367-368

D. R. Hanna, the, 339

Dallion, La Roche, 31-32, 43

Daniel, Father Antoine, 43; canonization of, 40; martyrdom of, 50

Darius C. Cole, the, 164

Darling, Dr. Paul, 185

Davost, Father Ambrose, 43

De Brosse, Chevalier, 296

De Casson, Dollier, 36-37, 150

De Chastes, Aymar, 25-26

Defoe Shipbuilding Company (Bay City), 366-368

Delafield, Major Joseph, 196, 197-198

De la Lande, Father St. John, 40

De la Ronde, 346

Delaware Indians, 68

De Noüe, Father Anne, 43

Desmond, *see* Port Huron, Mich.

Destiny, the, tug, 367

Detour passage, 90, 97, 336, 339, 340

Detroit, Mich., 65-67, 75, 207, 210, 237

Detroit, the, schooner, 347

Detroit *Gazette,* 69

Detroit River, 36, 37, 63-64, 68

Dick, Capt. James, 307

Dickens, Charles, 233

Dieppe, 25, 26, 50

Discovery, the, 29

Dominion Marine Association, 338

Dorchester, Lord, 115, 286, 287

Doubleday, Eliza, 188, 190

Dougall, John, 264

Douglas, Samuel, 273-274

Douglas, Silas H., 273

Dousman, Michael, 77, 78

Drummond, Lieut. Peter, 194
Drummond Island, 196-199, 221
Du Lhut, Daniel Greysolon, Sieur, 63
Dunlop, Dr. William, 120-125, 135; his will, 120-121
Dunmore, the, schooner, 288
Durham, Lord, 259

Eber Ward, the, Ward vessel, 160
Edison, Thomas Alva, 100-101
Edward U. Demmer, the, 339
Elizabeth Broder, the, 306
Elliott, Rev. Adam, 183
Emerald, the, 311
En-ar-co, the, tanker, former *W. S. Calvert,* 361
Enders M. Voorhees, the, 360 f.n.
Erie, the, 163
Erie Belle, the, 306
Erie Canal, 156
Erie Indians, 53
Etherington, Capt. George, 208
Evans, Rev. James, 117, 124, 134

F. B. Squire, the, 162
F. W. Gifford, the, 306
Favourite, the, later *City of Parry Sound,* 311
Fenian raids, 265-271
Fisheries, 98, 112-113, 133-134
Flower Pot Island, Ont., 132
Flying Cloud, the, 306
Flying Mist, the, 306
Foote, Capt. Robert D., 317, 319
Forest City, the, 355
Forest fires, 107-110, 340

Forest Queen, the, Ward vessel, 160
Forester, the, Ward vessel, 160
Forests, *see* Lumbering
Fort Erie, Ont., 87
Fort George, 86, 216
Fort Gratiot, Mich., 84, 98, 99, 123, 269; cholera at, 166-168
Fort Gratiot Lighthouse, 100, 101, 326
Fort Holmes, Mich., 86, 216
Fort Malden, *see* Amherstburg, Ont.
Fort Niagara, 201
Fort St. Joseph, 63, 100
Fox, W. Sherwood, 59
Fox Islands, Ont., 142
France, policy in America, 23, 37-38
Frances Smith, the, 308-309
Frank Rockefeller, the, whaleback, later the *South Park,* 358
Franklin, Sir John, 144-145
Fraser, Major Donald, 295
French River, Ont., 17, 19, 141, 245
French Settlement, Ont., 125-127
Fuller, Margaret, 226-228
Fur trade, 34, 72, 94, 192; at Detroit, 66, 69; at Mackinac, 67; British policy, 68; in Saginaw country, 103-104; in Saugeen River area, 116; *see also* North West Company, South West Company, John Jacob Astor

Galinée, René de Bréhant de, 36-37, 150
Gallatin, Albert, 93

Galt, John, 119-122

Garnier, Father Charles, canonization of, 40; martyrdom of, 53

Gauthier, C. W., 135

Gazelle, the, Ward vessel, 160

General Brady, the, 163

General Gratiot, the, 154, 163, 261

General Taylor, the, 275

Georgian Bay, 17, 137-147; place names, 147; shipping and sailors, 304-324; grain trade, 306-307, 315, 324; in wartime, 368-370

Georgian Bay Navigation Company, 310, 311

Gettysburg, Battle of, 299

Gladiator, the, tug, 169

Gladwin, the, schooner, 209

Gladys, the, later *Northern Belle,* 310, 323

Gleneagles, the, 315

Glenfinnan, the, former *Alva,* 315

Glengarry Light Infantry, 82

Glenislet, the, 315

Glenlivet, the, 315

Glenorchy, the, 339

Gloucester Bay, Ont., 139, 142

Goderich, Ont., 109, 119, 120, 122-125, 135-136, 267

Godley, John R., 351

Gold Hunter, the, 306

Golden West, the, 306

Gore, the, 307

Goshawk, the, 354, 356

Goupil, Father René, 40

Grain trade, 306-307, 324

Grand Bend, Ont., 126

Grand River, Ont., 36

Grant, Henry, 257, 260, 263

Gratiot, Capt. Charles, 98, 99

Gray, Capt. Andrew, 73-74

Great Lakes Navigation Company, 315

Great Lakes News, 170

Great Lakes Protective Association, 355

Great Northern Transit Company, 311, 317, 323

Green Bay, Wis., 30, 83

Grenolle, associate of Brulé, 30, 32

Greyhound, the, 164

Greysolon, Charles, 62

Griffin, the, 62, 148, 150, 205, 345-346

Groseilliers, Medard Chouart, 34, 203-204

Guelph, Ont., 120

H. B. Hawgood, the, 332

H. B. Smith, the, 331

Haldimand, Sir Frederick, 211, 287, 347

Hallen, Rev. George, 143

Hamilton, Henry, administrator at Detroit, 210

Hamonic, the, 353

Hanks, Lieut. Porter, 75, 76, 77, 79

Hanson, Capt. J. P., 172-173

Harris, Amelia (Mrs. John Harris), 291

Harris, John, 291

Harrison, General, W. H., 98

Harry A. Berwind, the, 162

Harvey H. Brown, the, 162

Harwood, Capt. Harvey, 113

Hawthorne, Nathaniel, 236

Head, Sir Francis Bond, Lieutenant Governor of Upper Canada, 132, 184

Hennepin, Father Louis, 62, 148

Henry, Alexander, 208-209, 245

Henry Clay, the, 166, 167, 349

Henry Cort, the, 342

Henry Steinbrenner, the, 162

Herman, Eugene, 170

Hiawatha, the, freighter, 356

Hiawatha, the, St. Clair River steamer, 164

Hill, James J., 353

Hind, Henry Youle, 307

Holland, Mich., 107

Hollands, Hulda T., 171

Holmes, Major Andrew Hunter, 84, 86, 216

Homer Alverson, the, 162

Hotel Dieu, Quebec, 52

Houghton, Dr. Douglas, 103

Howard, Capt. William, 209

Howard M. Hanna Jr., the, 331 f.n., 333

Hubbard, Bela, 103-104, 112

Hudson's Bay Company, 66, 70, 94, 204

Hull, General William, 75, 80

Hull cession (1807), 104

Hunter's Lodges, 259

Huron, the, schooner gunboat, 291

Huron, the, Ward vessel, 157, 163

Huron County, Mich., 108, 109

Huron Indians, trade with, 18, 24, 32; character, 40, 44; social conditions among, 45-46; destruction by Iroquois, 50-53; on Christian Island, 54-55; removal to

Huron Indians—*Cont.*
Quebec, 55

Huron Institute, 323

Huron lightship, 101, 326

Huron Tract, *see* Canada Company

Huron Union Society, 124

Huronia, 30, 33, 34, 39-60, 138; location, 41; life in, 45-46; population, 46-47; Iroquois attacks upon, 50-53; *see also* Sainte Marie I

Huronic, the, 353

Hydrus, the, 331 f.n., 334

Idlewild, the, 164

Ihonatiria, Huron village, 47

Illinois, the, schooner, 350

Illinois, the, steamer, 352

Imperial, the, tanker, 361

Impoco, the, tanker, 361

India, the, 170, 352

Indian cessions, in Michigan, 104 and f.n.; in Bruce County, 130-133; on Georgian Bay, 184 f.n.

Indian torture, 45

Indians, at Saugeen River, 128-129; on St. Clair River, 152; presents to, 178-182, 220; on Manitoulin Island, 179-187; at St. Ignace, 202-203, 206; at Fort Mackinac, 213, 220, 225, 226-227; *see also* Huron, Iroquois, Ottawa, Chippewa Indians

Industry, the, 347

International Boundary Commission, 199, 293-294

Iosco County, Mich., 113

Iron City, the, 352

Iron ore trade, 356; in wartime, 370-371

Iroquois Indians, 29, 33, 35, 49

Irving S. Olds, the, 360 f.n.

Isaac M. Scott, the, 162, 331 f.n., 332, 334

J. B. Neilson, the, 342

J.C.B., unidentified French officer, 202

J. C. Clarke, the, 164

J. H. Jones, the, 322

James, Thomas, 29

James Carruthers, the, 327, 329, 330, 331 f.n., 334

James H. Shrigley, the, 354

Jameson, Anna, 151-152, 158, 190-191, 222, 228, 230; at Manitoulin Island, 179-181; her tour of Lake Huron, 234-245

Jameson, Robert, 235

Japan, the, 170, 352

Jay Treaty (1794), 71, 93, 192, 286, 294

Jenks, W. L., 161

Jerome, Governor David H., 105

Jesuits, arrival in New France, 24; missions, 32-33, 34, 41-60, 206; archives, 39; training and character, 40; policy, 40, 41; martyrs, 40-48; canonization of martyrs, 40, 56; suppression of, 56

Jogues, Father Isaac, 33, 40, 177

John A. McGean, the, 331 f.n., 334

John B. Cowle, the, 162

John Ericsson, the, whaleback, 358

John F. Eddy, the, 355

John Owen, the, tug, 106

Johnson, Matthew, administrator in Illinois country, 210

Johnston, John, 183

Johnston, Mrs. John, 241

Jolliet, Louis, 35-37, 61, 150, 204-205

Jones, Father Edward, 58

Jones, Henry, 118-119

Jones, Rev. Peter, 118

Jones, Capt. Roger, 217

Julius D. Morton, the, 113

Kaloolah, the, later *Collingwood,* 307, 313

Kane, Paul, 127-129, 181-182

Kaskaskia, 211

Keating, Sergeant James, 83

Keller, Deane, 255

Kemble, Fanny, 236

Kerry, Capt. William, 262

Keweenaw, the, Ward vessel, 159

Keystone State, the, 308

Kizer, Capt. Howard H., 343

L. C. Waldo, the, 331

L. E. Block, the, 343

La Cloche, Ont., 142, 243

Lady Elgin, the, 308

La France, Capt. F. X., 319

Lahontan, Louis Armand de Lom d'Arce, Baron de, 63-64, 205-206

Lake Carriers' Association, 300, 332, 335, 363

Lake Erie, 20, 28, 31, 33, 36, 63

Lake Huron, discovery, 17; exploration, 28, 33, 35-37; in wartime, 366-372

Lake Michigan, 28, 30, 61, 300

Lake Nipissing, 19

Lake Ontario, 20, 33, 34-35

Lake St. Clair, 36, 37, 148, 288, 337

Lake Simcoe, 41

Lake Superior, 20, 61, 300, 325

Lakeland, the, former *Cambria,* 356

Lalemant, Father Charles, 32, 52

Lalemant, Father Gabriel, canonization of, 40; martyrdom of, 50-52

Lalemant, Father Jerome, 47, 52

Landmann, Lieut. George T., 193-195

Lapeer County, Mich., 109

La Salle, Robert Cavalier, Sieur de, 36, 205

La Vallée, French trader, 32

Lawrence, the, brig, 84, 86

Lawson, Surgeon General Thomas, 256

Leafield, the, 331, 332

Leavitt, Benjamin F., 274-275

Le Caron, Father Joseph, 19, 21, 22

Le Jeune, Father Paul, 24

Le Moyne, Father Simon, 35

Lemoyne, the, 307, 316, 343, 344

Leon Fraser, the, 344, 360 f.n.

Leonard B. Miller, the, 339

Limestone trade, 113-114

Livingston, Lieut. Robert, 83

Lockerbie, William, 318

London, Ont., 262

London Field Battery, 269, 270

"Lone shieling," *see* "Canadian Boat Song"

Long, John J., 310

Long, Thomas, 310, 323

Lora Bay, Ont., 146

Lorette, Quebec, 55

Louisiana, the, 331

Lovell, Surgeon General Joseph, 249

Lumber barges, 168

Lumbering, at Port Huron, 100; in Michigan, 102-107; on Georgian Bay, 106, 132, 139, 314

Lysons, Sir Daniel, 99-100

McCannell, Capt. James, 317

McCoskry, Rt. Rev. Samuel A., 238

McDouall, Lt. Col. Robert, 82-83, 85-86, 87, 90, 91, 92, 196

McDougall, Capt. Alexander, 356-358

McDougall, Rev. John, 146, 305

McElroy, Crocket, 163-164

MacGregor, Capt. Alexander, 133, 135

McKay, Capt. George P., 275-276

Mackenzie, William Lyon, 257

Mackinac, Straits of, 31, 61, 341

Mackinac Island, 37, 70, 111, 200-232, 240; trade, 68, 216; in War of 1812, 71, 74-81, 84-86, 90, 216; social life on, 218-219

Mackinaw City, Mich., 200

McKinley, President William, 353

McMurray, Rev. William, 183, 242, 244

McMurray, Mrs. William (Charlotte Johnston), 183

McNab, Capt. Alexander, 317

McTavish, Simon, 194

Madison, President James, 195
Magnetawan, the, 321
Maitland, Sir Peregrine, Lieutenant Governor of Upper Canada, 183
Maitland River, Ont., 119
Majestic, the, 311
Major, the, 331
Manistee, Mich., 107
Manitoba, the, 352
Manitou Islands, 111
Manitoulin, the, 311, 317-318
Manitoulin Island, 53, 55, 132, 176-187, 244
Manitowaning, Ont., 180, 184, 185, 186, 318
Mann, Capt. Gother, 115, 286-290
Mann, William, 108-109
Maple sugar, 116, 190, 305
Maplecourt, the, 353
Mapledawn, the, 60
Marine City, Mich., 149, 155-157, 163, 169, 172; shipbuilding at, 159-160
Marquette, Father Jacques, 35, 39, 204
Marryat, Frederick, 234
Martin, the, 355
Martin, Father Felix, 57, 58
Martineau, Harriet, 230, 234
Martyrs' Shrine, 57
Mary, the, St. Clair River steamer, 163-164
Mary A. McGregor, the, lumber carrier, 354
Matchedash Bay, 82, 84, 85, 289
Matoa, the, 331 f.n.
Matthew Andrews, the, 332 f.n.

Meade, General George Gordon, 299-300
Medical Society of Michigan Territory, 255
Merchant, the, first iron freighter, 170
Merrick, the, tug, 106
Meteor, the, passenger steamer, 272-276, 352
Meteor, the, former *South Park,* 358
Michigan, the, first iron vessel on the lakes, 355
Michigan Fencibles, 86
Midland, Ont., 41, 139, 314-316, 324; shipbuilding at, 315-316, 369
Midland King, the, 315
Midland Navigation Company, 315
Midland Prince, the, 315
Midland Queen, the, 315
Midland Railway, 314
Midland Shipbuilding Company, 315
Milford Haven, Ont., 189
Mineral Rock, the, 275
Mink, the, schooner, 85
Minneapolis, the, Ward vessel, 159
Minnehaha, the, 356
Missouri, Illinois and Eastern Trading Company, 264
Mitchell, Dr. David, 116, 220-221
Mitchell, Mrs. David, 221-222
Mohawk, the, 274
Monarch, the, 312, 352
Montreal, P. Q., 34, 35, 75
Montreal merchants, in War of

Montreal merchants—*Cont.*
1812, 73-74, 93
Moore, Capt. John, 314
Moore Township, Ont., 149, 153,
260-261
Moraviantown, 82
Morrison, Christine (Mrs. Albert
Fleming), 279-280
Morse, Rev. Jedidiah, 297
Muskoka, Ont., 139

Nancy, the, schooner, 87, 88-89, 99,
347
Negroes in Upper Canada, 123,
145, 146
Nelson Bloom, the, barge, former
Meteor, 276
Neutral Indians, 20, 31, 32-33, 34,
53, 115
Newport, *see* Marine City
Niagara, the, brig, 84, 87, 89
Niagara, the, 308
Niagara Patriot, 348
Niagara River, 33, 36, 63, 68
Nicolet, Jean, 17, 29, 30, 33
Nipissing Indians, 19
Noronic, the, 353
North Land, the, 353
North Shore Navigation Com-
pany, 311, 323
North West, the, 353
North West Company, 68, 72, 76,
84, 85, 87, 94, 192, 195, 243
North West Trading and Coloni-
zation Company, 307
Northern Belle, the, former *Gladys,*
310, 323
Northern Light, the, 352

Northern Navigation Company
of Ontario, 312, 352-353
Northern Queen, the, 311
Northern Railway, 306
Northwest passage, 18, 29, 209
Northwest Transportation Com-
pany, 311
Nottawasaga Bay, Ont., 41, 91, 289
Nottawasaga River, Ont., 53, 82,
87, 89, 99, 139
Nottingham, the, 331
Nute, Grace Lee, 204
Nye, Thomas, 110-111

Ogdensburg, the, 159
Ogilvy, John, 294, 295
Oil tankers, 360-361
Ojibwa, *see* Chippewa
Oliphant, Laurence, 129-131, 133,
186-187, 351
O'Meara, Rev. Frederick, 178, 186
Onoko, the, first metal bulk
freighter, 169, 355
Ontario, the, 352
Ord, General Edward, 268, 269
Oregon, the, Ward vessel, 158
Osler, Dr. William, 252, 253-254
Ossossané, Huron village, 47
Ottawa Indians, 80, 177, 206
Ottawa River route, 18, 34, 61, 138,
203; its difficulties, 18-19, 21, 43-
45
Otter, the, 347
Owen, Sir Edward William
Campbell Rich, 290
Owen, Robert, 118
Owen, Capt. William Fitzwilliam,
146-147, 290, 291, 292

Owen Sound, Ont., 128, 139, 312, 324; wartime shipbuilding, 370

PC boats, 367

Pacific, the, Georgian Bay steamer, 311, 312

Pacific, the, Ward vessel, 159

Palmer, *see* St. Clair, Mich.

Panic of 1837, 158, 259

Parkman, Francis, 128, 205, 207, 225-226

Parry Sound, Ont., 141, 309

Péan, Capt., 202

Pearl, the, Ward vessel, 159

Peerless, the, 275

Penetanguishine, Ont., 122, 142-144, 199, 242, 245, 322

Peré, Jean, 35

Perry, Capt. Oliver H., 71, 81

Petun Indians, 34, 53

Pewabic, the, 272-276

Piché, Pierre, 116

Picoté, Capt. Francis Marie, Sieur de Bellestre, 201-202

Pine River, *see* St. Clair, Mich.

Pittsburgh Steamship Company, 316, 342, 360

Pius XI, pope, 40

Planet, the, Ward vessel, 160

Playfair, James, 315-316

Playter, Capt. George, 318

Plymouth, the, barge, 331

Pollard, Rev. Richard, 193

Poncet, Father Antoine de la, 35

Pontanagipy, *see* Drummond Island

Pontiac conspiracy, 207-209

Port Arthur, Ont., 308-309, 313

Port Dover, Ont., 36

Port Huron, Mich., 98, 99-102, 336; shipbuilding at, 161-162; *see also* Fort Gratiot

Port McNichol, Ont., 139, 324

Porter, Peter B., 294

Potomac, the, 306, 307

Prairie du Chien, 83, 85, 92, 93

Presque Isle, Mich., 97, 111

Prevost, Sir George, 73, 76

Prince, Colonel John, 263

Prince Arthur's Landing, *see* Port Arthur

Pringle Barge Line, 170

Procter, Brigadier General Henry A., 81

Put in Bay, 71

Putnam, William, 262

Queen City, the, 308

Queenston Heights, 82

Quincy A. Shaw, the, 339

R. J. Hackett, the, first real bulk freighter, 355

R. L. Agassiz, the, 339

Radisson, Pierre Esprit, 34, 203-204

Rafts, 106, 170-171

Ragueneau, Father Paul, 33, 51, 53, 55

Rains, Major William Kingdom, 188-192

Raymbault, Father Charles, 33, 177

Rebellion of 1837, in Upper Canada, 99-100, 124, 185, 257-260

Récollets, 19, 21, 22

Red Crown, the, tanker, 361

Regina, the, 327, 329, 330, 331 f.n., 332, 334

Regnaut, Christophe, 52

Reid, Capt. Tom, 326

Renown, the, later *Beaumont Parks,* tanker, 361

Rescue, the, 307

Rich, the, DE boat, 368

Richardson, John, merchant, 88

Richardson, Major John, 99

Riley, James V., 104

Rising Star, the, 306

River aux Perches, Ont., 118

Robert Burns, the, brig, 162

Roberts, Lieut. Benjamin, 209

Roberts, Capt. Charles, 75-81, 84

Robinson, Capt. C. E., 343

Rogers, Major Robert, 201, 209

Roosevelt, President Franklin D., 176

Rosen, Dr. George, 254

Ross, Major A. M., 267, 268, 269

Royal Newfoundland Regiment, 83, 86, 91

Royal Ontario Museum of Archaeology, 57

Royal Proclamation of 1763, 66, 161

Ruby, the, Ward vessel, 159

S. R. Kirby, the, 333

Saginaw, the, Ward vessel, 159

Saginaw, Mich., 69, 103-104, 105, 106

Saginaw Bay, Mich., 64, 97, 105, 110, 113, 240

Saginaw River, Mich., 97, 103, 104, 105

Saginaw Treaty (1819), 104

Saginaw Valley, Mich., 69, 103, 105

St. Andrew, the, former *W. B. Hall,* 315

St. Clair, the, Ward vessel, 156

St. Clair, Mich., 239

St. Clair County, Mich., 109

St. Clair "Flats," Mich., 84, 171

St. Clair River, 97, 98, 148-174, 288-289, 326, 337; discovery, 35-37; cholera, 99, 166-168; French on, 149-150; settlers on, 149, 153-155; Indians on, 152-153; river boats, 163-164, 170; wood docks, 164-165; shipping, 168-171

St. Helen's Isle, 26

St. Ignace, Jesuit mission in Huronia, 49, 50-51, 58-60

St. Ignace, Michilimackinac, 64, 67, 200, 202-209; massacre at, 206-209

St. Jean, Jesuit mission, 53

St. Joseph, Jesuit mission, 49, 50

St. Joseph Island, 74-75, 77, 80, 85, 89, 90, 188-194, 215

St. Lawrence River, 35, 37

St. Leger, Colonel Barry, 347

St. Louis, Jesuit mission, 49, 50, 59

St. Martin, Alexis, 247-252

St. Mary's College, Montreal, 39

St. Mary's River, 28, 30, 61, 341

St. Maurice River, P. Q., 34

St. Michel, Jesuit mission, 49

Saint Paul, the, Ward vessel, 159

St. Sulpice, Gentlemen of, 35, 36, 61

Ste. Foy, 55

Sainte Marie I, Jesuit mission, 47-48, 53-54, 56-58, 138, 316

Sainte Marie II, Jesuit mission, 54

Sam Ward, the, Ward vessel, 160

Samson, the, tug, 169

Sanilac County, Mich., 108, 109

Sargent, Winthrop, 215

Sarnia, Ont., 116-117, 269

Sarnia and Plympton Library, 264

Saturn, the, Georgian Bay vessel, 310

Saturn, the, 339

Saugeen Fishing Islands, Ont., 133-134

Saugeen Peninsula, Ont., 116, 131-133

Saugeen River, Ont., 116, 128

Sault Ste. Marie, 33, 36, 68, 71, 74, 85, 233, 241-242, 275, 300

Savage, Capt. J. N., 277

Schoolcraft, Henry R., 110, 157-158, 179, 222-224, 228, 240, 295

Schoolcraft, Mrs. Henry R. (Jane Johnston), 183, 240, 241

Schoolcraft, James, 222

Schoolcraft, the, lumber carrier, 354

Schooners, 136, 349-350, 354-355; in the lumber trade, 106-107

Scorpion, the, schooner, 84, 87, 90-91, 93, 143

Scott, Archibald Hamilton, 189, 190

Scott, James, 323

Scott, Capt. Walter, 113

Scott, General Winfield, 166, 289

Scottish Hero, the, 362

Sea Bird, the, Ward vessel, 160

Second World War, 136, 366-372

Seelye, Alan, 343

Self-unloaders, 361-362

Separate lanes, 338-340

Severn River, Ont., 41

Sewall, Stephen, 294

Shanly, Colonel James, 269, 271

Shea, John Gilmary, 30

Shead, George, 104

Sheaffe, Major General R. H., 80

Sheldon Thompson, the, 166, 167

Shenango, the, 359

Sherman, General William Tecumseh, 268-271

Shiawassee River, Mich., 103

Shipbuilding, 347-348; at Port Huron, 100, 161-162; at Marine City, 159-160; at Midland, 315-316; in wartime, 366-370

Shirreff, Patrick, 123-124

Simcoe, John Graves, first Lieutenant Governor of Upper Canada, 73, 142, 214, 289

Simcoe, the, 311

Simpson, Melanchton, shipbuilder, 308

Sinclair, Capt. Arthur, 84-85, 88, 89

Sinclair, Capt. Patrick, 75, 160-161, 210-212, 214

Sioux Indians, 83

Smith, Milton, 328-329

Smith, Capt. W. H., 308

Sombra, Ont., 153

South Park, the, former *Frank Rockefeller,* whaleback, 358

South West Company, 195, 197

Southwold Earthwork, Ont., 32

Sovereign, the, 352

Sparta, the, 275

Spokane, the, first steel bulk freighter, 169-170, 355

Starin, Frederick J., 111-112

Stewart, Mrs. Rachel Mann, 109

Storm of 1913, 324, 325-334

Storrow, Samuel A., 98

Strathcona, Lord (Donald Smith), 313

Stuart, Capt. Charles, 145-146, 295

Superior, the, 166, 349, 350

Superior Shoal, 300

Surprise, the, former schooner *Tigress,* 91

Surveys of Lake Huron, 285-303; charts, 302-303

Susan Ward, the, Ward vessel, 160

Sutherland's Landing, Ont., 261

Swan, the, 347

Talbot, Colonel Thomas, 236

Talbot road, 264

Talon, Jean, 35

Tanner, John, 222

Tashmoo, the, St. Clair River steamer, 164

Tawas, Mich., 106

Teanaustayé, Huron village, 47, 50

Tecumseh, Shawnee chief, 72

Tenth Royal Veteran Battalion, 75

Thames River, Ont., 68, 82, 236

Thomas Jefferson, the, 237, 238, 350

Thompson, Charles, 189, 190

Thompson, David, 295, 297-298

Thornbury, Ont., 145

Three Rivers, P. Q., 34, 49

Thunder Bay, Mich., 64-65, 240, 341

Thunder Bay Island, Mich., 97, 111, 341

Thunder Bay River, Mich., 97, 110, 113

Tiger, the, schooner, 218

Tigress, the, schooner, 84, 87, 90-91, 93, 143

Tinkis, D. A., 278-280

Tobermoray, Ont., 131

"Toon o' Maxwell," *see* Jones, Henry

Tracy, Marquis de, 29

Traveller, the, Ward vessel, 159, 352

Treaty of Ghent, 86, 92-94, 196, 294

Treaty of Greenville (1795), 72

Tugs, 169

Turnbull, Robert, 327

Turner, Lieut. Daniel, 89

Turret Bay, the, 362

Turret Bell, the, 362

Turret boats, 362

Turret Cape, the, 362

Turret Chief, the, 331, 362

Turret Court, the, 362

Turret Crown, the, 362

Tuscola County, Mich., 109

Tuyle, Baron de, 125

Underground railroad, 146

Unique, the, St. Clair River steamer, 163-164

United Empire, the, 312, 352

V. H. Ketchum, the, 169, 355

Victoria, Queen of England, 243

Victory, the, first 400-footer, 359

Vidal, Alexander T. E., 154-155, 291

Vidal Shoals, 155

Vincennes, 210, 211

Von Egmond, Colonel Anthony, 124

Voyageurs, 79, 81, 138, 213, 241, 242-243, 244-245; Corps of Canadian Voyageurs, 81

W. B. Hall, the, later *St. Andrew,* 315

W. Grant Morden, the, 359

W. S. Calvert, the, later *En-ar-co,* tanker, 361

Wahcondah, the, 338

Walk-in-the-Water, the, first steamer on Lake Huron, 217, 348-349

Wanderer, the, British warship, 292

War of 1812, 71-94, 142, 143, 258, 289, 290, 347

Ward, Eber, 157, 160 f.n.

Ward, Eber Brock, 156-160

Ward, Samuel, 156-157

Waubuno, the, 309, 311, 320-321

Waymouth, Capt. George, 29

Wayne County Medical Society, Detroit, 255

Webster, Fletcher, 238, 239

Weld, Theodore Dwight, 145

Welfare of sailors, 363-364

Westcott Marine Reporting Agency, 336 f.n.

Western Herald (Sandwich, Upper Canada), 257, 262, 263, 264

"Western Sea," 23

Western World, the, 351-352

Westward movement, 66, 157-158, 236-237, 298-299, 304, 307-308, 347-348

Wexford, the, 327, 330, 331 f.n., 332, 334

Whaleback *101,* 357

Whalebacks, 356-358

White, D. L., 315

White Line, *see* Great Northern Transit Company

White Rock, Mich., 111, 112

Wikwemikong, Ont., 186

Wilkinson, General James, 215

William IV, King of England, 243

William B. Davock, the, 300, 333 f.n.

William H. Wolf, the, 172-173

William P. Cowan, the, tanker, 361

William P. Snyder Jr., the, 359

William Penn, the, 166, 167

Williams, David, 323

Winnebago Indians, 29, 30, 83

Wintemberg, W. J., 59-60

Wood docks, 164-165

Woodman, Elijah, 262, 263 f.n.

Worsley, Lieut. Miller, 87, 88, 90-91

Wright, Capt. William, 154, 260 f.n.

Wyandotte, the, first self-unloader, 361